The Stoy Hayward Guide to

GETTING INTO EUROPE

The Stoy Hayward Guide to

GETTING INTO EUROPE

Strategic planning for international tax, raising finance, and performance monitoring

RICHARD CITRON

STOY HAYWARD
Accountants and Business Advisers
A member of Horwath International

Horwath

KOGAN PAGE

Kogan Page Limited
120 Pentonville Road
London N1 9JN

British Library Cataloguing in Publication Data

A CIP record for this book is available from the British Library.

ISBN 0–7494–0274–1

Typeset by J&L Composition Ltd, Filey, North Yorkshire
Printed and bound in Great Britain by
Biddles Ltd, Guildford and Kings Lynn

Contents

Caveat

The Stoy Hayward Guide to Getting into Europe is a general guide to tax, finance and monitoring for a UK company expanding into Europe.

The law is as stated at 30 June 1990. However, by the time the book is published, undoubtedly some laws in some European countries, including the UK, will have changed. The book can never be used as a substitute for detailed professional advice, neither in the UK nor in the country of the overseas operation, nor sometimes in third countries – it is intended as a general guide only. In particular, many examples have been simplified and many conditions for given situations to apply have not been set out.

Acknowledgements

This book could not have been written without the help of very many people, in particular at Stoy Hayward, and especially Andrea Mudge, Ruth Baker, Zigurds Kronbergs, Brian Friedman, Peter Napier, John Dennison, Sue Kirby, Dermot McLellan, Ian Doe, Rick Sopher, Anton Hume, Alan Cinnamon, Rodney Taylor, Peter Webster, Ben Coleman, Tron Sanfeldt and Monique Ktourza-Granditer, whose help is gratefully acknowledged.

Thanks are due also to the following from Horwath International's European Regional Organisation offices: Bernhard Vanas of Vienna, Professor W Missorten of Brussels, Ole Nielsen of Copenhagen, Harry Lindberg of Helsinki, Blandine Leporcq of Paris, Dr Kurt Gratz of Stuttgart, Frank Sheedy of Dublin, Humberto Leal of Portugal, Margareta Wallin of Stockholm and Fernando Seglias of Zurich, as well as to Paul Godfrey and Pauline Goodwin of Kogan Page, John Jenkins and Mike Ranson of Lloyds Bank, Martin Brown of International Grant Services and last, but not least, Sarah Citron.

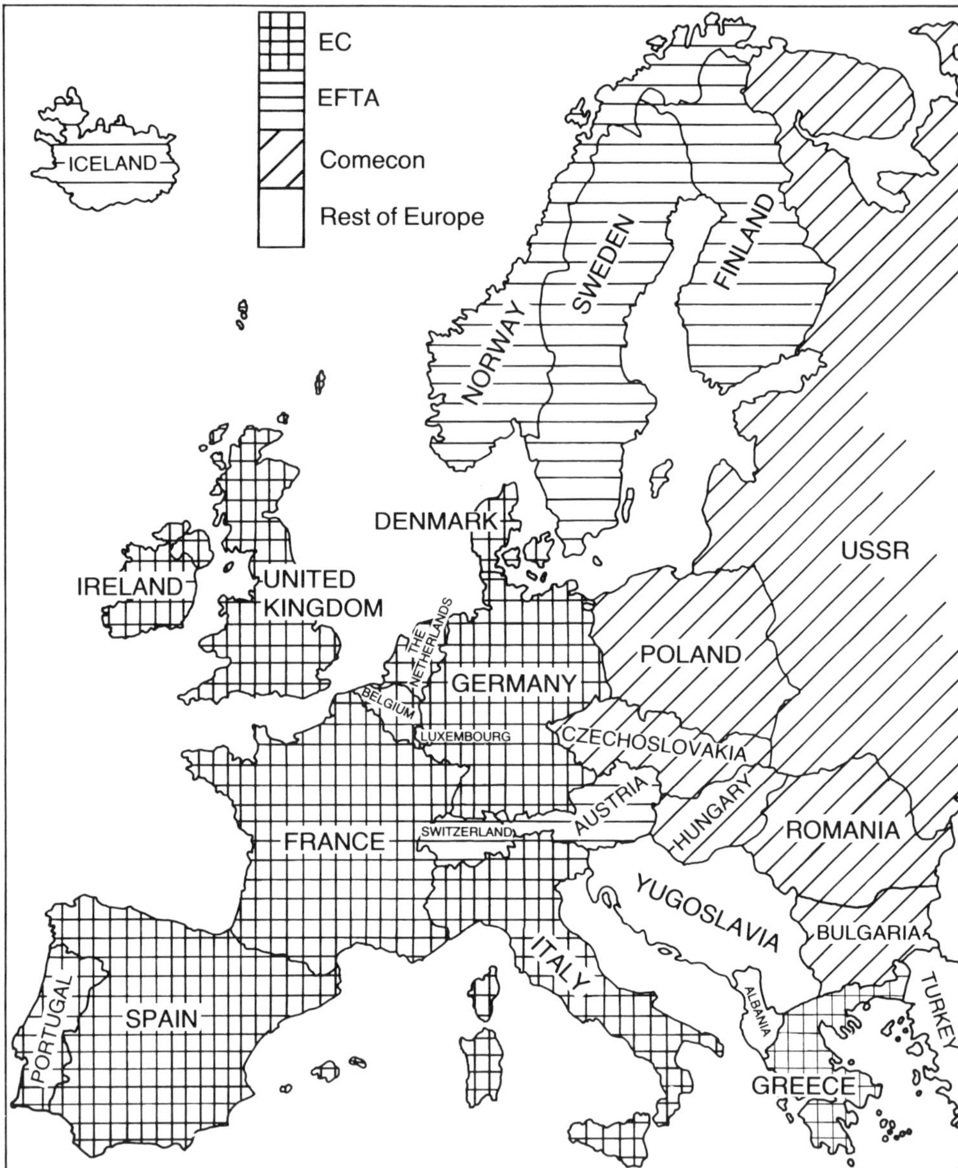

Trading blocs in Europe

List of Abbreviations

I have attempted to minimise the use of acronyms such as 'UK' for United Kingdom. However, I have had to use some abbreviations such as:

- EC — European Community – sometimes referred to as 'the Community' or 'EEC', made up of 'member states'
- ICTA 88 — Income and Corporation Taxes Act 1988
- ICTA 70 — Income and Corporation Taxes Act 1970
- CGTA 79 — Capital Gains Tax Act 1979
- FA 1988 — Finance Act 1988 etc
- ECGD — Export Credits Guarantee Department

Wherever possible, the use of acronyms and abbreviations has been avoided but, where necessary, these have been defined in the text within the relevant chapter.

INTRODUCTION

1

1993 and all that ...

1.1 Peering through the mist

This book is intended as a general guide to international tax planning, raising finance and management monitoring for UK companies considering expansion into Europe.

An ever-increasing number of UK companies are involved in the export of both goods and services. This trend will be accentuated by the forthcoming integration of the European Community on 1 January 1993, the Channel Tunnel, the continued lowering of worldwide tariffs and exchange controls, and by recent events in Germany and Eastern Europe. In 1993 and the years after, the attitude of British business must change. In the post-1993 Europe, UK firms will see themselves as potential exporters or owners of European operations even though they may be of a size which, up to now, has been considered to be merely 'domestic'.

By 1993 the European Community will be a single integrated market of 330 million people, a larger number than either the United States or Japan. By then the Single European Market may include the existing EFTA and Comecon countries, enormously increasing the scope for UK companies, presenting both a challenge and an opportunity for British business. However, the post-1993 environment will not only provide greater opportunity; there will also be greater competition in the UK home market. Indeed it could be said that by 1993 the 'home market' will become the Single European Market, allowing economies of scale in matters such as transport, finance, insurance, R&D and advertising. All barriers to selling within the European Community should have disappeared. There will be a removal of frontier controls resulting in freedom of movement of goods, services and workers. Artificial restraints on trade, such as import quotas and deposits, will disappear.

The costs of transport and insurance should fall. There should be a mutual recognition of qualifications and standards. Access to capital markets and freedom to invest in any Community country or currency will provide opportunities for United Kingdom business. The acquisition of European companies should be made easier as national company laws merge to become a single Community company law. Technical barriers to trade between member states will be removed. There will be protection for intellectual property rights which is currently not available within the UK. There will be an opportunity for UK exporters to tender for public sector contracts throughout the European Community through a common public procurement policy.

On the other hand, Europe will never be a true 'home market' in the way that the USA or Japan is a single market. Differences in taxation, law, language, culture, business customs, interest rates, business ethics, advertising techniques, markets, currencies, politics and history will all conspire to 'fragment' the Single Market. While these differences persist the addition of a European dimension to the existing domestic operation will cause the management of UK companies to face larger demands on their time, and add levels of complexity to their tasks. The years immediately following 1993 will be a period of change. During any period of change there are both opportunities and threats. The post-1993 world of the Single European Market will be a highly competitive environment. In a highly competitive environment change becomes difficult and expensive. UK companies must reorganise now to prepare themselves for post-1993 Europe.

The Single European Market will not ring the death knell for small UK companies. Strong evidence for this can be gathered from the fact that small companies prosper in similar large markets such as the USA and Japan. Small companies have the flexibility and lower cost base to enable them to compete with the giants. They can exploit narrow niches in the markets. They can be more focused in terms of geographic markets, or specific customer needs. The question is what the smaller and medium-sized UK company should do *now* to be ready for the new post-1993 environment of the Single European Market. UK companies which lack any corporate strategy will eventually lose out against their competitors, whether those competitors are UK or foreign. The question is: What should the strategy for post-1993 Europe be?

1.2 A strategy for post-1993 Europe

There is not just one strategy that a UK company can adopt for post-1993 Europe. The UK company could adopt a *defensive strategy*. It could concentrate on its niches, keeping costs and prices down and denying entry into that area of the market to new European competitors.

This also has the advantage of conserving financial resources. It may give the UK company time to look at its own product, production and pricing strategies, and reorganise.

The advent of the Single European Market may also spur a UK company to adopt a *UK strategy*. UK companies could combine to eliminate domestic competititon, and reduce costs such as transport, research and advertising.

UK companies may even adopt a *non-European strategy*. Europe may be seen as a very difficult nut to crack, and so UK companies realising that they need to expand their markets in order to lower their unit costs and spread their risks, may look to less competitive environments such as the Middle East, Far East (other than Japan), the English-speaking Commonwealth (Australia, Canada and New Zealand), the Third World and, most importantly, the USA. UK companies, given the history of these islands and their historical connections outside Europe, may see expansion into Europe as merely the first step to a *global strategy*.

In 1993 and beyond, the Single European Market will mean that even companies which have long established dominance in the UK home market will need to 'think international'. The UK market is large enough to encourage European entry, but it may be too small for a company to sell sufficiently to achieve the savings of scale to remain competitive in the new environment. UK companies will have to become internationally orientated to:

- take advantage of the economies of scale;
- spread the risk in terms of downturns in one product or economy;
- take the market sector away from foreign competitors;
- provide opportunities for joint venturing expensive matters such as research and advertising.

It is for this reason that there has been an upsurge in the number of small and medium-sized UK companies looking to adopt an *international strategy*. The question is whether the international strategy should be purely European focused, partly European focused, or anti-European focused.

This book concentrates on *the European strategy*. The opportunities provided by the Single European Market after 1993 cannot be ignored, and the European strategy may prove to be the most common strategy adopted. This will have the result that the number of UK exporters to

Europe will increase, while the size of the average exporter will decrease. Similarly the number of UK companies owning European subsidiaries will increase. If smaller UK companies are going to 'get into Europe', what will be their main concerns?

1.3 The three questions

The first three questions that the management of a UK company embarking on the journey into Europe asks are:

- How can we structure the trade to maximise tax opportunities and minimise pitfalls?
- How will we raise finance for our export trade or outward investment?
- How will we monitor the foreign operation?

It is these three questions which this book addresses, and which it seeks to answer.

1.4 Further questions

In any given situation the above three questions will become more specific. For example, your company may manufacture a product which you believe can be successfully exported to Germany. Management could ask the following questions:

- Will I be taxed in Germany?
- Must I charge VAT on the sales?
- How can I raise finance for the export trade?
- How will I be paid?
- Should I be paid in deutschemarks or sterling?

Once the company has successfully exported to Germany, management may wish to establish a more permanent presence in the local market. A host of further questions could be asked:

- Should the venture be structured as a German branch or subsidiary?
- If a subsidiary is formed who should own it?

- What permissions are required?
- Should the subsidiary be financed with shares or loans?
- Should the German patent rights be owned in Germany?
- How can the UK company fund the subsidiary?
- How can UK management monitor the German operation?

These are just some of the questions that need answering before any transnational operation is undertaken.

1.5 The importance of international tax planning

This book examines the need for UK companies doing business with Europe to undertake international tax planning. International tax planning is concerned primarily with minimising the overall tax paid, both UK and foreign. Tax-saving opportunities must be taken and tax pitfalls avoided. Properly integrated and cohesive tax planning is essential when business spans international borders. Without proper coordination the plan may save taxes in the foreign country but be tax-expensive at home, or vice versa.

Because of the pace of change in both domestic and international tax law and practice, regular review of the plan is also necessary. It is vital to keep abreast of tax planning techniques worldwide and to have instant access to changes in local legislation, bilateral treaties, and judicial interpretation and practice.

1.6 The importance of raising finance

Expanding into Europe, whether through export trade or outward investment, as with any expansion of your business, will require finance. This may be internally generated out of the business's own cash surpluses, but generally will need to come from outside sources, typically a bank. It is essential that the right type of finance is matched with the particular expansion process being adopted. There may be grants available in the UK or in Europe. In many parts of Europe strict exchange controls are still in force, and being paid can be a problem.

1.7 The importance of management monitoring of the foreign operation

An overseas operation will not run itself. Unless timely information is received back in the UK heavy losses can be incurred. The problems are both tangible, in terms of the hardware/software necessary to bring information back to the UK head office, and also intangible: language, business customs, a host of factors which very often can only be dealt with effectively by someone who lives in the country. But then how will the UK head office manage the foreign operation? What degree of autonomy should be allowed to foreign management? Given recent cost and technical advances in the field of accounting technology, there is no reason why a London head office should be less aware of what is happening in Barcelona than in Birmingham.

1.8 The need for professional expertise

International tax planning, raising finance and monitoring can be complex. Different professionals need to be approached to solve different problems. Tax would normally be the province of an accountant. On the other hand in terms of raising finance you would normally approach a bank. Solicitors would normally be the experts with respect to contracts involving foreign trade, or foreign laws. Questions regarding insurance would normally be dealt with by specialist brokers.

There has been a trend for the larger and more internationally minded firms of accountants and lawyers to provide 'one-stop shopping' so that some, but not all, of these problems can be dealt with by one firm of experts. Not all the problems can be answered by one professional adviser. Who, apart from the UK company's own management, should be involved in coordinating the UK group's expansion overseas? Remember, this may be the first time that you have considered expanding abroad, but someone else may have seen countless clients embarking on exactly the same journey as yours.

1.9 The book

The book has been written in a style which attempts to demystify its subjects. If I have simplified examples or have not set out all the relevant conditions for certain reliefs to be available then I make no apologies. I have written a book for the businessman, not his professional advisers. I have attempted to write this book in simple language but sometimes, of necessity, the points become somewhat technical. I have then attempted to illustrate those points by examples or diagrams. Most of what will follow is common sense. However, there are some topics, in particular the intricacies of the UK's anti-avoidance legislation, which have nothing to do with common sense and, in fact, very often make no sense at all.

We will look at a UK company which up to now has traded only in the UK, but which is now considering expanding abroad with Europe as the first stop. The comments apply equally to UK unincorporated businesses, but it is comparatively rare for such businesses to expand overseas other than through the medium of a company. Even where it is necessary, for professional body reasons, to trade in the UK as a partnership, it will usually be the case that overseas operations will be structured as a company, if only to gain the protection of limited liability.

The book is divided into three main parts. Part 1 deals with international tax planning, and considers the case of a UK company which commences trading with Europe through export, builds up overseas links through licensing and franchising, and then establishes a branch, then a subsidiary and finally a group. Apart from UK corporation taxation, VAT and Customs duty and the tax and NIC position of executives are discussed. There are also short chapters on the subjects of joint venturing, very often the first step on the European journey for UK companies, and real estate investment – a UK speciality.

Part 2 covers the question of raising finance, first for export, and subsequently to fund the working capital of, or to acquire, a European subsidiary. Under this section the very important subjects of debt insurance, payment and documentation are dealt with. Grants, exchange controls, and the effects of EC harmonisation of the monetary system are also covered.

Part 3 deals with management monitoring of the overseas operation: the hardware required, the human dimension, and the importance of recognising differing business customs within Europe.

The book concludes with six appendices. Appendix A sets out the main features of the tax systems of 16 different European countries in an easy-to-read format. The main points of their tax systems are set out, and special points relating to UK companies investing into and doing business with those particular European countries are highlighted.

Appendix B sets out the main points of personal tax for those same 16 European countries for a UK executive posted abroad, and his personal tax and NIC position is discussed at some length in the body of the book.

Appendix C sets out the latest position on Eastern Europe, an enormous potential market for UK exporters and investors.

Appendix D looks at moves towards further harmonisation of taxation and company law within the European Community.

Appendix E sets out in tabular form the withholding taxes on dividends, interest and royalties paid between European countries.

The book concludes with Appendix F, which is a list of useful addresses.

1.10 What happens next?

Let us now start out on our journey into Europe. So far your UK company has done business in the UK only. However, you feel that there could be a market for the company's goods or services in Europe, and that now is the time to reorganise for the Single European Market of 1993 and after. Your company wants to 'get into Europe'. What is likely to happen, and what can you do to protect yourself against adverse taxation?

Your UK company's first dealings with Europe are likely to be the simplest forms of doing business, such as exporting, licensing or franchising. These are discussed in the next Chapter.

PART 1

INTERNATIONAL TAX PLANNING

2

The Journey Begins

2.1 Trading with Europe

The UK company's first activity abroad will often take the form of pure export of goods or services. Commercially this often begins with the need to find a market for surplus production because of a downturn in the home market.

The exporter will usually use an *independent* agent (as will be seen, this is very important to avoid liability to local taxation), an *independent* transportation company to handle the shipping documents and transport of the goods, and an *independent* distributor to distribute the goods once they are shipped. The exporter may sell through a specialist export house or buying agency, whether private or public such as the Crown Agents. It is important to remember that the exporter is liable for any errors made by his agent in completing export declarations. The agent should be given all the details and background information concerning the exportation. The benefit of most Customs and Excise reliefs will be lost if export procedures are not correctly completed. Straight away, at the beginning of the journey, you have encountered the importance of correct documentation.

If a UK company is only operating in Europe by purchasing goods for importation back to the UK it is unlikely to be taxable overseas. Under general principles it is not generating profits overseas. Similarly it could set up an advertising office, or an office for seeking local information, without becoming liable to foreign tax.

Even if the UK company went further and licensed the manufacture of goods in Europe, or even franchised an operation throughout Europe, generally the monies flowing back to the UK would not be liable to foreign tax by virtue of the UK's double tax treaty network. That brings us to the next stage on the journey.

2.2 Licensing

The next stage after export is licensing. The UK company ('the licensor') could grant rights to another company to use a particular process or, possibly, a well-known UK company name. In return the licensee will pay a royalty back to the UK. Under the UK's double tax treaty network or, alternatively, foreign domestic law, many royalties paid back to the UK from Europe will carry no withholding tax, and hence the UK will receive the advantage of a gross cash flow. The type of matters which can be licensed include:

- names
- patents
- copyrights
- know-how
- show-how.

Licensing is useful where the UK company does not want to incur too great a risk in terms of the cost of establishing a branch or a subsidiary. In addition, particularly outside the EC, high rates of Customs duty, import quotas, exchange controls or technical barriers may make it expensive for a UK company to consider establishing local production. Also, the cost of transport to far-flung locations in Europe can render exporting economically unviable, and licensing far more profitable.

The whole question of the protection of intellectual property within the EC is in a state of flux. In due course it should be the case that a patent registered in one country will automatically be registered throughout the EC, or alternatively it may be that patents will have to be registered on an EC basis only. There are disadvantages as well as advantages, including competition by the foreign licensee with the UK company.

In addition, an inefficient licensee can devalue the trade mark or brand name or company name. The UK company may find it difficult to control quality at a distance.

It is vitally important that the UK company consults its lawyers to ensure that a contract is drawn up with the licensee; this would not only provide that the UK company will be effectively paid (very often the burden of withholding tax will be thrown on to the licensee in order to ensure that the UK company is paid gross, so that the foreign licensee will be responsible for, eg, filing forms with the UK's Inspector of Foreign Dividends), but would also protect the brand name. Very often this is the most valuable asset that a UK company can have.

2.3 Franchising

Franchising is yet another step on the journey prior to direct outward investment. Statistically franchised businesses stand a far greater likelihood of success than 'stand alone' businesses.

The same problems of quality control exist as with licensees. Care must be exercised to ensure that franchise fees can be repatriated gross back to the UK. Franchising can be an effective method of providing entry into markets without the risk of actually establishing an overseas operation of the UK company itself.

2.4 Permanent establishment

At this stage the profits will only be liable to UK tax. As a general principle of international tax law, and in particular by virtue of the 'permanent establishment' articles of the UK's extensive network of double tax treaties, there will be no foreign tax to pay until the UK exporter has a permanent establishment abroad. A permanent establishment will usually exist when the UK exporter has, as a minimum, a dependent agent who can sell in his name from a permanent office abroad. A permanent establishment will also exist if a UK company trades abroad through an office, factory or other premises.

If there is no permanent establishment overseas there is no foreign tax, so it can be seen that the UK's double tax treaties provide a vital source of relief and simplification for a UK business beginning to expand into Europe. It is therefore necessary to look at double tax treaties in some more detail.

2.5 Tax treaties

The UK has over 80 comprehensive double tax treaties with other countries – more than any other country in the world.

Tax treaties are bilateral agreements between two countries, which will normally overrule domestic law, whether UK or foreign. Treaties seek to avoid double taxation of income and gains, and reduce withholding taxes on passive income such as dividends, interest and royalties. Comprehensive treaties deal with a variety of different types of income and gain including permanent establishments, business profits, dividends, interest, royalties, capital gains and personal earnings. However, many countries have concluded double tax treaties which differ widely from the norm. For example the UK has 'tax sparing' negotiated into some of its treaties when tax exemptions are treated as foreign tax paid in the UK. This is discussed further in later chapters. The UK also has much shorter treaties which may only deal with a restricted range of topics, typically international shipping and air transport.

The UK has a comprehensive double tax treaty with every EC country, and with most European ones as follows:

Alderney	covered by Guernsey
Andorra	none
Austria	comprehensive
Belgium	comprehensive
Bulgaria	comprehensive
Cyprus	comprehensive
Czechoslovakia	comprehensive
Denmark	comprehensive
Finland	comprehensive
France	comprehensive
Germany	comprehensive
Gibraltar	none
Greece	comprehensive
Guernsey	arrangement
Hungary	comprehensive
Iceland	shipping
Ireland	comprehensive
Isle of Man	arrangement
Italy	comprehensive
Jersey	arrangement
Liechtenstein	none
Luxembourg	comprehensive
Malta	agreement
Monaco	none
Netherlands	comprehensive
Norway	comprehensive
Poland	comprehensive
Portugal	comprehensive

Romania	comprehensive
Sark	none
Spain	comprehensive
Sweden	comprehensive
Switzerland	comprehensive
Turkey	not yet in force
USSR	airline profits – not yet in force
Yugoslavia	comprehensive

Each treaty must be considered separately to see whether a particular activity will give rise to a foreign permanent establishment and hence foreign tax. They are all different, having been negotiated over a large period of time and many being in different formats.

2.6 Liability to foreign tax

If the UK exporter trades through a permanent establishment in Europe he will be liable to pay foreign tax. He is no longer merely trading *with* Europe, but trading *in* Europe.

This leads to the first point of international tax planning. The UK corporation tax rate is 35 per cent and this is now lower than most industrialised countries, although foreign tax rates are decreasing. Therefore the UK exporter could decide to retain an independent agent rather than switch to a dependent agent, in order to avoid having a permanent establishment which entails a liability to higher foreign taxes.

Rates of tax on corporate profits (including local tax)

UK	*35%*
EC	
Belgium	41%
Denmark	40%
France	37%
Germany	50%
Greece	46%
Ireland	43%
Italy	46%
Luxembourg	34%
Netherlands	35%

Portugal	40%
Spain	35%

2.7 Nominal and effective tax rates

As can be seen, only Luxembourg, Spain and the Netherlands have rates as low as, or lower than the UK's. These rates are a general guide only. Different countries have reliefs for different levels of profits (as in the UK), different types of profits (as in Ireland), different types of companies (as in Luxembourg), differing rates on distributed and retained profits (as in Germany) or do not tax certain types of income and gains from subsidiaries (as in the Netherlands).

Example

Belgium can provide a useful centre for coordinating foreign operations. Belgian coordination centres enjoy many tax privileges in Belgium. They can provide a useful tax deferral vehicle for UK companies with overseas operations. The profits are determined as a percentage of costs, and so the nominal Belgian tax rate of 41 per cent is simply not relevant.

Example

Germany taxes the profits of foreign branches at 56 per cent including local taxes, which is considerably higher than the UK's 35 per cent. Accordingly, before deciding to move from pure export to having a German permanent establishment, careful consideration should be given to the tax cost of doing so as opposed to the commercial advantages.

Quite apart from different companies being subjected to lower rates of tax, many countries grant special deductions, so that the nominal rate of tax is even less of a guide to the final rate of tax. Depreciation is one very important area for special deductions. Some countries restrict it to plant and equipment. Some extend it to buildings. Some allow depreciation of intangibles, for example goodwill, franchises, patents, copyrights, know-how and research and development expenses.

Some countries require that accounting and tax depreciation are in line. Other countries allow special tax deductions in respect of stock, along the lines of the UK's now defunct stock relief. Many countries have grants or allow rapid write-off of research and development. Some countries, especially in Scandinavia, allow tax deductions as specified investment reserves. In some countries, reserves for future pensions can be deducted even though no cash contributions are made. Other countries allow deductions for dividends.

Example

Austria	export-related investments and trade debts attract special deductions.
Belgium	acquired goodwill may be written off over five years.
Denmark	capital expenditure in respect of scientific research may be written off in the year incurred.
France	new subsidiaries need not pay tax for up to two years, and pay at reduced rates for the following 36 months (subject to certain conditions).
Germany	system of roll-over relief is available so that capital gains tax is not necessarily paid when fixed assets are sold.
Switzerland	an allowance against tax is available for the cost of buildings including land.

It can be seen that the nominal rate must be treated as a general guide only, but it does indicate the relatively low UK tax rate even when the various foreign incentives are taken into account.

2.8 Permissions

As with any journey, there may be formalities to complete before it can begin. First, one must consider exchange controls.

Since 1979 the UK has had no exchange controls, and since 1987 the Exchange Control Act has not been in force. Accordingly, it will be difficult for the UK to reintroduce exchange controls without at least some warning.

The mere fact that exchange control has disappeared in the UK and will rapidly disappear within the European Community is no guide to other areas of Europe. Other countries may have exchange control restrictions, or other restrictions on inward foreign investment, notwithstanding the worldwide trend for greater freedom of currency movement. In particular, Eastern Europe has very extensive exchange controls. Chapter 20 examines the exchange control systems of 17 European countries. As can be seen, there are residuary exchange controls in many Western European countries and substantial exchange controls in Eastern European countries. The broader questions relating to Eastern Europe are looked at on a country by country basis in Appendix C.

Apart from exchange controls, other permissions may be required. UK Treasury Consent is less relevant since 1988, but because it is a criminal offence to fail to seek consent where it is necessary, the question must be carefully considered. This is a point that is discussed in greater detail in Chapter 7.

Conversely, foreign countries may have inward investment approvals that are required before export trade can commence, let alone a branch or subsidiary be established. Careful advice should be taken with respect to exchange control restrictions, inward investment and repatriation of profits, foreign investment permissions, or local participation requirements.

2.9 Full operation

Having obtained the relevant permissions, and having established a permanent establishment overseas and hence become liable to foreign tax, the UK company must consider whether to expand its foreign presence to a full operation. The reasons for doing so include:

- commercial image – customers may wish to trade with a local entity;
- overcoming trade or exchange control restrictions;
- simplifying the acquisition of local companies;
- providing a vehicle to attract and employ local nationals which may be necessary to sell the product in the local market, particularly bearing in mind the lack of foreign languages among UK companies' management;
- in the case of acquisition, widening the range of products and markets;
- shortening transport distances;
- taking out a competitor's share;
- commitment by local staff to build the group's business in the relevant European country;

- dedication of the entire efforts of the group to that country rather than diffusing the efforts over a number of operations;
- better internal control of stock, cash and other resources.

There are disadvantages of course. These include the cost of making the investment, personnel management problems particularly bearing in mind differing language and customs, the increase in fixed overheads, political risks, exchange control risks, financial risks, not to mention the exposure to local taxation.

The UK group's management will automatically become a great deal more complex. Finally there is the very important danger of exposure to legal liability, although the use of a local subsidiary rather than a branch can help to overcome this particular problem.

This brings us to the next stage. Should the operation be structured as a branch or a subsidiary?

3

Branch or Subsidiary?

3.1 Trading in Europe

Having proceeded along the journey and established a taxable presence, 'trading *with* Europe' has evolved into 'trading *in* Europe'. Management has decided to develop the permanent establishment into a full operation. The next question to be considered is whether the operation should be run as a branch or a subsidiary. UK companies' decisions should not be governed by tax; they must carefully consider the commercial and strategic advantages and disadvantages of trading overseas through a branch or subsidiary.

3.2 Branch versus subsidiary – commercial reasons

In actual fact the decision of branch or subsidiary is not usually made on tax grounds but on commercial grounds. If the field of operations is, say, France it will generally be best to approach the French market by using a French company. It presents a better commercial image, and it will generally be easier to obtain local finance. Also, in some countries, as a matter of law, businesses must operate as local subsidiaries – sometimes with minimum local participation – especially in Eastern Europe. After 1993 these requirements should not be relevant within the EC, but may still be relevant in other parts of Europe.

Another major advantage of a subsidiary is that its shareholders (whether they are a UK company or individuals) will have limited liability. Sometimes the advantage of this limitation will be negated through the parent company being required to give guarantees for the debts of the overseas subsidiary. So important is this limitation of liability that even if tax considerations cause the operation to be structured as a branch, very often a separate UK company will be set up just to carry on the overseas branch, with no other activities. Other non-tax advantages of subsidiaries include the availability of local incentives and grants, which are often not available to a branch, and also limitation on disclosure. A subsidiary would generally have to disclose only its own results. A branch may also have to disclose the results of its head office so that the foreign tax authorities can apportion overhead expenses. It is often easier to justify overheads such as royalties and interest paid by a foreign subsidiary to its UK parent, as opposed to their payment by a foreign branch to its UK head office.

Among the advantages of a branch is that it is simple to operate. Requirements for filing and auditing accounts and complying with local corporate law are usually less onerous and this can lead to an economy of costs. Also, there are usually no foreign capital or stamp duties on branches. Most countries impose taxes on capital contributed into a foreign company. However, the EC is scheduled to abolish capital duty within the Community by 1992. The UK has not had capital duty for some time.

A foreign subsidiary sometimes may be required to have local shareholders and directors. A foreign branch will rarely need to have local managers.

3.3 Tax reasons

Finally we turn to tax. The essential tax-difference between a branch and a subsidiary is that the profits and losses of a branch are taxable and offsettable against UK tax, whereas those of a subsidiary are generally 'isolated' from UK tax in that profits are not taxed and losses are not available for relief.

The profits and the losses of branches will be consolidated with the UK's for both statutory accounts and corporation tax purposes. Relief will be obtained for foreign branch losses, especially in the opening years when losses are often incurred. Double tax relief will be available for foreign taxes imposed on the branch profits, and more rarely where there is a branch withholding tax. Where the overseas tax rate is greater than the UK's 35 per cent there will be a waste of foreign tax. This is a disadvantage of a branch.

On the other hand, the profits of an overseas subsidiary which is not resident in the UK will not be liable to UK corporation tax, until such time as the profits are repatriated back to the UK, typically as dividends but also as interest, royalties and management charges. This is subject to the UK's concept of residence, and also its anti-avoidance provisions with respect to foreign subsidiaries owned by UK companies (the controlled foreign company legislation) and income diverted overseas (Section 739 ICTA 1988). These are discussed in greater detail in Chapter 7 on anti-avoidance legislation. The isolation of the subsidiary means that profits are not taxed, but losses are not relievable.

Therefore, if a foreign operation will initially incur losses it may be advantageous to structure it as a branch. If it is likely to be profitable from an early date and foreign tax rates are low, it should probably be structured as a subsidiary. If the effective overseas tax rate is likely to be less than 35 per cent then tax may be deferred by profits being retained in a foreign subsidiary, which will not be the case with a branch.

An important distinction is that remittances of branch profits back to the UK head office will not usually attract foreign withholding tax, although this is rapidly changing and the US, France and Canada (to name but three) all impose branch withholding taxes. On the other hand, remittances of dividends from a foreign subsidiary to its UK parent will almost always attract a dividend withholding tax. However, double tax treaties can sometimes eliminate the branch withholding tax as in the case of the UK/France and UK/USA treaties, but, currently (see Appendix D) rarely eliminate dividend withholding tax and this can affect the branch/subsidiary decision.

Example

A UK company must decide between investing into France as a branch or a subsidiary.

By virtue of the UK/France double tax treaty the rate of withholding tax on profits remitted back to the UK head office by a French branch is now nil, whereas the rate of withholding tax on dividends remitted back to the UK parent of a French subsidiary is 5 per cent. Accordingly, there is a 5 per cent net tax advantage in trading in France as a French branch of a UK company as opposed to a subsidiary.

The dividend withholding tax represents an additional tax for a subsidiary rather than a branch. Of course, depending on the UK tax position, this extra tax might not be an extra burden if it could be used as a tax credit in the UK. However, with UK corporate tax rates generally lower than abroad, the withholding tax may not be usable as a credit, in which case it will become an extra overall tax. The UK also grants relief for 'underlying' tax – that is, tax on the profits of the foreign subsidiary out of which the dividend was paid. It is the combination of dividend withholding tax and this underlying tax that often leads to wasted double tax relief, ie an overall rate of double tax relief greater than 35 per cent, particularly bearing in mind the rates of tax prevalent in Europe.

It should be mentioned that some countries, for example Germany, reduce the tax charge on the subsidiary's profits by allowing dividends to be deducted, or by taxing distributed profits at a lower rate of tax. On the other hand, in some countries, for example Belgium, the rate of tax on the subsidiary's profits is lower than that applicable to a branch. This disparity may be alleviated by a double tax treaty, eg the UK/Belgium double tax treaty.

Reorganisation of the operation in the foreign country is often easier where the operation is carried on through a foreign subsidiary as opposed to a branch. On the other hand, single assets can sometimes be transferred more easily between branches and the UK, and indeed between the UK and branches. This is because there is no actual change in the ownership of the assets, and therefore there is generally no UK tax charge. However, there may well be a foreign tax liability. Similarly transfers of stock or services must always be made at an arm's-length price between a UK parent and its foreign subsidiary. From the UK tax point of view it need not be made at an arm's-length price between a UK head office and the branch. However, almost invariably the combination of the UK's transfer-pricing policy and the foreign country's transfer-pricing policy means that transactions between either head office and branch or parent and subsidiary must be on an arm's-length basis.

The ownership of assets as between branch and subsidiary also produces differing effects. Overseas capital gains made by a foreign branch will be taxed in the UK. The UK company will be liable to UK corporation tax at the normal 35 per cent on the resulting capital gain. Strictly speaking, a UK company is not liable to capital gains tax but to corporation tax on a capital gain, although the rules for computing the gain are identical for 'corporation tax on capital gains' and CGT. Double tax relief will be available with respect to any foreign tax paid on the disposal. On the other hand, in the case of a foreign subsidiary there will be no UK tax liability unless:

- the United Kingdom company is a 'close company' (most private companies are 'close');
- the gain is (essentially) a gain on the sale of an investment as opposed to an asset used in the trade.

Assets held by a branch which attract capital allowances will produce deductions both overseas and in the UK. This will not be the case with an overseas subsidiary, where the allowances will only be available abroad.

Another important distinction between the tax effect of branch and subsidiary relates to the sale of the business. If it is a branch, the sale of goodwill and other chargeable assets will usually be subject to foreign tax. At the same time the capital gain will also be taxable in the UK at 35 per cent and the foreign tax will be creditable against the UK tax. It could be that UK tax will be payable at a rate lower than the foreign tax because foreign tax is imposed at a higher rate, or because of UK tax losses or roll-over relief. In that event, the foreign tax will be a final additional tax.

On the other hand, if the foreign operation was set up as a subsidiary company the UK parent could realise the foreign business by selling the shares in the subsidiary. The UK shareholder would usually incur no foreign tax on selling the shares since most countries do not tax non-residents on sales of shares. However, the purchaser of the shares may require a discount for the inbuilt tax in the foreign subsidiary.

Generally, a foreign subsidiary affords much greater flexibility in the manner and timing of profit repatriation back to the UK. There is a choice with a subsidiary. Profits can be repatriated as a dividend, or as interest, or as a royalty, or as a capital gain on sale of the shares, or on liquidation, or even by a foreign subsidiary purchasing its own shares. The dividend or sale of shares can be timed so as to maximise double tax relief, or to set off a capital gain against UK losses. These choices are not usually available to a branch, where the profits are taxed as they arise.

A further advantage of subsidiaries is that many overseas countries permit consolidation of profits and losses between groups of local companies only. The foreign subsidiary could be part of a local group. Its profits can then offset profits and losses of other group companies in the same country, and very often assets can be transferred tax free between group companies. This is not usually available as between a foreign branch of a UK company and a foreign subsidiary of a UK company. The EC is trying to extend this system of 'group relief' to all EC subsidiaries.

3.4 Incorporation of a branch

Looked at from a pure tax point of view, it is very often the case that a UK company will wish to establish a foreign operation as a branch so as to offset early year losses against UK profits, and then once the operation becomes profitable incorporate the branch into a foreign subsidiary and then isolate the later profits. This incorporation may have tax implications.

Consideration should be given to the position of the accumulated losses. In the United Kingdom these may have been used up. However, in the overseas country the losses may be allowed to be carried forward against the future profits of the operating subsidiary. This is possible in Ireland, but not possible in France. Each situation should be looked at separately.

If a foreign branch is incorporated then assets will be transferred from the overseas branch to the overseas subsidiary. In the UK there will be a recapture of capital allowances based on the market value of the assets being transferred. Trading stock will be revalued to market value and a deemed sale made. Assets with an inherent capital gain including, in particular, goodwill (effectively the difference between what a third party would pay for the company and what the assets are worth), land and buildings will *prima facie* be subject to UK tax as if they had been sold at market value. However if the entire consideration for the transfer is shares or loan stock then any capital gain will be deferred until the shares are sold or the loan stock is redeemed.

The overseas tax position on the transfer of the branch assets will also need to be considered. In France, unless the transfer qualifies as a 'tax-free merger' there would be French tax, including tax on goodwill. This would make such a transfer very disadvantageous. However, in Belgium although unused tax losses cannot be carried forward into the new subsidiary, gains on the incorporation of the subsidiary may be deferred by reinvestment into Belgian fixed assets.

One solution to this problem will be to keep assets with an inherent capital gain (for example land, buildings and possibly even goodwill) in the overseas branch of the UK company, and merely transfer the other trading assets to a subsidiary. The new subsidiary would rent the premises and pay a royalty for the use of the goodwill. Under the UK's double tax treaties with most European countries the royalties should flow free of withholding tax back to the UK parent company (see Appendix E: European withholding taxes).

The foreign branch could sell stock to the foreign subsidiary on a consignment, ie sale or return basis. This would defer payment of tax until the stock was actually sold by the subsidiary. Care should be exercised to ensure that all necessary consents for the transfer, both UK and overseas, are obtained. It may be necessary to obtain Treasury Consent. This is a point that is discussed further in later chapters.

If the foreign legislation does not allow unutilised losses to be carried forward into the subsidiary, it may be advisable to delay incorporation until such time as the losses have been exhausted.

3.5 Acquiring assets or shares

When a business is acquired abroad, as opposed to set up *ab initio*, similar factors affect the question of whether to purchase assets or shares as opposed to setting up a branch or subsidiary. An existing operation can, of course, be acquired in a number of different ways. The assets of the business could be purchased, either singly or as an ongoing branch. A foreign branch of the UK company could purchase the assets. A foreign subsidiary of the UK parent could purchase the assets. Alternatively the UK parent could buy, directly or indirectly, the shares of an existing overseas company. The various different structures have radically different implications. In later chapters we will look at the use of the foreign holding company in order to obtain tax relief on acquisition debt. At the moment we will restrict ourselves to looking at the simple case of a UK company acquiring assets or shares.

There are usually allowances available on the purchase of assets, but there are nearly always no allowances on the purchase of shares. The purchase of shares brings with it any hidden or contingent liabilities in the company, whereas assets can be purchased more or less free of such encumbrances. The problem with buying assets as opposed to shares is that often the vendor will wish to sell shares, and if he sells assets he will expect a price which reflects the advantages to the UK purchaser. This is a question that must be looked at on a case-by-case basis.

The UK company may inherit latent foreign tax or other liabilities when it buys the shares of a foreign company. Normally the tax cost of the capital assets of the foreign subsidiary being purchased will be less than the value placed on them in arriving at a purchase price for the shares. If the foreign subsidiary eventually sells the asset, a tax liability may then arise by reference to their original cost to the company. If the UK company plans to sell off the assets immediately, the tax liability will be real rather than latent. In some countries this may not be a problem. For example, in Germany it is possible to 'step up' the value paid for shares to each asset by an internal sale. The disadvantage is that such a sale is liable to local tax, and this disadvantage must be set off against the longer term advantage of increased allowances on the enhanced value of the assets.

Similarly, the acquisition of the foreign subsidiary may not so much assume latent tax liabilities, but confer a tax benefit such as past tax losses. In many countries, Ireland, for example, these losses cannot be carried forward where there is a major change in ownership. In other countries they can be carried forward and will be of real value. The contract of sale may state that part of the purchase price is to be withheld until the losses are used.

When a foreign subsidiary is acquired as opposed to assets, there may be the foreign equivalent of the UK's stamp duty. Sometimes this may be avoided by reorganising the foreign subsidiary's share capital prior to acquisition. However, stamp-type duties may also be payable on the acquisition of assets. The two liabilities should be compared before a contract is signed.

In some countries, if a UK company purchases an ongoing branch, tax losses will be available to carry forward. This will be the case in Ireland. If this is not the case then it will always be possible to incorporate the operation into a new foreign subsidiary to acquire the business.

However, essentially the advantage of acquiring assets is the availability of deductions. For example, the purchase of stock will generate a tax deduction equal to the price paid. The cost of purchasing capital assets will produce relief in the UK according to the normal rules relating to capital allowances, and may also obtain depreciation deductions overseas.

3.6 Commercial versus tax reasons

There are a number of areas in which the tax treatment of a foreign branch and a foreign subsidiary differ. However, these differences will form only one of the criteria upon which the decision as to how to operate overseas will be based. The essential decision must be made on commercial grounds, which is why almost invariably the decision is in favour of a subsidiary, especially where the foreign operation is substantial. Throughout the rest of this book, unless otherwise stated, we will assume that the UK company has one, and in due course several, overseas subsidiaries.

In making the decision of branch versus subsidiary the old maxim 'the tax tail should not wag the commercial dog' must be followed.

Financing the Subsidiary

4.1 Choices

Having decided to trade abroad as a locally incorporated and resident subsidiary, the next question on the journey is how the subsidiary should be financed. No matter how extended the credit granted by the UK parent, there will almost invariably be a need for the foreign subsidiary to be put in funds. This is especially the case in the early years when losses are often incurred. In later years (it is hoped) the foreign subsidiary may be making upstream loans back to the UK parent! Let us look at the options available.

4.2 Local borrowings

First, the foreign subsidiary may be financed with borrowings from a local bank, by which is meant a bank local to the foreign operation. There are several advantages.

It is simple. Loans from outside the country may require exchange control approval. It is flexible. Further loans may be taken out or the loan repaid with relative ease. Generally interest will be paid to the local bank without any withholding tax. This may not be the case with interest paid on a loan from the UK parent.

A word of warning. Very often the extent to which a foreign subsidiary can borrow from a local bank is severely curtailed through local exchange control restrictions. This is the case, for example, in Spain and Italy. Certainly in these countries such restrictions should disappear in Europe beyond 1993.

A borrowing from a local bank to a local limited liability subsidiary will also have the effect of nominally isolating the liability from the UK. However, almost invariably the local bank will require a guarantee from the UK parent for any substantial borrowing, and possibly the borrowing may even have to be made on a back-to-back basis – that is, the UK parent will have to deposit an actual sum of money with the local bank's equivalent in the UK (or elsewhere) and a borrowing then be made locally.

Detailed professional advice must be obtained in selecting the currency of the loan. Generally, the first point of call in terms of a local bank will be the foreign correspondent bank of the UK company's United Kingdom bank. The question of raising finance generally is dealt with in greater detail in Part 2.

4.3 Loans or shares

The next question is whether the subsidiary should be capitalised with loans or shares. Usually it is more advantageous to finance the subsidiary with loans. This is because:

- interest on loans is tax-deductible whereas, usually, dividends on shares are not; where foreign tax rates are higher than the UK's, which is commonly the case in Europe, this will transfer profits from a higher tax to a lower tax jurisdiction, ie the UK;
- there are usually lower or no withholding taxes on interest as opposed to dividends, as can be seen from the following table:

Withholding tax to United Kingdom on:

	Interest	*Dividends (may depend on % of ownership)*
Austria	nil	5%/15%
Belgium	10%	5%/10%
Denmark	nil	nil/15%
Finland	nil	5%
France	nil	5%
Germany	nil	15%
Ireland	nil	nil
Italy	15%	5%/15%
Luxembourg	nil	5%/15%
Netherlands	nil	5%/15%
Norway	nil	10%/15%
Spain	12%	10%
Sweden	nil	nil/5%
Switzerland	nil	5%/15%

Example

A Netherlands subsidiary paying £100 to a UK parent would pay £100 interest but only £95 dividend. The other £5 would be available for double tax relief. At best it would represent a cash flow disadvantage. At worst it would represent an actual loss of income to the UK parent.

Appendix E sets out the withholding taxes imposed by various European countries when dividends, interest and royalties flow between them.

- Loans can be repaid more easily than shares. There will usually be capital gains tax, and sometimes even income tax, when shares are repaid. This can be overcome partly by the use of redeemable shares.
- It is easier to select the currency of loans and in some cases this provides good opportunities for tax planning. For example, in Switzerland and the Netherlands, in general a currency loss on a loan is deductible but a profit is either not taxable or only taxed when the loan is repaid.
- There are usually fewer stamp or capital duties on loans than shares.
- Loans can be converted easily into shares, but not vice versa.
- Loans are more flexible than shares. They may carry a low rate of interest compensated by a premium on repayment, or a discount on issue. They may even carry a zero rate of interest, a so-called 'zero coupon bond'.
- The European subsidiary's after-tax profits can be repatriated at no tax cost by repaying the loans it owes to the UK parent. However, a careful check must be made to ensure that the loan repayments are not classified as dividends in the European subsidiary's country.

4.4 Thin-capitalisation and debt:equity ratios

Because of the advantages of financing subsidiaries with loans, many countries have rules to deal with 'thin-capitalisation'. This is a term which describes the 'debt:equity' ratio, that is, the ratio of loans to shares and reserves. Where the debt:equity ratio of foreign-owned subsidiaries exceeds a certain figure, interest will generally be disallowed and treated as a dividend, and loan repayments may be treated as a distribution.

Some very rough guidelines to debt:equity ratios are as follows:

Austria	no guidelines
Belgium	no guidelines
Denmark	no guidelines
Finland	100:25–30
France	3:2
Germany	no guidelines
Ireland	no guidelines
Italy	domestic borrowings only
Luxembourg	3:1 for holding companies
Netherlands	6:1
Norway	no guidelines
Spain	domestic borrowings only
Sweden	no guidelines
Switzerland – financial	6:1
– property	4:1
– industrial	3:1
– commercial	2:1

Some countries may impose thin-capitalisation restrictions through exchange control or inward investment controls rather than through tax laws. In the Netherlands the ratio is effectively imposed through the advance tax ruling system. Even where there are no guidelines it is not necessarily the case that there are no debt:equity ratios. Excessive capitalisation with debt may lead to interest being disallowed under general anti-avoidance legislation.

As an example of how the lack of guidelines need not necessarily mean that there are no thin-capitalisation restrictions, one need look no further than the example of Germany.

Example

At present there is no law which specifies a debt:equity ratio. However, to avoid excessive capitalisation of foreign debts there is currently a proposal to introduce a 'new' tax law. This was announced by the Minister of Finance on 16 March 1987! Loan capital which is 'hidden' share capital, based on legal or economic considerations, for example, where economically it is essential that a company should have a certain level of share capital, will be treated as share capital and interest on such loan capital will be disallowed. It was to be the case that if a UK company capitalised a German subsidiary with a debt:equity ratio of more than 10:1, essentially the equity was less than 10 per cent of the total assets, and interest would be treated as a dividend. Similarly, repayments of loan capital would be treated as repayments of share capital and cause a German tax liability to crystallise. However, the Tax Court in Düsseldorf rejected the 10:1 ratio. At present tax reform is planned after the elections for a united Germany at the end of 1990, and debt:equity ratios may be included in these reforms.

It is often possible to avoid thin-capitalisation problems by back-to-back bank borrowings. As we have seen, this entails the foreign subsidiary borrowing from a local bank rather than directly from its UK parent. The borrowing will be secured (either formally or informally) by either a deposit by the UK parent with the same bank outside the foreign subsidiary's country or, alternatively, the UK parent's guaranteeing the subsidiary's bank borrowings. Under those circumstances the UK's transfer pricing legislation would mean that the foreign subsidiary should pay the UK parent a guarantee fee. Such exchange control restrictions and complex arrangements are particularly relevant in Eastern Europe, although that is, of course, a fast-changing area – see Appendix C.

4.5 Share capital can be good

It should not be forgotten that share capital has advantages. These include:

- maximising the foreign subsidiary's retained profits and minimising UK taxable income until such time as a dividend is paid; share capital will therefore be of advantage when tax rates overseas are lower than in the UK, and this could be either because the actual tax rate is lower or, for example, because the overseas subsidiary was incurring losses;
- certain tax incentives applying only to share capital and not loan capital; for example, in certain Swiss cantons there is a deduction based on share capital;
- if a sale of the foreign subsidiary's shares will be liable to foreign

tax, when there will be a larger deduction for the cost of shares as opposed to loans;

- some countries taxing distributed profits at a lower level than undistributed profits – for example, Germany; it may therefore be more efficient overall to repatriate profits from Germany as dividends rather than interest.

It should also be borne in mind that under the UK's system of double tax relief a UK company which owns more than 10 per cent of a foreign company will obtain underlying tax relief on a dividend repatriated to the UK: that is, the UK company will obtain double tax relief for the foreign tax on the profits out of which the dividend was paid. This means that in many instances dividends may be preferable to interest. Underlying tax relief is discussed in greater detail in Chapter 5.

A major advantage of share capital is that dividends can be paid where the foreign subsidiary is eligible for an exemption from foreign tax which the UK has agreed to treat as paid for the purposes of underlying tax relief. Such articles in double tax treaties are known as 'tax sparing' articles. The only countries in Europe with which the UK has concluded double tax treaties which contain tax sparing clauses are Cyprus, Malta, Portugal, Spain and Yugoslavia. An example may help to clarify tax sparing.

Example

A UK company owns 100 per cent of a Cypriot company. The Cyprus company earns 100 of profits. Normally it would be subject to 30 of Cyprus tax on those profits. However, because of certain specific exemptions in Cypriot domestic legislation the profits escape tax altogether. The Cypriot subsidiary pays a dividend of 100 to its UK parent. The UK company is taxed on the 100 of dividend at 35 per cent, making a liability of 35 in total. However, it receives a tax credit by virtue of the UK/Cyprus double tax treaty for the 30 of Cypriot tax that the Cypriot company never paid! It therefore pays only 5 to the UK Inland Revenue. (This example has been greatly simplified.)

4.6 Commercial rationale

There are many different methods of financing a subsidiary. These are discussed in further detail in Chapter 18 which deals with financing the overseas branch or subsidiary. The different methods of finance have different implications.

The overseas subsidiary can borrow locally. It can be financed with loans from its UK parent, or it could be financed with shares from its UK parent of different types, either ordinary shares or possibly redeemable shares. In later chapters we will look at how a group which expands further abroad can finance foreign subsidiaries through companies located offshore.

There are other ways by which a UK parent can finance a European subsidiary. For example, it may enter into a 'credit swap' whereby the UK parent will make available hard currency, such as sterling, to the subsidiary's local bank in exchange for lending on advantageous terms by the local bank to the European subsidiary. UK companies can even purchase government debt at a discount. In return, the foreign government will make local currency available at advantageous rates. Both of these techniques are of most relevance to Eastern Europe.

However, as with the choice of branch and subsidiary, it is often a commercial decision rather than a tax decision. Share capital projects a better commercial image. In addition the foreign subsidiary may need to have a significant equity base in order to raise outside borrowings. Also the UK company may not have sufficient borrowing power or internal cash resources to lend intra-group. There can be no hard and fast rules.

5

Double Taxation Relief

5.1 Setting the scene

A UK company is liable to UK corporation tax on its worldwide profits. If it has overseas sources of income (eg trading profits, dividends from overseas companies, interest and royalties) those sources of income may be taxable overseas, subject to the terms of the UK's double taxation agreements. This is a complex subject which is best illustrated by worked examples.

Let us look at the simplest situation: a UK company with a Swiss branch suffering 17 per cent effective Swiss (federal and cantonal) tax.

Example

UK company with Swiss branch

UK profits	1,000
Swiss profits	100
Swiss tax	17
UK tax 35% of 1,100	385
Double tax relief	17
UK tax to actually pay	368

If the branch had been German it would have suffered German tax at, say, approximately 50 per cent. The UK will only grant double tax relief against the 35 per cent UK tax on foreign income, and so 15 out of the 50 German tax will be wasted. In the UK, excess foreign tax cannot be carried forward or back.

Example

UK tax 35% of 1,100	385
Double tax relief limited to	35
UK tax to actually pay	350
Wasted German tax	15

Many countries, including the UK, give tax credits both under double tax treaties and unilaterally. Where, for example, a UK resident company has overseas income which has suffered foreign tax, the UK allows the foreign tax to be set against the UK tax liability on the same income. The UK does not allow double tax credits to be carried forward or back. Where the foreign tax exceeds the UK liability, the excess foreign tax is wasted.

5.2 Deducting the foreign tax

If the UK parent has losses, the foreign tax can be expensed rather than credited.

Example

UK company with Swiss branch

UK losses	(1,000)
Swiss profits	100
Swiss tax	17
If Swiss tax credited, losses carried forward	900
If Swiss tax expensed, losses carried forward	917

5.3 Underlying tax

Where a UK company receives a dividend from an overseas subsidiary which it owns to the extent of 10 per cent or more, double tax relief is given not only for withholding taxes deducted but also for underlying taxes suffered on the taxed income out of which the dividend is paid.

Example

UK company with French subsidiary.

French subsidiary	
Profits	100
Corporate tax paid, say	30
	70

Dividend – cash		66.5	
– 5% wht	(5% of 70)	3.5	
			(70)
Retained profits			nil

Received by the UK parent

Cash		66.5
Withholding tax		3.5
Underlying tax		30.0
UK company taxed on		100.0
Tax at 35%		35.0
Less: Withholding tax	3.5	
Underlying tax	30.0	33.5
UK tax to actually pay		1.5

If the rate of foreign tax, including foreign underlying tax, rises above 35 per cent then tax relief will be wasted.

Example

UK company receives a dividend of £100,000 from its Belgian subsidiary from which 5 per cent withholding tax is deducted (as per the UK/Belgium double tax treaty). The Belgian company had profits after tax of £200,000 on which Belgian corporation tax of £100,000 had been paid (effective rate 50 per cent). The UK liability is calculated as follows:

		£000
Net dividend received in the UK		95
Add: Withholding tax suffered		5
Dividend declared		100
Underlying tax (100/200 × 100)		50
Amount assessed to UK corporation tax		150
UK corporation tax at 35%		52.5
Less: Withholding tax	5	
Underlying tax	50	
	55	
Limited to UK tax liability		(52.5)
UK corporation tax payable		nil
Wasted foreign tax (55–52.5)		2.5

It is possible to 'spot' dividends by paying dividends out of profits for specified periods where companies have suffered high rates of tax rather than from other periods where the rate of tax may have been lower, irrespective of the nominal tax rate. Variances in the effective tax rate could be due to allowances and incentives, causing the actual rate paid to vary from the nominal rate.

Underlying tax relief is available not just for the tax on the profits out of which the dividend is paid, but also on a 'chain' through a corporate structure, so long as the 10 per cent ownership of each dividend-paying company is met. For example, if a UK company owns a foreign company ('F Co 1') which in turn owns another foreign company ('F Co 2') then when a dividend is paid by F Co 2 to F Co 1 and then by F Co 1 up to the UK parent, underlying tax relief will be available in the UK for the following:

- dividend withholding tax on the dividend from F Co 1 to the UK parent;
- underlying tax on the profits of F Co 1 out of which the dividend was paid back to the UK;
- underlying tax on the foreign tax on the profits of F Co 2 out of which a dividend was paid to F Co 1;
- dividend withholding tax imposed on a dividend between F Co 2 and F Co 1.

5.4 Case V Traps

A UK sub-holding company is a separate UK subsidiary of the UK parent which owns the foreign subsidiary.

It serves purposes which are both commercial and tax. From the tax point of view it helps maximise double tax relief. This is because the overseas dividend (or other income) should be received by a company which has no losses, especially non-trading 'losses' such as excess management expenses of an investment company. If, for example, an overseas dividend is received by a company with losses, double tax relief will be wasted. Therefore the dividend should be received by a UK company that carries on no other activities. Group relief can then be claimed as appropriate. Such companies are known as 'Case V Traps' because overseas dividends are subject to UK corporation tax under Case V of Schedule D.

An example of how a Case V Trap can avoid wasting double tax relief is set out below.

Example

A UK company has non-trading losses of 40 and receives a 'gross' dividend of 100 with combined underlying and withholding tax of 33.

UK Co is taxed on:

Non-trading losses	(40)
Dividend	100
Taxed on	60
Tax at 35%	21
Double tax relief limited to	(21)
Wasted foreign tax (33–21)	12
Losses carried forward	nil

If the UK company had incorporated a Case V Trap, the Trap would have been taxed on:

Example

Case V Trap received dividend of	100
UK tax at 35%	35
Double tax relief	(33)
UK tax to pay	2
Wasted foreign tax (33–33)	nil
Losses carried forward by UK Co	40

The loss could also be used for group relief to eliminate the UK tax of 2, but would not have been so available if no Case V Trap had been used. This illustrates another advantage of a Case V Trap. Just the right amount of group relief can be claimed to protect the loss carry-forward position and avoid wasting double tax relief.

Group relief can be allocated to sources of overseas income as appropriate. In the next example it is assumed that a UK company with subsidiaries in the USA, Netherlands and France has losses of (at least) 36. It receives dividends from its subsidiaries as shown.

Example

Case V sources – before group relief:

Dividend from:		*USA*		*Netherlands*		*France*
Dividend received (after wht)		95		47.5		57
Withholding tax		5		2.5		3
Dividend paid		100		50		60
Gross up for underlying tax		30		20		30
Gross income for UK purposes		130		70		90
UK Tax at 35%		45.5		24.5		31.5
Double tax relief:						
Underlying tax	30		20		30	
Withholding tax	5	(35)	2.5	(22.5)	3	(31.5)
UK Tax payable		10.5		2.0		nil
						(1.5 wasted)

Case V Sources – after group relief:

	USA	Netherlands	France
Gross income for UK purposes	130	70	90
Group relief surrendered	(30)	(6)	–
	100	64	90
UK tax at 35%	35	22.4	31.5
Double tax relief (above)	(35)	(22.4)	(31.5)
UK tax payable	nil	nil	nil
		0.1 wasted	(1.5 wasted)
Total group relief requirement	36		

A claim may be made for the exact amount of group relief (36) from the loss-making fellow group member, maximising not only group relief but also the loss situation.

5.5 Overseas holding companies

It is often advantageous to place overseas holding companies between the UK resident parent company and overseas operating subsidiaries.

The overseas holding company will usually be based in a different country from the operating subsidiary. This has several important advantages.

Most importantly, from the double tax relief aspect, if dividends from high-taxed and low-taxed subsidiaries are paid *first* to an overseas holding company, the high and low underlying tax rates can effectively be *averaged*, since the rate of underlying tax on dividends which the UK parent would receive from the overseas holding company will be a mixture of the high and low rates. This is known as 'mixing' and is a major reason for owning overseas subsidiaries through overseas holding companies.

On the other hand, if dividends from high-taxed and low-taxed overseas subsidiaries are repatriated directly back to a UK parent – ie not via an overseas holding company – tax is payable on the low-taxed dividend, but the higher underlying and withholding taxes of the second dividend will be wasted. This is because the UK's tax legislation will treat these dividends as income from two completely separate sources, double tax relief on which *must* be computed quite independently. Conversely, the UK's tax legislation regards the dividend from the overseas holding company as a single source and all the underlying taxes can therefore be effectively averaged.

The elimination of wasted double tax relief by 'mixing' is illustrated below.

Example

An *offshore holding company* receives a dividend of 100 (cash) from one foreign subsidiary funded out of profits of 165 on which tax of 65 has been suffered. The holding company also receives a dividend of 100 (cash) from a second subsidiary funded out of profits of 120 on which tax of 20 has been suffered. The cash received *is paid on to the UK parent* as a dividend, net of a 5 per cent withholding tax.

Received by UK parent

Cash received from offshore holding company	190
Withholding tax (5% on dividend of 200 paid by holding company)	10
	200

Underlying taxes

Offshore holding company	nil	
First sub	65	
Second sub	20	
		85
UK parent subject to tax on		285
Tax at 35% on 285		99
Less: Withholding tax	10	
Underlying taxes (65+20)	85	
		95
UK tax payable		4

If the dividends had been received directly by the UK parent, the UK tax payable would have been *nil* on the dividend from the first subsidiary and *22* (35 per cent of 120−20) on the dividend from the second subsidiary. *An extra 18 of tax (22−4) would have been payable* as compared to when mixing is available.

It is only when there is more than one subsidiary, and indeed widely differing effective rates of tax, that dividend mixing will be relevant. If there is more than one subsidiary with differing effective rates of tax then mixing will be advantageous. For mixing to be effective, one rate of underlying and withholding tax must be greater than 35 per cent and the other less than 35 per cent. This is not always the case in terms of UK companies investing into Europe.

In addition, when a UK company first begins to expand into Europe it will not have a clear idea of how far it will go. It will usually expand into only one country at a time, and until it acquires at least two subsidiaries dividend mixing will not be relevant. Nevertheless a UK company may still wish to have an offshore holding company for reasons that are discussed in greater detail in later chapters.

5.6 Netherlands holding companies

The Netherlands is often used as an offshore holding company location, especially with respect to UK companies expanding into Europe. This is because Netherlands holding companies, assuming that they satisfy all the right conditions, are not taxed either on dividends received from overseas subsidiaries or on a disposal of shares in overseas subsidiaries.

Interestingly, in the future, proposals currently being put forward by the European Commission might enable exempt Luxembourg holding companies to be used for investment into the EC with the advantage of no withholding tax on dividends paid outside the EC. The Netherlands imposes a dividend withholding tax of 5–25 per cent.

You will recall that in the opening chapters we discussed how the UK's tax rate – certainly its nominal tax rate – was generally lower than that of most other European countries. On the other hand, as discussed and illustrated, nominal rates are not necessarily a guide to actual rates of tax suffered.

Consider the next example where a UK company owns a Netherlands offshore holding company which, in turn, owns shares in a Danish trading company which is suffering 50 per cent effective Danish tax (nominal rate 40 per cent). The Netherlands offshore holding company also owns an Irish company suffering only 10 per cent effective Irish tax because it is a manufacturing company (normal rate 43 per cent).

Example

First, assume that the Irish and Danish subsidiaries are directly owned by the UK company.

A UK company receives two dividends, one direct from an Irish manufacturing company subject to 10 per cent, and one direct from a Danish company subject to 50 per cent tax. It is not possible for the tax on the dividends to be mixed to match the UK rate because they are received direct from abroad and are treated by UK tax law as two separate sources.

Dividend mixing – the problem

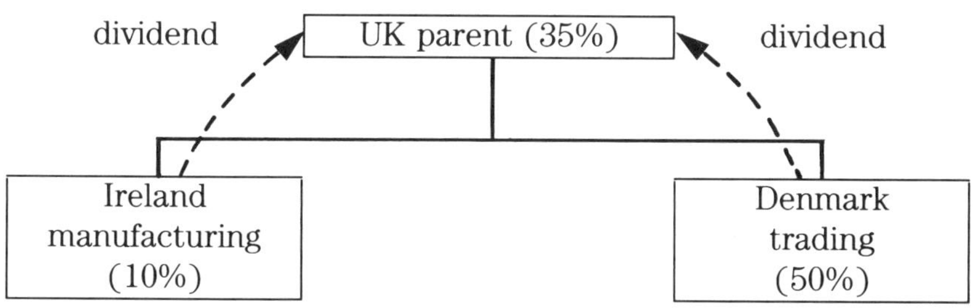

The dividends are considered as separate sources of income. The consequences are as follows:

- Dividend paid out of profits of 100 paid by Ireland
  Additional UK tax payable (35−10) = 25.
- Dividend paid out of profits of 100 paid by Denmark
  No relief for excess Danish tax paid UK tax to pay (35−35) = nil
  Wasted double tax relief (50−35) = 15

However, by using an offshore holding company such as a Netherlands holding company the rates of tax on the Irish and Danish companies can be 'mixed', as follows:

Dividend mixing – a possible solution

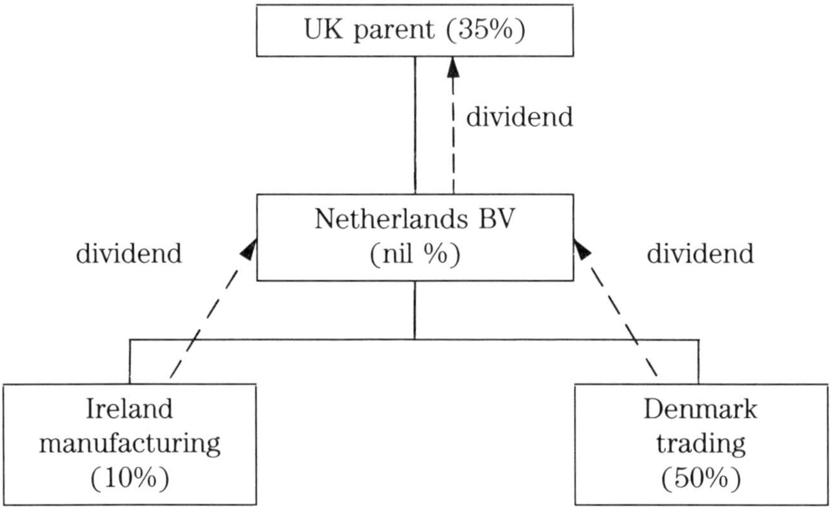

Netherlands BV receives

Cash from Ireland		90
Cash from Denmark		50
		140

Pays to UK parent

Cash	133	
Withholding tax of 5% of 140	7	
		140

UK parent taxed on

Cash received	133

Netherlands withholding tax	7
Irish underlying tax	10
Danish underlying tax	50
	200
Tax at 35%	70
Underlying and withholding taxes (7+10+50)	(67)
UK tax to pay	3
UK and overall tax saved by using Netherlands holding company (25−3)	22

The dividend from the Netherlands BV is considered as a single source of income. The dividends from Ireland and Denmark are 'mixed' in the Netherlands BV. By careful planning it should be possible to match exactly the UK corporation tax rate (35 per cent).

The dividends will not be taxable in the Netherlands provided the participation exemption applies. However, a 5 per cent withholding tax is payable on dividends from the Netherlands to the UK. As dividends from Ireland to the UK would be payable without a withholding tax, this represents an additional tax cost. No additional withholding tax arises on the dividend from Denmark as the Netherlands/Denmark treaty provides a nil withholding rate on dividends. Dividends paid direct from Denmark to the UK would normally be exempt from withholding tax under the Denmark/UK treaty.

5.7 Minimising withholding taxes

Overseas holding companies can also maximise double tax relief by minimising withholding taxes. In certain cases an intermediate holding company can be used to reduce withholding taxes on dividends flowing back to the UK.

Example

A UK company with a subsidiary in Spain would, under normal circumstances, suffer 10 per cent withholding tax on dividends under the UK/Spain treaty. By interposing a Netherlands holding company the withholding tax rate can be reduced to 9.75 per cent

(5% + (5% × 95)). While the percentage reduction appears small, the amount saved in cash terms may be considerable. This will increase the ability of the UK parent to avoid wasting double tax relief by keeping the overall rate of foreign underlying and withholding taxes below 35 per cent.

Appendix E tables withholding tax rates on dividends, interest and royalties paid between various European countries. The low rates of withholding on passive income such as dividends flowing into the Netherlands can clearly be seen.

5.8 Unremittable overseas income and gains

If a UK company earns profits overseas of whatever description and is unable to remit those profits back to the UK *due to foreign government action* then no UK tax need be paid on that income. Similar provisions apply to capital gains. This prevents a UK company with a foreign branch from being subject to tax on profits that it can never use to pay that tax.

Example

A UK company has a Brazilian branch. It earns £100,000 in Brazil. It pays 20 per cent effective rate Brazilian tax. It has a liability to tax at 35 per cent on the branch, and *prima facie* would owe a further £15,000 to the UK Inland Revenue. That £15,000 need not be paid until such time as the profits of the branch can be remitted out of Brazil. If they are blocked by Brazilian exchange controls then no tax need be paid.

In Europe these provisions are of most likely application to Eastern Europe. The question of exchange control is dealt with on a country-by-country basis in Chapter 20 and Eastern Europe is discussed in Appendix C.

5.9 Summary

To summarise, the UK's system of double tax relief is complex. The simplest relief is direct credit which will occur, for example, if a UK company trades overseas as a branch.

Remember that if there are losses foreign tax can be expensed rather than credited, but this is less efficient.

Underlying tax relief is available where a UK parent receives a dividend from its foreign subsidiary. The UK company receives double tax relief not just for foreign withholding tax directly imposed on the dividend, but also for the foreign tax on the profits out of which the dividend was paid.

A Case V Trap is a simple means of maximising double tax relief without complex restructuring.

Finally, remember the importance of using an offshore holding company to mix high- and low-taxed dividends.

6
Residence

6.1 The first stumbling block

Residence is of fundamental importance when thinking of establishing a subsidiary overseas.

If a company is incorporated overseas but managed and controlled from the UK, it will be resident in the UK and hence liable to 35 per cent UK corporation tax on its worldwide income and gains.

Mere incorporation of a company outside the UK is insufficient in itself to classify it as an overseas company. If the company's business is managed and controlled in the UK because directors' meetings are held here, or crucial decisions are taken here, it will be taxed as a UK company. Thus, even though a company is incorporated abroad, it may effectively lose any tax benefits of overseas status.

The Inland Revenue will not accept that a subsidiary of a UK company is non-resident unless:

- it is incorporated under the laws of a foreign country (since 1988 all companies incorporated under the laws of England, Scotland or Northern Ireland are United Kingdom resident);
- it is managed and controlled overseas.

6.2 Management and control

It is therefore essential to determine when a company incorporated overseas is managed and controlled from the UK. A series of decisions by the courts in the nineteenth and early twentieth century effectively determined what constitutes UK management and control and hence UK residence.

Lord Loreburn LC in the House of Lords set out the currently accepted test of residence in the case of *De Beers Consolidated Mines Limited versus Howe*. He said 'a company resides for the purposes of income tax where its real business is carried on ... I regard that as the true rule; the real business is carried on where the central management and control actually abides'. In the De Beers case, the company was incorporated in South Africa and held board meetings there. However, a majority of its directors were UK resident, and the London-based directors were in a position to control the company's affairs by virtue of the company's Memorandum and Articles. This they did in practice. The De Beers case established the importance of establishing the country where directors meet to exercise control in determining a company's residence.

Management and control is sometimes referred to as 'the superior and directing authority'. It must be distinguished from mere 'day-to-day' supervision of the company's business, although very often the directors carry on both functions. The superior and directing authority decides the highest level of general policy. It will take strategic or fundamental decisions relating to the direction of the company's affairs.

The distinction between ultimate management and control and day-to-day management and control may be illustrated by a series of nineteenth-century cases in which it was held that companies which were managed and controlled from the United Kingdom, and hence resident here, carried on trades of, *inter alia*:

- an Italian sulphur mine
- a Colorado hotel
- an Indian jute mill
- a Brazilian railway
- United States breweries
- United States cotton mills
- a series of gasworks throughout Europe.

Other case law determined that the place where directors meet is a very important indication of the country in which management and control is exercised, and hence where the company is resident.

In the case of *American Thread Co versus Joyce*, a company carried on business in the USA, held regular board meetings in the USA but reserved matters of major importance for UK board meetings. It was held that the company was UK resident. The Lord Chancellor said:

> ... it is clear that the directorate in Manchester was the directorate of *paramount authority* as is shown not only by the fact that the reserved

> subjects are kept for them in extraordinary session, but by this, that ... they were constantly supervising and guiding the policy of the company, even as regards matters which belong to manufacture and trading.

It is usually the case that if it can be determined *who* exercises central management and control, the question of the country in which it is exercised and hence *where* the company is resident will be obvious. Even where a board of directors delegates its power to a subsidiary board which meets overseas, but retains the right to revoke the delegated powers, central management and control may still rest with the delegators.

It should be noted that the mere fact that the foreign subsidiary is controlled in terms of ownership by a UK shareholder, whether corporate or individual, will not affect the question of its residence. Residence is determined separately for each legal entity, so that the parent may be resident in the UK and the subsidiary resident overseas.

6.3 General principles of management and control

The general principles of determining where a company incorporated overseas is resident in terms of the country in which it is managed and controlled may be set out as shown below:

- The question of who owns the shares of a foreign subsidiary will not be relevant in determining where the subsidiary is resident.
- The country of incorporation is only one factor to be considered in determining where a foreign subsidiary is resident, and is not a very important factor, but since 1988 it cannot be incorporated in England, Scotland or Northern Ireland.
- A company is resident where it is managed and controlled.
- Management and control is located in the country where the highest authority within the company is exercised.
- The location of where directors meet is a very important indication of where management and control of a company is carried on, and therefore of the residence of the company.
- Notwithstanding the country of incorporation and the internal constitution of the company, residence will be determined on the basis of where a company is actually managed and controlled, not where, for example, the internal constitution of the company purports that it is carried on.

6.4 Inland Revenue's attitude

The Inland Revenue have long recognised that the increase in sophistication of taxpayers and ease of communication mean that it is relatively easy for directors to meet overseas, even if between those meetings they are managing and controlling the company from the UK. Accordingly they have issued Statements of Practice. These are included on pages 80–88. The Revenue's 1983 statement stresses the need for a real commercial presence for a company to be considered to be resident overseas. The Revenue will not automatically accept that 'paper' companies can be managed and controlled from overseas where they are owned by UK residents. This was reiterated in the 1990 statement. Essentially, in order to demonstrate that a foreign subsidiary is not resident in the UK, it is essential to establish positively that it is resident in a particular overseas country.

Therefore the Inland Revenue will look to see where the real business of the company is carried on, and it will be very difficult to establish a company as resident overseas if it has no real commercial presence there. However they will also look at statutory matters, and among the matters that they will consider are:

- where meetings of the board of directors take place;
- whether the internal constitution demands that such meetings are held in the country of residence;
- the country of incorporation;
- types of decision reached by the board;
- the residence of the individuals constituting the board;
- where the books of account and corporate records, including minute books and other statutory documents, are kept;
- where shareholders' meetings are held, although this is not of paramount importance;
- minutes of directors' meetings.

It is essential that the conduct of the subsidiary's business, the composition of its board of directors, its internal constitution and its minutes will all tend to show that the company is not resident in the UK. The obvious danger is that a UK shareholder is effectively exercising central management and control over the company. The Revenue would closely examine the activities of a controlling shareholder to ascertain whether as a question of fact he could be said to run the company from the UK. The foreign subsiiary's internal constitution should therefore vest the powers of management in the directors. The company's internal constitution could specify that all powers rest with the board and that the board must meet in the country of residence and incorporation but, as discussed above, residence is determined as a question of fact and not as a question of paperwork.

Ideally, regular formal minuted board meetings should be held at the company's own premises. At such meetings major decisions should be made and contracts ratified. It is quite common for the Inland Revenue to require copies of minutes of such meetings.

The directors should be residents of the purported country of residence. Preferably there should be a totality of such non-residents of the UK on the board; if it is necessary to appoint UK-resident directors then they must be in a minority. The Inland Revenue's view is that if there is a majority of UK-resident directors then they can meet informally in the United Kingdom, and hence such companies will always be UK resident. The directors should hold an executive position with the subsidiary and include people with sufficient knowledge and competence to manage the business independently. They should be paid accordingly. The directors should not be mere professionals. They should have the expertise to run the type of company that they are managing. The overseas directors should not merely rubber-stamp decisions that are really made in the UK.

Care must be exercised with respect to the discretion and powers allowed to agents and officers by the board of directors.

The Revenue will look at the major decisions relating to a company's business to check that it is really being run from overseas. Examples of major decisions are:

- the acquisition or disposal of the company's trade or business or major changes in the nature of the company's business, eg the making or breaking of contracts with suppliers and customers;
- the sanctioning of capital expenditure, product research and development programmes;
- raising or repayment of finance, and the operation of bank accounts;
- approval of budgets;
- payment of dividends;

- approval of accounts;
- appointment of accountants and other professional advisers, eg lawyers and bankers;
- the making or disposal of material investments, including the acquisition and disposal of subsidiary companies;
- the hiring and firing of senior employees;
- the appointment and dismissal of agents.

Very often the Inland Revenue will ask whether a foreign subsidiary owns or rents premises in its country of purported residence, and whether it has full-time employees working for it. If neither of these can be answered in the affirmative then there may be problems in convincing the Inland Revenue that the company is not UK resident. To quote the words of a senior Inland Revenue official:

> It would be true to say that companies which are engaged in substantial trading with third parties and have a substantial presence in their country of residence have far less need to be concerned by the legislation than those which have a scanty real life and are in the main the creatures of their controllers.

With respect to European subsidiaries, it is normally the case that they will be liable to rates of tax which are roughly equal to, or more commonly exceed, the UK's rate. Under those circumstances the Inland Revenue will not usually look closely at the residence of such companies. However, companies such as Netherlands holding companies, companies in Monaco, or companies incorporated in jurisdictions such as Liechtenstein, Andorra or the Channel Islands will be closely scrutinised as to their residence.

6.5 Dual-resident companies

The UK's concept of central management and control being one of the tests of residence means that some overseas subsidiaries can be dual resident. For example, a company incorporated under the laws of the Netherlands but managed and controlled from the UK will be resident in the Netherlands for Netherlands tax purposes because it is incorporated under that country's laws, but also resident in the UK by virtue of being managed and controlled from here.

Dual residence has some advantages. The principle advantage is that where the company is a trading company (*not* a dual-resident investing company), its losses may be group relieved for UK corporation tax purposes. By way of completeness it should be mentioned that certain other reliefs are also denied to dual-resident companies.

However, there are also disadvantages to being dual resident. If a company incorporated under the laws of, for example, one of the states of the USA is held to be managed and controlled in the UK then the implications can be serious. Under some circumstances it is possible to end up with uncreditable withholding tax when dividends are repatriated back to the UK. This is because such a company would be said to be dual resident, and hence the Inland Revenue will not accept that what is being repatriated to the UK is in fact a dividend from a foreign source of income. This is a *prima facie* requirement for double tax relief to be available in the UK. The UK/US treaty has no provisions to relieve this problem. Other treaties with various European countries contain provisions to treat the company as resident in the UK or, for example, the Netherlands only for the purposes of the treaty. For instance some relief may be available for a dual UK/Netherlands company under the UK/Netherlands double tax treaty. However, relief may not always be immediately available, and it can be expensive, time-consuming and administratively burdensome to put matters right. As you might expect, detailed professional advice needs to be obtained.

6.6 Revenue statements of practice – an insight

There now follow the Inland Revenue Statements of Practice SP6/1983 and SP1/1990 referred to earlier.

These give an excellent insight into Inland Revenue thinking.

Statement of Practice

SP 6/83

Date 27 July 1983

INLAND REVENUE, SOMERSET HOUSE, LONDON

FURTHER COPIES OF THIS STATEMENT MAY BE OBTAINED BY WRITING TO (PLEASE ENCLOSE A STAMPED ADDRESSED ENVELOPE) OR BY CALLING PERSONALLY AT THE **PUBLIC ENQUIRY ROOM**, NEW WING, SOMERSET HOUSE, STRAND, LONDON WC2R 1LB

COMPANY RESIDENCE

1. Residence has always been a material factor, for companies as well as individuals, in determining tax liability. But statute law has never laid down any general rules for determining where a company is resident. The question has thus been left to the Courts to decide.

The case law test

2. The test of company residence is that enunciated by Lord Loreburn in De Beers Consolidated Mines v Howe 5 TC 198 at the beginning of this century:

> "A company resides, for the purposes of Income Tax, where its real business is carried on ... I regard that as the true rule; and the real business is carried on where the central management and control actually abides"

3. The "central management and control" test, as set out in De Beers, has been endorsed by a series of subsequent decisions. In particular, it was described by Lord Radcliffe in the 1959 case of Bullock v Unit Construction Company 38 TC 712 at page 738 as being:

> "as precise and unequivocal as a positive statutory injunction ... I do not know of any other test which has either been substituted for that of central management and control, or has been defined with sufficient precision to be regarded as an acceptable alternative to it. To me ... it seems impossible to read Lord Loreburn's words without seeing that he regarded the formula he was propounding as constituting the test of residence".

Nothing which has happened since has in any way altered this basic principle: under current UK case law a company is regarded as resident for tax purposes where central management and control is to be found.

THIS STATEMENT HAS NO BINDING FORCE AND DOES NOT AFFECT A TAXPAYER'S RIGHTS OF APPEAL ON POINTS CONCERNING HIS LIABILITY TO TAX

Place of "central management and control"

4. In determining whether or not an individual company is resident in the UK, it thus becomes necessary to locate its place of "central management and control". The case law concept of central management and control is, in broad terms, directed at the highest level of control of the business of a company. It is to be distinguished from the place where the main operations of a business are to be found, though those two places may often coincide. Moreover, the exercise of control does not necessarily demand any minimum standard of active involvement: it may, in appropriate circumstances, be exercised tacitly through passive oversight.

5. Successive decided cases have emphasised that the place of central management and control is wholly a question of fact. For example, Lord Radcliffe in Unit Construction said that "the question where control and management abide must be treated as one of fact or "actuality""(p.741). It follows that factors which together are decisive in one instance may individually carry little weight in another. Nevertheless the decided cases do give some pointers. In particular a series of decisions has attached importance to the place where the company's board of directors meet. There are very many cases in which the board meets in the same country as that in which the business operations take place, and central management and control is clearly located in that one place. In other cases central management and control may be exercised by directors in one country though the actual business operations may, perhaps under the immediate management of local directors, take place elsewhere.

6. But the location of board meetings, although important in the normal case, is not necessarily conclusive. Lord Radcliffe in Unit Construction pointed out (p.738) that the site of the meetings of the directors' board had not been chosen as "the test" of company residence. In some cases, for example, central management and control is exercised by a single individual. This may happen when a chairman or managing director exercises powers formally conferred by the company's Articles and the other board members are little more than cyphers, or by reason of a dominant shareholding or for some other reason. In those cases the residence of the company is where the controlling individual exercises his powers.

7. In general the place of directors' meetings is significant only in so far as those meetings constitute the medium through which central management and control is exercised. If, for example, the directors of a company were engaged together actively in the UK in the complete running of a business which was wholly in the UK, the company would not be regarded as resident outside the UK merely because the directors held formal board meetings outside the UK. While it is possible to identify extreme situations in which central management and control plainly is, or is not, exercised by directors in formal meetings, the conclusion in any case is wholly one of fact depending on the relative weight to be given to various factors. Any attempt to lay down rigid guidelines would only be misleading.

8. Generally, however, where doubts arise about a particular company's residence status, the Inland Revenue adopt the following approach:

(i) They first try to ascertain whether the directors of the company in fact exercise central management and control.

(ii) If so, they seek to determine where the directors exercise this central management and control (which is not necessarily where they meet).

(iii) In cases where the directors apparently do not exercise central management and control of the company, the Revenue then look to establish where and by whom it is exercised.

Parent/subsidiary relationship

9. It is particularly difficult to apply the "central management and control" test in the situation where a subsidiary company and its parent operate in different territories. In this situation, the parent will normally influence, to a greater or lesser extent, the actions of the subsidiary. Where that influence is exerted by the parent exercising the powers which a sole or majority shareholder has in general meetings of the subsidiary, for example to appoint and dismiss members of the board of the subsidiary and to initiate or approve alterations to its financial structure, the Revenue would not seek to argue that central management and control of the subsidiary is located where the parent company is resident. However, in cases where the parent usurps the functions of the board of the subsidiary (such as Unit Construction itself) or where that board merely rubber stamps the parent company's decisions without giving them any independent consideration of its own, the Revenue draw the conclusion that the subsidiary has the same residence for tax purposes as its parent.

10. The Revenue recognise that there may be many cases where a company is a member of a group having its ultimate holding company in another country which will not fall readily into either of the categories referred to above. In considering whether the board of such a subsidiary company exercises central management and control of the subsidiary's business, they have regard to the degree of autonomy which those directors have in conducting the company's business. Matters (among others) that may be taken into account are the extent to which the directors of the subsidiary take decisions on their own authority as to investment, production, marketing and procurement without reference to the parent.

Double taxation agreements

11. In general our double taxation agreements do not affect the UK residence of a company as established for UK tax purposes. But where the partner country adopts a different definition of residence, it may happen that a UK resident company is treated, under the partner country's domestic law, as also resident there. In these cases, the agreement normally specifies what the tax consequences of this "double" residence shall be.

12. Under the double taxation agreement with the United States, for example, the UK residence of a company for UK tax purposes is unaffected. But where that company is also a US corporation, it is excluded from some of the reliefs conferred by the agreement. On the other hand, under a double taxation agreement which follows the 1977 OECD Model Taxation Convention, a company classed as resident by both the UK and the partner country is, for the purposes of the agreement, treated as resident where its "place of effective management" is situated.

13. The Commentary on paragraph 3 of Article 4 of the OECD Model records the UK view that, in agreements (such as those with some Commonwealth countries) which treat a company as resident in a state in which "its business is managed and controlled", this expression means "the effective management of the enterprise". More detailed consideration of the question in the light of the approach of Continental legal systems and of Community law to the question of company residence has led the Revenue to revise this view. It is now considered that effective management may, in some cases, be found at a place different from the place of central management and control. This could happen, for example, where a company is run by executives based abroad, but the final directing power rests with non-executive directors who meet in the UK. In such circumstances the company's place of effective management might well be abroad but, depending on the precise powers of the non-executive directors, it might be centrally managed and controlled (and therefore resident) in the UK.

Conclusion

14. In outlining factors relevant to the application of the case law test, this statement assumes that they exist for genuine commercial reasons. Where, however, as may happen, it appears that a major objective underlying the existence of certain factors is the obtaining of tax benefits from residence or non-residence, the Revenue examines the facts particularly closely in order to see whether there has been an attempt to create the appearance of central management and control in a particular place without the reality.

15. The test examined in this statement is not always easy to apply in present day circumstances. The last relevant case was decided over 20 years ago, and there have been many developments in communications since then, which in particular may enable a company to be controlled from a place far distant from where the day-to-day management is carried on. As the statement makes clear, while the general principle has been laid down by the Courts, its application must depend on the precise facts.

Statement of Practice

SP 1/90

Date 9 January 1990

INLAND REVENUE, SOMERSET HOUSE, LONDON

FURTHER COPIES OF THIS STATEMENT MAY BE OBTAINED BY WRITING TO (PLEASE ENCLOSE A STAMPED ADDRESSED ENVELOPE) OR BY CALLING PERSONALLY AT THE PUBLIC ENQUIRY ROOM, WEST WING SOMERSET HOUSE, STRAND, LONDON WC2R 1LB

COMPANY RESIDENCE

1. Residence has always been a material factor, for companies as well as individuals, in determining tax liability. But statute law has never laid down comprehensive rules for determining where a company is resident and until 1988 the question was left solely to the Courts to decide. Section 66 Finance Act 1988 introduced the rule that a company incorporated in the UK is resident here for the purposes of the Taxes Acts. Case law still applies in determining the residence of companies excepted from the incorporation rule or which are not incorporated in the UK.

A. THE INCORPORATION RULE

2. The incorporation rule applies to companies incorporated in the UK subject to the exceptions in Schedule 7 FA 1988 for some companies incorporated before 15 March 1988. (This legislation is reproduced for convenience as an Appendix to this Statement). Paragraphs 3 to 8 below explain how the Revenue interpret various terms used in the legislation.

Carrying on business

3. The exceptions from the incorporation test in Schedule 7 depend in part on the company carrying on business at a specified time or during a relevant period. The question whether a company carries on business is one of fact to be decided according to the particular circumstances of the company. Detailed guidance is not practicable but the Revenue take the view that 'business' has a wider meaning than 'trade'; it can include transactions, such as the purchase of stock, carried out for the purposes of a trade about to be commenced and the holding of investments including shares in a subsidiary company. Such a holding could consist of a single investment from which no income was derived.

4. A company such as a shelf company whose transactions have been limited to those formalities necessary to keep the company on the register of companies will not be regarded as carrying on business.

5. For the purposes of the case law test (see B below) the residence of a company is determined by the place where its real business is carried on. A company which can demonstrate that in these terms it is or was resident outside the UK will have carried on business for the purposes of Schedule 7.

THIS STATEMENT HAS NO BINDING FORCE AND DOES NOT AFFECT A TAXPAYER'S RIGHTS OF APPEAL ON POINTS CONCERNING HIS LIABILITY TO TAX

"Taxable in a territory outside the UK"

6. A further condition for some companies for exception from the incorporation test is provided by Schedule 7 Para 1(1)(c) and Para 5(1). The company has to be taxable in a territory outside the UK. "Taxable" means that the company is liable to tax on income by reason of domicile, residence or place of management. This is similar to the approach adopted in the residence provisions of many double taxation agreements. Territories which impose tax on companies by reference to incorporation or registration or similar criteria are covered by the term 'domicile'. Territories which impose tax by reference to criteria such as "effective management", "central administration", "head office" or "principal place of business" are covered by the term 'place of management'.

7. A company has to be liable to tax on income so that a company which is, for example, liable only to a flat rate fee or lump sum duty does not fulfil the test. On the other hand a company is regarded as liable to tax in a particular territory if it is within the charge there even though it may pay no tax because, for example, it makes losses or claims double taxation relief.

"Treasury Consent"

8. Before 15 March 1988 it was unlawful for a company to cease to be resident in the UK without the consent of the Treasury. Companies which have ceased to be resident in pursuance of a Treasury consent, as defined in Schedule 7 Paragraph 5(1), are excepted from the incorporation rule subject to certain conditions. A few companies ceased to be resident without Treasury consent but were informed subsequently by letter that the Treasury would take no action against them under the relevant legislation. Such a letter is not a retrospective grant of consent and the companies concerned cannot benefit from the exceptions which depend on Treasury consent.

B. THE CASE LAW TEST

9. This test of company residence is that enunciated by Lord Loreburn in De Beers Consolidated Mines v Howe (5 TC 198) at the beginning of this century:

> "A company resides, for the purposes of Income Tax, where its real business is carried on ... I regard that as the true rule; and the real business is carried on where the central management and control actually abides".

10. The "central management and control" test, as set out in De Beers, has been endorsed by a series of subsequent decisions. In particular, it was described by Lord Radcliffe in the 1959 case of Bullock v Unit Construction Company 38 TC 712 at page 738 as being:

> "as precise and unequivocal as a positive statutory injunction ... I do not know of any other test which has either been substituted for that of central management and control, or has been defined with sufficient precision to be regarded as an acceptable alternative to it. To me ... it seems impossible to read Lord Loreburn's words without seeing that he regarded the formula he was propounding as constituting the test of residence".

Nothing which has happened since has in any way altered this basic principle for a company the residence of which is not governed by the incorporation rule; under current UK case law such a company is regarded as resident for tax purposes where central management and control is to be found.

Place of "central management and control"

11. In determining whether or not an individual company outside the scope of the incorporation test is resident in the UK, it thus becomes necessary to locate its place of "central management and control". The case law concept of central management and control is, in broad terms, directed at the highest level of control of the business of a company. It is to be distinguished from the place where the main operations of a business are to be found, though those two places may often coincide. Moreover, the exercise of control does not necessarily demand any minimum standard of active involvement: it may, in appropriate circumstances, be exercised tacitly through passive oversight.

12. Successive decided cases have emphasised that the place of central management and control is wholly a question of fact. For example, Lord Radcliffe in Unit Construction said that "the question where control and management abide must be treated as one of fact or "actuality"" (p.741). It follows that factors which together are decisive in one instance may individually carry little weight in another. Nevertheless the decided cases do give some pointers. In particular a series of decisions has attached importance to the place where the company's board of directors meet. There are very many cases in which the board meets in the same country as that in which the business operations take place, and central management and control is clearly located in that one place. In other cases central management and control may be exercised by directors in one country though the actual business operations may, perhaps under the immediate management of local directors, take place elsewhere.

13. But the location of board meetings, although important in the normal case, is not necessarily conclusive. Lord Radcliffe in Unit Construction pointed out (p.738) that the site of the meetings of the directors' board had not been chosen as "the test" of company residence. In some cases, for example, central management and control is exercised by a single individual. This may happen when a chairman or managing director exercises powers formally conferred by the company's Articles and the other board members are little more than cyphers, or by reason of a dominant shareholding or for some other reason. In those cases the residence of the company is where the controlling individual exercises his powers.

14. In general the place of directors' meetings is significant only insofar as those meetings constitute the medium through which central management and control is exercised. If, for example, the directors of a company were engaged together actively in the UK in the complete running of a business which was wholly in the UK, the company would not be regarded as resident outside the UK merely because the directors held formal board meetings outside the UK. While it is possible to identify extreme situations in which central management and control plainly is, or is not, exercised by directors in formal meetings, the conclusion in any case is wholly one of fact depending on the relative weight to be given to various factors. Any attempt to lay down rigid guidelines would only be misleading.

3.

15. Generally, however, where doubts arise about a particular company's residence status, the Inland Revenue adopt the following approach:

(i) They first try to ascertain whether the directors of the company in fact exercise central management and control.

(ii) If so, they seek to determine where the directors exercise this central management and control (which is not necessarily where they meet).

(iii) In cases where the directors apparently do not exercise central management and control of the company, the Revenue then look to establish where and by whom it is exercised.

Parent/subsidiary relationship

16. It is particularly difficult to apply the "central management and control" test in the situation where a subsidiary company and its parent operate in different territories. In this situation, the parent will normally influence, to a greater or lesser extent, the actions of the subsidiary. Where that influence is exerted by the parent exercising the powers which a sole or majority shareholder has in general meetings of the subsidiary, for example to appoint and dismiss members of the board of the subsidiary and to initiate or approve alterations to its financial structure, the Revenue would not seek to argue that central management and control of the subsidiary is located where the parent company is resident. However, in cases where the parent usurps the functions of the board of the subsidiary (such as Unit Construction itself) or where that board merely rubber stamps the parent company's decisions without giving them any independent consideration of its own, the Revenue draw the conclusion that the subsidiary has the same residence for tax purposes as its parent.

17. The Revenue recognise that there may be many cases where a company is a member of a group having its ultimate holding company in another country which will not fall readily into either of the categories referred to above. In considering whether the board of such a subsidiary company exercises central management and control of the subsidiary's business, they have regard to the degree of autonomy which those directors have in conducting the company's business. Matters (among others) that may be taken into account are the extent to which the directors of the subsidiary take decisions on their own authority as to investment, production, marketing and procurement without reference to the parent.

Conclusion

18. In outlining factors relevant to the application of the case law test, this statement assumes that they exist for genuine commercial reasons. Where, however, as may happen, it appears that a major objective underlying the existence of certain factors is the obtaining of tax benefits from residence or non-residence, the Revenue examine the facts particularly closely in order to see whether there has been an attempt to create the appearance of central management and control in a particular place without the reality.

19. The case law test examined in this Statement is not always easy to apply. The Courts have recognised that there may be difficulties where it is not possible to identify any one country as the seat of central

management and control. The principles to apply in those circumstances have not been fully developed in case law. In addition, the last relevant case was decided almost 30 years ago, and there have been many developments in communications since then, which in particular may enable a company to be controlled from a place far distant from where the day-to-day management is carried on. As the Statement makes clear, while the general principle has been laid down by the Courts, its application must depend on the precise facts.

C. DOUBLE TAXATION AGREEMENTS

20. In general our double taxation agreements do not affect the UK residence of a company as established for UK tax purposes. But where the partner country adopts a different definition of residence, it may happen that a UK resident company is treated, under the partner country's domestic law, as also resident there. In these cases, the agreement normally specifies what the tax consequences of this "double" residence shall be.

21. Under the double taxation agreement with the United States, for example, the UK residence of a company for UK tax purposes is unaffected. But where that company is also a US corporation, it is excluded from some of the reliefs conferred by the agreement. On the other hand, under a double taxation agreement which follows the 1977 OECD Model Taxation Convention, a company classed as resident by both the UK and the partner country is, for the purposes of the agreement, treated as resident where its "place of effective management" is situated.

22. The Commentary in paragraph 3 of Article 4 of the OECD Model records the UK view that, in agreements (such as those with some Commonwealth countries) which treat a company as resident in a state in which "its business is managed and controlled", this expression means "the effective management of the enterprise". More detailed consideration of the question in the light of the approach of Continental legal systems and of Community law to the question of company residence has led the Revenue to revise this view. It is now considered that effective management may, in some cases, be found at a place different from the place of central management and control. This could happen, for example, where a company is run by executives based abroad, but the final directing power rests with non-executive directors who meet in the UK. In such circumstances the company's place of effective management might well be abroad but, depending on the precise powers of the non-executive directors, it might be centrally managed and controlled (and therefore resident) in the UK.

23. The incorporation rule in Section 66(1) Finance Act 1988 determines a residence which supersedes a different place "given by any rule of law". This incorporation rule determines residence under UK domestic law and is subject to the provisions of any applicable double taxation agreement. It does not override the provisions of a double taxation agreement which may make a UK incorporated company a resident of an overseas territory <u>for the purposes of the agreement</u> (see 20 and 21 above).

6.7 Foreign company with a UK branch

As well as the danger of a company incorporated abroad being resident in the UK, care must be exercised that it does not have a branch in the UK. In that case its trading profits will be subject to UK tax. This can be a problem when, for example, a tax haven company is used to buy goods from overseas and sell them on at a profit to a UK company. Even if such a tax haven company can be said to be managed and controlled from overseas, and hence resident abroad, the Inland Revenue may be in a position to argue that its profits should be subject to UK tax on the grounds that it is selling its goods in the UK. In other words, it is trading *in* the UK and not merely *with* the UK.

6.8 The next obstacle

If a subsidiary can be shown to be incorporated *and* managed and controlled abroad *and* not trading in the UK then *prima facie* its profits will not be liable to UK tax. However, further probing is necessary. Will the overseas profits be liable to UK tax under the UK's anti-avoidance legislation? This is the subject of the next stage of our journey.

7

Anti-avoidance Measures

7.1 Major obstacles to saving tax

Even if you can succeed in making your offshore company non-resident, that is not the end of the story. UK anti-avoidance legislation can have the effect of subjecting the offshore profits to tax, either on the UK parent or on the individual shareholders of the UK company. Therefore, the principal advantage of non-residence, namely avoiding UK tax, will be negated.

The UK has extensive and highly complex anti-avoidance legislation. Anyone contemplating cross-border transactions should obtain detailed professional advice. The situation has been even more complicated by recent House of Lords' decisions in cases such as *Ramsay versus CIR*, *Furniss versus Dawson* and *Craven versus White*. Taken together these effectively seek to treat a series of transactions as a single composite transaction where steps have been inserted without a *bona fide* commercial reason into a pre-ordained series of transactions.

We must now look at some of the principal anti-avoidance provisions. I have attempted to simplify what is extemely complex, whichever way one approaches the problem.

7.2 Section 739

Section 739 Income and Corporation Taxes Act 1988 (formerly Section 478 Income and Corporation Taxes Act 1970) is an extremely widely-drawn section which applies in theory to most overseas operations. *Prima facie*, its effect is to automatically tax the UK resident individual shareholder at the end of the corporate chain on his share of any income accumulated inside the overseas company in which he owns a direct or indirect interest.

Section 739 will only apply where the individual shareholder was instrumental in setting up the structure overseas. Therefore it will generally *not* apply to public companies.

Example

A Jersey cross-invoicing company or a Netherlands Antilles royalty company owned by a private UK company or directly by UK individuals is likely to fall foul of Section 739, and hence its profits will be assessed on their UK owners. On the other hand, were they owned by a public UK company the shareholders would escape Section 739. However, the UK company would probably fall within other anti-avoidance legislation – in particular the controlled foreign company legislation.

Its obvious application is to tax a UK-resident individual who forms an overseas company in which he owns the shares direct. Therefore merely owning the foreign subsidiary outside the UK company or business will not avoid UK tax. Section 739 should also be read in conjunction with Section 740. Section 739 will automatically assess the income arising overseas on a UK shareholder as it arises year by year. Section 740 applies to UK individuals who were not 'transferors', that is, the individuals responsible for the setting up of the corporate structure. Under Section 740 such non-transferors are assessed only when they receive a distribution of income from the foreign structure.

Section 739 and Section 740 are of great relevance where trusts are concerned. Mere ownership of the foreign subsidiary through an overseas trust will not avoid liability to UK tax. Section 739 and other anti-trust legislation (known as Part XV because it is contained in Part XV of ICTA 88) will tax any settlor of a trust who retains an interest in the trust. If the settlor bars himself and his wife from benefiting under the trust, for example by settling what is known as an 'accumulation and maintenance trust' for his children, Section 740 will apply so as to tax the beneficiaries only when they receive a distribution out of the trust or the underlying company.

It should be noted that the transfer of assets abroad includes the creation of assets abroad. It will therefore apply when an offshore company derives income *ab initio* in a start-up situation, and not just when an income-producing asset or activity is transferred overseas. For Section 739 to apply, that transfer or creation of assets abroad must result in income becoming payable to a person resident abroad and the transferor must have 'power to enjoy' the income of the trust. 'Power to enjoy' is widely defined and includes:

- income actually being paid or payable for the benefit of the transferor or his or her spouse;
- an increase in the value of assets held by the transferor; therefore, leaving the income in the company will not avoid Section 739 because the value of the shares held by the individual will increase;
- either the transferor or his or her spouse controlling the application of the income – even if the income cannot be paid to the transferor, therefore, if he can exercise control over the destination of the application of the income (for example through powers in the trust) he will be held to have power to enjoy that income.

It is essential to examine the exemptions to Section 739 and 740. The first point to note is that for exemption from Section 739 to be available it is necessary for the taxpayer to show in writing *or otherwise* to the satisfaction of the Inland Revenue that the transfer or creation of assets abroad

either

- was not to avoid tax

or

- was for *bona fide* commercial reasons.

The second point to note is that if there is no liability to tax, the penalties for not disclosing to the Inland Revenue are nil or minimal. It is therefore a 'double or quits' situation. If the taxpayer wishes to avoid the threat of interest, penalties or even prosecution he would be well advised to disclose to the Inland Revenue, or to take detailed professional advice that the exemptions are available. I would add that the above exemptions are very much simplified.

The mere fact that the subsidiary is trading does not mean that Section 739 will not apply to the profits of the non-resident company. All the circumstances must be considered. In general, if there is a real commercial presence overseas it is likely that the Inland Revenue will accept that it was necessary for the income to be earned by a locally incorporated entity. Similarly, if the overseas entity suffers a relatively higher rate of tax it is unlikely that the Inland Revenue would seek to argue that avoidance of UK tax was behind the transaction. However, where income is diverted to companies paying low tax, especially companies which are mere 'paper' companies and do not have a real commercial presence overseas such as their own premises and staff, then the Inland Revenue are much more likely to invoke Section 739.

An important exemption from Section 739 is the 'multi-transferor' exemption. If there are very many transferors then Section 739 will not be invoked. This will normally apply in a public company situation unless there is a single large shareholder.

The use of overseas companies, while attractive at first sight, should be approached with considerable caution and the most careful tax-planning considerations, particularly by the closely-held company.

7.3 Controlled Foreign Company legislation

Section 747 Taxes Act 1988 *et seq* (Controlled Foreign Companies legislation) will automatically assess the income profits (not capital gains) of foreign subsidiaries on UK parents unless certain conditions are met. Under the Controlled Foreign Company (CFC) legislation, the income profits (not capital gains) of foreign subsidiaries will be assessed only on UK parent companies (not on individuals, trusts or any other entity).

The CFC legislation may be traced back to the suspension of UK exchange controls in 1979, which gave UK companies far more scope for tax planning in their international operations, Inland Revenue concerns over the taxation of company residence (see Chapter 6 – Residence) and the taxation of 'upstream loans'. Profits returning to the UK as loans from overseas subsidiaries to UK parents are not liable to UK tax. Although upstream loans return 'cash' to the UK they do not actually return profits into the accounts of the UK parent, and therefore cash from an upstream loan will not be paid out as a dividend unless there is some other source of profits.

We will now look at various questions relating to the CFC legislation. It is of necessity somewhat technical, but wherever possible I have attempted to use simple language. The first question to ask is: What is a CFC?

A CFC is defined as being a company which:

- is resident *outside* the UK (UK *resident* companies are liable to UK tax on their worldwide profits);
- is *controlled* by UK resident *persons* (control is effectively ownership which may be by a combination of UK resident companies, individuals and trusts; however, only *companies* are chargeable to tax on the profits of the CFC);

- is subject to a *lower level of taxation* in the *territory in which it is resident.*

First, it is necessary to determine the territory of the company's residence, defined as 'the territory (country) in which the company is liable to tax by reason of domicile (place of incorporation) residence or place of management'.

If the company is liable to tax in more than one country, the issue of where it is *resident* is decided by determining where the effective place of management is situated. If the company's effective management is located in two or more countries, residence is decided by the country in which the greater amount of its assets are situated. If, for whatever reason, the residence of the company is still not decided, the Inland Revenue have discretion to decide in which country the company should be regarded as resident.

The company will be considered to be subject to a *lower level of taxation* if the amount of tax paid under the laws of the country of residence in respect of profits arising in any accounting period is less than half of the corresponding UK rate. The profits of the foreign subsidiary must be computed according to UK rules, including arm's-length pricing.

It should be noted that only taxes on profits will be taken into account in determining whether the company is subject to a lower level of taxation, and not taxes on capital or net worth. In addition, it is only tax payable in the country of residence which is taken into account. Any tax paid in a third country (eg because of an overseas branch activity) will be ignored for these purposes.

If no country imposes tax on the company by reason of domicile, residence or place of management, the company is conclusively presumed to be resident in the country in which it is subject to a lower level of taxation.

Example

The profits of a Hong Kong company will *prima facie* be subject to the CFC legislation even if it pays tax at an effective rate of, for example, 18 per cent (ie over half the UK rate). Hong Kong does not tax on the basis of domicile, residence or place of management; instead Hong Kong taxes on the basis of whether income arises within Hong Kong.

Where a company is resident outside the UK and is subject to a lower level of taxation in the territory in which it is resident, the Board of

Inland Revenue may make a direction that the 'chargeable profits' and 'creditable tax' of the CFC be apportioned to certain UK corporate shareholders, who would therefore be liable to UK tax. Tax is not charged on any UK resident company, however, unless at least 10 per cent of the CFC's chargeable profits have been apportioned to it and/or persons connected or associated with it. If the chargeable profits of the CFC for a 12-month accounting period do not exceed *£20,000*, no direction can be made. This is the *'de minimis'* exemption.

Chargeable profits are, broadly, the amount of total profits of the company calculated in accordance with the principles of UK corporation tax. *Profits for these purposes do not include chargeable gains, which cannot be apportioned under CFC rules*, but are dealt with separately under Section 15 CGTA 1979.

Example

A Netherlands offshore holding company which is eligible for the 'affiliation privilege' will not pay Netherlands tax on gains arising from the disposal of foreign subsidiaries or on dividends received from foreign subsidiaries. The gain, although tax free, will not be assessed on the UK parent under the CFC legislation because it is a capital gain, not income.

On the other hand, a Netherlands offshore holding company which receives a dividend from subsidiaries must consider the activities of each of the foreign subsidiaries. If those foreign subsidiaries are CFCs, the Netherlands holding company must either pay the dividend back to the UK or its profits will be assessed on the UK parent. If the foreign subsidiary is not a CFC, the Netherlands company can retain the dividend free of Netherlands tax, so long as it is, again, eligible for the 'affiliation privilege', and also free of UK tax.

Creditable tax is, broadly, the amount of foreign tax credit which would be available for offset against corporation tax on the company's chargeable profits, computed in accordance with the normal double tax credit provisions.

There are a number of specific *exemptions* which apply to prevent a direction being made.

No direction can be made if the CFC follows an *acceptable distribution policy* – that is, it distributes to UK residents a specified proportion of its profits for an accounting period. For a trading company the specified proportion is 50 per cent, and for other companies the proportion is 90 per cent. The dividend received in the UK would, of course, be subject to UK tax. It is not sufficient merely to pay a dividend to a non-UK intermediate holding company. The dividend must be paid right up to UK residents.

As an additional requirement the dividend must not be paid out of specified profits. The reason for this is to prevent the CFC choosing highly-taxed profits from which to pay the dividends in order to maximise foreign tax credits in the UK. The company may, however, specify the accounting period to which the dividend relates. As we saw with double tax relief and underlying tax, specifying the accounting period can be very advantageous.

The dividends should be paid during, or not more than 18 months after, the end of the accounting period to which they relate, although the Inland Revenue has discretion to grant an extension to this.

The *exempt activities test* was once referred to as the 'genuine trading test'. Although it is designed to exempt from a charge to UK tax the profits of *bona fide* trading companies, the conditions are restrictive and it is likely that many trading companies will not satisfy the test. The conditions set out below must be met.

- The company must have a business establishment in the territory in which it is resident. For this purpose the company must have premises (eg an office, shop, factory etc) from which throughout the accounting period the business affairs in that territory are effectively managed.
- The business of the company must not consist of investment business. This will disqualify a company receiving dividends, interest or royalties, leasing companies and share dealing companies.
- The company must not rely for its business on transactions with connected or associated persons.
- The company must not receive a significant amount of dividends from companies unless they themselves are engaged in exempt activities.

The CFC could satisfy the *public quotation test*. No direction will be made against a CFC where at least 35 per cent of the voting power has been unconditionally allotted to the public and has been beneficially held by them throughout the accounting period. The shares must also have been dealt on a recognised stock exchange within the last year.

If the company does not satisfy any of the tests outlined above, no direction will be made if the company passes the *motive test*. In effect it is necessary to persuade the Inland Revenue that the CFC was not established with the purpose of achieving a reduction in UK taxation. A direction will not be made if it appears to the Inland Revenue that both of the following conditions are met:

- insofar as any transactions achieved a reduction in UK tax, *either*: the reduction was minimal *or*
- it was not the main purpose of the transaction to achieve the reduction; *and*
- it was not the main reason for the company's existence to achieve a reduction in UK tax by a diversion of profits from the UK.

The motive test is (as with the other let-outs) to be considered for each year. It is therefore possible for a CFC to pass the motive test in one year, but fail it in another. Although, strictly, there is no connection between the motive test and the other exclusions, the Inland Revenue appear to indicate in their explanatory notes that they may treat the test as passed if there has been a 'marginal and isolated' failure to satisfy other exclusions. *However, in practice the Revenue have hardly ever granted the motive test.*

The first *list of excluded countries* was published in July 1984, and is updated from time to time. An up-to-date list is contained in the latest Inland Revenue Press Release which is reproduced in full on pages 118–29. The list is subdivided into two sections: those countries not regarded as 'low tax', and those countries not regarded as 'low tax' but subject to qualifications for particular local tax exemptions or reliefs.

The list is non-statutory and should not be regarded as indicative that companies operating from such countries should be outside the scope of the CFC legislation.

Example

A Netherlands holding company will not satisfy this condition if it receives more than 10 per cent of its income from foreign subsidiaries, even though the Netherlands is on the list.

The list is designed to provide a basis for satisfying the motive test, but only if 90 per cent or more of a company's profits is derived from that country.

There is a CFC *clearance procedure*. Application may be made to a special unit of the Inland Revenue to establish whether a non-UK resident company falls within the CFC provisions. However, there is no formal statutory clearance procedure as there are with other tax sections or with Treasury Consents. Applications should be made to:

Inland Revenue
CFC Technical Unit
Somerset House
Strand
London WC2R 1LB.

It can be seen that in the case of residence, Section 739 and the CFC legislation there is a common thread. Where a UK business invests in an overseas subsidiary and that overseas subsidiary has a real commercial presence, it is relatively unlikely that there will be problems with the Inland Revenue regarding either the residence of the company, or an attempt to assess the profits of that overseas company on a UK individual or company. However, where the company pays low tax overseas and there is no real commercial presence then anti-avoidance legislation and the concept of residence are much more likely to be invoked by the Inland Revenue. This is not a statutory requirement (with the exception of the exempt activities of the CFC legislation). It is a matter of practice. Throughout all anti-avoidance legislation there are shades of grey and matters which are subjective, for example whether something has been set up to avoid tax or has arisen naturally in the normal course of business.

7.4 Offshore gains

Section 739 ICTA 1988 and the CFC legislation only tax the *income* profits of foreign subsidiaries. They do not address the question of a foreign subsidiary's *capital gains*. The anti-avoidance legislation relating to capital gains is contained in Section 15 Capital Gains Tax Act 1979 ('Section 15').

Section 15 automatically taxes shareholders who are UK-resident and domiciled on their respective shares of the realised but undistributed capital gains of overseas companies in which they have an indirect interest. Unlike Section 739, Section 15 applies whether or not the overseas company was set up to avoid UK tax. However, it applies only to closely-held (private) companies. Public companies and their subsidiaries are not liable under Section 15. Even private companies are eligible for a number of important exceptions. Gains on the realisation of tangible property used solely in an overseas trade are exempt from the section.

This exemption has the practical effect of generally exempting all gains on realisation of business assets, other than goodwill and shares in subsidiary companies. Other exemptions from Section 15 apply where there is repatriation of the gain back to the UK within two years or the gain is from a foreign currency bank account used in a foreign trade; or the foreign company is owned equally by more than 20 UK residents (ie less than 5 per cent each).

Section 15 can sometimes be a problem if a foreign country has imposed foreign tax on the gain. Strictly speaking, double tax relief is available by Inland Revenue concession only because the foreign tax is imposed on the UK company.

The concession is set out below:-

> *Non-resident companies (CGTA 1979, S15)*
> Where a UK shareholder in a non-resident company which would be a close company if resident in the UK is chargeable to capital gains tax on a proportion of a capital gain accruing to that company, the appropriate proportion of any overseas tax payable by the company in the country where it is resident in respect of its gain is regarded as deductible in computing the shareholder's capital gain (CGTA 1979, S11). Alternatively, tax credit relief may be allowable for the overseas tax (CGTA 1979, S10).

Many of the UK's double tax treaties with other countries will also avoid the worst effects of Section 15. Typically the capital gains article of the treaty will state that subject to certain exceptions capital gains will only be subject to tax in the country in which the seller of the property is resident. Since the UK has double tax treaties with most European countries, this means that the effect of Section 15 will be even further diluted.

7.5 Arm's-length pricing

The Inland Revenue have wide powers under Section 770 ICTA 1988 (formerly Section 485 ICTA 1970), to adjust inter-company pricing for tax purposes. Thus the diversion of profits abroad by the technique of underpricing sales and overpricing purchases from related companies can be counteracted. The Revenue also have powers to adjust inter-company items such as rents, royalties and interest which result in the diversion of profits away from the UK.

Generally speaking, these powers to adjust pricing for tax purposes also exist in overseas tax jurisdictions: for instance the US Section 482 of the Internal Revenue Code, and the German *Aussensteuergesetz*. Therefore although Section 770 *prima facie* only applies where sales are made at an undervalue or purchases at an overvalue, effectively it is essential to get the price absolutely right, or else there would be an adjustment either abroad or in the UK.

Arm's-length pricing applies not just to transfers of goods. It applies to intangibles so that the UK may have to charge a royalty for the use of know-how, a patent or a trademark; services, especially management services which are always a bone of contention with both the UK and overseas tax authorities; and loans and other types of credit facilities. The UK's arm's-length pricing rules will apply to lettings and hirings of property, grants and transfers of rights, interests, licenses and 'the giving of business facilities of whatever kind'. The Inland Revenue interpret this last phrase as meaning that the UK parent must recharge its overseas subsidiary market research, advertising, promotion, research and development costs incurred in the UK.

Even so, there is no reason why, for example, an overseas company buying in bulk from the UK group should not be given the benefit of bulk discount on the scale that would be granted to any non-related purchaser; or why an overseas company should not license a patent from a UK parent, which the overseas company exploits in its manufacturing business and from which it accordingly earns a large profit abroad; or why an overseas company should not require payment for the use of a name. The essential philosophy is that the UK company should make the scale of profit it would make on a sale to any non-related person. If the overseas company has manufacturing, marketing or technical resources of its own which enable it to earn a super-profit on resale of what it obtains from the UK, that is acceptable

With respect to how to compute arm's-length prices, official guidance may be found in a short memorandum published in 1981, a copy of which is set out below.

Although the following Notes on Transfer Pricing have not been superceded, the definition of company residence in paragraph 5 is no longer appropriate in view of the provisions of Section 66 of the Finance Act 1988. Although the notes have been amended to take account of the consolidation of the Taxes Acts 1988, the references in paragraphs 7 and 11 to Section 485 should be amended to Section 770. The full title of the consolidated legislation is Income and Corporation Taxes Act 1988.

OECD report on transfer pricing

THE TRANSFER PRICING OF MULTINATIONAL ENTERPRISES

NOTES BY THE UK INLAND REVENUE

1. Introduction

These notes are primarily designed for the guidance of overseas companies which have, or may be thinking of setting up, subsidiaries in the UK; but the law and practice described apply to UK resident companies generally.

2. General - the arm's length principle

Prices charged in transactions between connected companies in a multinational group (transfer prices) may be designed to meet the convenience of the group as a whole. They will not necessarily produce a figure of profit or loss which can be accepted for tax purposes. The UK law therefore, in common with that of many other countries, provides that these prices may be adjusted in arriving at the taxable profit or allowable loss of a UK taxpayer. The price to which they may be adjusted is the "arm's length price". This is the price which might have been expected if the parties to the transaction had been independent persons dealing at arm's length ie dealing with each other in a normal commercial manner unaffected by any special relationship between them.

3. Circumstances in which adjustments may be made to transfer prices

The relevant law is largely contained in Section 485 of the Income and Corporation Taxes Act ("ICTA" 1970. This provides the Inland Revenue with power, for example, to adjust a transfer price to the arm's length price in transactions between a resident and a non-resident body of persons when one controls the other or both are under common control.

4. Body of persons

A "body of persons" includes a partnership as well as a company.

5. Residence of a company

The general rule is that a company is resident where the central control and management of its trade or business is carried on. The application of the rule is a question of fact.

6. Control of a company

Control of a company has to be distinguished from the control and management of its trade or business. For the purposes of Section 485 it is defined in particular to mean, as in Section 534 of ICTA 1970, the power of a person to secure that the affairs of the company are conducted in accordance with his wishes, inter alia, by holding shares or possessing voting power in relation to that company (or any other company) or by virtue of any powers conferred by the articles of association or other document regulating that or any other company.

7. Scope of UK transfer pricing law

Section 485 applies to sales of goods and other property, lettings or hiring of property, grants and transfers of rights, interests and licences and the giving of business facilities of whatever kind. Loan interest, patent royalties, management fees, and payments for services are thus within its scope as well as payments for goods. Contributions by a subsidiary towards costs incurred by the parent company are similarly within its scope.

8. Tax returns - assessment of profits - onus of proof - rights of appeal

The UK system of taxing profits requires the taxpayer to make a return of his profits each year to the appropriate Inspector of Taxes. It is normal for his return to be accompanied by accounts and computations in some detail in order to substantiate the return. But the Inspector, if no return is made or if he is dissatisfied with a return which has been made, is however empowered to assess the liability to tax on the basis of his own estimate of the profits. The taxpayer has a right of appeal to independent Commissioners (and from the Commissioners, on a point of law, to the High Court and beyond) but it is for him in the first instance to disprove the correctness of the assessment in such an appeal and not for the Inspector to prove that it is correct.

9. Adjustment by agreement

If, however, the Inspector takes the view that it may be necessary to assess the profits on the basis of his own estimate he will normally seek, in any case where substantial amounts are at stake, to come to an agreement on the matter with the taxpayer either by correspondence or, very probably in a case where the adjustment of transfer prices is in point, by discussion round the table as well.

10. Requests for information

If it seems to the Inspector that it may be necessary to adjust a company's transfer prices for tax purposes he will normally, therefore, in the first place, ask the UK company for the information necessary to decide whether adjustments should be made and what sort of adjustments. There is no standard list of questions - each case will need to be looked at in the light of its own special features. But the Inspector will generally be interested in such matters as who owns or controls the company, what the nature of the trade is, how any group of which the company is a member is organised, what are the functions of particular companies in the group, what the results of the UK companies have been, how far they have come up to expectations and so on. The need for answers to more detailed questions may emerge as the discussions proceed.

11. Powers to require information

The Inland Revenue have power in certain circumstances to require the production of information for tax purposes and, in particular under Section 17 of the Finance Act 1975, they may require a company to produce information which is relevant to the adjustment of transfer prices (not necessarily its own transfer prices) under Section 485 of ICTA 1970. Powers provided under Section 17 also include in certain circumstances the power to require the production of information (including books and accounts) from a UK resident company, which is relevant to transactions with a 51% subsidiary resident outside the UK, including books and accounts of the subsidiary. This also applies where the transactions are between UK resident and non-resident companies both of which are 51% subsidiaries of the UK resident company. (The UK parent company may however appeal against the requirement to an independent body of Commissioners.) In addition, in certain circumstances the Board may require books and accounts and other documents or records which are relevant to a transfer pricing adjustment under Section 485 to be produced for examination by an Inspector of Taxes on the taxpayer's premises.

12. Confidentiality

Officers of the Inland Revenue are governed by very strict rules about the confidentiality of information received by them in the course of their duties. They are prohibited from disclosing such information except for tax purposes and, within that limitation, in very limited circumstances strictly defined by law.

13. Exchange of information with other countries

Disclosure is permitted (under strict safeguards) to other countries' tax authorities under agreements for the relief of double taxation and under the Directive concerning mutual assistance between tax authorities of the member States of the European Communities. (The Inland Revenue may also receive information from other countries under these instruments.)

14. Inland Revenue Organisation

The Inland Revenue maintains a network of local tax offices spread over the whole of the UK and normally the affairs of a taxpayer will be mainly dealt with by a local Inspector of Taxes. But transfer pricing problems involving substantial amounts of money or important matters of principle may be dealt with instead by a section of the central head office in London. (The affairs of oil companies including matters of transfer pricing are dealt with by a centralised Oil Taxation Office in London.)

15. Objectives and method of approach in adjusting transfer prices for tax purposes

The objectives of both central and local offices are however the same. The principal objective is to ensure that the UK taxpayer is paying the proper UK tax on its profits under the law. The Inland Revenue recognise, however, that answering the many detailed questions which may be necessary for the achievement of this objective may impose an onerous burden on the senior staff of companies or their advisers and they aim to keep these questions to a minimum by concentrating on the main pricing issues involved.

16. Methods of and considerations taken into account in arriving at arm's length prices

In ascertaining an arm's length price the Inland Revenue will often look for evidence of prices in similar transactions between parties who are in fact operating at arm's length. They may however find it more useful in some circumstances to start with the re-sale price of the goods or services etc and arrive at the relevant arm's length purchase price by deducting an appropriate mark up. They may find it more convenient on the other hand to start with the cost of the goods or services and arrive at the arm's length price by adding an appropriate mark up. But they will in practice use any method which seems likely to produce a satisfactory result. They will be guided in their search for an arm's length price by the considerations set out in the OECD Report on Multinationals and Transfer Pricing. (This Report examines the considerations which need to be taken into account in arriving at arm's length prices in general and also in particular in the context of sales of goods, the provision of intra group services, the transfer of technology and rights to use trademarks within a group and the provision of intra group loans).

17. Settlement of problems

The Inland Revenue recognise, as does the OECD Report, that the evidence needed to establish an arm's length price may be hard to come by and difficult to interpret and they recognise also that decisions on pricing in the arm's length situation would have had to be taken in the light of the facts which could have been known at the time when the decision was made. It is with considerations like this in mind that they are concerned to settle transfer pricing adjustments as far as possible by discussion and agreement with the companies concerned. They would hope as a result also to establish a reasonable basis of understanding with the companies for the future (possibly on the basis of a review after a number of years).

- 3 -

18. Consultation with other countries

The Inland Revenue recognise that transfer pricing adjustments may have a consequence not only for UK tax but also for foreign tax. They are able, under the terms of some seventy agreements for the relief of double taxation and the prevention of fiscal evasion, to exchange information with the tax authorities of their partner countries on transfer pricing matters among others and they often do this for the purpose of ensuring that tax is adequately charged in the UK. On the other hand, they are also able to consult and do consult with partner countries with a view to preventing unrelievable double taxation arising from (among other causes) the adjustment of transfer prices. A taxpayer who fears that unrelievable double taxation may result in his own case from some action of the tax authorities of a treaty partner may ask the UK Inland Revenue to enter into such consultations and they will do so whenever the need arises. All that such a taxpayer need do is to write a letter putting his request, and giving the relevant details, to the International Tax Policy Division of the Inland Revenue in Somerset House, London. For such consultation to be effective however it will usually be necessary for the request to be made in good time so as not to be frustrated by the expiry of legal time limits for tax adjustments either in the UK or in the other country.

19. Time limits for claims for credit

So far as concerns claiming relief for foreign tax against UK tax the normal rule is that a claim in respect of any income, must be made not later than six years from the end of the chargeable period for which the income is chargeable to UK tax. However where such credit has been rendered insufficient by reason of an adjustment to the other country's tax the time limit for a claim to additional credit is six years from the time when the adjustment was made - Section 512 ICTA 1970.

20. Status of these notes

These notes are for guidance only. They express the Inland Revenue's view of the law but they have no legal force and they do not affect any rights of appeal on points concerning a taxpayer's liability. Similarly any description in these notes of Inland Revenue approaches to the problem of transfer pricing or practices in dealing with this problem are not to be taken as limiting the Department to such approaches or practices in any particular case.

Inland Revenue
Somerset House
Strand
LONDON WC2

- 4 -

11/80

It refers to an OECD report on transfer pricing, published in 1979, which listed four general methods of ascertaining arm's-length prices.

- *The comparable uncontrolled price method*
  This method uses the open market value which an independent third party would pay for the same item.
- *The resale price method*
  This looks at the price at which the goods are sold by the end user and relates back using normal profit percentages.
- *The cost plus method*
  This is the reverse of the resale price method. An appropriate profit percentage should be added to the seller's costs.
- *Other methods*
  Any other method which is found to be acceptable, the so-called 'fourth method'.

The Inland Revenue have already stated that they will not look at any one particular method, although in general the first method is a very strong guide to what a transfer price should be. Its problem is that very often there is no clearly defined market for the product. The product may be unique or seasonal. This allows a measure of planning to be implemented.

It is also essential that any arm's-length pricing adjustments, whether in the UK or overseas, do not result in double taxation. A corresponding adjustment must be made in the buying or selling company where appropriate. This is recognised in some of the UK's double tax treaties, although not all of the UK's treaties allow for adjustment. The UK does not have any domestic provision to automatically compensate where a foreign tax authority has adjusted a transfer price, although it may be possible to enter a claim under Section 33 Taxes Management Act 1970 under the 'error or mistake' provisions. With respect to the special case of transfer pricing adjustments between companies resident in different member states of the EC, there is a directive which will provide for adjustment through a specific arbitration procedure (see Appendix D: EC Tax and Company Law Harmonisation).

It is of note that arm's-length pricing applies not just to corporation tax but also to other matters such as Customs duty.

7.6 Section 765

Section 765 is a section which makes it a criminal offence to undertake certain transactions without prior Treasury consent. Its maximum punishment is two years in jail and a fine of £10,000. It may be of some relief to the reader to know that since its introduction in 1951, no prosecution has been brought under Section 765 or any of its predecessors.

Section 765 Taxes Act 1988 (formerly Section 482 Taxes Act 1970) has been radically amended following the 1988 Budget.

It was previously an offence under Section 765 for a company to emigrate or to transfer its residence abroad without obtaining prior Treasury Consent. Following the 1988 Finance Act this is no longer a criminal offence. But if a company incorporated outside the UK now moves its central management and control abroad, a capital disposal of the company's assets will be deemed to occur and tax will be payable on its unrealised gains at the date of migration. (Following the 1988 Finance Act companies incorporated under the laws of England, Scotland or Northern Ireland will be resident in the UK for corporation tax purposes, irrespective of where those companies are managed and controlled so they can no longer emigrate.)

Section 765 Treasury Consents will still be required for certain transactions, for example for an overseas subsidiary of a UK-resident company to issue shares or debentures, or for a UK-resident company to transfer shares or debentures of a foreign subsidiary, but only under certain circumstances. Various General Consents have been issued and if a transaction falls within one of these then a special Treasury Consent will not be necessary. The General Consents were revised on and with effect from 15 March 1988. These are set out in full below. The references to Sections 482 and 258 predate ICTA 1988.

The new General Consents will allow one overseas subsidiary to issue shares to another overseas subsidiary which is either UK-resident or resident in the same country as its previous parent. Treasury Consent will still be required where, for example, shares are transferred to a company resident in a different country from the previous parent. This is one of the reasons why inserting a Netherlands holding company into an existing group structure will usually require Treasury Consent.

The following extract from The Treasury General Consents 1988 *has been reproduced with the kind permission of the Controller of Her Majesty's Stationery Office (HMSO).*

THE TREASURY GENERAL CONSENTS 1988

The Treasury, in exercise of the powers conferred on them by section 482(4) of the Income and Corporation Taxes Act 1970**(a)**, hereby give the following consents:

Citation and Commencement

1. These consents may be cited as the Treasury General Consents 1988 and apply to transactions on and after 15th March 1988.

Interpretation

2. (1) In these consents unless the context otherwise requires -

"company" means a body corporate;

"non-resident company" means the body corporate referred to in section 482(1)(c) or (d)**(a)** which is not resident in the United Kingdom;

"overseas group" means two or more companies, including the non-resident company, which are not resident in the United Kingdom and which -

(a) are liable to tax in the same territory outside the United Kingdom by reason of domicile, residence or place of management, and

(b) would be deemed to be members of a group of companies for the purposes of section 258 of the Taxes Act if, in subsection (7) of that section**(a)** -

---

(a)1970 c.10. By virtue of paragraph 21(3) of Schedule 30 to the Income and Corporation Taxes Act 1988 (c.1) on and after 6 April 1988 the reference to section 482(4) is to be construed as a reference to section 765(4) of that Act, the reference to section 482(1)(c) or (d) is to be construed as a reference to section 765(1)(c) or (d) of that Act, the reference to section 258(7) is to be construed as a reference to section 413(5) of that Act and the reference to the purposes of section 258 is to be construed as a reference to the purposes of Chapter IV of Part X of that Act.

(i) the words "resident in the United Kingdom" were omitted, and

(ii) a reference to a body corporate not liable to tax in the territory outside the United Kingdom by reason of domicile, residence or place of management referred to in sub-paragraph (a) above were substituted for the reference to a body corporate not resident in the United Kingdom in paragraph (c) of that subsection;

"redeemable", in relation to shares, means that the shares satisfy one or both of the following conditions -

(a) that, by virtue of the terms of their issue, the exercise of a right by any person or the existence of any arrangements, they are liable to be redeemed, cancelled or repaid, in whole or in part;

(b) that, by virtue of any material arrangements, the holder has a right to require another person to acquire the shares or is obliged in any circumstances to dispose of them or another person has a right or is in any circumstances obliged to acquire them;

and arrangements are material arrangements if the company which issued the shares or a company connected with that company is a party to the arrangements;

"resident company" means the body corporate resident in the United Kingdom referred to in section 482(1)(c) or (d);

"resident group" means those companies, including the resident company, which are deemed to be members of a group of companies for the purposes of section 258 of the Taxes Act;

"section 482(1)(c)" and "section 482(1)(d)" mean section 482(1)(c) and section 482(1)(d) of the Taxes Act, as the case may be;

"the Taxes Act" means the Income and Corporation Taxes Act 1970;

"territorial group" means two or more companies which are not resident in the United Kingdom and which -

(a) are liable to tax in the same territory outside the United Kingdom by reason of domicile, residence or place of management, and

(b) would be deemed to be members of a group of companies for the purposes of section 258 of the Taxes Act if, in subsection (7) of that section -

(i) the words "resident in the United Kingdom" were omitted, and

(ii) a reference to a body corporate not liable to tax in the territory outside the United Kingdom by reason of domicile, residence or place of management referred to in sub-paragraph (a) above were substituted for the reference to a body corporate not resident in the United Kingdom in paragraph (c) of that subsection;

"transaction" means a transaction of one of the classes described in section 482(1)(c) or (d) as the case may be;

and other expressions have the same meaning as in section 482 of the Taxes Act.

(2) The Interpretation Act 1978**(a)** shall apply to these consents as it applies to an Act of Parliament.

(3) In applying the provisions of section 258 of the Taxes Act for the purposes of the definitions of "overseas group", "resident group" and "territorial group" in sub-paragraph (1) above, the words "51 per cent. subsidiary" and "51 per cent. subsidiaries" shall be substituted for "75 per cent. subsidiary" and "75 per cent. subsidiaries" as the case may be, wherever they occur in that section.

(4) For the purposes of these consents, any question whether a person is connected with another shall be determined in accordance with the provisions of section 533(2) to (8) of the Taxes Act**(b)** (any provision that one person is connected with another being taken to mean that they are connected with one another).

(a) 1978 c.30. **(b)**By virtue of paragraph 21(3) of Schedule 30 to the Income and Corporation Taxes Act 1988 (c.1) on and after 6 April 1988 the reference to section 533(2) to (8) is to be construed as a reference to section 839(2) to (8) of that Act.

Consent to transactions within section 482(1)(c)

3. The Treasury consent generally to transactions of the class described in section 482(1)(c) which consist of -

(a) the creation of shares by the non-resident company;

(b) the issue of shares by the non-resident company -

(i) to another member of the overseas group, or

(ii) subject to the conditions prescribed by paragraph 4, to the resident company or to another member of the resident group, or

(iii) subject to the conditions prescribed by paragraph 5, to a person not connected with the resident company, or

(iv) subject to the conditions prescribed by paragraph 6, to all persons who are its shareholders at the time of the issue;

(c) the creation of debentures by the non-resident company and their issue -

(i) to another member of the overseas group, or

(ii) subject to the condition prescribed by paragraph 7, to the resident company or to another member of the resident group, or

(iii) subject to the conditions prescribed by paragraph 5, to persons not connected with the resident company;

(d) transactions of any kind described in subsection (1)(c) where the non-resident company -

(i) was incorporated after 31st December 1951,

(ii) is liable to tax in a Commonwealth territory other than the United Kingdom by reason of domicile, residence or place of management, and

(iii) was incorporated for the purpose of starting and carrying on a new industrial activity in that Commonwealth territory,

and in this sub-paragraph "industrial activity" means any productive, extractive or manufacturing industry, any public utility, fisheries or any form of husbandry.

4

4. The conditions prescribed by this paragraph are that the issue -

(a) is of shares that are not redeemable; and

(b) is made either -

(i) for full consideration paid in cash to the non-resident company, or

(ii) in or towards payment for any business undertaking or property acquired by the non-resident company for full consideration.

5. The conditions prescribed by this paragraph are -

(a) that the issue

(i) is for full consideration paid to the non-resident company, and

(ii) is not to a nominee or trustee for a person who is connected with the resident company;

(b) that no arrangements exist as a consequence of which the resident company or a person connected with the resident company, or a nominee or trustee for that person or that company, is or may become entitled to the shares or debentures so issued or to any of them or to any interest in them or in any of them.

6. The conditions prescribed by this paragraph are that the issue -

(a) is in respect of and in proportion to the shares held by the shareholders in the non-resident company at the time of the issue; and

(b) is either -

(i) of shares that are not redeemable, or

(ii) where no shares are issued to a company which is resident in the United Kingdom or to a nominee or trustee for such a company, for full consideration paid in cash to the non-resident company.

7. (1) The condition prescribed by this paragraph is that none of the circumstances set out in sub-paragraph (2) below are associated with, or are present in connection with, the issue of the debentures.

(2) Those circumstances are -

(a) that the debentures are issued at a discount;

(b) that arrangements exist as a result of which the non-resident company acquires property of any description from a company which is resident in the United Kingdom and the consideration, or some part of the consideration, for the acquisition remains unpaid;

(c) that a loan, whether or not of the same amount as that secured by the debentures, is made by a company which is not resident in the United Kingdom to a company which is resident in the United Kingdom;

(d) that any amount payable in respect of the debentures is determined by reference to the movement of an index of prices, earnings or any other indicator of an economic nature published in the United Kingdom or elsewhere.

Consent to transactions within section 482(1)(d)

8. The Treasury consent generally to transactions of the class described in section 482(1)(d) which consist of -

(a) the transfer by the resident company of shares or debentures of the non-resident company to another member of the resident group;

(b) subject to the conditions prescribed by paragraph 9, the transfer by the resident company or by a company which is not resident in the United Kingdom (in paragraph 9 referred to in either case as "the transferor company") of shares or debentures of the non-resident company to a person not connected with the resident company;

(c) the transfer by a company which is not resident in the United Kingdom of shares or debentures of the non-resident company to a company which is a member of a territorial group of which the first-mentioned company is also a member.

9. The conditions prescribed by this paragraph are -

(a) that the transfer -

(i) is for full consideration paid to the transferor company, and

(ii) is not to a nominee or trustee for a person who is connected with the resident company;

(b) that no arrangements exist as a consequence of which -

(i) the resident company, or

(ii) a nominee or trustee for the resident company, or

(iii) a person connected with the resident company, or

(iv) a nominee or trustee for a person connected with the resident company,

is or may become entitled to the shares or debentures transferred or to any of them or to any interest in them or in any of them.

Revocation of previous consents

10. All consents previously given generally by the Treasury to transactions of the classes described in section 482(1)(c) and (d) are hereby revoked.

Because Section 765 is a criminal section, punishable by up to two years in jail and/or a fine of £10,000, it is extremely important that any transaction which might require Treasury Consent does in fact obtain specific consent. In order to obtain specific consent the information detailed on page 116–17 must be sent to the Treasury in triplicate, although only the top copy requires accounts or supporting documents. The application should be sent to:

The Secretary
H M Treasury (AP)
Parliament Street
London SW1P 3AG.

If the application is urgent, two copies of the letter, both with accounts or other supporting documents, should be sent to:

Inland Revenue
International Division
Room 311
Melbourne House
Aldwych
London WC2B 4LL.

A letter should simultaneously be sent to the Treasury indicating that copies have already been sent directly to Melbourne House.

The application should give sufficient information to enable the Treasury to form a view on the transaction proposed. They will take into account the significance of any new factors or circumstances which are represented to require a proposed change and any compelling reason for such application, based on the efficiency and development of the applicant's operations. The Treasury will weigh against considerations of this kind the prospective loss of revenue or of foreign exchange to the country which the transaction, if permitted, would entail, and they will inform the Chancellor whether, on a balance of considerations, it would in their opinion, be in the national interest that permission should be granted.

As a result of the removal of Exchange Control, loss of foreign exchange is not a factor which is currently taken into account.

The commercial reasons for the proposed transactions should be fully explained and relevant background information given so as to enable the transactions to be understood in their proper context.

The letter should authorise the Commissioners of Inland Revenue to disclose particulars of the company's tax affairs to the Advisory Committee and, insofar as they are not disclosed by the application, to the Treasury.

The following information should be set out in an application for specific consent:-

For first time applications

1. The name of the applicant company (and, if it is a member of a group, the ultimate UK parent company).
2. The nature of the business of the company (and the group) and the place where the main activities are carried on.
3. Whether the company (and its UK parent) is a public or private company.
4. The extent of the shareholdings by non-residents in the company (or its UK parent) if these exceed 20 per cent.
5. The tax district (and reference) to which the company makes its corporation tax returns.
6. A copy of the latest accounts of the company (and its UK parent).

For subsequent applications

7. The name of the applicant company (and, if it is a member of a group, the ultimate UK parent company).
8. If any previous application related to the same overseas company as is referred to in the current application, the date and Treasury reference number for that application; otherwise, the date and Treasury reference number for the last application by the applicant company or another member of the same group.
9. Any significant changes in the information previously given under items 2–5 above, including the latest accounts.

For all applications

10. A description of the proposed transactions.
11. The name of the non-resident company, its country of incorporation and tax residence.
12. The nature of the business of the non-resident company.
13. The extent of the applicant company's control over the non-resident company (a) at present and (b) after the proposed transactions.

14. The name(s) of the person(s) to whom the issue (other than a public issue) or transfer is to be made, their country of residence, and full details of any direct or indirect connection by shareholdings or otherwise between such person(s) and the applicant company.
15. Full details of the consideration for the issue or transfer.
16. Where an issue is of redeemable shares (as defined in the General Consents), the terms of issue and of redemption.
17. If any sale is not at market value, the reasons for this.
18. The commercial reasons for the transactions with any relevant background information to enable the transactions to be understood in their proper context.
19. An estimate of the effect, if any, of the transactions on the UK tax position, indicating any difference in the tax payable at any time by the applicant company or any member of the same group as a direct or indirect result of the propsed transactions compared with the tax payable under existing arrangements.

With respect to companies investing into Europe, the Finance Act 1990 provided that certain transfers of shares between EC incorporated companies would not require specific consent. The implications of the Finance Act 1990 are complex, and if there is any doubt consent should be obtained. Professional advice in this very complex area is essential.

A word of warning. Section 765 is a criminal section. The normal rules of interpretation and judicial precedent that apply to other sections of tax legislation do not necessarily apply in this case. It will be governed by the rules of interpretation relating to criminal legislation, and therefore exceptional care must be exercised.

7.7 Other obstacles

We have looked at some of the principal sections of anti-avoidance legislation that a UK company expanding abroad may encounter on its journey. It should be noted that there is a host of other anti-avoidance legislation dealing with a variety of different subjects, some commonplace and others arcane.

In the next chapter we will look at how the anti-avoidance legislation discussed so far would apply in practice as the UK group expands overseas and develops a more complex international corporate structure.

INLAND REVENUE
Press Release

INLAND REVENUE PRESS OFFICE, SOMERSET HOUSE, STRAND, LONDON WC2R 1LB
PHONE: 01–438 6692 OR 6706

[3x] 20 October 1988

CONTROLLED FOREIGN COMPANIES: CHAPTER IV PART XVII INCOME AND CORPORATION TAXES ACT 1988 EXCLUDED COUNTRIES LIST

1. Following consultation the Government confirm the changes to the qualifications contained in Part II of the list of excluded countries, on which views were sought in the Press Release of 4 February 1988. The changes apply for all accounting periods ending after 4 February 1988.

2. A complete revised list is attached. As well as the above changes, this incorporates the further changes announced in the Press Release of 4 February which took effect immediately and were not subject to consultation. For ease of reference all provisions that are either new or revised are identified by underlining.

NOTES FOR EDITORS

1. The provisions on Controlled Foreign Companies are contained in Sections 747-756 and Schedules 24-26 of Income and Corporation Taxes Act 1988 (formerly Sections 82-91 and Schedules 16-18 of Finance Act 1984). They enable a charge to UK tax to be imposed on certain UK companies with interests in UK controlled companies in low tax areas. The purpose of the excluded countries list is to give an assurance that a company, if it is resident and carrying on a business in a listed country, will be regarded as meeting the conditions for exclusion set out in the legislation itself, subject to any qualification set out in the list for the country concerned.

2. The last fully updated list of excluded countries was published on 25 July 1985.

/ANNEX

ANNEX

CONTROLLED FOREIGN COMPANIES: LIST OF EXCLUDED COUNTRIES

Covering Note

1. This list relates to the provisions on Controlled Foreign Companies contained in Section 747-756 and Schedules 24-26 of Income and Corporation Taxes Act 1988 (formerly Sections 82-91 and Schedules 16-18 of the Finance Act 1984). Its purpose is to give an assurance that, if a company is resident and carries on business in one of the countries on the list, it will be regarded as meeting the conditions necessary for exclusion from the charge imposed by the legislation.

2. The list is split into two parts. Any company which is resident and carrying on business (see paragraphs 3 and 4 below) in a country on Part I of the list will be excluded from the application of the legislation. Where a company is resident and carrying on business in a country which appears on Part II it will be similarly excluded, provided that it does not benefit from any of the reliefs specified in column 2.

3. For the purposes of this list a company will be treated as resident in a country if, under local law, it is liable to tax there by reason of domicile, residence or place of management. Where a country does not impose tax by reason of one of these criteria, incorporation will be the test used. Thus, a company will be treated as resident in the country under whose laws it is incorporated, if otherwise it would not be resident anywhere for the purpose of this list.

4. A company will be regarded for the purpose of this list as carrying on business in a country if 90 per cent of its commercially quantified income is local source income. For this purpose:

a. "commercially quantified income" means the profits as determined according to generally-accepted commercial accounting standards, but disregarding any profits or losses of a capital nature; and

b. "local source income" means income which is treated under a country's own laws as accruing in, arising in, or being derived from that country and which is within its charge to tax - ie is actually chargeable there or covered by a specific exemption from the general charge. Income derived from a branch or agency outside a country will not in any event be regarded as local source income of that country.

5. The list will apply by reference to the overseas company's accounting period. No charge will arise if, throughout an accounting period, the company is resident and carrying on business either in a Part I country or in a Part II country but not entitled to any of the reliefs specified in column 2.

2

6. The fact that a company fails to gain exclusion from the charge by virtue of this list does not, of course, necessarily mean that it comes within the charge. A charge can arise only where all the conditions set out in Section 747 are present; and where they are all present, the company may escape through satisfying one of the statutory tests for exclusion in Section 748.

Changes to the list

7. The list will be amended from time to time, as necessary, to reflect tax changes made by the UK or by an overseas country or changes in the way in which the relevant laws are applied, or to reflect indications that the laws are capable of exploitation.

8. Where an amendment arises from a change in tax rates or tax law or practice, the Government will give notice of the proposed amendment and invite comments. If, in the light of consultations the list is revised, the change to the list will apply for all accounting periods ending after -

either a. the date on which the change in tax rates, or law or practice becomes effective;

or b. the date on which the Government gave notice of the proposed amendment to the list,

whichever is the later.

9. Where the need to amend the list arises from indications that a country's existing law or practice is capable of exploitation, the revised list will apply for all accounting periods ending after the date on which the revised list is published.

/Part I: Excluded Countries

Part I: Excluded Countries

Australia
Austria
Bangladesh
Bolivia
Botswana
Brazil
Bulgaria
Canada
China
Colombia
Czechoslovakia
Denmark
Dominican Republic
Falkland Islands
Fiji
Finland
France
Gambia
German Democratic Republic
German Federal Republic
Ghana
Honduras
Hungary
India
Indonesia
Italy
Ivory Coast
Japan
Korea, Republic of
Malawi
Mauritius
Mexico
Morocco
New Zealand
Nigeria
Norway
Papua New Guinea
Poland
Romania
Sierra Leone
South Africa (excluding the Homelands)
Soviet Union
Swaziland
Sweden
Thailand
Western Samoa
Yugoslavia
Zambia

/Part II: Excluded Countries, subject to qualifications

Part II: Excluded Countries, subject to qualifications

(1) Country		(2) Qualification
Argentina	:	companies obtaining exemption from tax on income from transactions, activities or operations carried on in, or from goods located in, tax free areas in accordance with Law 19640
Belgium	:	1. companies which are regarded as Foreign Sales Corporations by the United States and which therefore qualify for reduced Belgian taxation [accounting periods ending after 25 July 1985]. 2. companies approved under Royal Decree No.187 of 30 December 1982 as Co-ordination Centres (as defined by the original Royal Decree or by subsequent amending Laws) [accounting periods ending after 4 February 1988; with slightly modified wording, applied also to accounting periods ending after 25 July 1985].
Brunei	:	companies qualifying as "pioneer companies" under the Investment Incentives Enactment 1975
Chile	:	companies obtaining exemption from tax under Law 16,441 of 1 March 1966 on income from property located in the Department of Isla da Pascua or from activities developed therein [accounting period ending after 25 July 1985].
Egypt	:	1. companies outside the scope of Article III of Law 157 of 1981 because they do not "operate" in Egypt 2. companies to which Article 16 and 18 of Law 43 of 1974 (as amended by Law 32 of 1977) apply in circumstances where a dividend out of those profits to a UK resident company would not attract relief under Article 22(3) of the UK/Egypt Double Tax Agreement (SI No.1091 of 1980) on account of the proviso to Article 22(3)(b)

Part II (cont'd)

Faroe Islands	:	companies deriving interest from Faroese financial institutions from which tax is deducted at source under Law 4 of 26 March 1953
Greece	:	1. companies which have profits exempt from tax under Article 6(2)(c) of Law 3843 of 1958 (profits from the operation of ships under the Greek flag)
		2. companies having profits exempt from company income tax by virtue of Article 25 of Law 25/1975 as replaced by Article 28 of Law 814/1978, or by virtue of Law 89/1967 as supplemented by Law 378/1968 (profits from shipping and associated activities) [accounting periods ending after 25 July 1985].
Ireland	:	1. companies obtaining relief or exemption from tax under Part V of the Corporation Tax Act 1976 or Section 43 of the Finance Act 1980 (profits from trading within Shannon Airport)
		2. companies obtaining relief or exemption from tax under Part IV of the Corporation Tax Act 1976 or Section 42 of the Finance Act 1980 (profits from the export of certain goods) [accounting periods ending after 25 July 1985].
		3. companies obtaining relief or exemption from tax under Chapter VI of the Finance Act 1980 as amended by Section 17 of the Finance Act 1981 (manufacturing companies and their associates) [accounting periods ending after 25 July 1985].
Kenya	:	1. companies having income granted exemption from tax under paragraph 11 Schedule 1 of the Income Tax 1973
		2. companies obtaining investment allowance under paragraph 24(1)(a) or (c) or paragraph 25 Schedule 2 of the Income Tax Act 1973

Part II (cont'd)

Lesotho	:	companies obtaining initial, depreciation or investment allowances under Section 18 of the Pioneer Industries Encouragement Act 1969, as amended
Luxembourg	:	1. companies obtaining any special tax benefit under the law of 31 July 1929, decree of 17 December 1938 as amended or Grand Ducal Regulation of 29 July 1977 (holding companies) 2. companies carrying on any reinsurance business [accounting periods ending after 25 July 1985].
Malaysia	:	1. companies exempt from tax in accordance with Section 54A of the Income Tax Act 1967 (shipping) 2. companies subject to tax at 5 per cent in accordance with Section 60A of the Income Tax Act 1967 (inward reinsurance) 3. Companies deriving dividends from a company or companies deriving income from one or more of the activities mentioned above
Malta	:	companies entitled to exemption or relief from tax under a. Section 8(2) of the Income Tax Act 1948, or b. Section 6B of the Aid to Industry Ordinance 1959
Netherlands	:	companies which are regarded as Foreign Sales Corporations (FSC's) by the United States [accounting periods ending after 4 February 1988; with slightly modified wording, applied also to accounting periods ending after 25 July 1985]
Pakistan	:	companies deriving royalties, commissions or fees which are exempt from tax under paragraph 139, Part I, second Schedule, Income Tax Ordinance 1979

Part II (cont'd)

Philippines :	1. companies authorised under Presidential Decree 1034 or 1035, both of 30 September 1976, to operate an Offshore Banking Unit or a Foreign Currency Deposit Unit as defined in those decrees or the regulations thereto
	2. companies receiving interest on deposits with a Foreign Currency Deposit Unit, or other interest subject to the reduced rates of tax under Section 24(cc) of the National Internal Revenue Code
Portugal :	1. companies having income not charged to the industrial tax, but would have been so charged had the company been within group A of that tax
	2. companies which are investment or holding companies having a capital in excess of 100,000 Contos, and deriving dividends or interest from Portuguese securities
	3. companies obtaining the benefit of Article 44 of the Industrial Tax Code (reinvestment of reserves)
	4. companies obtaining a deduction from taxable income under Decree-Law 408/80 of 26 September 1980 (export incentives)
	5. companies obtaining any reduction in industrial, capital or complementary taxes by virtue of the Integrated System of Investment Incentives contained in Decree-Law 194/80 of 19 July 1980 or Decree-Law 132/83 of 18 March 1983 other than by way of accelerated depreciation [accounting periods ending after 4 February 1988 in relation to incentives under Decree-Law 132/83; earlier accounting periods in relation to incentives under Decree-Law 194/80].

Part II (cont'd)

		6. companies obtaining any reduction in industrial taxes by virtue of the investment incentives contained in Decree Law 197-C/86 of 18 July 1986 [accounting periods ending after 4 February 1988]
Puerto Rico	:	1. companies obtaining full or partial exemption from income tax or surtax under the Industrial Incentive Act 1978, in respect of income from a service industry or from property leased to and used by a business obtaining such exemption
		2. companies obtaining tax holidays in respect of income from exports, or in respect of the business of maritime transportation of freight or the lease or rental of property used in such transportation
Senegal	:	1. companies receiving income from "bons de caisse" which is not liable to the tax on industrial and commercial profits
		2. companies obtaining a reduction in the tax on industrial and commercial profits by reason of reinvestment of the whole or part of those profits
Singapore	:	1. companies subject to the concessionary rate of tax for insurance and reinsurance of risks outside Singapore by virtue of Section 43C of the Income Tax Act as amplified by the Income Tax (Concessionary Rate of Tax for Income from Insuring and Reinsuring Offshore Risks) Regulations 1980
		2. companies with Asian Currency Units having income: a. taxed at the concessionary rate by virtue of Section 43A of the Income Tax Act as amplified by the Income Tax (Concessionary Rate of Tax for Asian Currency Unit Income) Regulations 1979, or

Part II (cont'd)

Singapore (cont'd)		b. exempt from tax under the Income Tax (Income Arising from Syndicated Offshore Loans) Regulations 1984 [accounting periods ending after 25 July 1985]
		3. companies obtaining exemption from tax on the income of a shipping enterprise in accordance with Section 13A of the Income Tax Act
		4. companies obtaining relief from tax in accordance with Sections 37A to K of the Economic Expansion Incentives (Relief from Income Tax) Act, as amended (international trade incentives)
		5. companies obtaining relief from tax in accordance with Sections 46J to S of the Economic Expansion Incentives (Relief from Income Tax) Act as amended (warehouse and service incentives)
		6. companies with any income to which S43E of the Income Tax Act applies (headquarters companies) [accounting periods ending after 4 February 1988].
		7. companies deriving dividends from a company or companies deriving income from one or more of the activities mentioned above
Solomon Islands	:	1. companies having bank interest exempted from tax by Schedule 1(20) of the Income Tax Act (Chapter 61)
		2. companies carrying on life insurance business exempted from tax by Schedule 1(26) of the Income Tax Act
Spain	:	companies obtaining tax credit relief for investments under the following or similar laws -
		a. Article 32 Law 1 of 1979

Part II (cont'd)

		b. Article 34 Law 42 of 1979 c. Article 40 Royal Decree 3061 of 1979
Sri Lanka	:	companies obtaining relief or exemption from income tax under any of the following provisions of the Inland Revenue Act (No.28 of 1979) a. Section 8(c)(iv)- foreign currency banking units b. Sections 10(d) and 15(b) - income derived from approved bank accounts c. Section 10(e) - interest of newly resident companies d. Section 15(cc) - services rendered outside Sri Lanka e. Section 15(p) - re-export of approved products
Tanzania	:	1. companies relieved or exempted from income tax under Section 15(1) or (1A) of the Income Tax Act 1973 2. companies obtaining investment allowances under Schedule II Part V of the Income Tax Act 1973
Trinidad and Tobago	:	1. assurance companies carrying on long term insurance business and liable to corporation tax at 15 per cent on all or part of their profits in accordance with the proviso in Schedule III of the Finance Act 1966 2. investment companies as defined by Section 46(3) of the Finance Act 1966 obtaining exemption from corporation tax on profits in accordance with Section 46(1)(b)

Part II (cont'd)

Trinidad and Tobago (cont'd)		3. approved property development companies entitled in accordance with Section 55A of the Finance Act 1966 to a deduction of 15 per cent of capital expenditure incurred in the construction of a building used for commercial or industrial purposes by a lessee
		4. companies entitled to a deduction in computing chargeable income, in accordance with Section 2 of the Income Tax (In Aid of Industry) Ordinance 1950 (Chapter 33 No.2) on the capital expenditure on construction of a building or structure which has been or is to be an industrial building or structure occupied for the purposes of a trade carried on by a lessee
		5. companies deriving dividends from a company or companies deriving income from one or more of the activities mentioned above
Tunisia	:	companies obtaining exemption from or reduction of tax under Law 76 - 63 of 12 July 1976 (financial and banking institutions dealing with non-residents)
Turkey	:	1. companies obtaining investment incentive allowances under Article 8(9) of Law 5422 of 3 June 1949 and Chapter VIII of Law 202 of 19 February 1963
		2. companies obtaining export incentives under Article 8(4), (6), (7), (8) or (10) of Law 5422 of 3 June 1949
United States	:	Domestic International Sales Corporations as defined in Section 992(a) of the Internal Revenue Code 1954
Zimbabwe	:	companies carrying on a "growth point business" as defined in Schedule 14 of the Income Tax Act 1967 as amended.

12

8

Developing the Corporate Structure

8.1 Key

Having looked at the main principles underlying the tax on a UK company expanding into Europe, we should now consider more complicated international corporate structures. In order to simplify the explanation of what is happening the following symbols will be used:-

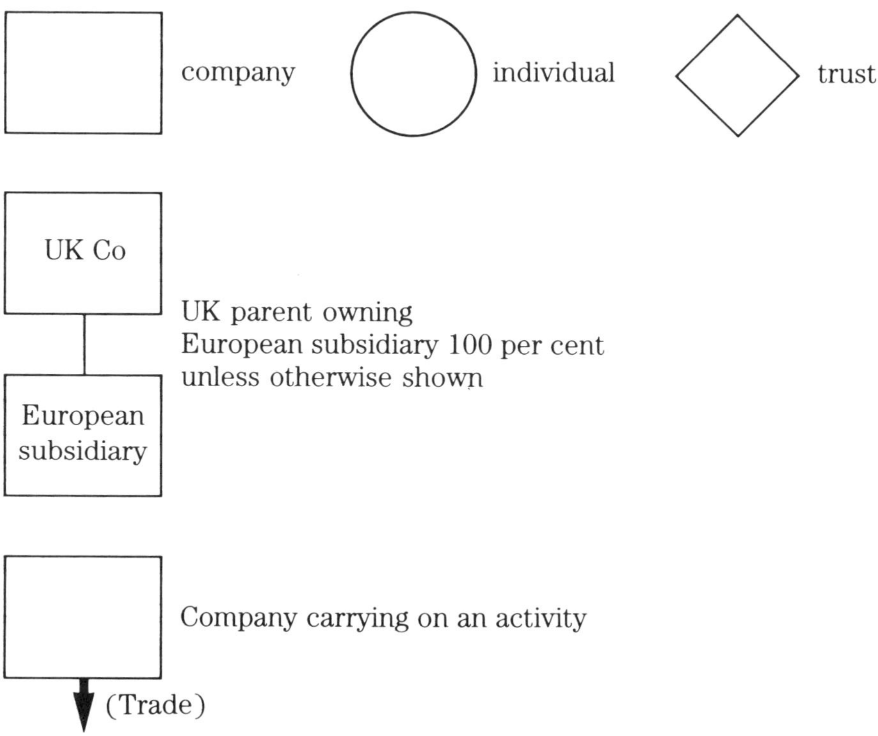

We will examine how an international corporate structure can develop in complexity over the years, and in particular how the UK's concept of residence and anti-avoidance legislation allows the Inland Revenue to attack overseas subsidiaries, especially where they lack commercial justification.

8.2 The simplest forms

The simplest international corporate structure is for the UK company not to have a permanent establishment in Europe and merely to trade with Europe rather than in Europe.

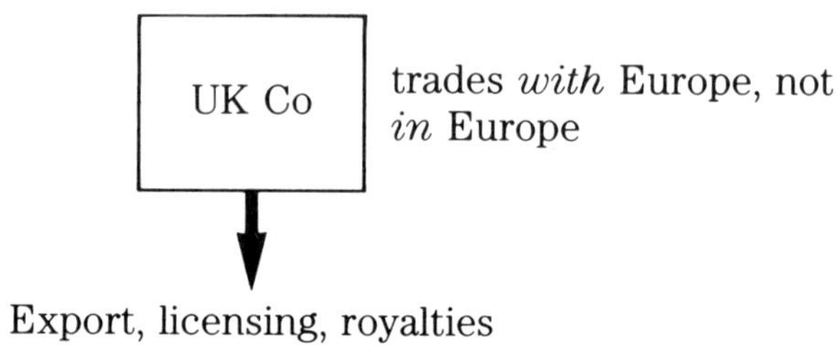

8.3 Foreign branch

The next stage is to have a foreign branch

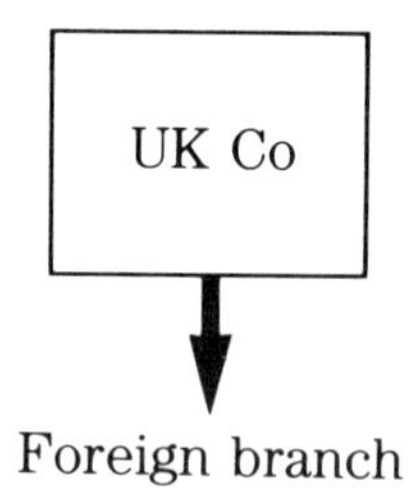

8.4 Foreign subsidiary

However, for the commercial reasons previously discussed, once it is liable to foreign tax usually the UK company will incorporate a foreign subsidiary.

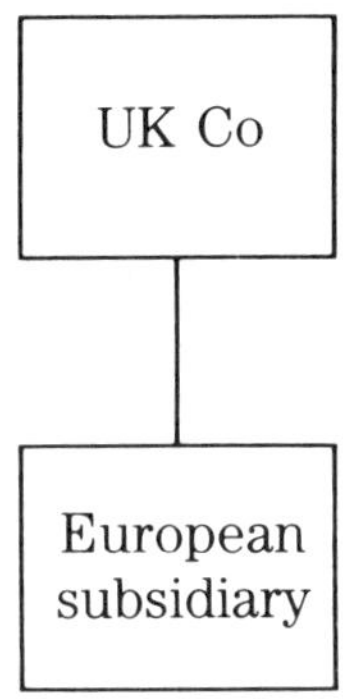

8.5 UK holding company

But what about more complex structures? We have already discussed the use of a UK sub-holding company (Case V Trap) under the heading of double tax relief.

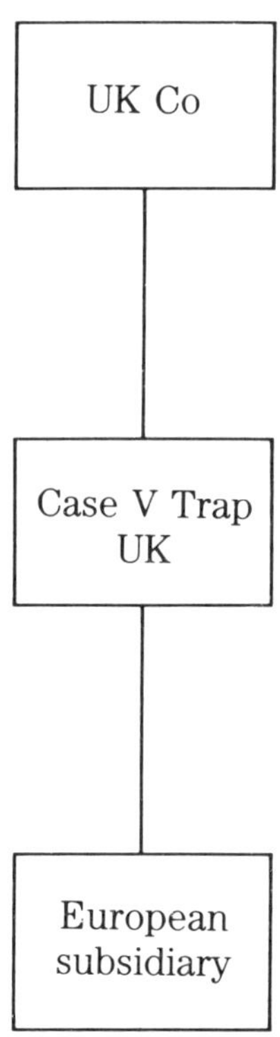

Let us recap why these are so useful.

A UK sub-holding company is usually formed to own overseas subsidiaries. This serves both commercial and tax purposes. From the tax point of view it helps to maximise double tax relief. This is because the overseas dividend (or other income) should be received by a company which has no losses, especially non-trading 'losses' such as excess management expenses of an investment company. If an overseas dividend is received by a company with such losses, double tax relief will be wasted. Also, just the right amount of group relief can be claimed by a separate company so as to maximise double tax relief. Therefore the dividend should be received by a UK company that carries on no other activities. Such companies are known as 'Case V Traps' because overseas dividends are subject to UK corporation tax under Case V of Schedule D. Case V Traps can usually be inserted into a corporate structure without having to obtain Treasury Consents and Inland Revenue clearances. This is because of the UK's domestic group taxing system. It is assumed, of course, that all companies in these structures are 100 per cent owned.

There are also non-tax advantages to such a structure. These include limitation of liability (distancing the UK assets still further from any foreign claims), the ability to appoint individuals as directors who are not main board directors, and the ability to bring in outside shareholders in a joint venture arrangement.

8.6 Overseas holding company

The next level of complexity is to have an overseas holding company, located in a third country.

The main advantages of owning overseas subsidiaries through an offshore holding company are:

- capital gains on the sale or part sale of subsidiaries may be realised tax-free;
- low- and high-taxed dividends may be mixed so as to maximise double tax relief. This has been discussed at some length in Chapter 5 on double tax relief;
- reducing withholding taxes along a chain of dividend payments, thereby maximising UK double tax relief – also discussed in Chapter 5;
- deferring tax on dividends from overseas subsidiaries (subject to the CFC legislation and Section 739 ICTA 1988);

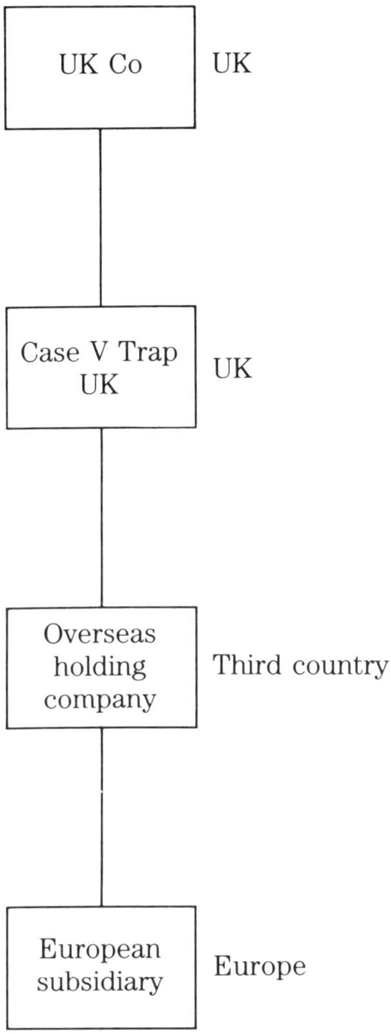

- protection against a reintroduction of UK exchange controls; although this is remote at present it could become more important on a change of government in the UK, although even the Opposition at present has indicated that it would not wish to reintroduce full exchange controls.

Example of capital gains deferral

A UK company owns an Irish subsidiary. The shares in the Irish subsidiary cost the UK company £100,000 and they are now to be sold for £200,000. Indexation on those shares is £20,000. If the UK company were to sell the shares in the Irish company it would realise a taxable profit of £80,000 which would be subject to tax at 35 per cent, ie tax of £28,000. On the other hand, if a UK company had a Netherlands holding company which in turn owned an Irish subsidiary, and the Netherlands holding company sold the Irish subsidiary, there would be no tax to pay. The group would therefore have saved £28,000 in tax until such time as the profits are repatriated to the UK, for example in the form of dividends.

Example of income deferral

A UK company owns a Netherlands offshore holding company which in turn owns a number of European subsidiaries. All the European subsidiaries have active businesses in those countries so that the CFC legislation does not apply. The UK company is a public company and therefore Section 739 does not apply. Dividends of £2 million per year are paid up from the European subsidiaries to the Netherlands holding company. They carry an underlying rate of tax of approximately 20 per cent (effective rate). Were those dividends to be repatriated back to the UK company they would suffer further corporation tax at 35 per cent with a credit for the 20 per cent underlying and withholding taxes, leaving a net liability of 15 per cent.

A UK company would therefore be liable to pay tax of £300,000 on a dividend of £2 million. By paying the dividends to a Netherlands holding company the dividends can be invested 'gross' of the £300,000 tax. The Netherlands company could even lend the funds back down to the European subsidiaries which could pay interest up to the Netherlands company, although that interest would in turn be subject to Netherlands tax, unless the Netherlands company was paying interest out.

The Netherlands company could lend to the European subsidiaries on a back-to-back basis. The Netherlands company could even invest in more sophisticated offshore funds which can provide a greater rate of return than a normal bank. This produces various other problems that need monitoring, for example the taxability of an exchange gain in the Netherlands and withholding tax.

Example of minimising withholding taxes

This is less of an advantage with UK parent companies than with most other countries, because the UK has even more double tax treaties than the Netherlands. Most countries do not have lower rates of withholding tax back to the Netherlands as opposed to the UK, although some do. For example, dividends from Austria to the UK attract a 5 per cent withholding tax. Dividends from Austria to the Netherlands have a nil withholding tax: similarly with dividends from Finland, Italy and Spain (under some circumstances). Under some circumstances there is a 10 per cent withholding tax on dividends from Norway to the UK but nil to the Netherlands. By minimising the withholding taxes along the chain of dividend payments the likelihood of keeping the overall rate of underlying and withholding taxes below 35 per cent is maximised, thereby avoiding wasting double tax relief.

8.7 Netherlands holding company

The Netherlands is often chosen as a location for an offshore holding company because of its extensive network of double tax treaties. This will allow passive income such as dividends to flow into and out of the

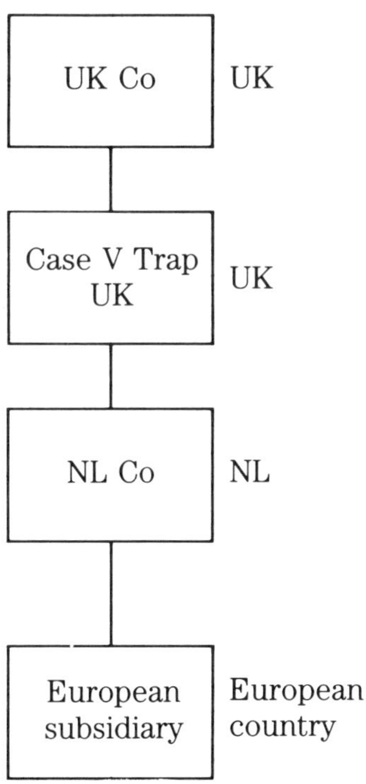

Netherlands with minimal withholding taxes. Appendix E illustrates the comparatively low rates of withholding tax on dividends paid to a Netherlands company. In addition it does not have the potential CFC and 1997 problems of Hong Kong, which has no double tax treaties.

Provided that the Netherlands company is eligible for the 'affiliation privilege', which should be confirmed in advance with the Netherlands tax authorities, it should pay no tax on dividends received from subsidiaries, and gains on the shares in subsidiaries should also be tax-free.

In order to interpose a Netherlands holding company into an existing structure, Treasury Consent under Section 765 ICTA 1988 and clearances from the UK Inland Revenue under Section 703 ICTA 1988 (transactions in securities) and Section 88 CGTA 1979 (tax-free share swaps) will be required. A *bona fide* commercial reason would need to be advanced as to why the overseas subsidiaries had to be transferred to a Netherlands holding company. In addition, foreign consents and clearances may be required. It would help greatly if the group had a real commercial presence in the Netherlands.

It should not be assumed that interposing a Netherlands holding company will always be advantageous. The UK treaties with many other countries (including Denmark, Italy, Switzerland, France and the US) all have a rate of 5 per cent dividend withholding tax. Routeing through the Netherlands would increase the effective rate to 9.75 per cent in the case of France and the USA. However, the effective rates of withholding tax on the dividends from Denmark, Italy and Switzerland would remain the same since all these countries have a nil withholding tax rate between themselves and the Netherlands. It can be seen that the dividend withholding tax position should be examined carefully before interposing offshore holding companies, whether Netherlands or other, between a UK parent and its overseas operating subsidiaries. As the rate of corporation tax in the UK is relatively low at 35 per cent, it may often happen that the UK liability is covered by underlying taxes borne on dividend payments with the result that the extra Netherlands dividend withholding tax of 5 per cent represents a real cost to the UK resident parent company.

8.8 Triple Netherlands structure

If the CFC legislation may apply to some of the UK group's overseas subsidiaries then a 'triple Netherlands structure' should be considered. The diagram set out below illustrates a triple Netherlands structure.

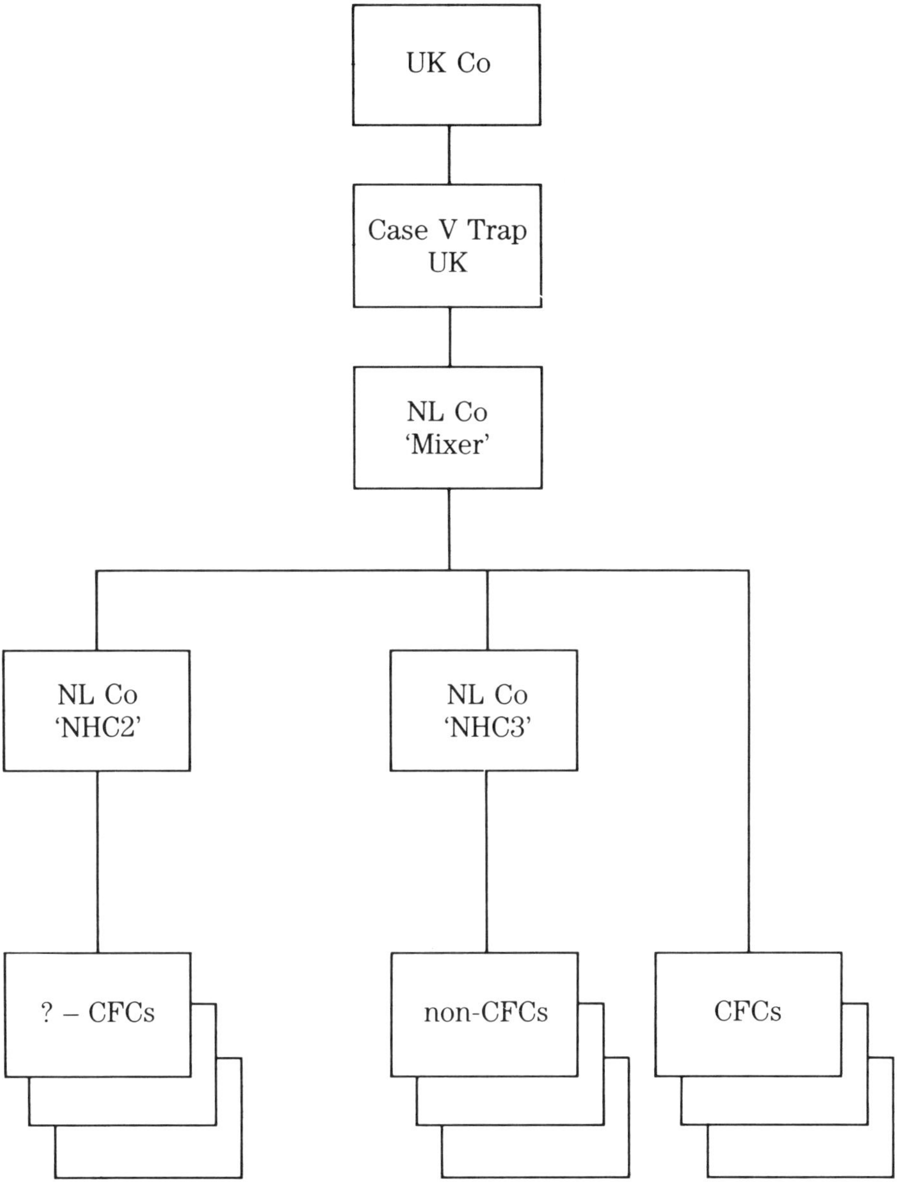

Because it will be necessary for subsidiaries which are definitely CFCs to repatriate their profits to the UK these are owned by Netherlands 'Mixer', which acts as a dividend conduit. Netherlands Holding Company No 2 (NHC2) owns shares in subsidiaries which may or may not be CFCs (in practice it is sometimes difficult to tell in advance) and

Netherlands Holding Company No 3 (NHC3) owns subsidiaries which are definitely not CFCs. Whereas income flows through NL Co Mixer, it is accumulated in NHC2 until the question of the CFC status of its subsidiaries is resolved, and may be accumulated in NHC3 without any adverse CFC implications.

The triple Netherlands holding structure is very rarely required in purely European situations. It is mostly relevant to large multinational groups which invest into countries with radically different tax systems. In most cases only a single Netherlands holding company will be required, but the situation must be kept under constant review.

8.9 Using the holding company as a conduit

A Netherlands holding company could also be used as an interest conduit by routeing the loans through the Netherlands. Interest may be paid gross between the UK and the Netherlands because the Netherlands does not domestically impose a withholding tax on interest.

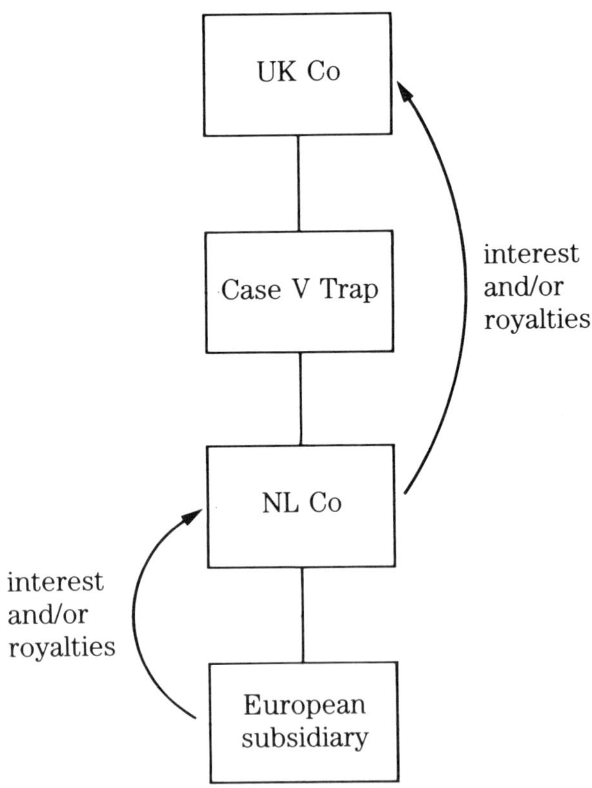

Interest could be paid gross or with minimal withholding taxes to the Netherlands company from the trading subsidiaries by virtue of the Netherlands' extensive network of double tax treaties. Appendix E also illustrates the low rates of withholding tax on payments of interest and royalties to a Netherlands resident company. Similarly, the Netherlands company could also act as a royalty conduit.

Note that interest and royalties are repatriated direct to the UK parent, thereby avoiding any possible loss of double tax relief in the Case V Trap.

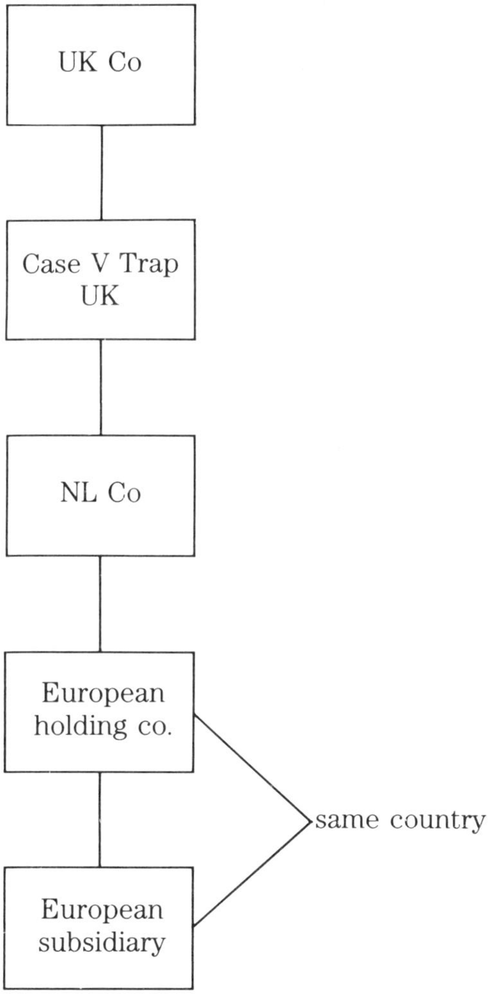

8.10 Foreign holding company

The next level of complexity is to have a foreign holding company in the structure.

Foreign holding companies are of most use in countries where groups of companies are taxed as single entities. Tax benefits can be gained by forming a foreign holding company which will incorporate or acquire a series of foreign subsidiaries. The advantages of forming a group under the 'umbrella' of a foreign holding company are not only the offset of profits and losses, although that is usually the most

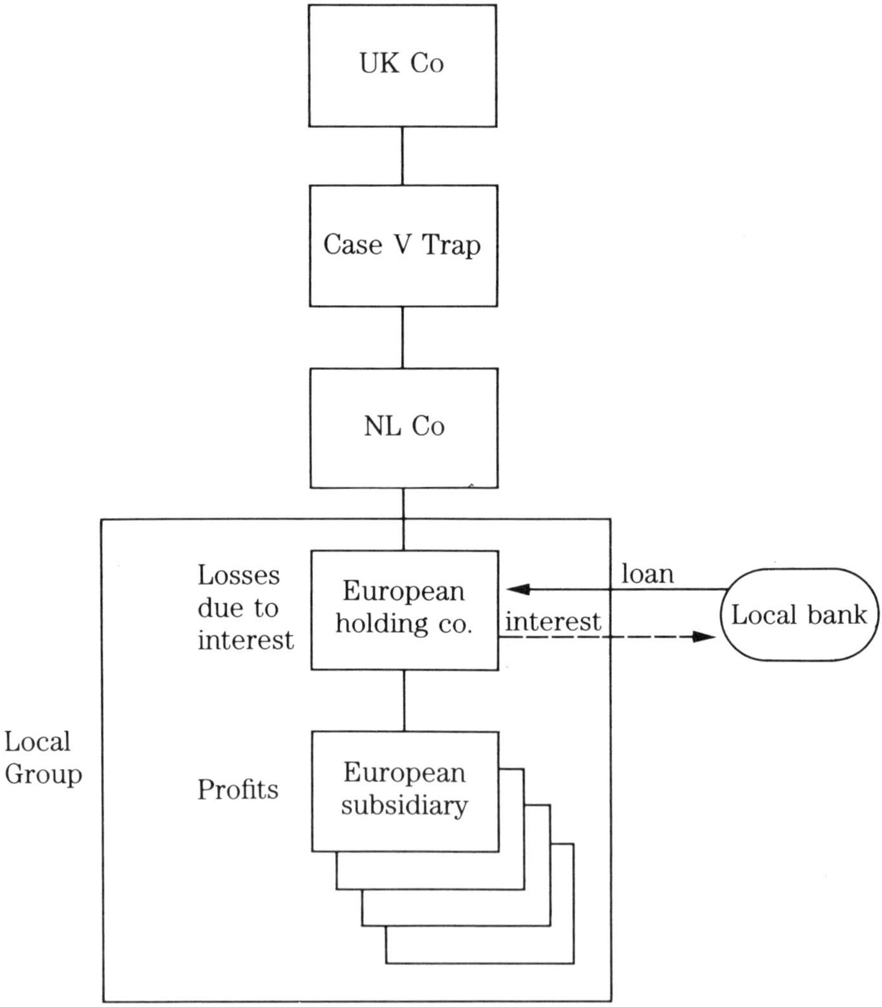

important point. In addition, assets may very often be transferred free of tax between groups of companies, and dividends may be paid free of taxes.

If there is a system of group relief and the foreign holding company borrows locally to acquire the target subsidiary, an offset will be available against the taxable profits of the foreign subsidiary in the form of group relief or a consolidated tax return.

It should be noted that different countries have differing percentages necessary to file group tax returns. In the case of the Netherlands it must be 99 per cent owned. In the case of Spain it need only be 90 per cent, but one must then wait two years before consolidated tax returns may be filed.

Country	*Group relief ownership % required*
Austria	not available
Belgium	not avaliable
Denmark	100%
Finland	90%
France	95%
Germany	50%
Greece	not available
Ireland	75%
Italy	not available
Luxembourg	99%
Netherlands	100%
Norway	90%
Portugal	90%
Spain	90% (deferred 2 years)
Sweden	90%
Switzerland	not available (but devaluation deduction available)

The EC is trying to harmonise these requirements. Currently a 50 per cent ownership test is proposed.

Even if a country does not have a system of group taxation (eg Austria under some circumstances) foreign holding companies can still be useful vehicles to make acquisitions. This is because many such countries recognise a system of merging the acquired vehicle into the acquiring vehicle. If the foreign holding company has borrowed (typically from a local, in this case Austrian, bank) then there will be relief for acquisition interest after merger.

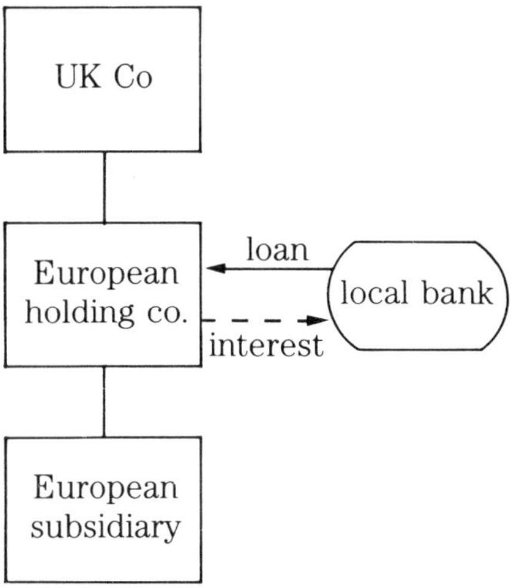

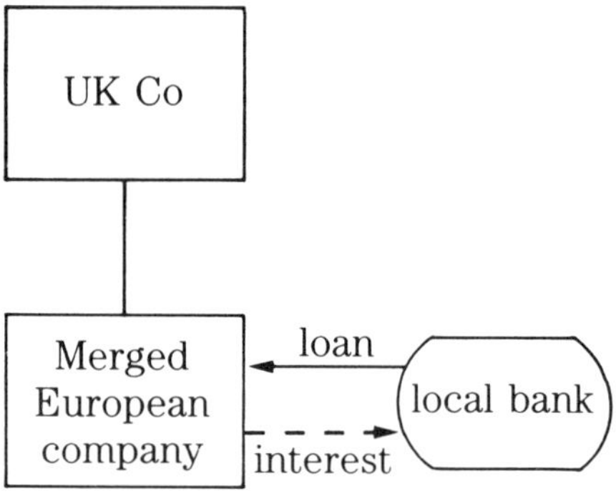

Sometimes, as in Germany, the merger will attract 'state' tax, even if exempt from national tax. In Austria the bank interest paid by the merged company will not be deductible for 'state' tax purposes.

Even if funds are not borrowed locally, it may be beneficial for the holding company to borrow them from the UK. If there are tax losses in the UK due to interest payments but profits overseas, then those overseas profits should be repatriated back to the UK.

This is an example of a very important international tax planning technique. It is necessary to decide where, in an international structure, interest costs should fall. If the interest deduction is required in the UK then the funds should be borrowed in the UK (they will normally be tax-deductible as a charge on income) and injected as share capital into the foreign subsidiary or its foreign holding company. If the interest deduction is required overseas because there are taxable profits there but not in the UK (or tax at a lower rate) then the foreign holding company or its subsidiary should borrow the funds.

Sometimes the use of a foreign holding company can be disadvantageous. This would be the case where a foreign subsidiary was to be sold. Generally a foreign holding company would be liable to tax on the sale of a foreign subsidiary at a gain. Under those circumstances it would have been better had the UK company held the foreign subsidiary direct under an offshore holding company, for example a Netherlands holding company, where so long as the affiliation privilege was available there would be no tax on disposal. Even if the UK company held the

either *or*

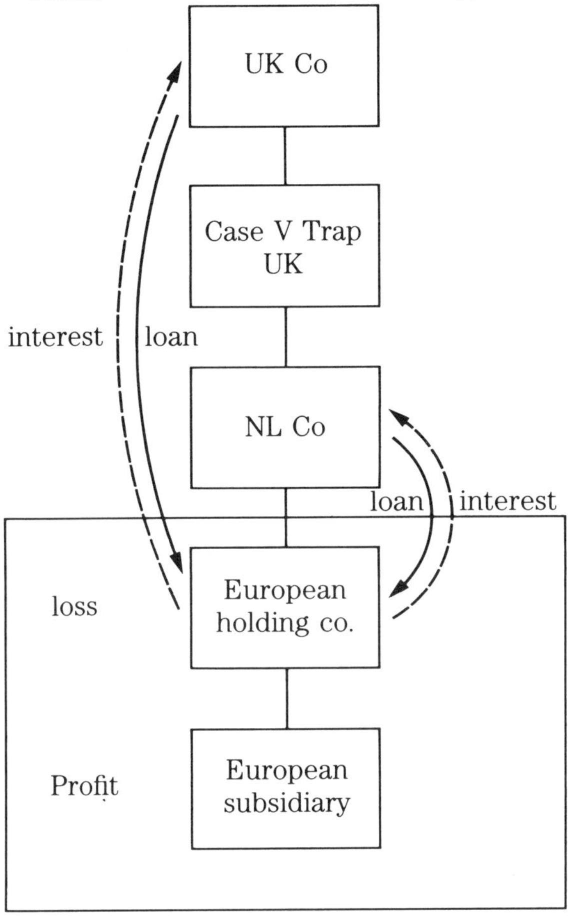
UK Co
Case V Trap UK
interest
loan
NL Co
loan
interest
loss
European holding co.
Profit
European subsidiary

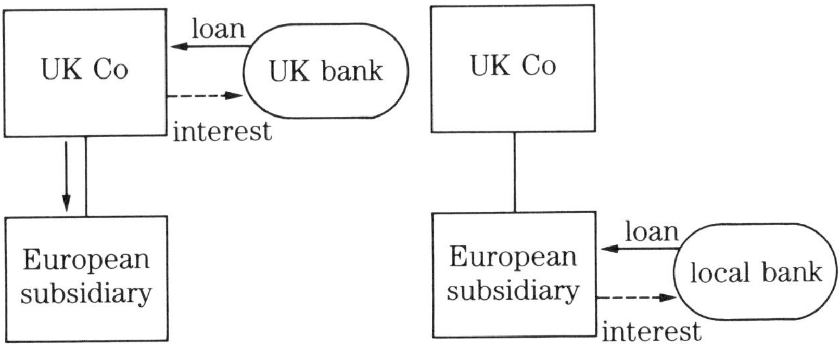
UK Co
loan
UK bank
interest
European subsidiary
UK Co
European subsidiary
loan
local bank
interest

shares in the foreign subsidiary direct there may be advantages. The UK will only tax the gain at 35 per cent and will grant indexation relief. The foreign country may have a higher effective rate.

A UK company, or rather its individual shareholders, can also be worse off investing through an offshore holding company where Section 739 applies. The reasons for this are complex but essentially they boil down to the following.

Section 739 taxes a UK individual on the income accruing to foreign companies as if it had been received direct by the individual. In many cases a UK individual will be worse off than a UK company in terms of what he is allowed to deduct against foreign income. For example, rents received from non-UK sited properties, where those rents are received by an individual, must be taxed without any relief for interest on a loan taken out to purchase that property. On the other hand, a UK company which receives such rent would obtain relief for a UK borrowing because generally it would be a charge on income. If foreign rents accrued to an offshore company, and those profits are assessed under Section 739 on an individual, then he will obtain no relief for interest. Had the income instead been diverted to a UK company there would have been no such problem.

Example

A Netherlands company borrows to acquire shares in a foreign subsidiary. The foreign subsidiary pays dividends to the Netherlands company. In due course the accumulated profits of the Netherlands company are subject to tax under Section 739 on the individual owner of the UK company which owns the Netherlands company. Under those circumstances the UK individual will be subject to tax on the dividends received by the Netherlands company without relief for the interest on the borrowing. Had the dividend been repatriated directly to the UK company it is unlikely that there would have been such a problem (although technically Section 739 could still apply).

8.11 Horizontal structures

More complicated corporate structures may be adopted involving 'horizontal' as opposed to 'vertical' structures. When a UK company has developed to a stage where it has a large number of overseas subsidiaries, it may then be possible to incorporate more complex corporate structures outside the vertical structure without falling foul of anti-avoidance legislation.

For example, offshore finance companies, patent holding companies, real estate holding companies or shareholding companies could be located in third countries. The use of third country companies involves not just UK anti-avoidance legislation but also foreign legislation.

8.12 Offshore finance company

The classic offshore finance company structure is as follows:

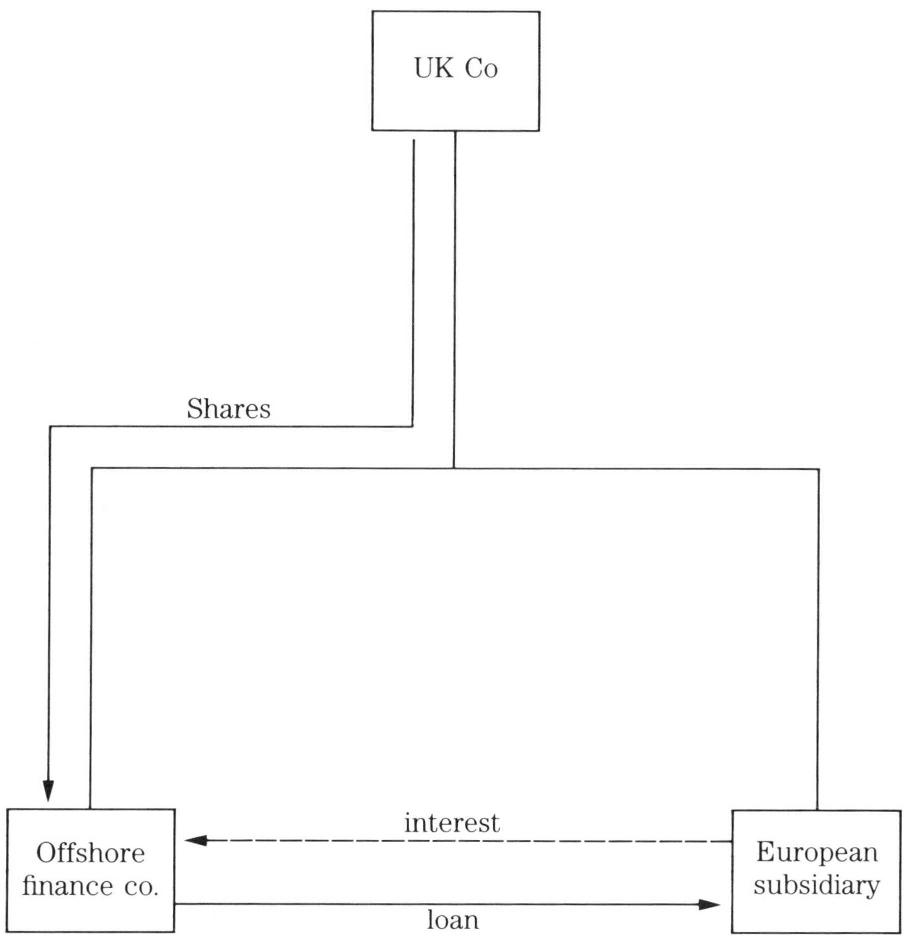

The UK parent will capitalise an offshore finance company with equity. The finance company will lend that equity to the foreign subsidiary which will pay tax-deductible interest to the finance company which will accumulate the income free of local tax. If the foreign country operates interest withholding tax, the finance company could lend its equity to a Netherlands conduit company which will then on-lend. Interest will be paid by the various foreign subsidiaries around the world through the Netherlands conduit company on to the finance company. The Netherlands' network of double tax treaties should minimise withholding tax on interest on the loans from the foreign subsidiaries. There is no domestic Netherlands withholding tax on interest paid out of the Netherlands; neither are there any debt:equity restrictions. The Netherlands authorities will agree an interest 'turn' of between 1/8 and 2 per cent, depending on the size of the loans.

Alternatively, the trading subsidiaries could borrow from a bank on a back-to-back basis against the collateral of a deposit made by the offshore finance company.

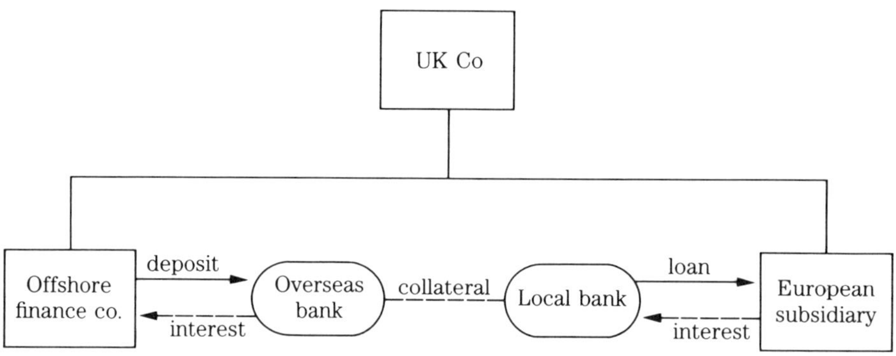

The finance company should be located in a country into which the group expands (so as to protect against Inland Revenue attack on residence and anti-avoidance legislation) which does not tax interest received, ie a tax haven, or which has a low rate of tax, for example Switzerland or Cyprus.

The problem with such finance companies since 1984 has been the controlled foreign company legislation, not to mention Section 739.

One method of avoiding the CFC legislation would be to take ownership of the actual finance company, and if necessary the Netherlands conduit company (which can also be a completely independent company acting for a fee) completely outside the group. For example it could be owned by the individual UK owners of the UK company.

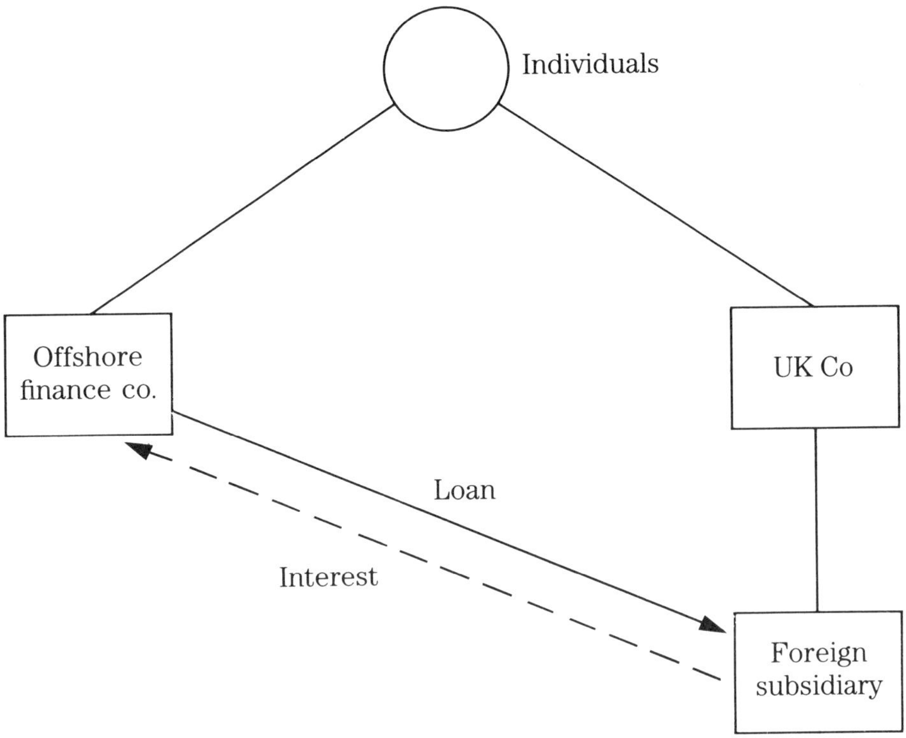

The next problem is that under such a structure the profits of the finance company would be subject to tax in the hands of the individuals under Section 739. Accordingly it may be necessary to interpose a trust (often an offshore trust) so that the shares of the finance company are held by a trust from which the individual UK owner of the company is irrevocably excluded from benefiting (as is his or her spouse). Such a trust could be an accumulation and maintenance (A & M) trust which we have previously discussed in the chapter on anti-avoidance legislation.

However, there are other possibilities. For example surplus cash may arise in due course overseas, so that it becomes appropriate to incorporate finance companies in jurisdictions which do not tax interest received where the group had a real commercial presence. When that type of set of commercial facts evolves, it becomes possible to plan around the UK's anti-avoidance legislation.

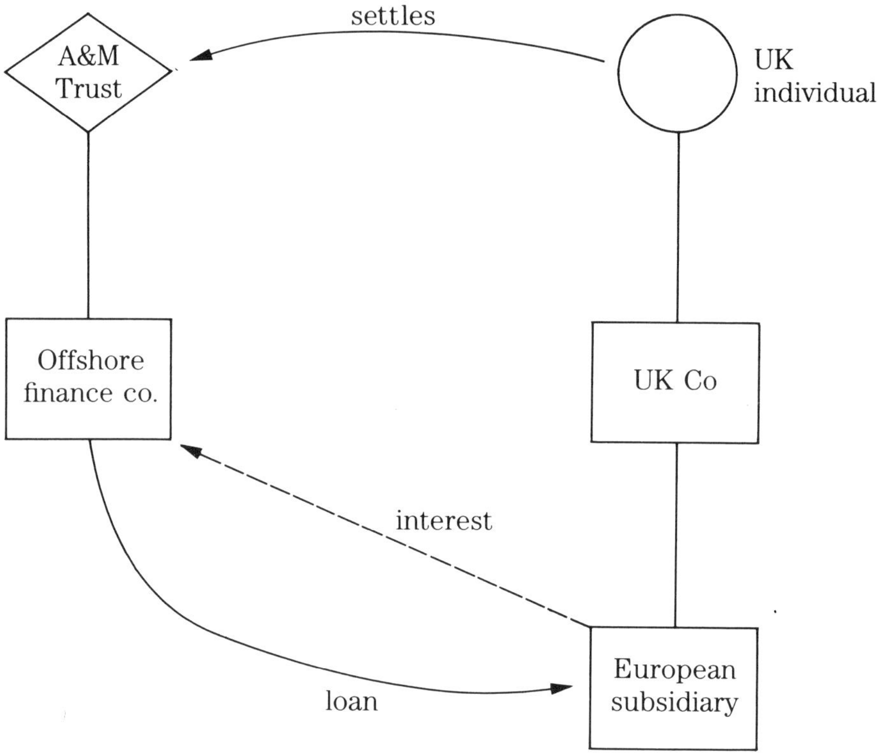

8.13 Offshore licensing company

Similar comments apply to an offshore licensing company. The UK group could utilise a licensing company located offshore to license rights around the world. Royalties could be paid so as to effectively shift profits from the foreign subsidiary to the offshore rights-owning company, which would be located in a jurisdiction where it pays little or no tax on the royalties received. In order to be outside the UK's anti-avoidance legislation (and indeed concept of residence) it is essential that the rights-owning company is situated in a jurisdiction where the UK group has real commercial presence, and that the structure has *bona fide* business credence.

The rights to the use of trade names, trade marks, know-how and other similar intellectual property could be placed into the ownership of an offshore licensing company. The company would then license these rights to other group subsidiaries in return for a percentage royalty based on their turnover, so that royalty income would arise in the offshore company free of tax.

Accordingly the licensing company should be located in a country into which the group expands where its royalty income will be exempt from tax or will suffer a low rate of tax. It will be necessary for the rights to be held by a company resident in a country which recognises the particular type of intangible rights in its judicial system.

A royalty conduit company will, on the other hand, have to be situated in a jurisdiction which has an attractive domestic taxation of royalties and also a substantial number of double tax treaties which will allow for a reduction of withholding tax applying on the payment of royalties from other treaty countries. Again, one of the most popular jurisdictions for royalty conduit companies is the Netherlands, because of the very favourable nature of the Netherlands double tax treaties, beneficial domestic legislation and the absence of any withholding tax in the Netherlands on royalties paid to non-residents.

Where the Netherlands company acts as a royalty conduit, the Netherlands authorities will tax an agreed margin of profit between royalties received and royalties and expenses paid which will vary between 2 and 7 per cent of the gross royalties received. The normal Netherlands corporate rate of tax is then applied to this spread.

Netherlands royalty conduit companies are very attractive for the routeing of certain types of royalties from the UK. This is because UK withholding tax on the payment of patent, copyright and certain other types of royalty is reduced from 25 per cent to nil under the UK/ Netherlands treaty. The relevant article of the UK/Netherlands treaty, however, contains a provision denying the treaty relief where the royalty rights have been created or assigned in order to take advantage of the treaty article rather than for *bona fide* commercial reasons. A commercial reason for its existence must therefore be present. This is an example of an anti-'treaty shopping' provision. Treaty shopping occurs where residents of one country invest into another country via a third country merely because that third country has a beneficial double tax treaty with the country of source of the income in question.

One important point to note. If the UK company transfers rights to the foreign rights-owning company then there might be UK tax on a deemed disposal. The types of rights that may be transferred include trademarks, copyrights, franchising rights and know-how.

8.14 Offshore selling or buying company

This is one of the most common forms of international tax planning, and in the experience of the author one of the most likely to fall foul of the UK Inland Revenue.

- *Selling company*
  An offshore sales company could be established to purchase goods from related companies in the group and sell them at a profit to customers abroad. Because of the UK's transfer pricing rules, commercial arguments would have to be sustained to support the price at which goods were purchased from related companies at a favourable price, enabling it to realise a profit on resale. For example the offshore company might have cash resources or access to credit facilities that would enable it to buy and sell at competitive prices.

- *Purchasing company*
  Similar advantages could be obtained by an international purchasing company, which would organise and coordinate the group's purchasing of goods from foreign suppliers for resale to group companies. The goods would be purchased at arm's-length prices but the ability of the offshore company to earn profits on resale might be justified by the fact that, for example, it had exclusive purchasing agreements enabling it to buy at low prices. It may be possible to demonstrate a commercial advantage in centralising these activities and in centralising international staff.

Another commercial justification for diverting profits from the UK by the use of a purchasing (or selling) company would be the grant of long-term credit to customers. A charge could be made for credit on normal commercial terms (eg 2 per cent per month). The overseas purchasing or selling company may require substantial equity funding, which could be provided by the UK parent, to enable it to finance the credit arrangements.

The typical arrangement may be shown diagrammatically as follows:

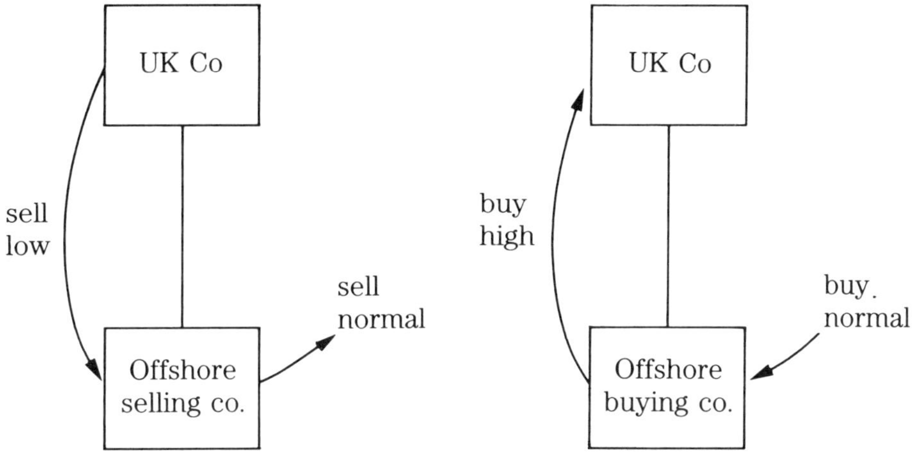

Very often the offshore company is not a subsidiary of the UK company but is instead owned by the individual shareholders of the UK company or separately under a trust.

Among the problems are:-

- residence
- the CFC legislation
- Section 739
- transfer pricing

The goods have to be purchased and sold at arm's-length prices. The ability of the offshore company to earn profits has to be justified by *bona fide* commercial facts: for example it has exclusive buying arrangements or lines of credit. This is usually very difficult in practice when the offshore company is under attack from the Revenue.

The controlled foreign company legislation and/or Section 739 severely curtail the use of such companies, but again, if there is a real commercial presence overseas, these may be avoided. For this reason it may be that all the functions of share-owning, financing, licensing and trading are carried out by the same offshore company, located in a suitable country in which the group operates.

8.15 Captive insurance company

A 'captive insurance company' insures and reinsures the risks of the group as an alternative to external insurers. It could be used to insure against risks which the normal insurance market will not accept or to provide certain types of insurance which commercial insurance companies do not have the flexibility to provide. It can also offer substantial savings in premiums provided the group's insurance record is better than average. Captive insurance companies are normally established for commercial insurance reasons, with tax considerations only a secondary factor.

Captive insurance companies are usually located in jurisdictions where premiums and investment income received from the investment of the funds can be accrued tax free, and where the company will not be subject to the same regulatory controls as insurance companies located in the UK.

A captive insurance company is paid premiums to insure risks around an international group (typically) and then reinsures those risks in the market. Reinsurance is usually cheaper than insurance. Over a period of time it will gradually invest and use those reserves to cease to reinsure until, assuming no claims are made over and above what is expected, a large sum of money is accrued overseas. Looked at on a worldwide basis, in most cases reserves for future claims are not deductible. However, the payment of a premium to a captive, which itself creates a reserve, allows the various companies in the group around the world to obtain tax relief.

It is essential to obtain specialist advice before a captive can even be considered. A feasibility study should be drawn up which should look at the minimum premium levels required to make a captive viable in terms of the professional costs. These are usually much higher than for setting up other offshore companies. A detailed implementation programme needs to be drawn up. Decisions need to be taken at the highest level within the UK parent. An operations manual should be drawn up. This should deal with matters such as risk acceptance, claims handling and the role of advisers.

Captive insurance companies present great difficulties to the Inland Revenue authorities. To quote a spokesman for the UK Inland Revenue: 'I would be less than honest if I tried to convince you that the Inland Revenue regard the offshore captive industry with particular favour. Our attitude is one of wary suspicion'.

Captives are usually used only by large multinational groups of companies. The commercial benefits are as set out below.

- Taking advantage of a better than average claims record: a group with a better than average claims record is effectively paying for the insurance of those with worse than average records unless it uses a captive – conversely, a captive is a positive disadvantage for a group with a poor claims record.

- Cover can be obtained for risks which would otherwise not be insured or can only be insured at uneconomic rates – this would include insurance in particularly volatile areas of the world (not Europe, it is hoped) or very often the first level of risk which is effectively very expensive to insure because insurance companies believe it quite likely that claims will fall in that size.
- Access to reinsurance markets – normally it is cheaper to reinsure than to insure risks.
- Greater control of the group's finance function.
- Smaller capital requirement than in the UK.
- Captives can be set up and running very much quicker abroad than in the UK.
- The cost and delay in meeting Department of Trade compliance requirements are avoided.
- The solvency margin can be smaller.

It is essential that any premiums paid to the captive are arm's-length.

The next problem is the CFC legislation. The Revenue have refused to agree that any captive can satisfy the motive test. In order to satisfy the exempt activities CFC test, at least 50 per cent of the income of the captive must be derived from outside the group. Even then, the captive must be in a country where it has local premises and employs real local people. Assuming that neither the motive test nor the exempt activities test is satisfied, it will be necessary for the captive to satisfy the acceptable distribution test and repatriate 50 per cent of its profits back to the UK within 18 months. This gives tax exemption to half the profits, and an effective 33-month deferral on tax on the other half which in itself is very valuable.

It may be possible to incorporate a captive in a territory on a list of CFC-excluded countries, for example Ireland's Customs House financial services area in Dublin.

Having raised the subject of the CFC legislation, and of anti-avoidance legislation generally, it would be timely to consider the lines of attack open to the Inland Revenue as the international corporate structure becomes more complex. Insofar as income has been diverted abroad, the Inland Revenue have numerous lines of attack. Some of these have been discussed in detail in previous chapters, in particular those on residence and anti-avoidance legislation.

8.16 Inland Revenue attacks

The UK Inland Revenue will be able to tax the profits diverted to offshore companies if they are successful in utilising any of the following lines of attack.

- *Residence*
  The Inland Revenue can determine the UK residence of a company on the basis of its management and control. If an offshore company is established which is incorporated overseas but the UK Inland Revenue determine that it is managed and controlled from the UK, the company will be treated as UK resident and thus liable to 35 per cent UK corporation tax on its profits, hence negating any potential tax benefits.

  Management and control is regarded as being exercised in the country in which important policy decisions relating to the company's affairs are taken and this is a question of fact. Central management and control is normally exercised by directors, and the UK Inland Revenue will first look to where directors' board meetings are held and also where the directors live. However, where management and control is exercised by somebody other than a director, the UK Revenue will argue that the country of residence is where he makes decisions with regard to the company.

  It is therefore important that for this, as well as other purposes, the company has a real commercial presence in the country in which it proposes to operate, so that 'real' management, rather than 'professional directors' such as lawyers, can be said to be making these decisions.

- *Trading in the UK*
  The offshore company must not trade in the UK through a UK branch or agency.

- *Anti-avoidance legislation*
  Even if it can be shown that the overseas subsidiary is resident outside the UK, the UK Revenue have extensive anti-avoidance legislation available to them which, if applicable, can subject the profits of the offshore subsidiary to UK tax.

- *Controlled foreign company (CFC) legislation*
  If it applies, the CFC legislation permits the UK Revenue to assess the profits of an overseas subsidiary on its UK parent company. The CFC legislation will make it very difficult to successfully

avoid UK tax on the profits of an offshore licensing or finance company located in a tax haven country with which the group has no connection.

There are various exemptions from the CFC legislation, one of which applies where the overseas subsidiary has a real commercial presence in the overseas territory concerned.

In the case of offshore selling and purchasing companies, even if they are established with real overseas premises, their profits are still likely to fall within the CFC legislation, broadly speaking because they will be buying from, or selling to, group companies. However, trading companies are able to avoid the practical impact of the CFC legislation by distributing 50 per cent of their profits as dividends to the UK.

In this way, the profits of an offshore trading company may be taxed effectively at 17.5 per cent, being 50 per cent of the normal UK rate of 35 per cent, to the extent that 50 per cent of its profits are retained.

The 50 per cent figure increases to *90 per cent* if the income is investment income as opposed to trading income. Therefore, in the case of licensing and finance companies some other exemption from the CFC legislation must be available if the profits are to escape substantial UK tax. If there is a substantial real commercial presence in the country in which the overseas subsidiary is incorporated, resident, managed and operating then the 'exempt activities' or 'motive' tests may be available. If the offshore subsidiary passes either of those tests, its profits will totally escape CFC assessment.

- *Arm's-length pricing*
  The UK tax legislation contains arm's-length pricing rules. The legislation applies to adjust the purchase or sale price to what it would be in an arm's-length transaction. Examples of the arm's-length pricing concept have been discussed above with respect to intra-group selling and purchasing companies.

- *Overseas income*
  Section 739 ICTA 1988 could give the UK Revenue the power to tax individual UK shareholders of the UK company on income diverted to overseas subsidiaries. In practice it is unusual for the UK Revenue to utilise Section 739 against a public company with a constantly changing population of shareholders, unless there is a single shareholder with a significant holding. However, Section 739 is of great importance with respect to private companies.

- *Overseas gains*
  The offshore gains of private companies are assessable under Section 15 CGTA 1979 on the UK parent company. Section 15 does not apply to public companies. Unlike Section 739 and the CFC legislation there are no '*bona fide* commercial' exemptions.

- *Treasury Consent*
  Treasury Consent is necessary only where a UK resident company permits a non-EC resident company over which it has control to issue shares or debentures or to dispose of any shares or debentures in a non-EC resident company that it controls. It is normally a matter of formality to obtain consent.

- *Real commercial presence*
  It can be seen from the above that the potential residence, CFC, Section 739 and other anti-avoidance legislation problems can be best avoided if the proposed offshore companies have a real commercial presence in their country of operation and residence.

In order to establish a commercial presence, the offshore company would *inter alia* need to establish its own premises and employ its own staff in the territory concerned. Generally the UK group should not establish an overseas subsidiary unless it has a real commercial presence overseas. The group could wait until natural growth produced a real overseas operation in a suitable location. Alternatively a group could consider renting or buying an office and employing staff as part of a deliberate decision to establish a presence in a particular location for tax reasons, but this would be expensive and almost certainly be less acceptable to the Inland Revenue than an office that had been set up for a genuine business reason.

Also, it would greatly help an overseas captive insurance, licensing or finance company to avoid Revenue attack over residence or CFC, if it received income from the UK as well as UK trading subsidiaries. Therefore such companies may have to wait until a group expands overseas, establishing subsidiaries in many different locations.

8.17 Tax haven companies

Certainly from the UK point of view, the use of no-tax 'paper' offshore companies located in 'tax-havens' to save UK tax has been severely curtailed by a mixture of anti-avoidance legislation, judicial decision against the taxpayer and increased vigilance and expertise on the part of the Inland Revenue. The Inland Revenue have set up specialised units and departments to deal with various topics over the last few years, and differing aspects of international trade have been carefully targeted. The use of 'tax havens' where the UK group has no real commercial presence has therefore been greatly reduced.

8.18 Repatriating the profits back to the UK

If the UK business is engaged in simple export, the profits will automatically accrue to the UK. Even if there is a foreign permanent establishment and there is a liability to foreign tax, generally profits can simply be passed back to the UK, normally with no tax effect but occasionally with a branch withholding tax. We have already looked at two other ways of repatriating profits back to the UK, namely interest on loans and dividends which are paid on shares. But there are other methods. As the corporate structure develops, these must be considered in terms of minimising tax. Very often, in practice dividends are not paid because the profits or cash reserves of the overseas subsidiary are repatriated back to the UK in the form of passive income or upstream loans.

Arm's-length royalties could be paid for the use of a name, or a patent, or a method of manufacture. The UK's double tax treaties often eliminate foreign withholding tax on royalties. Management charges could be levied by the UK parent and these can usually be paid gross. The UK parent could lease assets to its overseas subsidiary, although capital allowances may then be restricted.

Care should be taken in drawing up royalty and patent agreements to avoid payments made under such agreements being directly attributable to importations of goods. If this were the case, the royalty or patent fees might be added to the value of the goods for Customs duty and VAT calculation purposes.

The cash generated by the surplus profits of overseas subsidiaries could be repatriated as upstream loans. Upstream loans to the UK do not (at present) attract tax, although at one time the Inland Revenue did indicate a desire to tax upstream loans. Normally the UK will then be required to pay interest on the loans, under the foreign subsidiary's country's transfer pricing régime. This will have the effect of shifting profits out of the UK to overseas.

Instead of actually making upstream loans, another possibility would be to repay loans from the UK or, alternatively, to repay redeemable shares.

The foreign subsidiary could purchase assets from the UK parent, paying for them in cash. Depending on the UK tax position of the UK parent this may or may not attract a liability to UK tax. Some overseas countries may allow the company to purchase its own shares. In other cases this will not be legally possible, or may be possible only after formal permission has been obtained. Many countries treat repayment of share capital as dividend to the extent that the foreign subsidiary has retained earnings.

If profits are paid back to the UK parent by means of passive income payments such as interest, royalties or management charges then care must be exercised that they are paid at an arm's-length price. This is particularly the case with management services, where tax authorities throughout Europe will look closely to ensure that a proper fee is being paid and, conversely, that too great a fee is not being levied.

Profits may also be repatriated by means of the use of special companies, for example offshore trading companies, offshore licensing companies, offshore finance companies, offshore buying companies and captive insurance companies.

In due course consideration might have to be given to selling the foreign branch or subsidiary. The sale of a foreign branch will attract tax liabilities both in the UK and overseas. It is essential that foreign taxes are available for UK double tax relief. This is not always as straightforward as it appears and the situation must be carefully considered in advance. It may be possible to minimise the foreign taxes, or to defer payment, by selling the business on an instalment basis. In addition, if the foreign branch has unused losses it may be possible to sell these losses. However, in general it must be said that selling branches is much harder than selling subsidiaries, and it may be necessary to incorporate the branch into a subsidiary prior to sale.

Shares in foreign subsidiaries can very often be sold by non-residents without foreign tax arising. UK tax will also always be payable, based on the indexed costs of the shares being sold if the UK parent owns the shares directly as opposed to via an (eg) Netherlands holding company. However, as previously discussed the purchaser may require a discount for latent tax and other liabilities. It may be possible to reduce UK tax by paying dividends from the foreign subsidiary prior to sale. Under those circumstances clearance should be obtained from the UK Inland Revenue. The timing of the dividend in terms of maximising double tax relief must be carefully considered.

Some foreign countries do tax the sale of shares of their companies. Sometimes they will only tax the sale of a certain type of company, for example, a real estate company. The use of an offshore holding company, located in a suitable country should be considered, as treaty protection may be available.

8.19 Other paths on the journey

We have now seen the major rules relating to a UK company first exporting abroad and then setting up and developing a foreign corporate structure.

So far on our journey we have considered only direct taxation. However, other forms of taxation are too important to ignore. The next chapter looks at the major indirect taxes of VAT and Customs duty. This is of particular interest to UK companies expanding into Europe, because there is no Customs duty on intra-Community trading, and VAT is a tax created by the EC.

9

VAT and Customs Duty

9.1 Indirect taxes

So far we have discussed direct taxes only. However, any UK company considering expanding into Europe must give prime consideration not just to direct taxes but also to indirect taxes, in particular Value Added Tax (VAT) and customs duty. These are in the process of being harmonised throughout the EC: for example there is no customs duty on transfers of goods between EC countries.

9.2 Export of goods

Most exporters will know that the export of goods is zero rated for VAT purposes. In general a business can recover VAT paid on purchases and expenses if its sales of goods or services are either zero rated (no VAT) or standard rated (liable to VAT at 15 per cent).

Zero rating is therefore very advantageous and an incentive for UK companies to export. A pure exporter need not account for VAT on sales and may reclaim from Customs and Excise all the VAT charged on any expenses he has incurred.

Because of the the risk of fraud, Customs and Excise stringently enforce the requirements that export must be substantiated by evidence acceptable to them. This applies equally where goods are eligible for remission of VAT, customs duty or excise duty at exportation. Customs duty is a tax imposed on the importation of goods into the EC. Excise duty is a tax imposed on the importation of matches, lighters, alchohol, tobacco and hydrocarbon fuels into the UK. Failure to obtain satisfactory evidence of export will lead to the VAT or duty being called for by Customs and Excise.

The creation of an export company with its own VAT registration can achieve significant cash flow benefit by exploiting the difference between quarterly and monthly VAT returns. A 'repayment trader' can reclaim VAT on inputs each month by filing monthly VAT returns.

After 1993 all EC countries should have closer rates of VAT. Goods moving between EC countries are already customs duty-free. By 1993 frontier fiscal checks will be abolished.

An exporter should be aware that the material used to manufacture its products could have borne customs duty at first importation into the EC. Where those goods are processed and exported outside the EC, the exporter can arrange for his supplier to sell him the goods free of customs duty, thus lowering overheads.

The cost of clearing goods through customs can be reduced by operating one or more of the facilitating procedures, such as Local Export Control (LEC), Low-Value Goods Procedure (LVPG) or Pre-Authenticated Movement Certificates (PAMC).

Example

A UK exporter made significant cost savings by obtaining approval to operate Local Export Control, where his goods were cleared for export against the skeleton declaration, with full export details being sent to Customs and Excise on a periodic basis. Any physical examination of the goods required at exportation by Customs and Excise was carried out at his own premises rather than at the port.

Example

A UK exporter with a significant number of invoices, of a value of less than £600 each, saved himself £7,500 which he had previously been paying to a forwarder each year. This is because his forwarder had been charging for a full export declaration, when for goods of a value less than £600 a simplified clearance procedure could have been used, requiring a less detailed export declaration.

Example

A UK company exported goods to the European Free Trade Association (EFTA) countries (eg Sweden, Switzerland and Austria). The goods were eligible for the preference agreed by the EC, so the company completed form EUR1. Once the goods were authenticated by Customs at exportation the customer abroad could claim a lower rate of duty at importation, so the UK exporter's goods were more competitive in that market.

Although most of the extensive range of customs duty reliefs apply to imports, the exporter can also make customs duty savings. For example:

- Returned Goods Relief (RGR). Goods that were orginally exported, and now have to be re-imported, can be imported free of VAT and customs duty.
- Outward Processing Relief (OPR). An exporter may send goods for processing ouside the EC. OPR reduces the amount of customs duty payable on the subsequent re-importation of the compensating product.

Example

Company A manufactured computers for export outside the EC. The components used in production, although bought from UK suppliers B and C, were originally imported from 'third countries'. Because company A was approved for Inward Processing Relief (IPR), B and C could import the components free of duty under IPR and pass them, still free of duty, to company A. The rates of duty range from 4.9 to 14 per cent, depending on the nature of components.

Exporters should be aware that their goods may be subject to restrictions and controls, and an export licence may be required especially where electronic products or components are involved.

Before the opening of the Channel Tunnel reduces the time taken for goods to reach the continent, Customs and Excise should have introduced Customs Handling of Import and Export Freight (CHIEF). This computerisation of both import and export declarations will give a competitive edge to those firms prepared to take advantage of new technology in their accounting systems.

Planning for VAT and customs duty should be a primary objective for the management of any business involved with exporting goods. If further incentive were needed, the EC Commission's proposals for harmonisation by 1993 will mean changes in the operation of VAT and excise duties. Only those businesses that are prepared for the dismantling of the barriers to intra-Community trade by 1993 will be able to compete effectively in the Single European Market (SEM).

In 1993 and after, the current export procedures will remain for goods consigned to non-EC countries. However, along with fiscal barriers, the SAD (Single Administrative Document) will be abolished for intra-Community trade.

Goods consigned to another EC country will be relieved of VAT at export, but only if the *customer* can provide a certificate from his fiscal authorities showing that he is registered for VAT. In other cases, eg sales to private individuals or businesses not registered for VAT abroad, the supplier will have to charge VAT.

It will still be a requirement that the consignor must have satisfactory commercial evidence of shipment to support his claim to zero rating. Evidence of shipment will no longer be satisfactory to support relief from excise duty on goods consigned to another EC country. Goods liable to excise duty will have to be consigned under bond directly from one Customs-approved warehouse to another in the country of destination.

These new arrangements may prove difficult for those UK companies which sell goods abroad on an 'all taxes paid' basis since, after 1993, it will be the responsibility of the recipient of the goods to account to his fiscal authorities for taxes. Shippers will also find that they may well have to fill in a statistical return detailing the quantity and nature of the goods exported to EC countries – Customs currently collect details automatically from the SADs.

9.3 Export of services

Services may be exported by being rendered to non-residents, by being performed abroad, or by relating to non-resident matters.

Exported services are normally referred to as 'international services' and the words 'international services' might imply zero rating to the unwary. Exported services are not automatically zero rated. Many services are standard rated and some are exempt, and the rules governing liability are complex.

Different international services attract different VAT treatment. An exporter must carefully consider into which category the exported services fall, and professional advice may be required. The most important services are considered below.

- *Services related to land*
  Zero rating applies only to services invoiced by UK persons for services rendered with respect to land situated outside the UK. There must be a direct relationship between the services and the land. The relief applies particularly to construction, estate agencies, architects, surveyors, engineers, property management, conveyancing, surveys and valuations.

  Where the land element is incidental, the services are excluded from the relief unless zero rating is available under some other provision.

- *Hire of goods and the means of transport*
  The hire of a means of transport is zero rated only when the transport is for use exclusively outside the EC. The means of transport must also have been exported by the lessor, or be in place overseas at the time of hire.
  The hire of other assets is generally only zero rated when used outside the UK by someone in business who belongs outside the UK, or a private individual who belongs outside the EC. Where the goods are used in another EC country there may be a requirement to charge VAT locally.

- *Cultural, artistic, sporting, scientific, educational, exhibition or entertainment services and ancillary services*
  Zero rating is available with respect to the above services so long as the performance takes place outside the UK. Examples are the services of an actor or singer in making a film or a recording outside the UK, services related to filming or recording abroad, and any service provided to an exhibitor at an overseas trade fair or advertising exhibition. Again the VAT rules applying in other member states of the EC may require that the person performing the service be registered for local VAT.

- *'Schedule 3' services*
  Certain services listed in Schedule 3 VAT Act 1983 rendered to persons 'belonging' abroad are zero rated.
  Zero rating is only applicable under this heading where the recipient of the supply satisfies certain criteria. The supply to a person in his *business* capacity is only zero rated if he 'belongs' outside the UK. The supply to a person in his *private* capacity is only zero rated when he 'belongs' outside the EC.

A person 'belongs' in the UK if: he has a business establishment or other fixed establishment here (business establishment includes a branch or agency); *or* he has his usual place of residence here (*NB*: VAT definition of residence differs from the tax concept of residence); *or* he has establishments both in the UK and elsewhere and the establishment most directly concerned with the supply is in the UK.

The services specified in Schedule 3 VAT Act 1983 are:

Schedule 3 to the VAT Act 1983

1. Transfers and assignments of copyright, patents, licences, trademarks and similar rights.
2. Advertising services.
3. Services of consultants, engineers, consultancy bureaux, lawyers, accountants and other similar services: data processing and provision of information (excluding any services in relation to land).
4. Acceptance of any obligation to refrain from pursuing or exercising, in whole or part, any business activity or any such rights as referred to in 1 above.
5. Banking, financial and insurance services (including insurance but not including the provision of safe deposit facilities).
6. The supply of staff.

6A. The letting on hire of goods other than the means of transport.

7. The services rendered by one person to another in procuring for the other any of the services mentioned in 1 to 6A above.

Of these services, the most widely used is probably category 3, which deals with consultancy, professional services and information. Zero rating under this category requires careful consideration of exactly what is being supplied. It is often looked to by service companies raising management charges. However, management charges *per se* are not covered, unless they are of a type which fall within the definitions contained in category 3. Proper description in any document is therefore vital, and careful presentation is essential.

- *Valuing or carrying out work on goods*
  One of two alternative conditions needs to be satisfied before zero rating is available for valuation or work carried out on goods. The first requires the goods and place of performance to be outside the UK. The second is that the work to be carried out may take place in the UK provided the recipient belongs abroad, and the goods were specifically imported or acquired here for the work to be undertaken, and were subsequently exported.

- *Marine, aviation or transport (MAT) insurance*
  These and any related services may be zero rated with the condition that the supply is in connection with the carriage of passengers or goods to or from a place outside the EC.

- *Export insurance*
  Zero rating is given to approved insurers where the destination of the goods is outside the EC.

- *Export finance*
  Again zero rating applies if the destination is outside the EC.

- *Agency*
  All too often zero rating is presumed to apply when an agent acts on behalf of an overseas principal, but it is normally available only where the agent procures: an export of goods from the UK; *or* a supply of goods or services made outside the UK; *or* the supply of a service which is itself zero rated.

  Zero rating does not apply to services supplied by a person acting as a principal (such as taking title to goods) or acting as an intermediary in procuring a supply of goods in the UK.
  Also excluded are travel agency services where the place of enjoyment is within the EC.
  It is important to ensure that the services supplied fall within the agency provisions – failure to do so may expose the agent to financial loss.

These guidelines highlight some of the complexities of the zero-rating provisions. Simplistic assumptions can lead to expensive mistakes. Careful VAT and planning and professional advice are essential.

9.4 VAT on profits from subsidiaries

A UK parent could realise a profit from a subsidiary by selling its shares, receiving loan interest or receiving dividends. Each of these has important VAT implications.

The sale of shares to EC persons is normally exempt from VAT. Similarly, the receipt of interest from an EC person is also normally exempt from VAT. Accordingly there is a possibility of irrecoverable input tax, although usually the receipt of EC interest is effectively ignored for VAT purposes other than by financial institutions. However, sales of shares to, and the receipt of interest from, a company belonging outside the EC may be zero rated. Recovery of input VAT will therefore not be affected, even by a financial institution. To give two simple examples:

Example

A UK company sells shares to a Netherlands company and incurs VAT on costs of sale of £6,000. This input tax will normally be irrecoverable.

Example

A UK company sells shares to a USA corporation and incurs VAT on costs of sale of £6,000. The sale would be zero rated and the £6,000 VAT on costs will be recoverable.

Dividends received are outside the scope of VAT.

9.5 UK exporters and overseas VAT

Foreign VAT may not be deducted as an input on a UK VAT return. Instead there is a special refund scheme to allow refunds by the foreign equivalent of Customs and Excise. The method of reclaiming foreign VAT varies from country to country, but it is intended that in due course it will be harmonised throughout the EC.

To qualify for a refund under the scheme a UK business must not:

- be registered, liable or eligible to be registered in the relevant country;
- have a place of business or residence there;
- make any supplies there other than transport services related to the international carriage of goods.

Unfortunately, many EC countries do not allow refunds of VAT with respect to entertainment, hotels, meals or goods purchased for immediate export (which may very well qualify for zero rating in any event). No refund will be given by the foreign country if the VAT is not refundable under its domestic legislation.

Any repayment claim will need to be evidenced by:

- invoices;
- a certificate of VAT registration in the UK;
- a claim

There are even further difficulties in reclaiming this foreign VAT. Some countries will not accept claims below a certain value (which is different for different countries). Some countries will not accept refund claims submitted more than six months after the end of the calendar year in which the foreign VAT was incurred (and sometimes not later than six months after 30 June depending on what type of claim is being made).

To summarise, this is an area which requires detailed professional advice. It would be nice to think that, for example, a UK exporter would be able to reclaim VAT incurred overseas in the EC in building up his export trade. Unfortunately the practical difficulties in entering such refund claims are large. However, it may presage a unified EC VAT system. The obvious next stage would be to allow foreign VAT as an input against UK outputs.

9.6 General warning

VAT and customs duty are important taxes and must not be ignored when a UK company is considering expanding into Europe. There is no automatic zero rating when goods are exported, and even less automatic zero rating on the export of services. The importance of correct documentation cannot be overstressed.

10

Foreign Exchange Gains and Losses

10.1 The risk

Almost all businesses are exposed to exchange rate fluctuations, whether or not they actually do business direct with foreign markets. It goes without saying that the results of a UK exporter or outward investor will be affected by the performance of the pound against foreign currencies. This is true not only of the profit and loss account, where sales, purchases and stock values have to be translated into and out of sterling, but of the balance sheet also, where a foreign branch's fixed assets or a loan denominated in a foreign currency have to be expressed in sterling for accounting and tax purposes. An accounting standard (SSAP 20) sets out how exchange movements should be treated in accounts. Unfortunately there is no equivalent document governing the UK tax treatment of exchange gains and losses. Consequently it is one of the most complex aspects of international tax planning.

First I will try to explain how exchange gains and losses arise on foreign trade. A simple example may help.

Example

A UK company sells machinery to a German company. The sale price is stated as DM3 million. At the time DM3 = £1. The UK company realises a sale and sets up a debtor for £1 million in sterling terms. However, by the time the German importer pays for the goods the pound has dropped to DM2.75 = £1. Accordingly, when the German importer pays the UK exporter DM3 million the UK exporters realises sterling proceeds of £1,090,909. The UK exporter has realised a foreign exchange gain of £90,909. The question is, is that gain taxable or not?

10.2 Essential tax treatment

Essentially, the tax treatment of an exchange movement depends on the distinction between income and capital. Where an exchange movement relates to an income matter, it will normally be taxable or allowable. Where it is on capital account, it *may* be subject to capital gains tax or deductible (references to CGT include at all times references to corporation tax on chargeable gains), or left out of the tax net altogether.

Before going on to discuss this in more detail, it would be helpful to clarify certain terms. In dealing with exchange gains and losses it is sometimes necessary to distinguish between:

- open and closed transactions;
- translation and conversion of one currency into another;
- realised and unrealised gains and losses.

A foreign exchange transaction becomes *closed* when the final payment is acknowledged by the vendor; until that time, the transaction remains *open*. *Translation* is the process under which financial data denominated in one currency are expressed in another as, for example, where a US$ loan has to be expressed in sterling terms in a UK balance sheet. *Conversion*, on the other hand, involves the actual exchange of one currency for another. An exchange gain or loss becomes *realised* when the transaction is closed by final payment; until that time, it remains *unrealised*.

10.3 Revenue items

Exchange movements arising from normal trading activity are treated as part of overall trading income and are taxable or deductible. *Exceptional* transactions outside normal trading activity, but still of a revenue nature, will also be assessed but an exchange loss in this category may be set off against other exceptional income only and is not available against trading income.

10.4 Capital items

Where an exchange movement is on capital account, it is not recognised for income or corporation tax but it may be subject to capital gains tax. Capital gains tax will be applied only to movements on chargeable assets (and hence not on all assets) *and it does not apply to liabilities.* This can produce major problems. For tax to apply at all there must be an actual disposal of an asset. Hence, unrealised exchange movements will not give rise to a tax liability.

Example

A UK company has a debt of DM3 million. The exchange rate at the time the debt was incurred was DM3 = £1. In the company's year end accounts the exchange rate has moved to DM 2.8 = £1. At that rate the debt would realise £1,071,429 if repaid. At that time there is an unrealised exchange gain of £71,429. This is not taxable in the company's year end accounts, even though a profit on exchange may be brought into the accounting profit.

As far as capital liabilities (eg fixed or long-term debt) are concerned, exchange gains are not taxable at all and losses are not allowable. This strict position has been modified following the *Marine Midland* case, where foreign currency borrowings are matched with assets in the same currency.

The question must then be asked: What is a chargeable asset? An asset will be a chargeable asset unless it is specifically exempted. Thus a holding of foreign currency is a chargeable asset, but a debt is not a chargeable asset unless it is a 'debt on a security' (broadly, a freely marketable debt).

Where an asset is a chargeable asset, exchange gains on the disposal of that asset will be subject to tax, and losses will be allowable losses. Both cost and disposal proceeds must be translated into sterling at the exchange rate ruling at the date of the transaction concerned. This ensures that exchange movements between the dates of acquisition and disposal are fully taken into account.

This situation may be best summarised in the following table:

Item	Treatment of	
	Gain	Loss
Chargeable asset (including debt on a security)	chargeable	allowable
Other assets (including other debts	not chargeable	not allowable
Liabilities	not chargeable	not allowable

10.5 Movements on translation and conversion

Clearly, tax liability will depend on the point at which an exchange movement is recognised for tax purposes – whether translation profits and losses should be recognised or ignored until there has been a conversion. On translation, the Revenue's position is that, provided accounts have been drawn up in accordance with generally recognised accounting principles and have taken account of translation profits and losses, those profits and losses will be taken into account for tax purposes also, provided there is no specific reason to exclude them (eg because they are on capital account).

This approach is useful in that it avoids having to differentiate in the accounts between translation and conversion movements, but it suffers from the drawback that purely paper gains may be taxable.

10.6 Foreign currency borrowings

It is in the area of borrowings that many of the difficult tax issues arise. As we have seen, a 'forex' (foreign exchange) gain on a liability is not subject to tax. Any exchange loss arising on a foreign loan (as would happen where sterling depreciated against the currency of the loan by the time it came to be repaid) is also not recognised for tax purposes. If the borrowing can be treated as being on revenue account, however, any exchange loss will be treated as a trading loss. Conversely, an exchange gain will escape tax if the liability is a capital liability and will be taxable if the liability is a revenue liability. Unfortunately, the distinction between capital and revenue in this area is far from clear.

The essential distinction between capital and revenue liabilities is between loans that could be said to add to the capital base of the UK company borrower (capital liabilities) and those designed to provide more temporary finance (revenue liabilities). Clearly, a long-term loan is far more likely to be a capital loan, whereas a short-term loan will often be revenue. However, the accounting distinction between what is short term or what is long term (a loan of less than 12 months' duration is regarded as a short-term loan) does not carry over into tax law. Following the recent case of *Beauchamp versus F W Woolworth plc*, the types of loan that may be regarded as on revenue account have been restricted further. According to the House of Lords in that case, a fixed amount borrowed unconditionally and for a fixed period will be a capital borrowing, regardless of the taxpayer's intention in taking out the loan or the use to which it is actually put. Only temporary or fluctuating borrowings (including overdrafts) incurred in transacting business could be revenue transactions.

If the object of a borrowing was to deal with a temporary cash shortage, but the solution actually adopted was to make an addition to liquid resources sufficiently permanent to constitute an accretion of capital, then a loan will be capital. It is only where there is no fixed term of repayment that the use to which the money is actually put might throw light on whether it constituted an accretion to a company's capital or not.

10.7 Hedging

Very often, businesses will attempt to 'hedge' against exchange movements on a foreign currency loan. Hedging involves establishing an offsetting position to the underlying transaction, so that a gain or loss on that transaction is offset by an opposite gain or loss on the hedging transaction.

Example

A UK company sells machinery to a German importer for £1 million when £1 = DM3. Payment will be received in three months' time. The UK exporter buys deutschmarks forward at £1 = DM3. In three months' time the pound has fallen to £1 = DM2.75 and the German importer pays £1 million. The UK company exercises the option and uses the £1 million to buy DM3 million which it needs for its business. Without the option it could only have bought DM2.75 million. the UK company has therefore avoided spending DM250,000 (£90,909 at current exchange rates) to reach the same position.

A variety of hedging instruments (eg forward contracts, options, futures and currency swaps) is offered by the financial markets. For example, forward purchases of the same or different currencies might be undertaken so as to balance any loss on repayment of the loan with a gain on the forward transaction. As will be seen, the hedge may well be only partially effective after tax. If the loan is a capital liability, any loss will not be recognised for tax purposes, whereas the forward purchase of currency is a chargeable asset so the gain on that contract will be liable to CGT.

There may thus be a net tax charge when there is no overall actual gain or loss. It might be possible to make the hedge fully effective after tax by grossing up the currency purchased to take the tax payable into account. This problem, where the tax treatment of the hedge differs from the treatment of the underlying transaction, is known as *fragmentation.*

The same fragmentation problems will apply where hedging is undertaken against foreign currency assets. Thus a business investing abroad by acquiring shares in an overseas company may hedge that investment (or, indeed finance it) by borrowing in the same currency. An exchange loss on the borrowing would not be allowable, whereas any gain on the eventual disposal of the shares would be liable to CGT (after indexation).

10.8 Capital lending

Where a company finances an overseas subsidiary with a loan, the loan will not be made in the course of the company's trade (unless it is a finance company). The loan will constitute a capital asset. Whether it is a chargeable asset depends, as has been stated, on whether the loan is a debt on a security. If a gain is anticipated on repayment of the loan, the company should ensure that the loan is not a debt on a security, so that the gain will be free of tax. The tax-free gain should compensate for any unrecognised loss on borrowing to finance the loan. Where a loss on the loan is likely, the technique would be the reverse, ie the lender should ensure that the loan is a debt on a security. Unfortunately, that may be difficult in a private company situation.

An investment in shares will always be a chargeable asset, so the debt on a security option is not available in this instance. An answer is to use overseas holding companies or to form special purpose finance companies to finance overseas acquisitions (see Chapter 8 on developing a corporate structure). These finance companies can be located either offshore or in the UK. The problem with the UK as a location is highlighted by the *Overseas Containers (Finance) Ltd versus Stoker* case, in which a speciallly formed UK-resident finance company, which took over substantial deutschmark loans from other group companies, was denied loss relief on those loans. The court held that since the sole purpose of forming the company was to translate losses on capital account to revenue losses eligible for group relief, its transactions could not be regarded as trading transactions.

10.9 Matching, Marine Midland and SP1/87

It was stated earlier that the Revenue departs from its strict position on capital borrowings where capital liabilities are matched by assets in the same currency.

The Revenue's position in these and other circumstances is set out in Statement of Practice SP1/87. This was issued in the light of the House of Lords decision in *Pattison versus Marine Midland Ltd* and subsequent consultations.

Marine Midland was a bank, but the Statement applies to all trading companies. It provides that where foreign currency borrowings are matched by assets in the same currency, no attempt is made to distinguish the nature (whether capital or revenue) of the borrowings but that gains on one will be taken as cancelling out losses on the other to the extent that the value of the foreign assets and foreign liabilities is the same. This is so whether capital borrowings are matched by current assets (as in Marine Midland) or capital assets by current borrowings.

It is accepted that, in practice, foreign currency assets and liabilities are not exactly matched in every currency throughout an entire accounting period. Strictly speaking, therefore, the company must exclude, disallow or add back any unmatched exchange movements relating to capital items in its tax computations. However, because of the practical difficulties that might be involved, the statement proposes a practical method for calculating the effect of matching.

- First, ascertain the aggregate of exchange movements on capital assets and liabilities.
- If this is zero, no further action is necessary.
- If the net movement is a loss and the net movement taken to the profit and loss account is a loss, the smaller of these is the amount to be disallowed in the tax computation.
- Similarly, if the net movement on capital account is a profit and the net movement in the profit and loss account is a profit, the smaller of these is the amount to be deducted in the tax computation.
- Where the net movement on capital account is a loss but the net movement taken to the profit and loss account is a profit, or vice versa, no adjustment is made.

Where more than one currency is involved, the same principles must be applied separately to each currency. Taxpayers who adopt this practical method must accept that it will produce results at times more, and at times less, favourable than the strict method, but must apply it on a consistent basis from year to year.

If hedging transactions are undertaken, however, the statement provides special rules.

- Where forward exchange contracts or currency futures are entered into for hedging purposes, these are taken into account in considering whether there is a matched pool of currency, but the hedging transactions must be reflected in the accounts on a consistent basis and in accordance with accepted accounting practice.
- Where a foreign currency swap agreement is entered into to exchange borrowed currency for an equivalent amount of another currency (sterling not excluded) for a fixed period, the two transactions are regarded as matched for the duration of the swap. The underlying liability in the first currency is effectively treated as a liability in the second currency. When the swap is terminated, if the currencies are exchanged back at the spot rate prevailing at the beginning of the swap, there is no exchange movement in the original currency for tax purposes.
- Foreign currency options are not regarded as matching.

The statement makes it clear that the matching principle applies only to individual trading companies and cannot be extended to a group of companies as a whole.

10.10 Future changes

Of course, the Statement merely represents the Revenue's view of the existing law, and begs the question of what is a capital asset or liability which, as we have seen, is by no means a straightforward question. Consultations have continued about possible changes to the law, and the latest stage in those consultations is represented by the Revenue's consultative document, *Tax Treatment of Foreign Exchange Gains and Losses*, issued in April 1989. Several bodies have published their responses to the document, but no indication has come from the government or the Revenue as to whether any legislation is intended and, if so, when.

In the meantime, certain basic strategies suggest themselves, even though the circumstances and requirements of individual businesses will obviously differ. Provided that commercial realities allow for it, it is advisable to match currency assets and liabilities to as great an extent as possible at the beginning of each accounting period. Towards the end of the period it should become apparent (unexpected crises always excepted) whether the year-end rate of the currency in question will be up or down on the previous year's figure, and appropriate action (eg a degree of unmatching) can then be taken. For example, if a company has made a dollar loan to a subsidiary in the form of a debt on a security and has dollar borrowings on capital account, and the dollar appreciates against sterling over the accounting period, it is best to match the assets and liabilities as closely as possible so that the otherwise disallowable loss on the liability can be used to net off the gain on the loan to the subsidiary.

Within a group of companies, to the extent that matching is deemed necessary, the group should ensure that each company has the required complementary asset or liability. Denominating inter-company loan accounts in the appropriate currency may be sufficient to ensure this.

10.11 Depreciating currencies

Much of the discussion so far as been on the premise that the foreign currency in question is appreciating against sterling in the long term. However, the same principles apply, in reverse, if the currency (eg the Yugoslavian dinar) is depreciating against sterling. For example, if the sterling value of a dinar loan that is a chargeable asset depreciates over the period, matching should generally be avoided, as the loss on the loan would be an allowable loss for capital gains purposes, leaving the uncancelled profit on any unmatched dinar borrowings tax free.

Example

A UK company sells machinery to a German company. The sale price is stated as DM3 million. At the time DM3 = £1. The UK company realises a sale and sets up a debtor for £1 million in sterling terms. However, by the time the German importer pays for the goods the pound has *risen* to £1 = DM3.2. Accordingly, when the German importer pays the UK exporter DM3 million the UK exporter realises sterling proceeds of £937,500. The UK exporter has realised a foreign exchange *loss* of £62,500 which can be offset against taxable profits.

10.12 Forex management

Managing foreign exchange movements is a complex task requiring a great deal of sophistication, and it is important to remember that it needs to be subordinated to the overall objectives of the company or group. It may well be that the optimum tax strategy for exchange movements conflicts with the other requirements (debt against equity, optimum group structure etc) discussed elsewhere in this book and it is then a question of setting priorities and adapting them to changing circumstances.

11

Joint Ventures and Partnerships

11.1 The first tentative step

Many businesses will make their first venture into Europe beyond exporting by entering into a joint venture with a locally based business entity, either as an alternative or as a prelude to establishing a branch or subsidiary.

The decision to enter into a joint venture may be made from political as well as commercial or fiscal considerations. Whereas in Western Europe there are few or no restrictions on the form of business entity through which non-residents may do business, the joint venture with a state enterprise has until recently been the *only* form of vehicle for doing business in the Eastern bloc. Restrictions on foreign direct investment in Comecon countries are being progressively lifted or removed entirely (see Appendix C) but the joint venture remains as either the only, or to date the principal, business vehicle for UK companies throughout most of 'Eastern Europe'.

A joint venture may take one of several forms, and its tax treatment, both in the UK and the country of operations, depends on that form.

11.2 European trends

Over the last five to ten years there has been a trend towards joint venture and partnership arrangements. The reasons are obvious.

- It is a strategy of minimising risk.
- It overcomes financial constraints due to high interest rates (a UK constraint) or exchange controls (European constraint).
- The need to comply with ever-expanding local regulations, especially environmental regulations. Very often these will not be apparent to UK management, and a local partner will be needed to deal with them.

- The need for local expertise at the highest level.
- Regulations requiring minimum local ownership (rare in Europe, other than in Eastern Europe).
- Commercial image. A joint venture company or partnership is more likely to be perceived as local rather than foreign. This can be particularly important where government or local government attitudes are important, for example in Italy where the local administrations have tended to be biased against foreign inward investment.
- Ease of language and culture problems.
- Ease of raising local finance.
- Pooling of complementary skills. For example there have been very many excellent Western European/Japanese joint ventures. The Japanese partner brings technical, product and R&D knowledge. The UK company brings knowledge of the European market, English language and culture, which is the predominant business culture to a large extent in Europe, and flair for marketing.

In the longer term, most joint ventures or partnerships involving small/medium companies either dissolve, or become wholly owned.

11.3 B–C net

B–C Net is the European Community's Business Cooperation Centre. This seeks to put companies in touch with each other throughout Europe, especially in the area of new technologies and innovation through the Sprint programme.

11.4 Cooperation

The joint venture may be limited to an agreement between two or more businesses to cooperate towards a common goal, while retaining their present legal form and without creating a new legal entity. In such instances, each party will continue to account for its own income and expenditure in its own way. Both in the UK and in most other countries, tax on the results of the venture would continue to be charged on each entity separately.

An alternative would be to allow one party to run the project and retain the profits in return for a consultancy fee, based on profits. If partnership status is to be avoided in the UK, care must be taken, for example, for the consultant party not to finance the project and not to share any losses arising. For a partnership to exist in UK law, there does not have to be a partnership agreement, nor is it sufficient for the parties concerned to declare that one does not exist, if the objective facts indicate otherwise.

An advantage in operating this minimal form of joint venture lies, as far as the UK tax position is concerned, in the ability to use losses brought forward against the profits of the venture. Where a new entity, either a partnership or a company, is created, the joint venture parties cannot transfer any brought forward losses to the new entity. If the parties continue to be assessed separately, this advantage is not lost. However, to ensure the continued availability of past losses, the joint venture's trade and the trade in which the losses arose must be the same. The joint venture cannot therefore represent a radically different departure from the venturer's existing trade. The UK Revenue sometimes take the line that any joint venture trade is *per se* a new trade, but this contention can successfully be resisted provided that the joint venture activity closely resembles the trade already carried on by the venturer, and that the venturer's role in that activity is similar to its customary role in its own trade.

11.5 Partnerships generally

It is normal for joint ventures to be conducted as partnerships or through the medium of a joint venture company.

In general English law, a partnership exists whenever persons carry on business in common with a view of profit. However, for tax purposes the net is cast somewhat wider. Any two or more persons jointly carrying on a trade or profession constitute a partnership for tax purposes. Income tax on their profits is computed and assessed jointly in one sum and separately from any other tax chargeable on them.

Whether or not a partnership exists for tax purposes has been a question considered in a long line of cases. The principles that can be deduced from them are that:

- the existence of a partnership agreement is not conclusive;
- the sharing of profits indicates a partnership but is not conclusive in itself;

- the sharing of losses is strongly suggestive of a partnership but not conclusive;
- the mere joint ownership of property does not give rise to a partnership.

In England, Wales and Northern Ireland, a partnership is not a separate legal persona but consists of individuals carrying on business in partnership with each other. In Scotland, on the other hand, a partnership (a 'firm') does have a separate legal status from the individuals comprising it. Whereas the Scottish position is closer to that adopted by most European countries for tax as well as general legal purposes, it is of no consequence as far as UK taxation of a partnership is concerned.

Whether partnerships constituted under foreign law are regarded as partnerships for UK taxation purposes depends on the facts. Most German partnership structures – eg the KG (*Kommanditgesellschaft*) or general partnership (*offene Handelsgesellschaft*) – would be regarded as partnerships for UK purposes. The French *société en nom collectif* is regarded as a partnership in practice, although in a single decided case a *société en nom collectif* was held to be a body corporate.

11.6 Residence of partnerships

There are special rules for determining the residence of a partnership. Although, except under Scottish law, a partnership is not a separate legal entity, nevertheless the question of where it is resident is determined separately from the residence of the partners. The residence of a partnership is determined entirely by where the management and control resides. If a partnership is managed and controlled in the UK then it is resident here, no matter how many of the partners may themselves be resident abroad. Conversely, if a partnership is managed and controlled abroad then it is resident abroad, no matter how many of the partners may be resident in the UK. Where management and control is deemed to reside is a question of fact, determined in much the same way as for a company (see Chapter 6 – Residence).

It follows that if the aim is to ensure that the partnership is non-resident, the partnership agreement should have a provision that partners' meetings where all the central decisions are taken must be held abroad, and that voting control rests with the non-resident partners. However, as with the residence of companies it is a question of fact as to where the partnership is managed and hence resident, and not a question of paperwork.

11.7 UK-resident partnerships

Where a partnership is resident in the UK, the UK-resident partners are assessable on their share of the worldwide profits. Non-resident partners are taxable only on UK-source income and gains, but it is the Inland Revenue's view that this is a concession. In their view non-resident partners in a UK-resident partnership are, strictly speaking, in receipt of UK-source income and gains with respect to their worldwide profit shares. Where the partnership has permanent establishments in one or more foreign countries, the tax paid in those countries on the partnership profits is available as a tax credit against UK tax.

11.8 Non-resident partnerships

Where control and management is situated abroad, the partnership is deemed to be resident abroad. A UK-resident partner in a non-resident partnership is assessed to UK tax. Losses from a non-resident partnership may *not* be set off against profits from UK sources. The partner will be assessed on his share of the partnership profits and capital gains, irrespective of any double tax treaty provisions.

11.9 Partnerships involving a company

Most UK partners in a joint venture partnership with European partners will be companies. There are special rules for taxation of partnerships where one of the partners is a company.

As far as corporate partners are concerned, the profits of a company partnership are computed for corporation tax purposes as if the partnership were a company with a year end that of the partnership. The computation departs from the normal corporation tax computation in the ways set out below.

- Distributions are ignored. This means, in effect, that payments of interest linked to the profits of the partnership, which would otherwise constitute a distribution and cause a company to be liable to ACT (Advance Corporation Tax – payable on account of the final corporation tax liability when a company pays a dividend) and be non-deductible against profits, are not so treated and will be treated as any other interest payment.
- No addition or deduction is made for capital allowances, balancing

charges and charges on income. Charges on income will include most interest payments, except those made to a UK bank.

- Pre-trading expenditure is not allowed.
- No deduction is made for losses of any period other than the current period.
- Losses may not be carried forward to a future accounting period of the partnership; however, they may be relievable by the partners.
- Changes in the membership of the partnership are ignored as long as there is continuity of at least one corporate member before and after the change. If, after the change, none of the corporate members was a member before the change, the trade of the partnership is treated as transferred to the new corporate member(s).

The corporate member's share of the partnership profit or loss is calculated according to the profit-sharing ratio in force during the year. Its share of items excluded from the computation earlier (ie capital allowances, charges on income, prior losses, pre-trading expenditure) is calculated in the same way. Where the corporate partner's year end does not coincide with the partnership's, the results are time-apportioned over the respective accounts of the company partner.

Once the company partner's share of the profit or loss is calculated, it can be treated as the profit or loss of any other trade it carries on. In the case of a profit, it can thus be:

- reduced by current period losses of other trades carried on by the company;
- reduced by losses claimed from other group companies by way of group relief;
- reduced by losses of the partnership trade brought forward from previous accounting period.

In the case of a loss, the loss can be:

- set against current period profits of other trades or other current period income and gains;
- carried back against profits from the partnership trade in the previous accounting period;
- surrendered to other group companies by way of group relief;

- carried forward against future profits from the partnership trade.

Where the company partnership is controlled and managed abroad, but one or more of the partners is a UK-resident company, the partnership is treated as if it were UK resident for the purposes of assessing the UK-resident corporate partners. That is to say, all the above rules apply unchanged. As far as the non-resident partners are concerned, the general rules already described for the taxation of non-resident partnerships apply.

11.10 Joint venture companies

Another way of structuring a joint venture is to set up a new company, referred to here as a JVC (for Joint Venture Company) in which the venturers all hold shares. For UK taxation purposes, the JVC may be a consortium company, the special rules pertaining to which will be discussed below. As it is a company, the rules described in Chapter 6 apply to determine where it is resident. If it is not to be resident in the UK it must be incorporated abroad and its management and control must be located abroad. Although most of the advantages of dual-resident companies have been removed by legislation, they are still useful in certain situations (see paragraph 6.6). It is worth bearing in mind that whereas most bodies corporate constituted as such under foreign law are treated as companies for UK tax purposes (eg the French *société à responsabilité limitée* and the German GmbH), this is not invariably the case.

A consortium exists where 75 per cent or more of the ordinary share capital of a company (the consortium company) is owned by two or more other companies (the consortium members). Each consortium member must effectively own at least 5 per cent of the consortium company's shares.

For UK taxation purposes, consortia are treated similarly to groups, with the necessary adaptations, but for any of the group provisions (eg group relief) to apply, it is necessary for the minimum shareholding requirements to be satisfied by UK-resident companies.

Thus dividends, interest and other charges may be paid by the consortium company to members of the consortium without ACT or a deduction of income tax only where the consortium company is UK resident, at least 75 per cent of its shares are held by UK-resident companies and the recipient company is UK resident. This is, of course, of no consequence where the consortium company is non-resident, since, provided the UK-resident consortium member owns at least 10 per cent of the consortium company, it will obtain double tax relief on foreign withholding tax and underlying tax on the consortium company's profits in the normal way.

Similarly, the facility to surrender losses down to the consortium company or up from the consortium company to consortium members or fellow group members of the consortium members depends on the same UK-residence requirement. This means that, as far as UK consortium members are concerned, the losses of a non-resident JVC are locked in, in much the same way as those of a foreign subsidiary. Under the European Commission's corporate tax harmonisation proposals, however, losses would be transferable across EC boundaries between parent and subsidiary. For this purpose, a 20 per cent or 50 per cent (depending on purpose) holding would suffice to establish a parent–subsidiary relationship (see Appendix D). This would be of direct assistance in many JVC situations, but of course within the EC only. The Commission is expected to publish its draft directive to this effect in the autumn of 1990 and wishes it to have effect from 1 January 1993.

11.11 European economic interest groupings

The European Economic Interest Grouping (EEIG), or 'earwig' as it has been dubbed, is a new entity designed to ease cross-border joint venture activities within the EC. The EEIG is based on the French *groupement d'intérêt économique* which, in France, can elect to be taxed as either a company or a partnership.

Legislation has been introduced in the Finance Act 1990 to provide a taxation régime in the UK for EEIGs. An EEIG is formed under Community law, specifically Council Regulation 2137/85 of 25 July 1985. Its members must belong to two or more EC states and may be individuals, partnerships or companies carrying on business. The purpose of the EEIG is to facilitate or develop the economic activities of its members, but its activities are not allowed to be anything other than ancillary to those of its members. It is not meant to be a profit-making body, so is unsuitable as a vehicle for trading activities. The sorts of activity envisaged for an EEIG are packaging, processing, marketing and research.

An EEIG must have its 'official address' (registered office) in a member state of the EC, where its own or a member's central administration is located and it is governed by the law of the member state where its official address lies. It is up to each member state to determine the legal status of an EEIG in its territory. In the UK, an

EEIG is regarded as a body corporate with separate legal status and must register with the Registrar of Companies. However, for tax purposes it is fiscally transparent as it is regarded as the agent of its members. Where it carries on a trade, the members are treated as carrying on a trade in partnership so that the company partnership rules apply.

11.12 Non-tax considerations

Where a UK company joint ventures or goes into partnership in order to export or expand into Europe, it will give up a measure of control. Many UK businessmen might resent this loss of control. Sometimes these feelings of frustration can be compounded if the joint venture/partner is foreign, with concomitant language difficulties or differing business customs.

A joint venture is often a first step, prior to 'doing the thing properly'. Statistically, in the longer term most joint ventures dissolve or become wholly owned. Joint ventures can, of course, be very successful and large in their own right; very often venturers will bring differing assets into the equation, for example one venturer may provide the finance and another venturer the expertise. The form of the joint venture or partnership must be carefully chosen, and not just from a tax point of view.

12

Investment in Foreign Real Property

12.1 Investment versus trading

Much UK investment into Europe is not into active trading ventures, but is instead into passive investment into foreign real estate. The tax implications of such investment are markedly different from the tax on trading-type activities. For example, by owning the real estate through a UK company and borrowing locally foreign tax on both rents and a capital gain on the sale of the land may be avoided. However, many European countries have anti-avoidance legislation relating to foreigners owning land; in particular they wish to tax a disposal of land.

Set out below is a brief country-by-country outline of the treatment of non-business related real estate. For discussion of the taxes mentioned, see under the appropriate entry in Appendix A. Except where explicitly stated, it is assumed that the investor is a UK company.

12.2 Austria

- The purchase of real property in Austria by a non-resident person or the Austrian subsidiary of a non-resident requires formal permission from the authorities.
- Property investment profits will not normally be liable to trade tax, but property dealing profits will be.
- A 3.5 per cent transfer tax is payable on purchase, plus a 1 per cent registration duty.
- Interest payable on loans to acquire or develop the property is normally tax deductible for corporation tax purposes but non-deductible for trade tax.

- Net rental income is subject to 30 per cent corporation tax in the hands of a non-resident investor. Where a tax loss results from an excess of interest and tax-deductible expenses over rental income, it may be carried forward for set-off against all sources of income and gains for the next seven years, where the rent accrues to an Austrian permanent establishment or subsidiary. There is no withholding tax on rental income. Rental income derived by a non-resident is not subject to trade tax unless the non-resident has a permanent establishment in Austria.
- There is no withholding tax on rental income.
- The 'assessed value' of the property net of borrowings is liable to annual net worth tax.

Gains on the disposal of real property by a non-resident are subject to corporation tax (but not 30 per cent trade tax) if the disposal takes place within 10 (sometimes 15) years of acquisition. VAT is payable if the property is sold within nine years of development or refurbishment.

12.3 Belgium

- There are no special restrictions on the purchase of real property by non-residents.
- The purchaser of a newly constructed building may be charged VAT (at 17 per cent). An investor who uses the building for letting cannot recoup this VAT. Where VAT is not chargeable, the purchaser faces a registration tax of 12.5 per cent. The rate is reduced to 5 per cent if the purchaser is a real estate company.
- Interest payable on loans for acquiring or constructing real property is normally tax deductible. Where the source of the loan is outside Belgium, the interest remains tax deductible provided that the loan was raised specifically for the purchase.
- A non-resident's net rental income is subject to the non-resident's corporation tax, at a maximum rate of 43 per cent. Any net loss on rented property is treated as a normal trading loss.
- There is no withholding tax on net rent derived by a non-resident.
- A property tax, based on a notional net rental value of property, is payable, but it may be partly credited against the non-resident corporation tax liability.

- Capital gains from the disposal of Belgian real property are not taxable whether or not the investor has a permanent establishment in Belgium.

12.4 Denmark

- There are no special restrictions on the purchase of real property by non-residents.
- Interest payable on loans to purchase or construct real property is tax deductible where secured by mortgage, but no deduction is available to the extent that the loan exceeds 80 per cent of the property's market value.
- Net rental income is liable to corporation tax at 40 per cent. Where net rental income is negative, the loss is treated as an ordinary trading loss.
- There is no withholding tax on rents derived from Danish real property by a non-resident.
- An annual communal land tax is levied on the value of real property.
- Gains arising on the disposal of real property by a non-resident are liable to 40 per cent corporation tax. The full rate is payable if disposal takes place within three years of acquisition. For disposal within four to seven years, a tapered rate applies and an inflation allowance is available. For disposal after seven years, the gain is tax free. Stamp duty of 1.2 per cent is payable by the vendor of real property.

12.5 Finland

- A non-resident is generally not permitted to acquire real property in Finland for investment purposes.

12.6 France

- There are no special restrictions on the purchase of real property by non-residents.

- The purchaser of real property is not generally liable to any special taxes.
- Interest payable on loans to purchase or construct real property is generally tax deductible.
- Net rental income in the hands of a non-resident corporate investor is liable to corporation tax at 42 per cent. Where net rental income is negative (ie interest and other deductible expenses exceed rents), the loss may be carried forward against future rental income only.
- Capital gains paid over directly to a non-resident are liable to withholding tax of 33.3 per cent on the gross amount.
- Non-resident companies owning French real property (where this constitutes 50 per cent or more of their total French assets) are liable to an annual tax of 3 per cent on the market value of the property. Exemption may be conferred by some of France's tax treaties, for example the UK/France treaty.
- A registration tax of 16.6 per cent is payable by the vendor of real property, and capital gains are also subject to corporation tax.

12.7 Germany

- There are no special restrictions on the purchase of real property by non-residents.
- There are no special taxes payable by the purchaser of real property.
- Interest payable on loans to purchase or construct real property is generally tax deductible.
- Net rental income in the hands of a foreign corporate investor is liable to corporation tax at 46 per cent. Where net rental income is negative, the loss may be offset in the normal way against other income liable to corporation tax.
- There is no withholding tax on rents derived from German real property.
- An annual net worth tax is payable on the specially assessed value of real property.

- Speculative gains on the disposal of real property within two years of acquisition are liable to corporation tax at 46 per cent. If the investor has a permanent establishment in Germany to which the gain accrues, it will also be subject to the local trade tax. A transfer tax of 2 per cent is also payable by the vendor of real property. Contrary to popular belief, mere ownership of the land for a period of more than two years does not confer automatic exemption from German tax on a sale. If the UK property-owning company has a German permanent establishment to which the disposal can be attributed, the gain will be taxable even if the property is held for more than two years.

12.8 Greece

- There are no special restrictions on the purchase of real property by non-residents.
- Net rental income derived by non-residents is liable to corporation tax at 46 per cent.
- There is a withholding tax of 25 per cent on payments of rent to non-residents.
- An annual property tax is levied on the value (net of liabilities) of real property. The first Drs 40 million (£151,500) is exempt and the balance is charged at 1.5 per cent.
- There is no capital gains tax and no corporation tax on the gain arising from disposal of real property. However, a transfer tax of 11 per cent (9 per cent if the property is situated in an area without adequate fire protection) is payable by the vendor.

12.9 Ireland

- There are no special restrictions on the purchase of real property by non-residents.
- A stamp duty of 6 per cent is payable by the purchaser of property exceeding IR£60,000 (£54,725). VAT may also be chargeable.
- Interest payable on loans to purchase or construct real property is generally tax deductible.

- Net rental income derived from Irish real property by a non-resident corporate investor is liable to income tax at the basic rate of 30 per cent. Where net rental income is negative, the loss may be carried forward against future rental income only.
- Rents paid direct to a foreign investor are subject to a withholding tax of 30 per cent. Where the rents are paid to an Irish resident agent, withholding tax is not deducted but the agent will withhold sufficient sums to cover the investor's likely liability against final settlement.
- There are special rules relating to development land gains which are taxed at 50 per cent (regardless of period of ownership) with a restricted indexation allowance and loss relief. Development land is defined as land and buildings situated in Ireland, the consideration for the disposal of which, or the market value of which at the date of disposal, exceeds its current use value, at that date.
- Foreign investors are liable to capital gains tax on disposals of Irish real property. The rate of tax depends on the length of ownership.

12.10 Italy

- There are no special restrictions on the purchase of real property by non-residents.
- A 10 per cent registration tax is payable by the purchaser of real property, and VAT may also be chargeable.
- Interest payable on loans to purchase or construct real property is generally tax deductible.
- Net rental income is liable to approximately 46 per cent IRPEG and ILOR (national and local corporation tax) in the same manner as other income.
- There is no withholding tax on rents paid directly to non-residents.
- INVIM, the property gains tax, is also payable as a property tax on every tenth anniversary of the acquisition of Italian real property.
- Capital gains arising from the disposal of real property by a non-resident are liable to approximately 46 per cent IRPEG and ILOR. INVIM is also payable by the vendor on the transfer of real property.

12.11 Luxembourg

- There are no special restrictions on the purchase of real property by non-residents.
- Interest payable on loans to purchase or construct real property is generally tax deductible.
- Net rental income is subject to corporation tax at 34 per cent. Where net rental income is negative, the loss is treated as a trading loss. If the property constitutes a permanent establishment, the communal business tax is also payable on rental income.
- Net worth tax is payable at 0.5 per cent on a company's net worth, including real property. The net worth element of communal business tax will be due where the property constitutes a permanent establishment. In addition, there is a communal real property tax on 5 to 10 per cent of the value of real property, charged at various rates not exceeding 8 per cent.
- There is no withholding tax on rents derived from Luxembourg real property by a non-resident.
- Capital gains arising on the disposal of real property are subject to 34 per cent corporation tax and, where the property constitutes a permanent establishment, to communal business tax. A real estate transfer tax of 6 per cent (9 per cent in the city of Luxembourg) is payable by the vendor.

12.12 Netherlands

- There are no special restrictions on the purchase of real property by non-residents.
- Either 6 per cent purchase tax is payable by the purchaser of real property, or VAT will be payable at 18.5 per cent.
- Interest payable on loans to purchase or construct real property is generally tax deductible.
- Net rental income is liable to corporation tax (currently at 35 per cent). Where net rental income is negative, the loss is treated as a normal trading loss, available for carry back or carry forward as applicable.

- There is no withholding tax on rents derived from Netherlands real property by a non-resident.
- Real property is subject to an annual local property tax.
- Capital gains arising from the disposal of real property are taxed as part of normal income at 35 per cent. Taxation of the gain may be deferred by creating a deductible reinvestment reserve, where appropriate.

12.13 Norway

- The purchase of real property by non-residents or the subsidiaries of non-resident companies is subject to government approval.
- There are no special purchase taxes payable by the purchaser of real property, and VAT is not normally chargeable on the purchase or sale of real property.
- Interest payable on loans to purchase or construct real property is tax deductible.
- Net rental income is liable to approximately 50 per cent corporation tax in the same manner as other income. Where net rental income is negative, the loss is treated in the same manner as a trading loss.
- No withholding tax is deducted from rents derived by a non-resident from Norwegian real property.
- A communal real property tax is payable at rates of between 0.2 and 0.7 per cent, and is deductible for corporation tax purposes. There is also a communal net worth tax on Norwegian *situs* assets (including real property) levied at a rate of 1 per cent and a national net worth tax of 0.3 per cent. This latter is not payable by residents of a country (eg the UK) which has a non-discrimination article in its tax treaty with Norway.
- Capital gains arising from the disposal of real estate by non-residents are subject to corporation tax. Where the property is not business property, a special overall rate of 32 per cent applies.

12.14 Portugal

- As from 1 January 1990, there are no special restrictions on the purchase of real property by residents of the EC.
- Net rental income derived by non-residents without a permanent establishment in Portugal is subject to corporation tax at a special reduced rate of 25 per cent. Companies with a permanent establishment are liable to corporation tax at the full rate of 40.15 per cent (including the local surcharge of 10 per cent).
- Gains arising on the disposal of real property are subject to corporation tax at a rate of either 25 per cent (in the absence of a permanent establishment) or 40.15 per cent (where there is a permanent establishment).

12.14 Spain

- There are no special restrictions on the purchase of real property by non-residents.
- There are no special purchase taxes on the purchase of real property.
- Interest payable on loans to purchase or construct real property is tax deductible.
- The taxation of net rental income of non-residents varies according to whether the property is held through a Spanish permanent establishment. If it is so held, net rental income is liable to corporation tax at the normal rate of 35 per cent. If the property investment is not deemed to be a permanent establishment, no corporation tax is payable but the gross rental will be subject to 25 per cent withholding tax.
- Capital gains arising from the disposal of real property by a non-resident are liable to corporation tax at 35 per cent.
- VAT is normally chargeable at 12 per cent on the transfer of real estate, except for private residential property for which the rate is 6 per cent. Where the vendor is not within the VAT system, transfer tax at 6 per cent is charged.

12.16 Sweden

- The purchase of real property in Sweden by non-residents is subject to government permission. Where the property is not business property, permission is not automatically obtained.
- Subject to the above, stamp duty of between 1.5 and 3 per cent is payable by the purchaser of real property. VAT may also be chargeable.
- Interest payable on loans to purchase or construct real property is generally tax deductible, irrespective of the source of the loan.
- Net rental income is liable to 30 per cent national income tax. Where net rental income is negative, the loss may be carried forward against future profits from that property.
- There is no withholding tax on rents derived by a non-resident from Swedish real property.
- Unless the non-resident investor is a resident of a country with which Sweden has a double tax treaty, local net worth tax is payable on the value of the property at rates of between 1.5 and 3 per cent.
- Capital gains arising from the disposal of real property by a non-resident are liable to national income tax (30 per cent).

12.17 Switzerland

- There are no special restrictions on the purchase of real property by a non-resident; they vary from canton to canton. Swiss real estate for investment is very difficult for a non-resident to acquire. A non-resident may have to buy an existing Swiss company which owns land.
- There may be cantonal purchase or registration taxes payable by the purchaser of real property.
- Interest payable on loans to purchase or construct real property is normally tax deductible.
- Net rental income is subject to federal, cantonal and communal income tax. Where net rental income is negative, the loss may be carried forward against future rental income only.

- There are no withholding taxes on rents derived from Swiss real property by a non-resident.
- Federal and cantonal net worth tax is payable on the value of real property. In certain cantons, cantonal and communal property taxes may be payable, in addition to the net worth tax.
- Capital gains arising from the disposal of real property by a non-resident are liable to federal and cantonal income tax.
- The overall rate will vary greatly from canton to canton.

12.18 European real estate generally

In most European countries, the tax treatment of investment in real property that is not used as premises for the investor's own business, but as an investment in its own right or as part of a property-owning business as such, is markedly different. The normal treatment of business premises for a trade is covered within the general text of the book, and in particular in Appendix A with respect to each European country. However, with respect to the subject of real estate special rules apply. As with many other aspects of international tax planning, detailed professional advice should be obtained.

13

Director/Employee Remuneration

13.1 The personal aspect

By 1993, immigration and passport controls within the EC are scheduled to have disappeared, especially with respect to matters such as work permits. A UK company expanding into Europe will find it substantially easier to send employees abroad.

Working abroad for substantial periods can provide opportunities for income tax, inheritance tax and national insurance planning for the individual. However, the greatest care must be exercised to ensure that pitfalls, both UK and foreign, are avoided. In this respect the UK's extensive network of bilateral double tax treaties and social security agreements can offer useful protection.

13.2 One year out – the 100 per cent deduction rule

Someone going abroad for one year, but who remains resident and ordinarily resident in the UK, can avoid UK income tax on his earnings (salary and benefits) if he satisfies the 'one-sixth' rule, essentially if he spends less than one-sixth of his time in the UK. He can also be protected against foreign tax under a double tax treaty.

This is the so-called '100 per cent deduction'. Where it applies, there is a deduction of 100 per cent against salary and benefits in kind, so that there is no UK income tax liability on earnings. However, liability to UK tax on all other income and gains remains.

To qualify for the 100 per cent deduction, the duties must be performed wholly or partly outside the UK. There has to be a 'qualifying period' of at least 365 days, of which 5/6ths is spent abroad.

Return visits to the UK are permitted provided that:

- a visit to the UK does not exceed 62 days in length; *and*

- the number of days in the UK does not exceed 1/6th of the 'qualifying period'.

This second restriction is cumulative, so that at the end of each period spent abroad (that is, just before each return visit to the UK) it is necessary to ensure that both conditions are satisfied. If they are, a 'qualifying period' is being constructed; if not, then counting must start again. Once the qualifying period exceeds 365 days the 100 per cent deduction can be claimed. It may help to consider the concept of a sandwich, with the 'bread' representing periods outside the UK and the 'fillings' representing periods in the UK.

Example

A	Out of UK	28 days	bread
B	In UK	10 days	filling
C	Out of UK	53 days	bread

A+B+C = a qualifying period of 91 days because period B (10 days) is less than 1/6th of 91 days (15 days)

Example

A	Out of UK	28 days	bread
B	In UK	10 days	filling
C	Out of UK	53 days	bread
D	In UK	4 days	filling
E	Out of UK	27 days	bread
F	In UK	18 days	filling
G	Out of UK	4 days	bread

A + B + C + D + E = a qualifying period of 122 days because periods B and D (14 days) are less than 1/6th of 122 days (20 days)
A + B + C + D + E + F + G = not a qualifying period because the total of UK days (32) is more than 1/6th of total days (144)
In the second example there will be no deduction.

A day outside the UK is one on which an employee is outside the UK at midnight. The Inland Revenue's attitude is that a day on which an employee arrives in the UK at 00.01 and departs *the same day* at 23.59 counts as a day *outside* the UK for this purpose. It is where you are at midnight that counts! Interestingly, there is a different definition of day when determining matters such as residence. Therefore the day of departure from the UK is treated as a qualifying day and the day of return to the UK as non-qualifying. Days abroad, not necessarily connected with the individual's employment, also count as days overseas for the purposes of the 100 per cent deduction; indeed days may be spent overseas on leave at the beginning or end of an overseas secondment to form part of a 365-day qualifying period. One of the few pieces of case law relating to this subject, however, held that a period spent in the *UK* during a contract of employment, but not followed by a period abroad under the contract, could not form part of a qualifying period. Nevertheless, if a period of leave in the UK immediately follows a qualifying period then the emoluments for that period of leave are attributed to the qualifying period and therefore generally qualify for the deduction.

Where the duties of an employment are performed wholly abroad and a qualifying period of 365 days or more is achieved, the 100 per cent deduction is given on earnings for the qualifying period.

13.3 Duties partly in the UK and partly overseas

If the duties are performed partly in the UK or wholly abroad, but there is an associated employment in which duties are performed in the UK, the 100 per cent deduction is allowed on only a 'reasonable proportion' of the total earnings from the employment and all other associated employments. The 'reasonable proportion' is a fraction which is shown to be reasonable, taking account of the nature and time devoted to the duties undertaken in the UK and outside the UK and of all other relevant circumstances. One employment is associated with another if they are with the same employer or with employers under common ownership. *Prima facie* this may be found by apportioning the emoluments by the ratio of the number of days the individual spent working abroad to the number of days for which the relevant employment is held.

Example

An example may help to illustrate how a qualifying 100 per cent 'one year out' deduction is constructed where an associated employment is held under which duties are performed in the UK.

An individual who is resident and ordinarily resident in the UK but is seconded to the employer's Brussels office for a period of

370 days spends the following days in the UK and overseas during the period.

A	Out of UK	75 days all working
B	In UK	16 days all not working
C	Out of UK	90 days all working
D	In UK	18 days all working
E	Out of UK	60 days, 30 days working/30 days not working
F	In UK	24 days all working
G	Out of UK	87 days all working

Test 1
No return visit to the UK exceeds 62 days

Test 2

- *First return visit to the UK.* The 'one-sixth' test must be considered in conjunction with the periods abroad on either side on each return visit to the UK. Sixteen days is less than one-sixth of 181 (75 + 16 + 90).
- *Second return visit to the UK.* The cumulative number of days spent in the UK by the end of the second return visit (ie 16 + 18 = 34) is less than one-sixth of 259 days (ie 181 (above) + 18 + 60).
- *Third return visit to the UK.* The cumulative number of days spent in the UK by the end of the third return visit (ie 16 + 18 + 24 = 58) is less than one-sixth of 370 (ie 259 (above) + 24 + 87)

Emoluments for the total qualifying period (including UK duties) amount to £100,000. The following illustrates the emoluments chargeable to UK tax on a simple time apportionment basis:

Example

UK duties

Days on UK duties	42 (D + F)	
Days on UK and overseas duties	324 (A + C + D + 30 of E + F + G)	
Earnings liable to UK income tax	$\frac{42}{324} \times$ £100,000 =	£12,963
Earnings not liable		£87,037
		£100,000

13.4 PAYE ruling

It is essential that before the employee goes abroad the UK company obtains an 'NT' (which stands for 'no tax') PAYE ruling. This will allow the UK company to pay the employee gross. A UK company cannot pay without deducting PAYE unless prior permission is obtained. The employer's payroll section should not simply assume that the employee is non-taxable.

Someone who is eligible for the 100 per cent deduction will escape tax on his salary and benefits. It is important to remember that in order to qualify for the 100 per cent deduction he must remain both UK resident and ordinarily resident. If necessary, steps should be taken to ensure that he is so resident. However, notwithstanding that the employee will escape tax on earnings and benefits, he will remain liable to UK tax on all his other income and gains.

13.5 Treaty protection

The great advantage of the 100 per cent deduction is that the employee can take advantage of one of the UK's double tax treaties. Typically this provides protection against foreign tax if the following conditions are satisfied.

- First, the employee spends less than 183 days in the foreign country's tax year in that country. Most European countries have 31 December tax year ends as opposed to the UK's 5 April.
- Second, the employer is not resident in the foreign country (under some treaties the employer must be UK resident).
- Third, the employee is resident in the UK for the purposes of the treaty. In practice this will nearly always be the case. Although an employee may be resident in the UK for UK tax purposes (which he *must* be to be eligible for the 100 per cent deduction) he may also be resident in another country under its tax rules. However, in practice the dual residence article of the double tax treaty will normally ensure that, by virtue of a series of tests, *for the purposes of the treaty only,* he is to be treated as resident in the UK alone. The UK has double tax treaties with many European countries which contain both earnings and dual residence provisions. An example may help to make this clearer.

Example

An individual who is UK resident and ordinarily resident goes abroad to work and satisfies the rules for the 100 per cent deduction. He is resident in the UK for UK tax purposes. However, he also buys a German property and the circumstances of his life are such that he becomes resident in Germany for German tax purposes. Under Article 2 of the UK/Germany double tax treaty he would be assumed for the purposes of the treaty only to be resident in the UK. By virtue of Article 11 he would not be liable to German tax so long as he spends less than 183 days in Germany in a calendar year, is employed by a non-German employer, and his remuneration is not charged to a German permanent establishment. This brings us to the fourth condition.

- The employee's remuneration is not charged to a permanent establishment in the foreign country

Example

A UK company decides to commit a senior executive to working abroad in the EC for one year. The executive leaves the UK on 30 June and works for subsidiaries in France for three months, Germany for three months, the Netherlands for three months, Italy for three months and Portugal for three months. Accordingly he spends less than 183 days in each country. He remains an employee of the UK exporting company. He remains resident and ordinarily resident in the UK. By virtue of the UK's '100 per cent deduction' rules, he also escapes UK tax on his salary. Accordingly, he pays no tax on his salary in the UK. The UK company has a branch in France, and his salary is paid by the branch and deducted for French tax purposes. Under the terms of the UK's comprehensive double tax treaty his salary would escape tax in Germany, the Netherlands, Italy and Portugal. However, he would be *potentially* liable to tax in France because the fourth condition is not satisfied. The word 'potentially' is used because the employee's tax position would be dictated by French domestic law.

13.6 Personal residence in Europe

It can be seen that so long as he satisfies the treaty rules, an individual may not become liable to European tax until he ceases to be UK resident and becomes resident overseas. The rules as to what constitutes residence for an individual in each European country are different. In Belgium, for example, an individual will be resident if he stays more than 183 days, or he has a permanent home in Belgium, or his centre of vital economic interests is there. Nearly all European countries have a rule that anyone staying six months will be resident there. On the other hand, Denmark has no concept of 'centre of vital interest'. Very few European countries, if any, take any cognisance of nationality. Other countries have special rules. For example, an individual will be resident in France if he performs professional activities there on a regular basis. On the other hand, Sweden will treat as a resident anyone whose 'genuine domicile' is in Sweden or who has 'substantial connections' with Sweden. Some countries, for example Ireland, will tax an individual as resident if he merely has a permanent home there (unless other conditions are satisfied).

13.7 Overseas tax systems

The example raises the question of the way that foreign countries tax UK executives posted there. Appendix B sets out, in tabular form, the foreign taxation of UK executives posted to Austria, Belgium, Denmark, Finland, France, Germany, Greece, Ireland, Italy, Luxembourg, Netherlands, Norway, Portugal, Spain, Sweden and Switzerland.

Detailed advice is required, both in the UK and overseas, in order to determine the tax position of a UK employee being sent overseas, and to take any necessary planning steps to minimise his overall tax liability.

13.8 Expenses

Where an employee who is resident and ordinarily resident in the UK carries on the duties of an employment abroad, certain expenses which are not usually available may be claimed.

Where the duties are performed wholly outside the UK, the cost of both travelling between the UK and overseas to take up the overseas employment, and board and lodging outside the UK, may be tax deductible.

Where the duties are only partly performed outside the UK, the rules are a little harder to fulfil. Travelling facilities provided or reimbursed by the employer between the UK and overseas to perform the duties of an employment are deductible if the duties can *only* be performed outside the UK and absence from the UK is wholly and exclusively due to the performance of those activities.

Where an individual carries on more than one employment and at least one of them is performed wholly or partly outside the UK, travelling expenses incurred by the employee in travelling from one place of employment to another are deductible.

Where an employee's absence from the UK amounts to a continuous period of 60 days or more, the payment or reimbursement by the employer of travelling facilities for the spouse and any children under the age of 18 accompanying the employee at the beginning of the period of absence, or visiting him during that period, may be deductible; there is a limit of two outward and return journeys per person in any tax year.

Example

Harry is a married man who is resident and ordinarily resident in the UK. He is employed by Employer plc at a salary of £100,000 per annum and is involved in the commissioning of petrochemical plants. He spends the following periods overseas:

3 July to 20 September 1989 (80 days) in Alaska
30 October to 20 December 1989 (53 days) in Spain
5 January to 15 May 1990 (132 days) in Hungary

Travel expenses incurred in 1989-90 are as follows:

		Paid by Harry £	*Amounts paid by Harry and reimbursed by Employer plc* £	*Paid by Employer plc* £
2.7.89	Birmingham–Heathrow Airport	80		
3.7.89	Heathrow–Alaska (H)			1,100
15.8.89	Birmingham–Alaska (wife and children)			2,500
26.8.89	Alaska–Birmingham (wife and children)	2,500	2,500	
20.9.89	Alaska–Birmingham (H)	1,200	1,200	
30.10.89	Birmingham–Heathrow (H)			80
30.10.89	Heathrow–Spain (H)			150
20.11.89	Birmingham–Spain (wife and children)			350 (b)

28.11.89	Birmingham–Spain (wife and children)	350 (b)	350 (b)	
20.12.89	Spain–Birmingham (H)			160
5.1.90	Birmingham–Heathrow (H)	80	80	
5.1.90	Heathrow–Hungary (H)			400
28.2.90	Birmingham–Hungary (wife)	100 (c)		300
		£4,310	£4,130	£5,040

Harry will be assessed as follows:	£	£
Salary		100,000
Cost of expenses incurred by Employer plc		5,040
Reimbursed travel expenses		4,130
		109,170
Deduct: Allowable part of expenses incurred by Employer plc	4,690	
Allowable expenses incurred by Harry	3,860	
Personal allowances	4,375	
		12,925
Taxable		£96,245
Income Tax		
on first £20,700 at 25%		5,175
on balance of £75,545 at 40%		30,218
		£35,393

Notes

(a) A deduction is allowed for travelling expenses of the employee from any place in the UK to take up the overseas employment.

(b) As Harry is away for less than 60 days in Spain he cannot deduct the cost of his family's trip.

(c) In November 1989 the part of the cost of his wife's trip to Hungary not reimbursed cannot be deducted.

Similarly, tax relief is available to non-UK domiciled employees in relation to travelling facilities provided or reimbursed in respect of journeys to and from the UK in relation to duties performed in this country.

13.9 Emigration

Someone going abroad for a longer period may lose UK-residence and ordinary-residence status entirely. Whereas he would then be able to realise tax-free capital gains, he would have no treaty protection against foreign tax.

13.10 Residence

In order to lose UK-residence status an individual must:

- not be present in the UK for more than six months in a UK tax year (year to 5 April);
- not be present in the UK for an average of more than three months per UK tax year over a four-year period;
- unless he is in full time employment abroad, not have available accommodation available for him in the UK; if he does, he will become resident as soon as he sets foot here. This makes it particularly difficult for people who are not in full-time employment abroad. It is therefore necessary to consider what this means.

An individual is in 'full-time employment abroad' when he devotes substantially most of his working time to his job while overseas. Accordingly, someone who merely retires overseas will not be in full-time employment abroad. Under no circumstances will the Inland Revenue accept that an individual is in full-time employment abroad if:

- he attends a board meeting in the UK as a director of a UK company;
- he attends a partners' meeting in the UK in his capacity as a partner;
- he spends more than three months in the UK in a tax year for any reason.

Where visits to the UK are necessary they must be incidental to the overseas duties, for example to report or to receive fresh instructions. Great care should be taken when drawing up contracts to ensure that they make clear that an individual is not employed in the UK.

It can be seen that it can be a much longer-term process for an individual to become non-resident than to qualify for the 100 per cent deduction.

In order to escape capital gains tax an individual must be both non-resident *and* not ordinarily resident.

13.11 Ordinary residence

'Ordinary residence' looks to where an individual will be living over a period of three to five years, whereas 'residence' looks at where an individual is living on a year-to-year basis. A person will normally be treated by the Inland Revenue as ceasing to be ordinarily resident in the UK if he leaves the UK to work full-time abroad, and UK duties are only incidental, provided that the employment covers a complete UK tax year to 5 April. The individual must also spend less than three months in the UK in that year.

13.12 Capital gains

Provided that an individual is both not resident and not ordinarily resident he may escape capital gains tax on the sale of investments, wherever they are situated.

If an individual wishes to take advantage of becoming not resident and not ordinarily resident in order to avoid CGT, he would be well advised not to realise a capital gain until after 5 April following emigration. This is because UK tax years are only split by concession. If the taxpayer does not want to rely on Inland Revenue concession (and it is best not to do so, since the Inland Revenue will not apply a concession where they consider that tax avoidance is involved) then he should defer making the gain until after 5 April following emigration. Similarly, when returning to the UK, he should avoid realising a capital gain at any time in the tax year in which he returns to the UK.

13.13 Domicile

If an individual leaves the UK to work abroad permanently, effectively forever, he may cease to be UK domiciled. It is, however, often difficult for individuals to lose their UK domicile status if they were born with what is known as a 'domicile of origin' in the UK (strictly England and Wales, Scotland or Northern Ireland). This is particularly so for a UK employee, because the intention to abandon a UK domicile must be demonstrated by positive actions which will include cutting as many ties as possible with the home country (including a continuing employment with a UK company). The onus of proof of a change in domicile of origin would be (in this case) with the individual.

The main advantage of losing a UK domicile is that the individual concerned will then cease to be liable to UK inheritance tax on non-UK sited assets. A non-resident but UK-domiciled individual remains liable to UK inheritance tax on his worldwide assets.

Example

Edward has ceased to be domiciled in the UK for inheritance tax purposes and is neither resident nor ordinarily resident in the UK. He dies on 30 April 1990 with the following estate:

	£
Land in Lincolnshire	250,000
House in Marbella, Spain	200,000
UK-registered shares	100,000
Foreign currency account with Grindleys Bank, London	50,000
UK company bearer shares held by Banco de Bilbao, Spain	70,000
Chattels situated in Marbella home	30,000
Total worldwide estate	£700,000

His UK inheritance tax liability (assuming he has not made any chargeable lifetime gifts in the previous seven years) is calculated as follows:

Land in Lincolnshire	250,000
UK registered shares	100,000
Chargeable estate	£350,000
IHT charge	*Tax*
128,000 at 0%	nil
222,000 at 40%	88,800
	£88,800
£350,000 UK estate	

Notes

- Bearer shares and securities are situated where the title document is physically kept.
- A foreign currency account with the Bank of England, the National Savings Bank or any other recognised bank in the UK is not liable to IHT *on death* if held by a non-UK domiciled, non-resident and non-ordinarily resident person.

If Edward was not UK resident or ordinarily resident *but continued to be UK domiciled* on death for UK IHT purposes, his chargeable estate would amount to £700,000 and the IHT payable by his executors would be as follows:–

		Tax
		£
128,000	at 0%	–
572,000	at 40%	
£700,000	Worldwide assets	£228,800

At present, inheritance tax is effectively a voluntary tax, in that so long as an individual gives away his assets more than seven years before he dies there is no inheritance tax to pay. However, this may change in the future, and obviously the employee does not usually know when he is going to die! Insurance for any inheritance tax liability is therefore very important and detailed professional guidance is essential.

13.14 MIRAS

MIRAS (mortgage interest relief at source) is a system under which a home owner pays only 75 per cent of the nominal interest rates on the element of loans up to £30,000 to buy a main residence. Even if sent abroad for fairly lengthy periods, possibly up to four years, an expatriate may still be eligible for MIRAS, although where the borrower's taxable income is insufficient for him to benefit from the full amount of his personal allowances (where available) the amount by which his personal reliefs exceed his total income is deducted from the gross mortgage interest figure before calculating the tax deducted at source. This is a very important point that should not be overlooked when the expatriate is sent abroad.

13.15 Renting

Very often an individual employee sent abroad will wish to rent out his UK house while he and his family are overseas. The rent remains liable to UK tax, and he should appoint a managing agent in order to avoid application of UK withholding tax at the 25 per cent basic rate by the tenant. A managing agent is liable for the landlord's income tax liability. He has to actually manage the property. If possible, it is usually best to agree in advance that managing agents will be accepted as such by the Inland Revenue: very often they are estate agents who will charge between 7.5 and 15 per cent of the rent so to act.

Example

Hubert is a British citizen resident in Portugal and receives rental income of £50,000 per annum from the letting of his Bristol house. Hubert is single. He originally obtained a mortgage from Lloyds Bank for the purchase of the property and paid interest of £20,000 on the loan during 1990–91. His other outgoings in respect of the property are £5,000 (assumed to be fully allowable for tax purposes).

No managing agent
If Hubert does not have a UK managing agent, the tenant will be required to pay the rent net of 25 per cent withholding tax.

Hubert will receive £37,500 and the tenant will need to account for £12,500 withholding tax to the UK Inland Revenue. Hubert would then need to file a UK return of the rental income for 1990–91 at the year-end as follows:–

Rent	50,000
Less: outgoings	(5,000)
	45,000
Less: Interest	(20,000)
	25,000
Less: Personal allowance	(3,005)
	£21,995
Income tax on £20,700 at 25 per cent	5,175
Income tax on £1,295 at 40 per cent	518
	5,693
Less: Tax withheld	12,500
Tax overpaid–repayable	£6,807

Notes

- Because Hubert is not UK resident he would normally not be entitled to UK personal allowance. However, as a British citizen he *can* benefit from UK personal allowances. UK personal allowances are available to the following categories of non-resident:

(a) Commonwealth citizens or citizens of the Republic of Ireland; *or*
(b) individuals who are or who have been employed in the service of the Crown, or who are employed in the service of any missionary society or in the service of any territory under Her Majesty's protection; *or*
(c) residents in the Isle of Man or the Channel Islands; *or*
(d) individuals who have previously resided in the UK and are resident abroad for the sake of their health, or for the health of a member of their family resident with them; *or*
(e) widows whose late husband or widowers whose late wife was in the service of the Crown;
(f) residents of certain countries with which the UK has concluded double tax treaties with specific types of non-discrimination articles.

- The Inland Revenue will not pay repayment supplement (interest) on late repayment of any tax overpaid to a non-resident.

Managing agent
If Hubert has a UK managing agent, the tenant will not be required to withhold tax. The managing agent will submit a UK tax return after the year end (5 April) and account for the following tax (chargeable income as before £25,000 less managing agent's fees of 10 per cent of rent, ie 10 per cent of £50,000, ie £5,000: therefore chargeable income now £20,000):

Chargeable income	£20,000
Income tax	£5,000

The managing agent would normally withhold £5,000 from the rent paid to Hubert. He may withhold more until Hubert's accountants have agreed his income tax liability with the Inland Revenue.

The employee must take legal advice on the implications of renting. He must ensure that his house will be available to him on his return to the UK and that he will not be faced with a 'sitting tenant'.

13.16 Selling the house

Sometimes the employee is abroad and wishes to sell the house. Normally he would be both not resident and not ordinarily resident and hence he can sell the house free of capital gains tax.

If for some reason he is either resident or ordinarily resident, and hence potentially liable to CGT, there are substantial exemptions for employees working abroad which would mean that the house would still qualify as a 'main residence' which would be exempt from capital gains tax.

13.17 Tax equalisation

Very often the employer will be required to make good any extra tax or NIC under the employee's remuneration package. Such extra remuneration is known as 'tax equalisation'. The employer must compute what the tax on the employee would have been had he remained in the UK and compensate him for the extra foreign tax. This extra foreign tax may itself become liable to foreign tax and therefore a grossing-up exercise will be required.

Example

Sean works for a UK employer and is to be seconded abroad for two years. His current salary is £100,000, on which his accountants advise he will suffer UK tax and national insurance of £35,000 in the current tax year; his annual tax-home pay would therefore amount to £65,000. The foreign federal and local taxes and social security contributions will apply at a higher rate than that previously in the UK but, everything else being equal, the employer intends to pay Sean a salary that will correspond to his current take-home pay. The effective rate of tax and social security applying overseas is 50 per cent overall. Therefore Sean must be paid £130,000 so that he is in no worse a position, ie he is left with £65,000 net of tax.

13.18 The employer's position

The employer must bear in mind both the UK and the overseas tax positions. As we shall see in the next chapter, the employer must also bear in mind the NIC and foreign social security contributions positions.

14

National Insurance Contributions

14.1 Introduction

In the UK, social security contributions are referred to as 'National Insurance Contributions' (or 'NIC' for short). This is an important tax, although the government continues to insist that it is not a tax but an insurance payment, and is particularly important for an employer sending someone overseas. As a matter of interest to the reader it should be mentioned that the UK's system of NIC is divided into two separate systems, one for 'Great Britain' (England, Scotland and Wales) and the other for Northern Ireland. All other taxes such as income tax, corporation tax, VAT and inheritance tax are levied on a United Kingdom basis.

14.2 Minimising the cost to the employer

NIC is divided into four classes. Employees are liable to Class 1. This in turn is divided into two types of Class 1 contribution, the 'primary' contribution which is paid by the employee, and the 'secondary' contribution which is paid by the employer. Liability to secondary Class 1 NIC is a cost to the employer and must be minimised. Since 1985 there has been no 'upper earnings limit' – that is, cut-off point – for secondary Class 1 NIC. Accordingly it is essential for an employer to ascertain when an employee will be liable to Class 1 NIC when going abroad, because if the employee is not liable to primary Class 1 NIC the employer will not be liable to Class 1 secondary NIC. Secondary Class 1 NIC is currently 10.45 per cent of salary.

Example

A UK company pays an employee a salary of £100,000 per year. The employee has to account for primary contributions of £1,470.56 (1990–91 standard figure) out of his salary of £100,000. The company, on the other hand, has to pay £10,450. The primary figure is comparatively low because there is an upper earnings limit. No matter how much the employee earns above the equivalent of £350 per week he will pay no more than £28.28 (or £22.20 if he is 'contracted out'). However, there is no upper earnings limit for secondary contributions. Were the employee to earn £1 million the employer would be liable to pay £104,500.

Sometimes a UK parent will become involved with overseas employees posted back to the UK, and this will bring its own NIC complications.

Example

A UK company exports to Italy. It established an Italian subsidiary some years ago. An Italian employee of that subsidiary was required to work in the UK at the UK parent's offices. Because he worked for less than one year in the UK he was able to avoid UK National Insurance under the terms of the EC social security agreement. Accordingly the UK company's unlimited 10.45 per cent secondary Class 1 NIC liability under the 'intermediate employer' regulations was also avoided. The employee was only liable to pay Italian contributions.

Class 1 contributions are payable with respect to an employed earner's employment. An 'employed earner' is 'a person who is gainfully employed in Great Britain'. Therefore no Class 1 NIC will be due unless the earner is gainfully employed in Great Britain. However, if he is 'resident or present in Great Britain (or, but for any temporary absence, would be present) at the time of that employment, or is then ordinarily resident' then he will still be liable to NIC, even if he is temporarily working abroad.

The general rule is that where an employed earner leaves Great Britain to work overseas, liability to Class 1 NIC will cease immediately. However, there is an exception.

- If the employment would have been an employed earner's employment but for the fact that it is outside Great Britain; *and*

- the earner is ordinarily resident in Great Britain; *and*
- immediately before the commencement of the employment he was resident in Great Britain; *and*
- the employer has a place of business in Great Britain,

then Class 1 NIC will be payable for the first 52 weeks of the employment.

Under those circumstances it may be advisable for the employee to cease being employed by the UK parent and instead to be employed by the foreign subsidiary, which must have no place of business in Great Britain even within the extended definition given by the legislation, regulations and case law. However, the employee may then become liable to the foreign equivalent of NIC, usually referred to as social security contributions.

The position with respect to Europe is particularly complicated by the fact that there are bilateral agreements with individual European countries and within the EC generally. In most cases an employee will be liable to pay contributions in the EC state in which he is employed unless he falls within the temporary employment rule, so that:

- he is sent by his employer to work abroad for the same employer; *and*
- he is not being sent to replace another person with similar duties; *and*
- the employment is not expected to last for more than 12 months.

Generally, under the social security agreements with non-EC countries an employee sent abroad from the UK *may* voluntarily remain liable to Class 1 NIC (and hence his employer liable to NIC). Strictly speaking this should be for only a year and then possibly a further year, but in practice, and with the mutual agreement of all the relevant social security authorities, the period may be extended indefinitely. This makes sense for an employee who has no particular wish to contribute to a foreign social security scheme merely to avoid liability to Class 1 NIC when Class 1 NIC will guarantee certain rights, and where the employer does not object to the secondary Class 1 liability. There can be a conflict of interest. The employee may wish to continue paying Class 1 NICs in order to avoid liability to foreign social security contributions and to protect his benefit rights. On the other hand, the employer wants to minimise his 10.45 per cent secondary Class 1 NIC liability.

There are bilateral agreements with the following European countries:

Austria, Cyprus, Finland, Iceland, Malta, Norway, Sweden, Switzerland, Turkey and Yugoslavia.

In addition, there are individual reciprocal arrangements which have been superseded by the EC arrangements with Belgium, Denmark, France, Germany, Gibraltar, Ireland, Italy, Luxembourg, Netherlands, Portugal and Spain.

The benefits which are available as a result of Class 1 contributions are:

- unemployment benefit
- sickness benefit
- invalidity pension
- invalidity allowance
- maternity allowance
- widow's payment
- widowed mother's allowance
- widow's pension
- category A and B retirement pensions.

Category A pension is retirement pension claimed on a person's own contribution record. Category B pension is a retirement pension claimed on the record of a spouse.

14.3 National Health Service (NHS)

Medical expenses incurred while working abroad will not be paid by the NHS. The NHS is only available to people living in this country.

Once an individual is sent to work permanently abroad and becomes resident abroad, he will no longer be able to get free NHS treatment, even in this country.

Many overseas countries, and most European countries, have reciprocal health agreements with the UK, but the benefits provided are not exactly comparable with those available under the NHS. It is essential to take out private health insurance to ensure full medical attention both abroad and back in the UK.

14.4 Child benefit

Generally speaking, child benefit will cease once the individual has left the United Kingdom. Most EC countries have their own equivalent social security legislation, and generally an individual would be entitled to the local family allowances. Temporary absences of up to eight weeks will not restrict child benefit.

Even if an individual leaves the UK for more than eight weeks, if in that UK tax year (year to 5 April) at least half his earnings were liable to UK income tax, then child benefit may continue to be paid.

14.5 Multi-state employment

Where a person carries out duties of employment in two or more EC states there are regulations to ensure that contributions are paid to the correct state. Again, if prior mutual agreement of the various social security authorities is obtained he can remain liable to Class 1 NIC.

14.6 Allowances concession

Expatriate remuneration arrangements usually pay the employee not just a salary; there will also be separate payments for cost of living, accommodation, child education, foreign taxation and various other allowances. Under these circumstances, strictly speaking the DSS is entitled to ask for secondary Class 1 NIC with respect to these payments as well. Therefore, as already stated, many UK companies posting an employee overseas will ensure that he will immediately cease to be employed by the UK company and instead become an employee of a foreign subsidiary with no UK presence. Alternatively it is possible to agree with the DSS that certain specific computed payments are to be treated as a reimbursement of expenses, and not as round sum or scale rate amounts which would attract Class 1 NIC.

14.7 Voluntary contributions

An employee sent abroad who ceases to pay Class 1 NIC may pay Class 3 NIC, which is voluntary and much cheaper; at current rates it is only £3.95 per week. Class 3 NIC will entitle an employee to count years towards his retirement pension, and may also entitle an employee to the following benefits:

- widow's payment
- basic widowed mother's allowance
- basic widow's pension.

There is no employer's Class 3 contribution.

It is an extremely cheap method of funding the state pension. As can be seen by comparing this list of benefits against those granted by Class 1 contributions, the benefits are not as numerous.

Employees may prefer to pay Class 1 rather than Class 3, because first, Class 1 entitles the employee to better benefits; more importantly, however, Class 1 can exempt the employee from paying foreign contributions, which may be higher, but which will also not usually give the employee any benefits.

14.8 Self-employed earners

Self-employed earners are liable to Class 2 and Class 4 contributions. *Class 2* contributions are due in respect of (self)employment in Great Britain but will be payable only if the self-employed earner is ordinarily resident in Great Britain or if he has been resident in 26 of the immediately preceding 52 weeks. When a self-employed earner leaves the UK, generally there will be no further liability to Class 2 unless he has been resident in Great Britain for a continuous period of three years or he has paid certain minimum amounts of contributions in any previous three years. Again, the effect of the UK's bilateral agreements and the EC agreement should be carefully considered.

A self-employed UK individual sent abroad may wish to continue paying Class 2 in much the same way as he might wish to continue to pay Class 1. Class 2 is relatively cheap: currently £4.05 per week.

However, *Class 4* contributions are effectively another form of income tax, being 6.3 per cent of earnings between £5,450 and £18,200. Liability for Class 4 will not arise unless the earner is resident for income tax purposes. The definition of residence and ordinary residence for national insurance contributions is more or less the same as for income tax, and therefore a self-employed earner should carefully ensure that he is not resident when he goes to work abroad.

14.9 The next stage of the journey

NIC is an important tax. It brings in more revenue to the Treasury than any other tax apart from income tax. It must not be ignored when a UK company begins to expand into Europe and individuals are posted from the UK to Europe and vice versa.

We have now looked at various types of UK taxes when a UK company embarks on the journey into Europe. We have considered direct taxes, in particular corporation tax. We have looked at the indirect taxes of VAT and customs duty. We have also looked at the taxes that apply to individuals, in particular income tax and national insurance contributions. We have even briefly considered inheritance tax. We have also looked at NIC in its form as a tax on companies.

The importance of international tax planning should now be obvious. It is essential that any outward investment into Europe is correctly structured so as to minimise overall tax rates, both in the UK and overseas, and possibly in third countries as well.

The next part of the book looks at the important question of raising finance for the export trade or outward investment.

PART 2

RAISING FINANCE

15

Export Finance and Insurance

15.1 The middle passage

We have now reached the middle passage of our journey. Part 1 dealt with international tax planning. Part 3 will deal with management monitoring of the overseas operation. Here in Part 2, we will deal with the vital question of how a UK company can finance an export trade or outward investment. Also covered are the subjects of how to be paid from abroad, the various documents that may be encountered in transnational business, grants, exchange controls, and the implications of European monetary union.

Once a UK businessman has established that there is a market for his product or service in Europe, he has to establish a method of financing the export trade. It is important to match the correct type of finance to the particular circumstances of the UK company's European expansion drive. In this regard the advice of a bank is absolutely essential. Banking transactions are far more complex for pure export than for transfers intra-group, eg between a UK parent and its European subsidiary. That is because there is an element of risk and lack of trust, and especially difficulties in enforcement, in exporting to third parties which do not exist on internal transfers of funds. External export trade usually needs to be accompanied by insurance.

15.2 Export finance and insurance generally

Over the years many sophisticated techniques have been developed by the banks to provide suitable finance. Banks will normally lend to finance export trade, but will usually require confirmation that the debts have been insured before doing so.

The government has developed its own export finance insurance service, the Export Credits Guarantee Department (ECGD). This is a separate government department currently responsible to the Secretary of State for Trade and Industry, but which is in the course of being given greater autonomy within the public sector, possibly in preparation for privatisation.

ECGD provides insurance for three main categories of risk:

- creditworthiness of the buyer
- transfer risk
- political risk

ECGD will operate within the guidelines contained in the Berne Union of credit insurers. If a bank is lending to a UK company to finance the European operation, it will usually collateralise its loan by an assignment of the insurance cover provided by ECGD.

Transfer risk relates to the difficulty in transferring money out of countries which may not have a sophisticated banking system like that which exists in Western Europe. This would be particularly relevant with respect to Eastern Europe. Obviously both Western and Eastern Europe could provide bad debts. The creditworthiness of the European buyer must be assessed by the UK seller, and this is one of the factors to be taken into account when fixing risk insurance premium levels.

Careful attention must be paid to the political and economic conditions in the country to which export will be made. This is unlikely to be a problem with most countries in Western Europe but, again, could be a problem in Eastern Europe, particularly in the current fluid situation. The British Overseas Trade Board will be able to supply relevant information. In addition the exporter's bank should be able to provide up-to-date reports on economic conditions, import regulations and exchange controls.

15.3 ECGD insurance for exporters

ECGD provides many different types of insurance for exporters. It is essential to match the correct insurance with the relevant risk.

Where trade will be conducted over a number of years with a similar range of goods and services and with regular buyers with a wide spread of risk, ECGD will provide a *comprehensive insurance policy.* There is a *Comprehensive Short Term Guarantee* policy providing cover for goods exported on credit terms of up to 180 days. Under such a policy the UK company can insure against non-payment for goods from the date of a contract, even prior to the goods being exported ('the pre-credit risk') provided that the goods are to be exported within 12 months of the date of the contract. ECGD need only be informed if there are substantial delays in payments or when an event occurs which is likely to cause a loss. The UK company will ensure that its debts from each European buyer are kept below a pre-agreed limit. Normally ECGD would require its pre-agreement to a substantial line of credit to a new European customer, or an increase in credit to an existing customer.

The Supplemental (Extended Terms) Guarantee policy is available for goods sold on credit terms in excess of six months – normally heavy engineering goods. It is usually available only to exporters already in possession of a comprehensive short-term guarantee policy. Because of the large size of individual transactions of this nature, the supplemental (extended terms) guarantee will normally have to be agreed on an individual contract by contract basis with the ECGD. Credit will not normally be extended beyond five years, and again the goods must be delivered within two years.

Specific policies are available. This type of policy is normally appropriate to very large, single exports such as large items of industrial equipment. Specific policies must be agreed in writing with the ECGD at the time that the contracts are being negotiated with the European importer.

15.4 Export finance from banks

Banks provide a prime source of export finance.

Medium term bank guarantees (supplier credit). In many cases exports of heavy capital goods require a UK exporter to include credit terms as part of the sales package. Credit terms of between two and five years are often offered. The exporter will normally arrange an overdraft facility with his bank, backed by an ECGD guarantee. The UK company will pay interest at a fixed rate for the period that the overdraft is in existence. Negotiable instruments such as Bills of Exchange will be necessary to enable effective payment.

Buyer credit guarantees and lines of credit. A UK bank can lend to the overseas buyer. Normally banks will only deal in contracts of more than £1 million, and the terms of the loan would normally be five years in length. The loan can be denominated in any currency. The loan could be made in low interest rate currencies (LIRCS). This is a recent development and an exporter should meet with his bank before entering into negotiations with the European importer.

Tender to contract cover. ECGD will insure to a certain extent against exchange losses during the period between tendering and signing the contract. Many contracts will be denominated in a currency other than sterling, introducing an exchange risk.

Smaller exports scheme. Many banks have schemes for companies with relatively small export turnovers, typically in the region of £0.5–£2 million. Cash will usually be available on shipment against the relevant documents, relieving a relatively small exporter from the administrative burden of collecting payment from his European customers. This also has the advantage of extending credit to the European buyers up to 180 days, making the UK company's goods or services more attractive. Most banks will offer a smaller exports scheme only if ECGD cover is available under the exporter's own policy. As an alternative, 'umbrella' cover may be available, eg Unicol of Lloyds, for a fee under a master policy with ECGD taken out by the umbrella insurer.

Confirming house facilities. If an exporter exports only occasionally, and does not wish to be involved in the administrative burden of negotiating complex and unusual financial arrangements with the overseas customer, and if the exporter would prefer not to be involved in direct negotiations with ECGD, he may wish to utilise a confirming house facility provided by his bank. For a fee the confirming house will pay the exporter on shipment against presentation of the shipping documents. This removes the risk to the exporter.

Euro currency loans. If the overseas buyer requires finance, a UK bank may be willing to provide a loan through the euro-currency market. The loan will normally have to be repaid within the life of the related ECGD credit.

Bond support. ECGD may be able to guarantee banks to enable those banks to issue *tender bonds, performance bonds* and *advance payment bonds* for certain specific types of UK export trade. The exporter will be able to 'call' the bond (on demand) without having to prove that the importer has failed to comply with the terms of the contract.

Pre-shipment finance. The exporter's UK bank may be willing to provide pre-shipping finance at commercial rates to the exporter. This may relieve cash-flow problems during the period between signing the contract and commencing manufacture and/or selling.

15.5 Export houses

Small or medium-sized UK companies may wish to make use of an *export house.* Some export houses buy goods and will then sell them in Europe through their own organisation. This will eliminate the complications of documentation and being paid from abroad. Other export houses only deal with the documentation on behalf of the small exporter. Some specialist confirming houses act on behalf of the European importer, but they will undertake to guarantee that the UK exporter receives payment on shipment of the goods. Export houses tend to specialise in a particular type of product or market and therefore they have niche knowledge which can be very valuable. It is important that the exporter is matched with the correct export house. Export houses will usually have close relations with banks and therefore they will be able to arrange tailored packages of finance and credit for the UK exporter. Other export houses are effectively factors, and will buy the export debts off the UK company subject to certain conditions, at a discount.

We have looked at how a UK company can finance an export trade, and also insure the risk of its foreign debts. But what happens if a UK company goes further than mere export and establishes an overseas subsidiary? This requires finance of a different order. The next Chapter looks at how a UK company can finance a European branch or subsidiary.

16

Financing a European Branch or Subsidiary

16.1 Introduction

We have looked at the finance and insurance of export trade. When a UK company goes further than mere exporting and begins to set up a substantial presence overseas, consideration must be given as to how it will finance its overseas branch or subsidiary. It is always easier to raise finance before a project commences, rather than to meet existing liabilities. Planning is essential.

16.2 Internal finance

The UK company could finance the overseas operation through internally passing funds in the form of loans or shares. The tax implications have been discussed in some detail. The loan could be denominated either in sterling, or in the foreign currency of the European operation or, exceptionally, in ECU or a third country currency. The shares could be ordinary shares, or preference shares which if they are redeemable provide ease of repayment, although redemption may have overseas tax implications.

Management of the UK company needs to think about what proportion of finance needs to be internal as opposed to external. This depends on the type of borrowing, the cashflow and profit trend of the business, and the nature of the UK and European business assets. The impact of further interest payments on external borrowings in terms of the effect on the profit and loss account, and the ability of the UK company to raise further finance for other matters, must also be considered.

16.3 External finance

If the overseas operation requires further finance than can be provided internally within the group, it must look to external sources for further finance. Usually the UK company's bank will be the first port of call. The local correspondent bank of the UK bank will be the next stop if local borrowings are required.

It is important that the terms of the borrowing are matched with the cash-flow. For example, it is inadvisable to take out a five-year loan to construct a building which will be used for 25 years, unless the cash-flow generated from the building will allow the UK company to repay the loan. A longer-term or permanent loan would be required under those circumstances. As we have already seen, the question of whether loans are permanent or not can affect the taxation of foreign exchange gains (see Chapter 10). On the other hand a three- to five-year loan from a bank would be suitable to finance the purchase of a large item of plant, or even the acquisition of a new subsidiary. Such an investment would produce cash-flow which would match the repayment terms of the loan.

The simplest form of further external finance would be a bank overdraft. The UK bank would normally seek a fixed charge over specific assets, and/or a floating charge over all the assets of the group. A UK company should be aware of providing too much security, because this will reduce its ability to negotiate new borrowings in the future as the operations both in the UK and overseas expand. As always, UK manager/owners should attempt to avoid giving personal guarantees, and the UK parent should try to avoid giving guarantees to the overseas subsidiary as that will tend to negate the advantage of limited liability.

It is vital that the level of bank borrowings are controlled as the UK and overseas businesses grow. Good relations with the lending bank manager are obviously essential. The UK company must always stay within its agreed bank overdraft limits. Management accounts (and audited accounts) should be provided when demanded. Forecasts and cash-flows must be realistic, and the UK company must predict when additional finance would be required.

The parent company's UK bank may lend to the UK company, which will then pass those funds on to the subsidiary in the form of loans or shares. This has the effect of causing an interest deduction to arise in the UK rather than overseas. Very often this will be useful in the opening years of the overseas operation, as there will be taxable profits in the UK but not overseas. The normal criteria by which UK banks lend to UK companies will apply with respect to monies passing to the overseas operation. The bank will look at:

- management
- the business (both in the UK and overseas)
- the return
- the bank's exit in terms of repayment of the loan.

It is vital to ensure from the beginning that the overseas subsidiary is adequately capitalised. As the overseas operation expands, the internally generated profits, both UK and overseas, must be sufficient to allow for further expansion without continual extra borrowings leading to continually higher interest costs. The more rapid the growth, the greater the need for share capital.

Irrespective of whether a loan is sought from a local bank or a large international institution, it is essential that the application for the loan is submitted in a well prepared, concise yet comprehensive and attractive presentation. Professional advice is essential, and the corporate finance departments of firms of accountants should be involved. Among the matters contained in a presentation would be:

- background to the business
- shareholders
- departures from the norm in the Memorandum and Articles of Association
- description of goods or services sold
- market
- strengths, weaknesses, opportunities and threats
- management organisation
- accounting systems and policies
- significant contingent liabilities such as unsettled litigation
- details of existing borrowings and security given
- latest accounts
- profit projections
- cash-flows

- new projects
- details of matter for which loan is required
- interest terms
- currency of the loan
- repayment terms
- effect on cash-flows
- sensitivity of assumptions on which forecasts are made

16.4 European Investment Bank

Larger projects can be financed with loans from international institutions such as the EC itself, the World Bank and European Investment Bank. For example, the European Commission has adopted a five-year plan beginning in 1989 and ending in 1994 to provide financial support for small and medium-sized companies through 24 independently operated 'seed funds'. Where Business Innovation Centres (BICs) are available, the aid will usually be channelled through them.

The European Investment Bank is the EC's own development bank. It was established in 1958 and is funded and managed by the member states. It has a triple 'A' rating in international finance. The bank makes no profit, and charges no fees for arranging loans.

It was established with the aim of helping to finance projects in both the private and the public sector. Loans are for capital investment in industry, infrastructure, and energy provided they are in the general interest of the EC. Funds for industrial development are largely restricted to the less prosperous regions of the Community. Funds are more generally available for large infrastructure projects of interest to the Community and there is a particular emphasis on environmental projects, and investments in advanced technology. The bank has arrangements through an Agency Loan system for smaller loans to be available to small and medium-sized companies. Anyone with a suitable project can apply but direct loans start at about $1 million, are available in most currencies including ECU's, or a cocktail of currencies, and interest rates will reflect the rate at which the bank borrows.

16.5 Local borrowing

The advantages of local borrowing are that the interest can normally be paid gross, and there are no thin-capitalisation restrictions. However sometimes local borrowing is circumscribed by exchange control provisions. Very often the local bank will want the UK company either to guarantee the foreign borrowing (in which case the subsidiary should pay an arm's-length guarantee fee back to its parent under the UK's transfer pricing rules), or exceptionally it may even require a back-to-back deposit.

16.6 Venture capital

Venture capital can be obtained from several different sources. Some could be obtained from the existing shareholders of the UK company. Some could be obtained from external sources, such as 3i plc. In this country the clearing banks rarely take share capital in their client companies, although it is much more common overseas in countries such as Germany.

A UK company can also raise finance for major acquisitions through the issue of new shares, to wealthy individuals via a merchant bank, or to financial institutions including 3i plc. Shares could be ordinary shares, preference shares, redeemable preference shares, convertible preference shares or redeemable convertible preference shares, or the UK company could grant options over shares.

16.7 Minority shareholdings

There are advantages and disadvantages in bringing in minority shareholding finance. It gives away independence and flexibility, which are highly prized in small to medium-sized companies, many of which are owned by a single individual. He may have little or no experience of working as a partner. On the other hand he will have gained a powerful new business partner who will be available for help and advice, and who may be experienced in expansion into Europe.

It may be the case that help and advice is better obtained through professionals, which then does not involve giving away part ownership, from which part management may then follow.

16.8 Joint ventures and partnerships

In Chapter 11 we looked at the tax implications of joint ventures and partnerships. One of the reasons for undertaking such joint ventures was that one of the partners may have finance and the other partner the expertise.

A joint venture is an effective method of financing one-off transactions without giving up the independence enjoyed by an owner/manager who owns 100 per cent of his company. It is an extremely flexible form of doing business, allowing different ownership and different profit-sharing arrangements to be undertaken with respect to different deals. The EC has several different schemes to encourage joint ventures and partnerships within the Community.

The Venture Consort Pilot Scheme is intended to encourage the growth of small and medium-sized companies by forming transnational syndicates of venture capitalists. Support is available for full members of the European Venture Capital Association (EVCA). *Eurotech Capital* is a scheme designed specifically for small and medium-sized companies promoting transnational higher-technology projects (THTPs). *EC research funding* is available to co-finance research programmes which involve transnational cooperation. Its aim is to promote European integration and to make research more effective within the EC by minimising wasteful duplicate effort.

16.9 Eurobonds

The raising of finance through Eurobonds is usually undertaken only by substantial UK companies. Eurobonds are a device whereby the bonds, which may be bought and sold on European stock exchanges, are taken up by investors (who may or may not be UK resident) who are then paid gross. Normally a UK company would need to withhold tax on interest paid abroad (unless there was a double tax treaty between the UK and the country of residence of the bondholder, and the bondholder had filed the relevant form with the Inspector of Foreign Dividends), but Eurobond interest may be paid gross.

16.10 Public companies

If the UK company is quoted on the full stock exchange or the unlisted securities market (USM) then new shares can be issued by way of a rights issue. Even private UK companies can raise finance by issuing new shares to outside investors willing to provide equity, although, again, that is obviously a drastic step for the situation of a UK company which is wholly owned by its chief executive. Sometimes a UK company will look to flotation, and subsequent sale on to a large company as an exit route. This may have been the sole reason for undertaking overseas investment in the first place, ie the UK company embarked on a strategy involving an exit route of a capital gain as opposed to an income stream of profits.

16.11 Acceptance credits

If the UK company merely has a short-term requirement for temporary finance, for example to meet a large export order or because the overseas subsidiary only requires a single injection of working capital, a merchant bank can arrange for an *acceptance credit*. This is a Bill of Exchange drawn on a merchant bank which is guaranteed by the UK company's normal bank. The Bill of Exchange can be sold in the market at a discount reflecting current interest rates. When the export order is paid, the UK company will repay its bank, which will then meet the Bill of Exchange. Acceptance credits may provide a cheaper form of financing than bank overdrafts for short-term finance over £50,000.

16.12 Interest rate strategy

The question of what currency the loan should be is a separate issue on which the advice of a bank should be sought.

There is plainly an exchange risk in trading overseas and this is discussed in greater detail in the next chapter. With the entry of the UK into the ERM the tendency of some UK companies to borrow in foreign currencies, typically the deutschemark, and to pay at the lower deutschemark interest rates, may well increase. The normal downside risk of such a borrowing – the higher repayments were the pound to fall against the deutschemark – will now be much reduced since the amount by which the pound can depreciate against the deutschemark is strictly limited to 6 per cent, reducing to 2.25 per cent. However, it is not impossible for the pound to undergo further changes in parity, as did the French franc in the five years following its entry into the ERM in 1979. The normal disadvantage of not matching a currency in which income is received, against the currency in which interest is paid therefore partly disappears. This is an interesting strategy discussed further in Chapter 21 on European monetary union and related matters.

As can be seen, the typical ways of raising finance are fairly obvious. If the UK company has funds of its own it could pass these to the overseas operation in the form of loans or shares. Further finance can be provided by local borrowings. Failing that, the UK company will need to convince a bank to lend to it, so that it can then pass the funds down to its subsidiary, or obtain finance from some other outside source.

The next chapter deals with the very important subject of how a UK company is going to be paid for export trade, or intra-group trading with its subsidiary. Even the repatriation of profits from a subsidiary by way of a dividend has certain difficulties when the subsidiary is located in a different country from the UK parent. There is also the exchange risk to be considered.

17
Being Paid

17.1 Introduction

Obviously, it is essential for a UK company dealing with foreign customers to ensure that debts can be easily paid. The three main methods of paying for export trade are open account, documentary collection and documentary credit.

17.2 Open account

The UK company will be paid by *cheque*, *electronic transfer* or by *International Money Transfer*. However this is subject to a high degree of risk. The cheque could bounce or the buyer could default and it would be expensive and administratively difficult to sue the importer in a foreign country. This method of payment is best when there is a high degree of mutual trust built up over a number of years, or the amounts involved are very small. It is also used on transfers of funds between European subsidiaries and the UK parent where the risk of default is not relevant.

17.3 Documentary collection

This is normally carried on through a bank. All the relevant documents will be delivered to a UK bank which will then send them to its correspondent bank in Europe. The importer will then obtain the documents from that bank only if he pays there and then, or accepts a *Bill of Exchange*.

17.4 Bills of Exchange

The legal definition of a Bill of Exchange is an unconditional order in writing:

- addressed by one person (the drawer)
- to another (the drawee)
- signed by the person giving it (the drawer)
- requiring the person to whom it is addressed (the drawee, who when he signs becomes the acceptor) to pay
- on demand or at a fixed or determinable future time
- a sum certain in money
- to, or to the order of, a specified person or to bearer (the payee).

Put another way, a Bill of Exchange is a demand for the payment of a particular amount of money on a specific date. It will either be drawn *at sight* or *at usance*. At sight means immediately, and at usance means payment must be made at a future specified date. If a Bill of Exchange is issued at usance and the European importer defaults, the same difficulties regarding collection of the debt would be in point as with open account. The exporter will have the expense and inconvenience of unpaid goods being returned to the UK. This is expensive in terms of transport costs at any time, but is especially serious with perishable goods such as food. Insurance is available to guard against this eventuality. Bills of Exchange are also sometimes referred to as 'sight drafts' when payment must be made immediately by the importer on presentation of the Bill of Exchange, or 'time drafts' which means the importer will pay at a future specified time.

17.5 Discounting

Bills of Exchange can be sold to Discount Houses. Generally the bill will be sold at slightly less than its face value; hence the expression 'discounting'. The amount of the discount is a function of the level of risk and the time between paying the UK company and the Bill maturing. It is a useful method of laying off a risk by a UK company, in exchange for receiving slightly less money, and improving cash flow.

17.6 Irrevocable documentary credit

This is the most secure method of payment. The European importer will arrange for his bank ('the issuing bank') to issue a documentary credit. His bank will undertake to make payment to the UK company at another bank ('the advising bank' – usually the UK company's bank) on presentation of documents specified in the documentary credit. This is conditional on the documents presented being *precisely* as specified in the documentary credit. The UK company may arrange for a UK bank to *confirm* the documentary credit. A UK bank will join in the undertaking to confirm the credit and honour the obligations, even if the issuing bank does not. Confirmation would usually be relevant in circumstances under which a UK exporter was unsure of the substance of the issuing bank, or if there were political or currency problems in the country of import. It depends on the creditworthiness of the overseas bank, and is especially relevant to Eastern Europe. The resulting *letter of credit* is known as a *confirmed letter of credit.* If the bank's guarantee is irrevocable the resulting letter of credit is known as a *confirmed irrevocable letter of credit.* This confers the greatest level of assurance to a UK exporter. In practice nowadays nearly all credits are confirmed irrevocable letters of credit. Most UK banks will not advise an exporter to be paid on any other basis.

Documentary acceptance drafts (*D/A*) allow goods to be released to an importer once he accepts the obligation to pay the UK exporter. This is suitable for importers in which the UK company has a degree of trust. If there is less trust, the UK company can ask for payment on payment drafts (*D/P*) which means that the UK exporter must be paid before the goods are released.

17.7 Avalising

As an alternative to documentary credits, a UK exporter could consider 'avalising'. This is a technique under which an exporter exports goods, and then after the event bears risk for a period of time until a bank underwrites the Bill of Exchange, in exchange for a fee. Avalisation is a half-way house between no bank guarantee and a full guarantee. Its advantages for the exporter are quickness, simplicity, no detailed checking of documents, and cheapness. It is widely used in the EC, but until now has not been widely used in the UK. After 1993 it may become more widespread in this country.

17.8 Forward foreign exchange market

Rates for forward foreign exchange are based on a mathematical calculation of interest rate differentials and should not reflect the feelings of the market or of an individual dealer as to what the rate might be in the future.

Under a *forward foreign exchange contract* the UK company will sell or buy a specified amount of foreign currency, normally simultaneously with entering into a contract to sell goods or services overseas. The currency will be delivered at a pre-agreed date, which will be the date that the UK company expects to receive a foreign currency receipt. The risk is thus removed, but either at a fee or for a charge in the form of an exchange rate differential. The exchange rate differential could be either a premium or a discount according to the currency involved and the market situation at the time. There is therefore an opportunity for the UK exporter to realise a gain or the risk of a loss. Fees are usually charged on smaller forward contracts. The normal types of forward foreign exchange contract are 'fixed' as described above, and 'option' where foreign exchange will be delivered to the UK exporter between a range of dates on completion of the contract.

17.9 Currency option contracts

Currency option contracts are an insurance against exchange rate changes. The UK company will buy a currency option which will give it the right to buy and sell a specific amount of currency at a given exchange rate at some time in the future, but unlike a forward foreign exchange contract it is not obliged to exercise the option. The UK company may let the option lapse. The option contract is paid in the form of an up-front premium. This ensures against an adverse rate movement, within limits, while it may be possible to profit from a favourable currency exchange movement.

17.10 Swaps

The UK exporter and the European importer may agree to a currency swap. This is often the case where the UK company already owns an overseas subsidiary and it is selling to the overseas subsidiary prior to the overseas subsidiary selling on locally. The UK company and the overseas subsidiary reach an agreement to swap currencies now, and then to swap them back at some time in the future.

Another type of swap is the *credit swap*. The UK company, instead of lending to the local subsidiary, may make foreign currency available to the bank of the subsidiary. The local bank will then lend in local currency to the subsidiary. When the subsidiary repays the local bank the UK company will be repaid by the bank in sterling (or some other hard currency). This is another method of financing a subsidiary.

17.11 Government debt

In some cases, especially when dealing with Eastern Europe, UK companies can purchase government debt at a discount. In return, the foreign government will make local currency available at advantageous rates.

17.12 Currency of payment – the risk

In any form of international trade, either the importer or the exporter will have to carry a currency exchange risk. If the importer agrees to pay in sterling he will bear the risk, otherwise it must be passed to a bank at a cost. If the UK exporter agrees to sell in a foreign currency then he will bear the risk. UK exporters, given the volatile history of the pound, may prefer to 'hedge' any potential exchange gain or loss. This can be done by using the forward foreign exchange market to buy (or more usually sell) in the case of exporting or outward investment, foreign currency or sterling, at a price given at the time of purchase for future delivery.

The importance of the forward market is to protect a UK company against an adverse move in the exchange rate. Effectively, the rate of exchange for a transaction can be fixed, and the risk is then passed on to the bank, but at a fee. There is normally a difference between *spot* and *forward* rates which is known as the *spread in the forward market*. The width of the spread is symptomatic of the expectation of the level of fluctuations between currencies.

Once a UK company begins to operate overseas, whether by export or outward investment, it will encounter the risk of foreign exchange loss or the opportunity of foreign exchange gain. With the UK's entry into the ERM (see Chapter 21), these risks and opportunities are now greatly reduced *vis à vis* the other EC currencies.

17.13 Exchange rates

An *exchange rate* is the amount of currency needed to buy one unit of another currency. They fluctuate constantly.

Exchange rates may be quoted as *spot rates* or *forward rates*. The spot rate applies for an immediate transaction. Forward rates are those quoted for *future delivery*, that is a rate quoted for conversion into a foreign currency in the future. There are also *cross rates* where an exchange rate between two currencies is calculated by virtue of their rates against a more commonly traded currency, typically dollars or sterling. This is less usual in Europe than outside, but may apply to Eastern Europe.

Rates may be quoted in *direct* terms or *indirect* terms. A direct quote would be £0.35 = DM1. An indirect quote would be DM2.85 = £1. In international trade there are two rates of exchange: the *bid rate* and the *offer rate*. The bid rate is the rate at which a bank buys foreign exchange from a UK company. The offer rate is the rate at which the bank will sell foreign currency to a UK company. A UK company which converted £1m into lire and then the next instant reconverted the lire back into pounds would lose a significant proportion of its £1m, say £20,000.

17.14 The importance of documentation

Having looked at the question of how a UK company can be paid for foreign debts incurred in an export trade, or from its foreign subsidiary, it will be obvious that the *documents* involved in doing foreign business are of vital importance. This is a point that has already been covered in Part 1 when looking at, for example, VAT and customs duty. The various documents needed to trade with and within Europe are the subject of the next chapter.

18
Documentation

18.1 Introduction

Exporting will involve a substantial amount of paperwork. It is essential in exporting, particularly goods, that every document is in perfect order. Many VAT and Customs duty reliefs depend on the documentation being in good order.

18.2 Contract

This should be drawn up with the help of the UK company's lawyers. The importance of correct wording has already been illustrated. The contracting parties will be listed. The law governing the contract will be stated. An arbitration and disputes procedure will be laid down. The contract must specify the currency of the deal. It should make clear which party will bear any withholding taxes. It must ensure that royalties will not be part of the price of goods, otherwise extra customs duty could be payable. It must define the terms of shipping, so that it is clear when ownership of the goods passes. Payment and delivery dates must be scheduled. The burden of obtaining permissions should rest with one or other of the parties. Losses may be paid for only when used. The UK company may seek protection of its company or brand name. There may be anti-competition or secrecy clauses. The contract may contain extensive warranties and indemnities. The contract may be an informal letter or a detailed document. Whatever its format, legal advice is essential.

18.3 Bill of Lading

A Bill of Lading relates to transport by sea, and is a document showing title to the goods. The Bill of Lading will show details such as the name of the ship, the ports of embarkation and destination, the goods, and the terms and conditions of carriage. Bills of Lading are usually issued in sets of two or three originals: one set will be sent to the importer, so that he may claim the goods when they arrive. One method of helping the UK company's cash-flow of the export trade is for the UK exporter to retain title to the goods by not releasing the Bill of Lading until payment is received, thereby providing an incentive for speedy payment by the importer.

18.4 Invoices

Many countries have a legal requirement as to what information must be contained in an invoice. For example in the EC invoices will generally have to bear a VAT number. Invoices issued by a UK company will carry the name and address of the UK company, its VAT number, the address of the buyer, a description of the goods, details of the price and shipment terms. Sometimes invoices may have to be legalised or notarised by the relevant embassy in the UK. Goods may not be cleared through the overseas Customs if this formality has not been carried out, because that may be the method of levying import duties overseas.

18.5 Certificate of Origin

A Certificate of Origin of goods being shipped abroad may be required. Very often such a form needs to be certified by a Chamber of Commerce in the UK, and possibly legalised or notarised by the relevant overseas Embassy. It is important in determining customs duty rates. There is of course no customs duty on intra-EC trade.

18.6 Certificate of Insurance

Depending on the terms of shipping, the UK company may be responsible for insuring the goods until they pass into the ownership of the European importer. A Certificate of Insurance may be required by the overseas importer to ensure that the goods have been insured at the time that they come into his ownership. This, in turn, will depend on the terms under which the goods are shipped. When a Certificate of Insurance is not called for by the European importer, it is worth considering the implications of relying upon insurance being covered by the importer. What proof does the exporter have that the goods are insured? If the importer does not or cannot pay, the goods will revert to the exporter. If they are not insured by the importer then it is the UK exporter who will be at risk (for example the goods may be perishable). For a modest premium an exporter may take out 'seller's interest' insurance to protect himself from loss should the buyer's promised insurance prove ineffective.

18.7 Waybills

This may be used as a substitute for a Bill of Lading. It will not be necessary to present a Bill of Lading in order to obtain release of the goods. All waybills carry the disadvantage that the UK exporter is unable to retain legal ownership of the goods until payment is received. In some instances a bank in the importer's country will guarantee the importer's liability.

- *Sea waybills*
  If the goods are accompanied by a sea waybill then they will be released automatically.
- *Air waybill/air consignment note*
  This is the air equivalent of the sea waybill.
- *Road waybill*
  This is the road transport equivalent of the sea waybill.
- *Rail consignment note*
  This is the rail transport equivalent of the sea waybill.
- *Combined transport waybill*
  This is the 'multi-modal transport' equivalent of the sea waybill.

18.8 Price terms

If goods are being transferred, it will be necessary to show when goods leave the ownership of the exporter and enter the ownership of the importer. This will depend on the terms of trade. The International Chamber of Commerce has codified a list of such arrangements ('Inco Terms'). These could be as follows:

- *Ex-works*. Once the goods have left the factory they belong to the importer.

- *FAS* (Free Alongside). Goods leave ownership of the exporter once they are next to the ship in the UK port.
- *FOB* (Free on Board). Goods leave the ownership of the UK exporter once they are loaded on to a ship in the UK port.
- *FOA*. The air equivalent of FOB.
- *FOR*. The rail equivalent of FOB or FOA.
- *C&F* (Cost and Freight). This includes the cost of sea carriage to the importer's port. Ownership changes when the ship ties up in the foreign port.
- *CIF* (Cost Insurance Freight). Again, the goods remain in the ownership of the exporter until they reach the importer's port. However, in this case the cost will include insurance cover during shipment.
- *FRC* (Free Carrier). The exporter will be liable for costs up to the delivery of goods to the importer at a named point. At that point ownership changes.
- *CIP* (Carriage and Insurance Paid). Costs including insurance will be borne by the exporter to a named destination. At that named destination ownership changes.
- *Delivery*. Costs will be borne by the exporter until the goods are in the ownership of the importer at the importers' own premises, at which point in time ownership will change.

18.9 Accounting

The importance of when ownership changes is that the goods will leave the stock and work-in-progress of the accounts of the UK company and become a sale. This means that in many instances a profit can be taken. It is of vital accounting significance. Imagine a UK exporter of machinery exporting goods throughout the world. In determining when for tax and accounting purposes a sale is made on goods which may have just left his factory, be loaded on board a ship, be in transit or have arrived at his customer's premises, it is vital to ascertain when he has actually sold the goods and when they remain in his ownership.

18.10 Other aspects of financing European operations

We have looked at how to raise finance for an export trade and an overseas subsidiary, how to be paid and the documentation involved. The rest of Part 2 deals with the related questions of the grants available to a UK company exporting and investing overseas, exchange controls still in force in Europe and, in the longer term, the effects of European monetary union on questions pertaining to financing the UK company's European business.

19
Grants

19.1 Introduction

A variety of grants and assistance is made available to a UK company looking to export or invest directly abroad by the British Overseas Trade Board (BOTB), an arm of the Department of Trade and Industry (DTI). Almost invariably, the investee country also offers some form of assistance by way of grants, subsidies or tax concessions, although in some cases this is limited to investment in specially designated areas (eg the Mezzogiorno of Italy). In the case of the European Community, additional grants can often be obtained from the Community itself.

Grants fall into several categories:-

- business and technical advisory grants (consultancy schemes);
- employment and training;
- export promotion;
- innovation (including research and development);
- investments;
- general.

It is essential that grant applications are made through professional organisations such as IGS or Lloyds Bank Grantfinder who know the correct formats, people to approach etc. (see Appendix F, paragraph F.4).

19.2 DTI grants

The DTI has two very important grants which a UK company may wish to take up, especially when implementing a management monitoring information technology system (see Part 3: Performance monitoring).

The first is a grant of up to two-thirds (assisted areas) or half (non-assisted areas) against total costs to pay consultants to advise on choosing the best system. The importance of choosing the correct system is obviously vital, and is discussed in greater detail in Part 3.

The second grant is a £15,000 Business Training Grant from the Training Council in order to train employees of the UK company to use the system!

19.3 BOTB grants

The British Overseas Trade Board (BOTB) acts as a central point for any firm considering export or wanting to increase its existing export market. Assistance is provided both financially and in the form of expert advice and guidance, contacts and information. BOTB can make financial assistance available to overseas department stores towards the cost incurred in promoting UK goods in their stores through advertising, instore displays, exhibitions and personality visits. Useful information on many aspects of exporting can be found in BOTB's *Export Intelligence Service and Trade Promotions Guide.*

19.4 BOTB contact points

Northern Ireland
Industrial Development Board
IDB House
64 Chichester Street
Belfast
BT1 4JX
Tel: 0232 233233

Wales
Welsh Office Industry Department
Cathays Park
Cardiff
CF1 2NQ
Tel: 0222 823185

Scotland
Scottish Export Office
Alhambra House
45 Waterloo Street
Glasgow
G2 6AT
Tel: 041–248 2855

North East
Stanegate House
2 Groat Market
Newcastle upon Tyne
NE1 1YN
Tel: 091–232 4722

North West
Sunley Tower
Piccadilly Plaza
Manchester
M1 4BE
Tel: 061–236 2171

Yorkshire and Humberside
Priestley House
Park Row
Leeds
LS1 5LF
Tel: 0532 443171

East Midlands
Severns House
20 Middle Pavement
Nottingham
NG1 7DW
Tel: 0602 506181

West Midlands
Ladywood House
Stephenson Street
Birmingham
B2 4DT
Tel: 021–631 6181

South East
Bridge Place
88–89 Eccleston Square
London
SW1V 1PT
Tel: 071–215 5000

South West
The Pithay
Bristol
BS1 2PB
Tel: 0272 272666

Advice on specific markets:

Western Europe: 071–215 5336
Eastern Europe: 071–215 5258

19.5 Export Marketing Research Scheme (EMRS)

This scheme can provide assistance for research projects relating to export markets. Grants can be provided in any of the ways detailed below. In all cases the giving of the grant is discretionary.

Using consultants

A grant will be available for up to 50 per cent of the costs of employing consultants to carry out a research assignment in an overseas market. The consultants must be approved by BOTB and competitive quotes must be obtained.

Using in-house researches

BOTB will meet up to 50 per cent of the travel costs of one member of staff with the ability and experience to carry out an export market research project. In addition, up to 50 per cent of an interpreter's fees and a daily allowance may be payable. However, there are two conditions before a grant is available under this heading:

- The grant is available for projects relating to non-EC countries only;

- the research must be of a high standard and involve extensive report writing.

Published research

BOTB will pay for up to one-third of the costs of purchasing published marketing research material. However, it should be noted that Trade Associations can obtain grants of up to two-thirds of the costs if they carry out the research on behalf of an individual firm. There are conditions to be met before grant is available.

- The company, firm or group applying must employ less than 200 people (divisions within companies are not eligible).
- Each firm is allowed support for a maximum of three projects. (This maximum takes into account any projects undertaken since 1 January 1990.)
- Only two projects can be supported per firm within one year.
- Only two published market research reports can be purchased with BOTB support in any one year.
- Only one study per country is allowed.
- Sales and promotional trips are not classified as market research.

For individual companies there is a maximum of £20,000 per project and £40,000 per year in aggregate.

For Trade Associations the amounts are:

First project: 75 per cent of costs up to £60,000
Second project: 66⅔ per cent of costs up to £53,000
Third and any subsequent project: 50 per cent of costs up to £40,000

Further information may be obtained from:

The Association of British Chambers of Commerce
4 Westwood House
Westwood Business Park
Coventry CV4 8HS
Tel: 0203 694484

19.6 Inward and outward missions for exporters' schemes

BOTB can also provide grant support for groups interested in organising events to promote the export of British goods and services. There are two schemes, depending on whether the mission is overseas or in the UK.

Outward missions scheme

BOTB can provide a contribution to missions organised by approved non-profit making bodies or trade organisations towards the travel costs of groups visiting a potential export market. Missions to Western Europe are not eligible. The group must have between 10 and 20 participating members. One representative plus one mission coordinator can be supported, and firms can claim for up to four trips. Applications should be submitted at least six months before the estimated departure date.

Inwards missions scheme

BOTB will provide a Trade Association or other approved body with a grant of up to 50 per cent of the costs of bringing to the UK 10 to 20 businessmen, journalists or others who are able to affect the level of purchase of UK goods and services. The grant covers the following items:

- 50 per cent of travel costs in the UK, interpreters' fees (not translators' fees), average hotel costs in the UK, costs of a reception or dinner, direct economy class return by British carrier. These rates apply to visitors from Western Europe, Cyprus, Finland, Gibraltar, Malta and Yugoslavia.
- 75 per cent of costs of same items for visitors from elsewhere.

Individual delegates can be supported or, alternatively, up to 60 delegates for a single event. Six to eight months are needed for the application procedure. Further information may be obtained from:

British Overseas Trade Board

(1) Fairs and Promotions Board – Tel: 071–212 0093/6277
(2) Inward Missions Section – Tel: 071–212 8758

19.7 Trade fairs and exhibitions for exporters' schemes

There are three schemes operated by the BOTB to provide assistance to UK companies seeking to exhibit abroad.

Joint venture schemes

Display schemes and stands at overseas exhibitions can be made available to UK firms at attractive rates.

First-time exhibitors: 60 per cent discount
Second-time exhibitors: 45 per cent discount
Third-time exhibitors: 25 per cent discount.

Exhibitions must be organised by an approved sponsor, such as a Trade Association or Chamber of Commerce. Applications should be submitted to BOTB at least nine months before the exhibition takes place.

Pavilion schemes

BOTB organises pavilions at various international trade fairs. Fees are as follows:-

First-time exhibitors: 45 per cent of BOTB costs
Second-time exhibitors: 60 per cent of BOTB costs
Third-time exhibitors: 80 per cent of BOTB costs.

Stands are available to individual firms.

All British exhibitions

These are organised by BOTB when sufficient demand exists. Fees are:

For approved sponsors: 55 per cent of BOTB costs
For non-approved sponsors: 60 per cent of BOTB costs.

On all schemes travel grants can be available for events taking place outside Western Europe.

19.8 EC Grants

Many different grants are available from the EC. The principal grants are available from:

- European Regional Development Fund (ERDF)
- European Social Fund (ESF)
  (These first two schemes are not currently of much relevance to UK companies – money under these schemes is administered via the investee country.)
- The Guidance Section of the Agricultural Fund (EAGGF)
- European Coal and Steel Community (ECSC)
- European Investment Bank (EIB)

The funds can be used for a number of different purposes, in particular broad assistance to small and medium-sized companies which are defined as companies employing up to 500 employees with fixed assets of up to £50 million. Grants are available for a number of specific projects including, but not limited to:

- Public works such as roads, telecommunications, airports, ports, inland waterways such as canals, dams, vocational training centres, facilities for transport operators, tourist facilities and advisory and support services for businesses;
- investment in the processing and marketing of food, fish, construction, plant and machinery, computer software, studies and reports;
- recruitment;
- training;
- marketing in agriculture and forestry;
- regional aid schemes.

The rates of grant in the case of ERDF and ESF can vary between 50 per cent of public expenditure and 75 per cent of total cost, but only in certain parts of the EC. These include parts or all of Greece, Spain, French overseas dependencies, Italy, Portugal, Ireland and Northern Ireland. In other geographic areas the rates of ERDF and ESF will be between 25 per cent of total public expenditure and 50 per cent of total cost. There are also specific schemes, such as schemes to assist the regeneration of:

- Ship building areas ('Renaval');
- Coal areas ('Rechar');

- Steel areas ('Resider');
- Research and technology ('Stride');
- The environment ('Envireg');
- Fisheries and agriculture.

Many of the EC grants come on a 'first come, first served' basis, and when the fixed amount allocated for that grant has been utilised no further grants will be available under that heading.

19.9 Other sources of grant

We have looked at UK and EC grants. There are over 500 grants available just from UK sources for companies wishing to export or establish a presence in Europe. In addition there are a vast number of grants from the EC itself. The other major source of grant would be the European country into which the UK company expands. It is essential that detailed professional advice is obtained from specialists, who should have a network of correspondents throughout Europe so that they can advise on grants in the relevant European country, and should also have good contacts with Brussels.

20
Exchange Controls

20.1 The UK position

Since 1979 the UK has had no exchange controls, and since 1987 the Exchange Control Act has not been in force. Accordingly, it will be difficult for the UK to reintroduce exchange controls without at least some warning. Even the Opposition parties have adopted policies of no controls.

20.2 The non-UK position

However, other countries may have exchange control restrictions or other restrictions on inward foreign investment, notwithstanding the worldwide trend for greater freedom of currency movement.

Careful advice should be taken with respect to exchange control restrictions, inward investment and repatriation of profits, foreign investment permissions, or local participation requirements.

By 1993, within the EC there should, of course, be complete freedom of movement of capital – the situation which already exists in the UK. However, at present there are still controls in some EC countries, even more controls in non-EC Western European countries, and a full system of exchange controls in Eastern Europe.

The position with respect to exchange controls as they affect both inward and outward investment in the major European countries outside the former Eastern bloc (for which see Appendix C) is set out below on a country by country basis. Details are based on the position at July 1990; the general movement, both inside and outside the EC, to ease or abolish exchange controls may render the information out of date in a relatively short time. Where future developments are reasonably certain they are referred to, but readers are advised to take advice regarding the latest position.

The position is first given in tabular form and, where further information is necessary, is given under the appropriate country. The table is set out below.

Country	Controls	
	Outward	*Inward*
Austria	No	No
Belgium	No	No
Denmark	No	No
Finland	Yes	Yes
France	No	No
Germany	No	No
Greece	Yes	Yes
Ireland	Yes	Yes
Italy	Yes	Yes
Luxembourg	No	No
Netherlands	No	No
Norway	Yes	Yes
Portugal	Yes	Yes
Spain	Yes	Yes
Sweden	No	No
Switzerland	No	No
UK	No	No

20.3 Austria

Outward: No controls now exist on investment abroad, nor is there any minimum percentage of profits that must be repatriated. Reporting of foreign investment to the Austrian National Bank may still need to be made for statistical purposes.
Inward: There is no restriction as such on inward investment but the Austrian branch of a UK company or an Austrian subsidiary of a UK parent will require prior permission for foreign borrowing from non-banking sources.

20.4 Denmark

Outward: No controls exist on outward investment from Denmark but investments of over DKr 60,000 (£5,320) need to be reported to the National Bank of Denmark.
Inward: No controls exist on inward investment into Denmark.

20.5 Finland

Finland is in the middle of a process of scrapping many of its controls.

Outward: Prior permission from the Bank of Finland is generally no longer required for Finnish resident persons (including companies) wishing to invest abroad. Where permission is required, it is generally granted if the investment is likely to promote Finnish exports. Long-term (ie one year or more) foreign currency borrowings are permitted. The profits of foreign operations must be repatriated, where lawful, to the extent they are not required to finance operations.

Inward: Approval for inward investment need no longer be obtained from the Bank of Finland. Generally, permission is not available for investment by non-residents in Finnish real property, except where it constitutes the fixed assets of a business. Supplier credits and prepayments in respect of Finnish imports from the UK are no longer required.

20.6 Greece

Inward: There are generally no restrictions on foreign direct investment from the EC or on repatriation of earnings and capital. Non-EC investors may import capital freely through the Bank of Greece but free repatriation is only possible for investments registered as 'productive'.

20.7 Ireland

Outward: Strict exchange controls are still operated on investment outside Ireland, although Ireland is committed to abolition *vis-à-vis* the EC by 1993. In the interim, prior permission must be sought from the Central Bank of Ireland, and profits earned abroad must generally be repatriated where the law of the foreign country permits.

Inward: Inward investment in excess of IR£1 million (£912,150) requires prior permission from the Central Bank of Ireland. Permission is usually granted. Approval is also needed for the repatriation of profits, whether by way of dividend or otherwise. These controls are to be removed for investors from the EC by 1993.

20.8 Italy

Outward: Italy is committed to the abolition of all controls *vis-à-vis* the EC by 1993. In the interim permission is not required for direct investment in OECD (Organisation for Economic Cooperation and Development – essentially the industrialised world) countries or for direct investment in entities engaged in the same line of business in non-OECD countries. Investment in foreign holding or financial companies is not considered direct investment.

Inward: There are already few controls over inward investment. Unrestricted repatriation of income and capital is available where investment has taken place in so-called 'productive enterprises'. There are some residuary controls on local borrowings.

20.9 Norway

Outward: It is necessary to buy foreign shares through a Norwegian broker.

Inward: At least half of the board members of a Norwegian resident trading company must be Norwegian residents of a minimum two years' standing. Special approval must be obtained for the purchase or long-term lease of real property or for the acquisition of over 20 per cent of the share capital of an established Norwegian company.

20.10 Portugal

Inward: Foreign direct investment generally requires clearance from the Portuguese Foreign Trade Institute (IECP), but an acquisition of a holding of up to 20 per cent in a Portuguese company is exempt, provided the investor does not intend to establish permanent economic links and is not acquiring direct or indirect control over management. Where foreign currency is involved, prior authorisation by the Central Bank must be obtained. Repatriation is generally unrestricted, provided investment and tax rules have been complied with.

20.11 Spain

Outward: In common with its EC partners, Spain is committed to removing exchange controls *vis-à-vis* the EC by 1993. Meanwhile, outward direct investment still requires verification by the Directorate General of External Transactions (DGTE), and repatriation of profits from abroad, after a reasonable retention for reinvestment in the foreign business, is generally obligatory.

Inward: Inward investment of Pts 25 million (£134,500) or more requires the prior approval of the DGTE. Special controls exist over foreign investment in gaming, defence, the broadcast media and air transport. There are some residuary controls over local borrowings.

20.12 Other currency restrictions

Apart from classical exchange control there are other types of currency restriction, especially in Eastern Europe. Sometimes certain types of income (for example authors' royalties) can only be spent in a foreign currency.

Licensing can be used to allocate foreign exchange to importers based on what a country sees as priorities. Therefore a UK company exporting must ensure that the importer will have access to foreign exchange.

Multiple exchange rates can be used to encourage inward investment and to discourage outward investment. The UK had such a system for many years through the 'dollar premium'. *Import deposits* may be required when a UK company exports abroad. They are often introduced in order to dissuade importers from maintaining high stock levels.

Barter trade. Some countries, again especially in Eastern Europe, follow a system of bartering instead of trading through money. This can take the form of *compensatory trade*, or *counter trade*. For example, some countries such as Spain have in the past insisted that UK companies which buy Spanish companies must in turn export Spanish-made goods into the UK.

In all of these matters advice from banks with experience of international trade is essential.

21

European Aspects of Finance

21.1 The European dimension

Just as there is a European dimension to international tax planning, with European countries' tax systems converging, so in the field of international finance Europe is gradually merging into a single entity.

This can be seen in the use of the ECU (European Currency Unit) as a currency. Whereas the UK has suggested that the ECU should be used alongside national currencies such as sterling, the long-term aim of the Delors plan is that the ECU should *replace* national currencies, and sterling along with other national currencies would disappear.

UK companies can raise loans denominated in ECU to finance export trading or outward investment. They are not common now, but they may be in the future.

Only Greece and Portugal now remain outside the ERM (exchange rate mechanism). By joining the ERM the UK Government hopes to reduce interest rates and inflation, but possibly at the price of either high unemployment in the UK or net emigration. Finally, there is complete monetary union, now seen by some as inevitable. The views of Nicholas Ridley on the effect of a very strong Germany in the event of monetary union are well known. Ironically perhaps, the German Bundesbank also has deep misgivings at this stage.

21.2 ECU

The ECU is a 'basket' currency, composed of weighted amounts of each of the EC member states' currencies. The weighting is based on factors such as GNP, interest rates and the strength of the individual member currencies. Its composition is reviewed every five years.

The EC's institutions have used the ECU as the unit of account in drawing up their budgets since 1978. All Community revenue and expenditure is accounted for in ECU and it is the sole unit of account for fixing and collecting specific customs duties, levies, refunds and other intra-Community payments. The European Investment Bank issues public loans in ECU, thereby contributing to the development of a private capital market in ECU. Several pan-European companies, such as Fiat, use the ECU for internal accounting purposes and show ECU equivalent figures in their public report and accounts. Some European companies quote ECU prices to their non-domestic customers, thus shifting the burden of the exchange rate risk to the customer. The ECU is also being used as a hedging instrument as an alternative to a variety of hedges in individual currencies. UK businesses might also consider operating in ECU for large-scale trade with the USSR and the former Eastern bloc. As payment for larger business projects may be spread over several years, the UK's inflationary pressures might otherwise place them at a disadvantage compared to German or Japanese competitors. For smaller projects, however, it seems that Eastern European customers prefer to deal in US dollars, sterling and other major currencies. The four major UK clearing banks, the Co-operative Bank and TSB all offer ECU banking facilities, as do the London offices of a number of foreign banks.

21.3 ERM

The ERM (or exchange rate mechanism) is an agreement between 10 of the 12 member states (Greece and Portugal excepted) to tie their individual currencies into a fixed band of parities, relative to each other. Changed parities within the ERM require a formal realignment with the agreement of all members. To join the ERM, participants must deposit 20 per cent of their gold and US dollar reserves with the European Monetary Cooperation Fund (EMCF). In exchange, they are credited with ECU. These deposits take the form of revolving three-monthly swaps, requiring members' central banks to make adjustments necessary to maintain the 20 per cent deposit. At the same time, the volume of ECU issued is adjusted for changes in the price of gold and changes in the exchange rates.

21.4 European monetary union

European monetary union, as envisaged by the Delors Report, would involve two aspects. First, the creation of a European Central Bank, to which the central banks of the member states would be subsidiary.

Second, there would be a single European currency like the ECU, which would replace the individual currencies of the member states. The first stage would entail adhesion to the ERM by the remaining two member states – Greece and Portugal. Once the currencies were locked together in the ERM, they could gradually be replaced by a single, common currency. There is general agreement that the single currency would have to be managed by a European Central Bank, in the running of which all member states' central banking authorities would have a say.

If the Delors Report's recommendations were to be fully implemented, EC governments would no longer have access to the monetary printing press, and 'spendthrift' economies would be denied their favourite remedy for overborrowing.

The UK government is well known as an opponent of stages two and three of the Delors report. It has suggested that, instead, there should be a common currency, the existing ECU, used alongside with, but not replacing, the currencies of the individual member states.

21.5 The window of opportunity

The lack of a common EC currency restricts the ability of UK companies to move funds around the Community unhindered, whereas the running of any pan-European business will involve the movement of funds to pay for goods, services, investment and loans. There are already large disparities between the relative costs of financial services. In 1993 and after, new entrants in banking, insurance and factoring should be able to provide cheaper services to the smaller UK company. The EC's commitment to abolishing exchange controls and hence liberalising capital movements is well known. In addition, it is hoped that banks will be able to undertake a wide range of activities throughout the EC. Eventually a 'European Financial Area' will be established where, to all intents and purposes, a single currency and a single bank will reign, where banking and other financial services can be carried on by any resident of a member state and where there is complete freedom of exchange control.

The lack of common currency and EC central bank tends to fragment the Single European Market. Variations in foreign exchange distort trade and hide uncompetitive sectors. They also increase foreign exchange risks for UK companies operating in the EC. This, in turn, causes disjunctions in interest and exchange rates. Efficient foreign businesses are put at a competitive disadvantage and inefficient ones at an advantage. This can of course work either to the advantage or the disadvantage of the UK company, protecting the home market while causing a barrier abroad. This is one of the reasons why UK companies should strategically reorganise *now*, to be ready for the harsher climate of post-1993 Europe.

21.6 The last stage of the journey

We have looked at the first two of the three issues that raise questions among UK management when setting out on their journey to Europe:

- international tax planning
- raising finance.

It is now time to look at the third issue, the last stage of the journey. How does management, back in the UK, monitor the overseas operation from a distance?

PART 3
PERFORMANCE MONITORING

22

Organising for 1993

22.1 The need to organise

As UK companies prepare for the advent of the Single European Market after 1993, and develop European and possibly international structures, management must take a hard critical look at its method of operation and the group's internal organisation. The group must become more competitive and more responsive. Very often these are contradictory objectives. The corporate culture must change to become more international, whereas previously it may have been narrowly focused on the UK market, or even a geographic area of the UK market. Management of people will have to be considered carefully, as will the management of change and growth. The problems of managing change in a small company with limited management resources are many.

When the UK company first starts to export, it may have few executives with international experience, and no overseas structure. The same will apply to licensing and franchising. This is why, quite apart from tax reasons, the company will look to independent agents, forwarders and distributors. Those UK executives involved in the export trade will become the nucleus around which management of the overseas branch or subsidiary will be centred.

As commitment to the overseas business develops, a company may institute a separate international division, providing a central focus for international matters.

Eventually, when the UK company establishes overseas subsidiaries, organisational changes will again be necessary. There is the question of the degree of local autonomy to be allowed to the subsidiary. What will be the level of management in terms of local management as opposed to management sent out from the UK? Will there be a greatly increased cost because the UK company is now acting as a headquarters?

Structured correctly, the increased sales generated by an overseas subsidiary can provide savings. However, this involves exploiting economies of scale and maintaining quality standards. These controls must be carried out without stifling local initiative, and without producing over-centralisation. There is an obvious need for ensuring that internal communications run smoothly, particularly given differing languages and customs. The use of an exchange programme can help greatly.

The problems will multiply as the UK company acquires not just one European subsidiary but many, and possibly subsidiaries outside Europe as well. The foreign holding company can produce not just a tax 'umbrella', but also a management centre. It can be a channel of communication through which that country's problems are focused. Similarly an overseas holding company can provide a focusing of all foreign problems, and be a management centre of its own. It can provide an opportunity to appoint directors who otherwise would not be directors of the UK parent (but always bear in mind the UK's concept of residence). On the other hand it is also the case that, as the group grows, its management organisation will bear progressively less resemblance to its corporate structure. This is probably more problematic in the field of tax than management.

22.2 Planning for 1993

A plan for change to meet the new competitive business environment of post-1993 Europe, and a timetable for action, must be drawn up. Before drawing up a plan, UK management should undertake a review of its business and industry. This could address questions such as:

- What are the local and overseas competitors doing?
- Where do the company's products or services fit into the European market?
- What are customers' expectations?
- What is the state of the particular industry?
- Are legislation changes likely to have an impact on the industry?
- Where is the company at its strongest – and also at its weakest?
- What is the market position of the company?

Under each of the above headings a considerable amount of investigation work needs to be carried out. To undertake the review properly also requires a particular frame of mind. Management may believe that it will be able to 'see off' any new competition, but underestimating the strength and determination of the opposition in the Single European

Market, and overestimating a company's products' or services' competitiveness and customers' loyalty, are areas where many organisations fail. UK management must ask, 'Are we really providing our customers with exactly what they want or are we merely the best of a not-so-impressive bunch currently in the market-place? If there is any hint of not providing customers with exactly what they want (invariably a modern, cost-effective, reliable and timely service backed up by more-than-adequate customer care), there is a gap which will be exploited by the opposition eager to steal customers.

Once management has carried out an investigation and arrived at an honest assessment of the UK company's position and potential vulnerability, it will be in a position to formulate a strategy. The strategy adopted will be dependent upon position in the market, resources, threats and opportunities.

22.3 Simple actions

Irrespective of the strategy adopted, the UK company should consider taking actions which do not cost too much money. These could include matters such as:

- becoming aware on an international basis what is happening in the industry and what the major players are doing;
- membership of the appropriate trade association and an active role in its activities – a trade association can be a very effective vehicle for lobbying the EC, which unfortunately is not done nearly enough by United Kingdom business;
- carrying out research on customers in order to ensure that management knows exactly what they want and can ensure that their requirements are met;
- investigating whether a customer care course for staff would be a good investment;
- investigating whether a strategic alliance with an overseas or local company would enable maintenance or even improvement in market position;
- investigating the benefits of modest diversification: single product companies will be more vulnerable to having their markets stolen;
- looking at the financial position of competitors – this is particularly easy in the UK because of our disclosure requirements.

Especially watch for competitor companies which may be for sale. This may present an opportunity for a foreign company to move into the UK market. UK management may have to seriously consider acquiring a domestic competitor in order to prevent its falling into the hands of a bigger foreign competitor.

22.4 Drawing up the plan

A plan for change to meet the new post-1993 environment must be drawn up and implemented. The plan could cover:

- the corporate mission;
- objectives;
- creating a database;
- strategies for production, pricing, people and products;
- research and development where applicable;
- budgets;
- risk analysis.

This is just the beginning. The objectives and details of the plan must be diffused throughout the organisation, both in the UK and in Europe. The internal organisation of the company may have to change to meet the new environment in which businesses will be operating. Any response must be led from the top. The chief executive of the UK company must be involved in formulating the strategy, but the strategy must in turn embrace all levels of the company.

It must be stressed that the options available will vary significantly from company to company and from industry to industry. There is a fine line between defensive and offensive actions, and it is a well known fact that sometimes the best form of defence is offence. This will be one of the driving forces behind companies adopting a European strategy to meet the challenges of the post-1993 régime of the Single European Market.

The next stage is for a UK company to look before it leaps, and to undertake a detailed feasibility study, and then a location study.

22.5 The need for a feasibility study

It is essential that before the UK company proceeds to set up overseas in any major outward investment, it commissions a *feasibility study*. In any event the banks will often require such a study before lending. The feasibility study will usually be prepared by independent professionals. By definition, management will already have taken a decision that an investment should be made, and therefore is inherently biased. Independent counsel may advise against what could be a disastrous drain on the company's resources. Matters dealt with in a feasibility report are as set out below.

- The likely market for the product or service.
- Other players in the market place and their strengths and weaknesses.
- The ability of the UK operation to devote the resources, both financial and human, to establish and run the European operation.

Example

A UK company with two senior executives should not acquire a German subsidiary with 100 employees. UK management would not have sufficient time to run both operations efficiently.

- The control and financial requirements of the new operation.
- An examination of the alternative corporate structures available. This could include whether the operation should be run as a branch, subsidiary or joint venture. International tax would certainly be one consideration. There may be local participation requirements. There may be local exchange controls preventing repatriation of profits back to the UK. Inward investment permissions may be required. The regulatory environment needs to be examined, expecially environmental controls.
- An estimate of the cash flow demands of the new operation, and its effect on borrowing limits for the group as a whole.
- An estimate of the profitability of the new venture, and the timing of those profits.
- An assessment of the operational needs in terms of labour skills, raw materials, premises, accommodation for the work force etc, and the availability of resources to satisfy those needs.

22.6 The need for a location study

A *location study* should also be undertaken. This can either be incorporated in the initial feasibility study or be prepared as a follow-on study after the general viability of the project has been determined.

Most new ventures will have a choice of operation locations, and the correct choice will have a material bearing on the overall success of the venture. A location study takes over from the general feasibility study and focuses on all the issues which are location sensitive. These could include:

- availability and cost of labour with the required skills;
- transport and communications infrastructure;
- availability and cost of raw materials and/or components;
- proximity of customers;
- availability and cost of suitable accommodation for workers;
- local planning considerations with regard to noise, noxious odours, etc;
- the image required.

Example

Many hi-tech businesses like to set up near each other in 'science parks'. Some countries have a better image than others for particular products (Germany for cars, Japan for electronic consumer goods, France for wines, Italy for fashions, Switzerland for watches, the UK for advertising).

- the overall attractiveness of the area as somewhere to live and work;
- availability of support functions such as office supplies and professional services;
- the local attitude to UK companies setting up business in the locality;
- industrial relations practices;
- future development plans for the area;
- grants and other financial incentives (see Chapter 19 on grants).

The location study is a detailed assessment allowing an informal decision to be made on the choice of location. It also provides essential information on how the operation will work in the chosen location in greater detail than the feasibility study. In some instances, the location study can have such an influence on the overall viability that it will be included in the initial feasibility study.

Having looked at the alternative strategies, reorganised, commissioned feasibility and location studies, and eventually decided to proceed with establishing a European operation, management must monitor the overseas operation. In the rest of the last part of this book we will look at how UK management can monitor what is happening abroad, and the problems it will face.

23

Hardware and Software

23.1 The importance of the correct monitoring equipment

There is an obvious importance in having the correct monitoring equipment in the purely technical sense of an information system. These days, this means having the correct computer accounting system, which in turn means having the correct hardware and software to enable UK management to be aware of what is happening overseas, and in particular to make an early diagnosis of problems.

23.2 Information systems generally

Your information system should furnish the right information to the right people at the right time, at the right cost.

There were times in the not-too-distant past when the computer problems associated with international operations were both complex and expensive. It was thought inadvisable for smaller UK companies to become involved in the financial and management problems inherent in installing transnational systems. Cost and technological advances mean that many of the problems are now in the past, and adherence to a limited number of fairly simple rules should keep problems to a minimum.

There is no point in transplanting the UK domestic accounting system into the European operation. All that will develop is a disjointed network of different systems which over time will grow in a random manner, unable to communicate with each other and unable to effectively integrate.

The information system must take into account the accounting, legal and tax requirements of the European country. Many UK systems are, of course, biased towards UK requirements. Any system that is implemented will take time to develop before it becomes fully effective in terms of giving what is needed. Development must be based on input from both the UK and European management.

Up to 15 years ago, information generated on overseas computer systems could only be easily integrated into the UK system by producing permanent records or tapes which then had to be re-input. However the last decade has seen a quiet revolution through the use of *comms* (short for communication lines) such as telephone communication links, to produce instant access between the UK and the European accounting system.

With the use of an inexpensive modem at each end of a telephone line, any line as long as it is of reasonable quality can be used to transmit information between computers. Such an approach is, however, relatively slow and is not to be recommended for transmission of a large volume of data.

When telephone links are of poor quality, or are over a long distance, it pays to invest in better quality modems. These should incorporate some form of error correction facility, capable of detecting noise on the telephone link which may corrupt the received data. Modems with this facility will retransmit the data affected by the interference in order to ensure they are received intact.

International standards for modem operation have been defined by CCIT (an international body belonging to the United Nations). The subject is necessarily complex, and apart from recommending that modems from the same manufacturer be used at either end of the line, advice can only be given with respect to a specific configuration for a specific accounting and monitoring requirement.

The simple modem approach is obviously inadequate if more than one person needs access to the remote computer at the same time, eg on VDUs (visual display units). If multiple access is required, a multiplexer needs to be installed at each end (in addition to the modem). This 'black box' allows simultaneous use of a single telephone link to a remote computer, eg for enquiry or input by several individuals.

If the volumes of data to be transmitted are high, the 'dial up' line described above will be inadequate. In this instance private leased lines may be more cost-effective and will certainly be more efficient. These lines which may, like all telephone links, involve a combination of wire, microwave, fibre-optic or satellite links, are permanently connected and thus no dialling is required. The lines may be specially conditioned for data transmission and are therefore capable of transmitting data at higher speeds than normal dial-up lines. The maximum speed achievable is determined by the type of circuit, with International Kilo Stream and International Megastream offering the highest speeds.

In the UK, only British Telecom and Mercury Communications are licensed by the government as carriers for voice and data traffic and have the capability of offering links to overseas networks.

New legislation now permits third parties to offer the use of the BT or Mercury circuits so long as they add value to the use of the circuit. This value may include linking with overseas networks to provide for European communications. Such options now give a choice of channels to would-be purchasers of communications systems.

There is a disadvantage to instantaneous access systems, and that is a lessening of security, eg from hacking. To secure systems from hacking, various security options are available ranging from shielded and dedicated comms lines through to ring-back modems and encryption. However, the only computer which is totally safe from hacking is one which is not connected to a comms line. Any other computer is vulnerable and must be protected. Apart from computers, coded telex transmissions, faxes and satellite telecommunications need to be thought of.

23.3 Hardware

With regard to hardware, the best solution is still to have the same equipment in both locations. Quite apart from the obvious benefit of making life that little bit easier, it avoids the possibility of buck-passing whenever problems occur. There are very few instances where one computer cannot be made to 'talk' to another. Given the option of having identical hardware or having hardware well supported with good technical back-up by a local supplier, it is always preferable to go for the good back-up and then resolve the communication problems back in the UK. It is essential to select hardware which is well accepted in both the European country (as well as internationally) and the UK.

23.4 Software

To a certain extent software is more difficult. The selection of a system (ie hardware and software) should always be driven by the software and not the hardware. The majority of operations can now be adequately satisfied by packages (standard programs) rather than specially written programs. As the UK company will now be dealing in currencies other than sterling it is essential to have an accounting software package which properly handles multi-currencies, and which is not biased towards UK accounting principles, corporate disclosure requirements and tax. The benefits of having the identical package at the overseas location, as is used at the UK head office, are numerous – not the least being that in an emergency, staff from head office can travel to Europe and run the system. This can be important when you may have a relatively small overseas office with only one person competent on the computer. A sudden resignation of the only operator can cause a problem if no one can easily take over.

23.5 The need for independent professional advice

As in many areas, relying on biased suppliers who will always assure you that everything will be all right can lead to considerable problems. Beware of the UK suppliers who say that they can service your equipment in Italy when in reality they have no facility there and the equipment is not generally available. The situation will almost certainly end up causing considerable problems and expense.

If in any doubt, take independent professional advice. Do not ask a computer supplier which computer to use.

24

Liveware

24.1 The human factor

A UK company expanding into Europe deals primarily not in goods and services, or even in information, but *with people.*

The human factor overrides all other considerations. No matter how efficient the hardware and software, it is the *liveware* on which UK management must ultimately depend for the successful operation of the European subsidiary.

Your European operation will not run itself. No matter how good local management is or, rather, no matter how good its reputation is, it is essential that UK management keeps its finger on the pulse of what is happening overseas.

24.2 Who should head up the operation?

The most difficult question to answer is whether the operation should be headed by a local man or by someone sent out from the UK. Very often the ideal is to use someone used to both business cultures. For example, a Spaniard working for the UK company could head up a new Spanish operation, or an expatriate working in Spain would also be ideal. Both should be familiar with English and Spanish, which must be the first essential.

Interestingly, large multinationals find less problems in sending quite random nationalities overseas to fill positions at all levels. This merely shows that, as with everything else, experience helps.

24.3 The north-south divide

Many people with experience of UK companies expanding into Europe will say that Europe is not only divided into Western Europe and

Eastern Europe, but that Western Europe is divided into Northern Europe and Southern Europe.

Northern Europe includes Austria, Belgium, Germany, the Netherlands, Scandinavia and Switzerland. Southern Europe includes Greece, Spain and Portugal. France and Italy are special cases in that the northern parts can be said to be Northern European, whereas the southern parts are more Southern in their nature.

The Northern European business culture can be thought to be more like that of the UK. The attitude is materially different in Southern Europe. Very often a local man can be appointed to head up an operation in Northern Europe, and to run it without the essential presence of UK senior staff. On the other hand, it is essential to send someone from the UK to be on site in Southern Europe. In that case, however, the 'number two' must be local so that, *inter alia*, the local bureaucracy can be negotiated.

As with all people issues these are sweeping statements. The UK company, especially the smaller firm, will be dealing with individuals and must make judgements on an individual by individual basis.

24.4 Autonomy and control

Throughout the development of the UK's overseas structure, there will be conflicts of interest between allowing autonomy for subsidiary companies and controlling them. A low level of autonomy will help standardisation, and hence the economies of scale. It will help to protect the UK company's good name. The likelihood of poor decisions being made by a subsidiary's management will be reduced. On the other hand, there will be the danger of low morale overseas, and the likelihood of making an incorrect decision because the decision is being made in the United Kingdom rather than locally. It is an unresponsive structure. It may also create the wrong corporate culture.

There are no hard and fast rules as to the degree of autonomy that should be allowed. However, whatever the degree of autonomy, UK management must constantly monitor the overseas subsidiaries to ensure that they are financially healthy. With current advances in technology there is no reason why the best of both worlds should not be possible. Local subsidiaries can have a high degree of autonomy, so that local initiatives are encouraged allowing the greatest of flexibility to changes in market and other conditions. On the other hand, UK management must have its finger on the pulse to detect any signs that a subsidiary is on the wrong track.

Apart from any other matters, as UK companies grow, senior management will simply not have sufficient time in the day to undertake detailed investigations into what is happening overseas. They will have to rely on exception reports and summaries. Nevertheless, key financial data – for example cash balances – can still be produced on a daily basis allowing management to act swiftly when a problem arises.

24.5 Reporting requirements

It is essential that the UK company receives regular reports from its overseas operations. It should receive regular management accounts, regular cash-flow statements and forecasts and even regular bank reconciliations, if necessary on a daily basis. If the UK company has an internal auditing function then that must be extended to encompass the foreign operation. There should be regular meetings between the UK and the management of the foreign operation, and reciprocal regular visits. Budgets must be set and any variance must be rigorously investigated. The variance between budgets and reported profits will alert management back in the UK that there may be a problem. Regular management accounts should be produced. These should show:

- the profitability of each operation of the overseas subsidiary;
- the cash-flow position;
- the stock position;
- the order position;
- debtors and any potential bad debts;
- the level at which the business is operating as a percentage of capacity.

The management accounts must be regularly audited internally where such a capability exists – certainly more regularly than an annual audit.

Sometimes figures have to be estimated, for example an estimated gross profit margin may be used. Under these circumstances it is essential that stock is accurately counted. Normally this should be done quarterly, or at least half-yearly, and not just at the time of the annual audit.

24.6 Exchange programmes

Some groups swap staff, not necessarily at the highest level but at different levels, for periods of up to six months. This helps to inculcate an international culture among all the employees of the group, and also helps to avoid repeating mistakes made in one country in another country. Conversely, the successes in one country can be repeated elsewhere.

24.7 Continuity

No matter how carefully the UK company plans its expansion into Europe, there is no substitute for having done it before. The next best thing is to ensure that your professional advisers have done it before. It will help continuity to keep the same professional advisers. UK companies setting up European operations will usually use the same accountants, lawyers and bankers, assuming they have opposite numbers in the relevant European countries.

Once a single operation has been established successfully overseas, it is usually the case that others follow. On the other hand, if a UK company 'gets it wrong' the first time then not only will it find it very difficult to repeat the operation successfully at a later date, but the losses that can be incurred in the overseas venture can have a damaging impact on the UK company, even leading to its demise. Any failure will have a dampening effect on the desire of UK management to progress a European strategy further. There are risks in expanding abroad as well as rewards. Very often a UK company would be well advised to consider a minimum risks strategy when first going abroad, for example by ensuring there are no cross guarantees with the UK parent, using a separate subsidiary to limit liability, or joint venturing with a larger partner who can provide the substantial finance that may be required.

25

Business Customs in Europe

25.1 The need for understanding

In order to monitor and manage the overseas operation effectively it will be necessary to work with people of a different nationality. Working with other nationalities can be difficult. Cross-border effectiveness is dependent on the cooperation and understanding of people. Understanding means not only of the words spoken, but also of attitudes, etiquettes, dress codes and the things people do. These will affect performance and, ultimately, business results. The manager who identifies, accepts and can work with cultural differences will ultimately achieve more both personally and for the company.

25.2 Some specifics

Set out below are areas which need careful attention. This can never be a complete list. It only provides examples of how misunderstandings can occur.

- **Question your own attitude, value system and expectations.** These colour your view of people and occurrences. We tend to like those who are like ourselves. Business abroad is an exercise in patience. Don't pre-judge if you are angry or upset at something which has happened; it might be a simple misunderstanding.
- **Translations.** To check the correctness of the translation, have it re-translated by somebody else, a native speaker of the language, back into English, then talk through the differences.
- **Learn the language.** There's no better form of insider dealing than knowing how people think (and speak) even if you conduct business in English. For example, does 'Yes' mean 'No' or 'Perhaps' or 'Maybe'? Agreements in public can be merely a politeness. To some, blunt decisiveness can sound brusque and rude; to others,

saying 'thank you' is a sign of weakness and servility. Pick up hints from your language lessons.

- **Make regular visits.** Misunderstandings can grow in proportion when all contact is by telephone. Non-verbal communication such as body language can convey more than words. Watch how people work and behave for understanding intention and meaning.
- **Shaking hands.** In France, it is normal to shake hands at the beginning and end of each meeting. In other countries, shaking hands at the end of a meeting signifies that you've agreed on the deal, a misunderstanding that can land you in court.
- **Dress with care for the office.** In the Netherlands, dress is more casual than in the UK. In the UK, shirt sleeves indicate a man hard at work. A German, however, will not remove his jacket in the office in meetings.
- **First-name terms are best kept at home unless you are invited to use them.** Using the correct title can also be important. When in doubt use a business card. In business abroad, the boss/worker relationship can be more formal than in the UK. Inappropriate informality can be seen as weakness and can make subordinates feel uneasy. In Germany first names are never used in business; people are addressed formally. In the USA first names are nearly always used.
- **Don't prejudge ethics or moral behaviour.** Corporate entertaining might be seen as bribery and corruption overseas; cheating the tax man as a moral duty. Social policing such as telling people off for crossing the road at a red pedestrian light or mowing their grass on a Sunday in Germany is acceptable (in Bavaria – maybe not in Hamburg), whereas showing up intoxicated is definitely 'out' in France.
- **Punctuality.** To be late or not to be late can be a question of respect. In America, be early; in Germany be on time.
- **Status is deceptive.** In France, government workers are part of the social elite. Engineers in Germany carry more status than financial executives. In Italy, cultural education can show social standing. In the UK, status is deduced from the size of your company car. You also need to be careful of age. In parts of Europe, youth is seen as being dynamic; in others, immature.
- **Be cautious of humour.** A serious demeanour and commitment to work can be expected and jokes are often unacceptable,

especially in the workplace. As humour doesn't cross borders easily, it is better to watch and wait before attempting to amuse.

- **Team working.** In competitive societies, individual technical excellence can be prized above an ability to work in teams. In looser organisations, as in the UK, the team player can be the one who gets on.
- **Xenophobia.** Where there are strong nationalistic feelings, a foreign businessman might never get on. It might be wiser to recruit a local. However, exercise caution. Will he feel isolated, or independent? How often do you need to communicate with him before your instructions are seen as interference. An alternative is to find expatriates with experience of success in the industry in the chosen country.
- **Attitude.** Working long hours can be seen as commitment through to incompetence and an inability to control or manage your time. Take care if calling a colleague at home – it may be considered an intrusion. In addition, talking business at social occasions can be a social gaffe, where private and personal lives are kept separate from the workplace.
- **Meetings.** Formal or informal, most meetings will follow a well-defined format around content and participant behaviour. Individual contributions might be acceptable – or not; presenters can be challenged without offence – or not; consensus agreement might be sought – or not; decision-making might be expected at the meeting or before in private discussions; and the Chairman's recommendations might be accepted – or not!
- **Communication.** Whatever language is used for discussions, written business communications should be in the language of the recipient. In addressing the recipient, formality is less likely to offend. Some people will expect written confirmation of every decision. For others, written instructions imply lack of trust.
- **Paying for performance.** If trust, company loyalty and a belief that the employee should strive for perfection are part of the work ethic, paying for performance can indicate lack of trust, or can be seen as unfair or as wasted money. Investigate before making a decision.
- **Appointments.** In some countries the meeting should be arranged initially by letter – sometimes in English, more often in the local language. Beware of the necessity to write in a local

dialect such as Flemish. In other countries the first contact should be by telephone.

- **Meetings.** Some meetings can be conducted in English, others in the local language. Handshaking, small talk, the level of formality and the time of the meeting will vary throughout Europe.
- **Entertaining** In some countries breakfast meetings are normal, in other they would be considered rude and intrusive.
- **Gifts.** In some countries gifts are normal business custom. In others, extravagant gifts will be rejected and seen as an attempt to 'bribe'.
- **Women.** Women have achieved high positions in business in very few countries in Europe. The acceptability of sending a woman executive out to meet a potential European customer will vary from country to country, as will the reaction of the European importer or client.
- **Working hours.** These will vary from country to country. In particular, public holidays are taken on different days; a business diary will normally tell you when any particular European country is closed. In some countries attempting to meet people outside normal working hours is considered intrusive.
- **Marketing, media and consumer preferences.** These vary greatly from country to country. It is these inherent cultural differences which are the greatest fragmenter of the Single European Market. Different countries spend different amounts on different things. They buy different types of goods. Detailed local advice will be necessary to penetrate the local market.

25.3 Europe versus the world

As can be seen, different parts of Europe have differing business customs. However, the Northern European/Southern European gap, or even the Western/Eastern European gap, cannot match the gaps in customs between the United Kingdom and the world outside Europe (eg Japan, parts of Africa, the Middle East), where much more radical differences are apparent. Within Europe, both within and outside the EC, young peoples' attitudes and fashions are becoming harmonised, or possibly Americanised. It may be that in due course, as these young people move into positions of responsibility, European countries will grow so that they eventually resemble each other in their business customs, as well as the other matters that are being harmonised by the EC.

26

Interaction of Monitoring Finance and Tax

26.1 The end in sight

If you have followed our journey from the beginning, you will have seen that the management of a UK company about to embark on export, and thence on to direct investment overseas, will be looking primarily at international tax planning, raising finance and monitoring the overseas operation. There are, of course, other matters to consider, including legal and insurance angles. None of these matters can be dealt with in isolation.

26.2 Monitoring, finance and tax

We have seen that the concept of residence can be a stumbling block. Companies must be managed and controlled from overseas to escape UK tax. If they are managed and controlled from the UK they will be liable to UK corporation tax at 35 per cent on their worldwide income and gains. In addition, if they are incorporated abroad they may become dual resident which will bring its own problems. On the other hand, we have just discussed the importance of monitoring the overseas operation to ensure that any problems that arise are dealt with promptly, and do not fester. Care must be exercised to ensure that UK management merely monitors an investment, and does not run a business. The dividing line can be fine. Furthermore, as groups grow and develop more complex corporate structures, the management structure of such multinationals can bear little or no resemblance to actual corporate structure, so that the question of who exercises management and control with respect to any particular company can be uncertain. The board of directors of the overseas subsidiary must not meet merely to 'rubber stamp' decisions taken by the UK company as a result of its monitoring process. There must be a degree of autonomy.

This is recognised by the Inland Revenue, but they will always look to see whether there is a real commercial presence in the purported country of residence, and they will take this into account in deciding whether UK management is merely monitoring, or actually managing and controlling.

We have discussed the importance of a feasibility study before a UK company commits its resources into substantial overseas investment. The feasibility study will have international tax considerations as one of its inputs. Such a feasibility study will also be required before a bank will lend to finance the overseas trade or outward investment.

This, in turn, leads to the question of how the operation should be financed. There are detailed tax considerations as to whether the overseas subsidiary should be financed with shares and loans from the UK, local borrowings or by an offshore finance company. This then leads to questions such as whether there is withholding tax on interest paid back to the UK, and whether exchange controls in the overseas country can have an effect in determining the method of finance.

26.3 No man is an island

In all these matters, both looked at individually and taken together, management of the UK company should not be too proud or penny-pinching to take the best professional advice available. As we have already discussed, there is no substitute for having 'done it before'. If this is the first investment into Europe, then advice should be obtained from outside.

CONCLUSION

27

Journey's End

We have now reached 'Journey's End'. The UK company, which began as a purely domestic animal, has looked across the seas to Europe. It began by exporting and decided to undertake more major outward investment, establishing a subsidiary. Now the UK company is the parent of a large group.

Whatever strategy you wish to adopt, even if it is staying within the UK domestic market, by 1993 the increasing internationalisation of business means that the UK businessman must be aware of what is going on in the outside world, and what he can do about it. This increased competition will result in the UK company having to consider not just whether or not to get into Europe, but also other matters. What about pricing policy? Should more be spent on product development and research in order to compete with what are now more technologically advanced environments, eg Germany and Japan? What about advertising? What about a strategy of acquiring UK competitors to strengthen position in the home market? None of these questions can be avoided as we rapidly approach the world of post-1992 Europe.

Management must decide now on how the group will be run after 1992. One major question is the degree of autonomy allowed to subsidiary companies. Control and autonomy must be balanced. Too much central control will lead to stifling of local initiative. Too much local autonomy will lead to subsidiaries going their own way and diversifying into areas which may not be to the overall benefit of the group. However, the enhanced power and reduced cost of information technology has allowed greater autonomy, while still allowing the centre to monitor rather than to manage and control.

The changes in 1992 should be a 'prod in the back' for UK companies. 1992 will provide a unique opportunity for UK companies to look at their corporate strategy, their internal communications, and their people matters such as training. Even if they were not thinking of looking at their corporate strategy, 1992 will force them to think where they are going into 1993. 1992 can be used as a springboard for 1993, to motivate management, to look for new markets, to consider new products and to think of how the UK company will respond to the European challenge. 1992 will be the lever to make the management think about getting into Europe by 1993.

We have now come to Journey's End. What will your strategy be? Will you adopt a strategy of inaction, or one of action? If so, will it be European, part-European or non-European? No matter what path your UK company is now setting out to follow, by 1993 the Single European Market will have some effect. Act now, but think before you act.

APPENDICES

Appendix A:

European Corporate Tax Systems

Introduction

This Appendix contains concise summaries of the corporate tax systems of all the major Western European countries. Eastern Europe is dealt with in Appendix C. The countries covered are Austria, Belgium, Denmark, Finland, France, Germany, Greece, Ireland, Italy, Luxembourg, Netherlands, Norway, Portugal, Spain, Sweden and Switzerland.

The information concerning each country is set out in an identical format, allowing for easy comparison. The features covered are:

1. the tax year; nature and rates of tax(es);
2. residence and territoriality;
3. the tax base;
4. treatment of dividends;
5. anti-avoidance measures;
6. treatment of losses;
7. treatment of capital gains;
8. treatment of groups;
9. treatment of branches;
10. other taxes.

Austria

Average rate of exchange y/e 31.3.90: £1 = AS 20.472.

1. The tax year; nature and rates of tax

(a) The tax year is the calendar year. The profits of an accounting period ending other than on 31 December are taxable in full for the tax year in which the period ends.

Accounting year ended 30 September 1990. Profits AS 1,000,000
Taxable: AS 1,000,000 in tax year 1990 (ending 31 December 1990)

(b) The corporation tax (*Körperschaftsteuer*) is levied at a rate of 30 per cent (on both distributed and undistributed income).

2. Residence and territoriality

Companies resident in Austria are liable to corporation tax on their worldwide income and gains.

A company incorporated in Austria is resident there, as is a company incorporated elsewhere but whose activities are directed from Austria.

3. The tax base

(a) *Method of calculation.* Taxable profits are calculated on an increase in net worth basis, by comparing net assets at the beginning and end of the accounting year.
(b) *Disallowable items.* The main disallowable items are: most entertainment expenses, transfers to most reserves, 50 per cent of supervisory board (*Aufsichtsrat*) members' fees, expenses relating to non-taxable items, corporation tax itself. For interest, see (d) below.
(c) *Exempt income/special deductions.* Dividends received from Austrian companies and foreign companies qualifying for the affiliation privilege (see 4 below) are exempt.
(d) *Interest paid.* Normally deductible on the accruals basis. Disallowed interest includes interest on borrowings used to acquire a shareholding qualifying for the affiliation privilege, interest on long-term borrowings (for trade tax purposes only) and interest in excess of arm's length rates paid to connected persons.
(e) *Stock.* Stock and work in progress is valued at the lower of cost or

'going concern' value. FIFO is generally acceptable but LIFO only if it reflects the company's actual practice. There is no 'stock relief' for inflationary increases in value.

(f) *Depreciation.* Mostly straight-line basis only, within a range of acceptable rates for different types of asset. Book depreciation usually matches tax depreciation. There is no pooling of assets. Many assets qualify, in addition, for an investment allowance of up to 20 per cent in the year of acquisition.

4. Treatment of dividends received and paid

(a) *Dividends received from Austrian companies.* Exempt from tax.

(b) *Dividends received from foreign companies.* Taxable, except where the Austrian company's holding in the paying company is 25 per cent or more throughout the entire fiscal year, in which case the 'affiliation privilege' (*Beteiligungsertragsbefreiung*) exempts the dividend from tax. The affiliation privilege is not available for holdings in foreign companies more than 25 per cent of whose assets are directly or indirectly invested in securities.

(c) *Dividends paid to Austrian and non-resident shareholders.* Withholding tax of 25 per cent must be deducted from dividends paid except where paid: (1) to Austrian resident companies holding 25 per cent or more of the equity; (2) on liquidation distributions and (3) to non-residents covered by a tax treaty specifying a different rate. Generally, non-residents must apply for a refund or reduced withholding tax.

5. Anti-avoidance measures

Austrian law recognises the general *fraus legis* (or *abus de droit*) principle, whereby transactions that are regarded as an abuse of the statutes can be nullified.

Thin-capitalisation rules are operated by the revenue authorities. Where the debt equity ratio exceeds the region of 4:1 or 5:1, interest paid may be treated as a dividend. These rules are often invoked where shareholders' loans are granted on unusual terms (especially where repayment is unlikely).

There is no special accumulated earnings tax (cf UK close company apportionment). However, payment of dividends reduces a company's net worth and hence its net worth tax (*Vermögensteuer*) liability (see 10 below).

6. Treatment of losses

(a) *Current period.* Trading losses and capital losses may be set off against both trading profits and capital gains of the same period.
(b) *Carry back.* Losses cannot be carried back.
(c) *Carry forward.* Losses may be carried forward (to the extent that they remain unrelieved in the current period) against future profits for a maximum of seven years.
(d) *Transferability of losses.* Provided the same business continues to be carried on, there is no restriction of loss carry forward when the ownership of a company changes.

7. Treatment of capital gains

(a) *Treatment.* Capital gains are treated as income.
(b) *Computation.* The gain (or loss) is computed by deducting depreciated cost from sale proceeds. There is no allowance for inflation.
(c) *Roll-over.* There is no general roll-over or deferral, but where fixed assets held for at least seven years are disposed of, the tax on any capital gain may be deferred if the sale proceeds are used to acquire other assets located in Austria. The replacement asset must be of the same nature (ie a tangible asset if the old asset was tangible, intangible if the old asset was intangible). Acquisition of the new asset must take place within three years of disposal. Any amount deferred reduces the depreciable cost of the replacement asset.
(d) *Special treatment for shares.* Gains from disposals of shares in foreign companies qualifying for the affiliation privilege (see 4 above) are exempt. Gains on the disposal of shares in Austrian companies are not exempt, whatever the level of holding.

8. Groups of companies

There is no general 'fiscal unity' concept, so each member of a group of companies is treated separately, with no facility for pooling profits and losses or tax-free transfers of assets. However, there is an exception for 'integrated companies' (*Organschaften*), which may file consolidated tax returns. To qualify, subsidiaries must be financially, organisationally and economically integrated with the parent company, which must hold at least 75 per cent of the shares in each subsidiary. An agreement to pool profits and losses must be in force. The subsidiaries must be resident in Austria and be subsidiaries throughout the accounting period concerned.

9. Treatment of branches

An Austrian branch of a foreign resident company is treated for tax purposes exactly as if it were an Austrian resident company. There is no special branch profits tax and no withholding tax on remittances of profits from the branch to head office. Branches are also liable to the trade tax and the net worth tax (see 10 below).

10. Other taxes

Other taxes include:

(a) *Taxes on income and gains.* There is a trade tax (*Gewerbesteuer*) levied as a local business income tax. The trade tax has a similar base to the corporation tax. The trade tax payable is deductible in calculating the trade tax itself, as is the net worth tax (see below), but the corporation tax is not. Branches of foreign companies are also liable to the tax.

The rate of the tax is 4.5 per cent times a multiple fixed by the province itself. The multiples are currently in the range 300 to 400 per cent. The resulting liability is about 13 per cent of income before tax.

(b) *Taxes on capital.* Companies are subject to a net worth tax (*Vermögensteuer*) at a rate of 1 per cent on 90 per cent of the value of net assets worldwide. Some assets (eg holdings in Austrian companies and holdings in foreign companies qualifying for the affiliation privilege – see 4(b) above) are excluded from the net worth tax base. Corporation tax, trade tax and the net worth tax itself are all deductible (on an accruals basis, so long as the year-end date is 31 December) in computing the net worth tax liability.

Subject to a double tax treaty, Austrian branches of foreign companies are liable to the tax on their assets situated in Austria, except shareholdings in Austrian companies. Where the shares in the company are owned by another company, a further tax (*Erbschaftssteueräquivalent* – substitute inheritance tax) is levied at 0.5 per cent.

(c) *Turnover taxes.* There is a value-added tax (*Mehrwertsteuer*) of 20 per cent, with a reduced rate of 10 per cent and a luxury rate of

32 per cent. Exports are zero rated. Services performed in Austria are liable to VAT, even if there is no branch or permanent establishment. Non-residents may elect for exemption from VAT where their customers in Austria are trading businesses (but not banks or insurance companies).

(d) *Payroll and social security taxes.* There is a payroll tax (*Lohnsummensteuer*) of about 4.5 per cent of gross salaries, on a monthly basis. In addition, employers pay social security contributions of about 19–23 per cent on salaries below AS 394,800 (£20,150) per annum. There is also a separate local payroll tax of 2 per cent.

(e) *Transaction taxes.* There is a share capital duty of 2 per cent on new share issues (based on proceeds not par value), a loan capital duty of 0.8 per cent, stamp duties on share transfers and other conveyances and a land transfer tax of 3.5 per cent.

Belgium

Average exchange rate y/e 31 March 1990: £1 = BFr 60.943

1. The tax year: nature and rates of tax

(a) The tax year is the calendar year. The profits of an accounting period, whether or not a calendar year, are wholly taxable in the year following that in which the accounting period begins.

Accounting year ended 30 September 1990. Profits BFr 5,000,000

Taxable: BFr 5,000,000 in tax year 1990 (ending 31 December 1990)

Accounting year ended 31 December 1990: taxable in tax year 1991

(b) The corporation tax (*impôt des sociétés*; *vennootschapsbelasting*) is levied at a standard rate of 41 per cent in the tax year 1991 (39 per cent in 1992) on both distributed and undistributed income. The standard rate applies to profits (1991) above BFr 14,800,000; for smaller profits, there are intermediate rates of 29 per cent and 37 per cent. Intermediate rates are not available to 50 per cent subsidiaries, companies with over 50 per cent of net worth represented by investments in other company shares or where distributions exceed 13 per cent of the paid up capital.

Some capital gains are taxed at a special rate of 20.5 per cent (19.5 per cent in 1992) – see 7 below.

(c) *Special régimes*. Special taxation treatment is accorded to Belgian-based administration or liaison offices of foreign companies. The most important of these is the so called 'coordination centre' (*centre de coordination*; *coördinatie centrum*) of an international group of companies. Briefly, a coordination centre:

(1) is part of an international group, with minimum consolidated equity of BFr 1,000 million (minimum equity outside Belgium of BFr 500 million – or 20 per cent of group equity), minimum consolidated turnover of BFr 10,000 million (minimum outside Belgium of BFr 5,000 million – or 20 per cent of group turnover) and susidiaries in at least four different countries;

(2) employs at least 10 persons in Belgium at the end of its second year of operations;

(3) is engaged in activities such as advertising, information, centralisation of administration, accounting or financing operations;

(4) must not be engaged in direct industrial, manufacturing or commercial activities.

Once recognition has been obtained, the coordination centre enjoys certain tax advantages.

(1) Liability to corporation tax is based not on actual profits but on a notional percentage of certain expenses (excluding financial and salary costs) incurred. The actual percentage is negotiable but varies between 4 and 10 per cent. The tax base cannot be less than the aggregate of expenses not normally allowable as professional charges, non-allowable directors' fees and 'gratuitous advantages' (eg excessive management charges) transferred.

(2) Dividends paid by coordination centres are not subject to withholding tax. Belgian companies in receipt of a dividend from a coordination centre are entitled to a refundable tax credit of 25 per cent (10 per cent in the case of interest).

2. Corporate residence rules and territoriality

Companies resident in Belgium are liable to corporation tax on worldwide profits or gains.

Companies incorporated in Belgium are resident there, as are companies having their principal place of management (significance is also given to the location of shareholders' meetings and board meetings) in Belgium.

3. The tax base

(a) *Method of calculation* Taxable profits are based on the income reported in the annual accounts. Income includes all profits and losses, capital gains, and non-trading income such as dividends, rents, interest etc.

(b) *Disallowable items.* The main disallowable items include some entertainment expenses, 25 per cent of most costs related to motor cars (including depreciation), transfers to reserves and accruals not representing expenditure incurred in the period. Limits are placed on the deductibility of bad debt provisions (eg the general provision may not exceed 0.2 per cent of total debtors).

(c) *Exempt income and special deductions.* 85 per cent or 90 per cent of dividend income from permanent participations is exempt (see 4 below). Investment allowances (see (f) below) are deductible.

(d) *Interest paid.* Interest is normally deductible on an accruals basis. Where not paid to banks or financial institutions, allowable interest may not exceed a rate 3 per cent above the National Bank's government bond discount rate. A withholding tax of 10 per cent (25 per cent if the loan predates 1 March 1990) is deductible from interest payments unless made to Belgian financial institutions, the Belgian state or to non-residents for whom a tax treaty prescribes a different rate.

(e) *Stock.* Stock and work in progress is valued at the lower of cost and market value. Most recognised accountancy valuation principles (eg FIFO, LIFO) are permissible. There is no stock relief for inflationary increases in value.

(f) *Depreciation.* Either the straight line or the reducing balance basis may be used, depending on the accounts treatment. There is a generally accepted range of values for different types of asset. There is no pooling of assets. Many assets qualify in addition for an investment allowance of between 4 and 11 per cent of cost (for 1991).

4. Treatment of dividends received and paid

(a) *Dividends received from Belgian companies.* Subject to withholding tax of 25 per cent and included in taxable income, but a credit or refund is given. If the shares have been owned for the entire accounting period (a so-called 'permanent participation'), 90 per cent of the gross amount is exempted (85 per cent if the recipient is a financial company). Where the shares are not owned throughout the accounting period, there is no exemption but an additional tax credit of 50 per cent is available.

(b) *Dividends received from abroad.* If the shares have not been owned for the entire accounting period, the dividend (net of foreign withholding tax) is liable to corporation tax, grossed up at 15/85. Provided tax has actually been paid abroad on the dividend, a fixed foreign tax credit of 15 per cent is given, regardless of the actual foreign tax paid. For permanent participations, the same treatment (85 or 90 per cent exemption) applies as for Belgian source dividends. The exemption is not available in respect of holdings in foreign companies unless those companies are subject to a corporation tax similar to Belgium's. The fixed foreign tax credit may soon be replaced by a credit for the actual tax paid.

(c) *Dividends paid.* Withholding tax of 25 per cent is deductible from dividends paid to resident and non-resident shareholders.

5. Anti-avoidance measures

There are no taxes on accumulated earnings and no debt-equity restrictions. Note, however, the general limit on deductible loan interest (see 3(d) above). Transfer pricing rules exist to impose arm's-length prices on dealings with foreign affiliates and with non-affiliated foreign companies based in jurisdictions with substantially lower tax régimes. There are no provisions corresponding to the UK's controlled foreign company rules, but the tax authorities may ignore transfers of assets such as shares, patents etc to jurisdictions where the income generated by those assets incurs a substantially lower rate of taxation. In such a case, the income will be taxed as if the assets were still located in Belgium.

6. Treatment of losses

(a) *Current period.* Trading losses may be offset against all income and gains of the current period.
(b) *Future periods.* Trading losses may be carried forward for set-off against future income and gains indefinitely, as may losses incurred before 1 January 1990, except losses of the first five years following incorporation and losses corresponding to depreciation and investment allowances (see 3(f) above), which may be carried forward for a maximum of five years only.
(c) *Past periods.* There is no carry back of losses to prior periods.
(d) *Transferability.* There is no restriction on loss transfer on a change of ownership, provided merely that the company carries on its operations.

7. Treatment of capital gains

(a) *Treatment.* Capital gains are treated as income.
(b) *Computation.* Gains are computed by deducting cost from sale proceeds.
(c) *Roll-over.* Roll-over exists for a wide variety of assets, but the rules are complicated and depend on length of ownership.
   (1) The gain from financial fixed assets (investments, shares and other participations) held for more than five years but not qualifying for roll-over is included in taxable income at the end of the third year after disposal and taxed at half the corporation tax rate (currently at 20.5 per cent).
   (2) Gains from financial fixed assets qualifying for roll-over are fully exempt.

(3) Gains from other fixed assets qualifying for roll-over are deferred and taxed over the depreciation period of the replacement assets in proportion to the depreciation claimed.
(4) Gains from other fixed assets not qualifying for roll-over are subject to tax at the full corporation tax rate.
(5) Gains from business assets held for more than five years qualify for roll-over where the replacement asset is located in Belgium and reinvestment takes place within three years of the beginning of the accounting period of disposal.

(d) *Special treatment of shares*. See (c) above. Where a tax treaty is in force, 75 per cent of the gain from foreign shares is exempt and the remaining 25 per cent is taxable at the full rate of corporation tax.

8. Treatment of groups

There is no concept of fiscal unity, so every company in a group must be treated separately.

9. Treatment of branches

A Belgian branch of a non-resident company is taxed on the same basis as a Belgian resident company. However, the corporation tax rate payable by branches is 43 per cent; this is reduced to 41 per cent (the normal corporation tax rate) where the head office is located in a country with the appropriate non-discrimination clause in its tax treaty with Belgium. Among the countries with such treaties are: the United States, Japan, Austria, Denmark, Germany, Greece, Italy, Norway, Portugal, Spain, Sweden and Switzerland. The branch tax rate will be reduced to 42.85 per cent in 1991 where the head office is in France, the Netherlands or Luxembourg. However, the full 43 per cent is payable by companies with head offices in, *inter alia*, Australia, Canada, Finland, Ireland and the UK.

Roll-over of capital gains is available to branches on the same terms as for Belgian resident companies (see 7 above). Where the half or full rates are payable, the appropriate rate for the branch is taken; eg where gains made by the Belgian branch of a French company are payable at the half rate, that rate will be 21.425 per cent. The same gains would be taxable at 21.5 per cent if the branch belonged to a UK company.

10. Other taxes

(a) *Taxes on capital.* There is no net worth tax but there is a property tax levied at the communal, provincial and national levels on all property situated in Belgium. The tax is based on a notional rental value of the property. Provincial and communal rates vary.

(b) *Turnover taxes.* There is a value-added tax (*taxe sur la valeur ajoutée*; *belasting over de toegevoegde waarde*) charged on the supply of goods and services and on imports. There is a standard rate of 19 per cent, reduced rates of 6 and 17 per cent and luxury rates of 25 and 33 per cent. Exports are zero rated.

(c) *Transaction taxes.* A capital duty of 0.5 per cent is levied on capital contributions to companies. A registration tax of 12.5 per cent is payable by the purchaser of immovable property. The rate is reduced to 5 per cent if the purchaser is a real estate company.

(d) *Payroll taxes.* A social security tax is payable by employers on gross salaries. The minimum rate for employers is 34 per cent.

Denmark

Average exchange rate y/e 31 March 1990: $1 = DKr 11.282

1. The tax year: nature and rates of tax

(a) The tax year is the year ending 31 March. The profits of an accounting period are wholly taxable in the year following that in which the accounting period ends.

Accounting period ended 30 September 1990. Profits DKr 500,000
Taxable: DKr 500,000 in year 1991 (ending 31 March 1992)

(b) Companies pay corporate income tax (*indkomstskat af aktieselskaber*) at a flat rate of 40 per cent (before tax year 1991, the rate was 50 per cent) on distributed and undistributed income. A reduced rate of 16 per cent is payable by some production and marketing cooperatives.

2. Residence and territoriality

Danish resident companies pay tax on their worldwide income. The decisive factor in determining residence is entry in the Danish register of companies. A company with an entry in the register will almost invariably be resident in Denmark for tax purposes.

3. The tax base

(a) *Method of calculation.* Taxable profits are based on the profit reported in the accounts.
(b) *Disallowable items.* The major disallowable items are formation expenses, 75 per cent of entertainment expenses and provisions for unquantifiable anticipated losses.
(c) *Exempt income and special deductions.* For dividends, see 4 below. Foreign trading relief is available as a reduction in the company's overall tax liability. The tax liability on the company's total income (including the foreign trading income – *virksomhed i utlandet*) is reduced by 50 per cent of the tax attributable (calculated as a proportion of gross foreign trading income to total income) to the foreign trading income. The relief applies equally to the income of a foreign branch and from a share in a foreign partnership. It is also given even where the income is actually exempt from Danish tax under the terms of a treaty. For the treatment of foreign subsidiaries, see 8 below.

(d) *Interest paid.* Interest is deductible on an accruals basis but, where payable to connected persons, is limited to arm's-length rates. Interest on loans to acquire subsidiary companies within the tax group (see 8 below) is deductible only against the acquiring company's own income.

(e) *Stock.* Stocks may be valued either at market value at the end of the accounting period, gross purchase price, or cost of production. Different categories of stock may be valued by different methods. LIFO is not acceptable.
Stock relief of up to 30 per cent may be claimed as a deduction each year. The amount claimed must, however, be added back to taxable income of the following period.

(f) *Depreciation.* Different rules apply.

(1) Plant and machinery. All plant forms one pool for depreciation purposes. Depreciation is applied to the net book value of the pool as brought forward from the previous year, less disposal proceeds of plant sold during the year (this balance being adjusted annually for inflation), plus five-sixths of the cost price of assets purchased during the year. The remaining one-sixth is added to the pool the following year. The maximum rate of depreciation is 30 per cent. Plant costing less than DKr 5,000 (£440) (this amount is adjusted annually) and plant with a useful life of less than three years may be written off in the year of purchase, up to an overall limit of DKr 200,000 annually. Accelerated allowances are available for ships.

(2) Buildings. A maximum of 6 per cent on cost until 60 per cent has been written down (a minimum of ten years); 2 per cent thereafter. Hotels and cinemas have reduced rates of 4 per cent (until 40 per cent has been written down) and 1 per cent thereafter. The depreciable base (where the building was acquired after 31 December 1982) is adjusted annually for inflation. Retail, storage and industrial premises all qualify for depreciation (*skattemaessige afskrivning*); office buildings in general do not.

(3) Initial allowances (*forskudsafskrivning*) is available for both buildings and plant being built or manufactured under contract. When a contract is awarded, the excess of the price over DKr 700,000 (£62,000) may be depreciated at a maximum of 15 per cent a year, limited to 30 per cent in total over four years.

(4) Other rates apply for various types of asset (eg patent rights, scientific research).

4. Treatment of dividends

(a) *Dividends received from Danish companies*

   (1) Where less than 25 per cent is held in the paying company, the dividend received is taxable. Dividends are normally subject to 30 per cent withholding tax. The dividend received plus a tax credit of 25 per cent is included in taxable income and the 30 per cent withholding tax, together with the 25 per cent tax credit, are deductible from the resulting tax payable. Pure investment companies quoted in Denmark are exempt from tax on all dividends. The sole object and activity of these companies must be the holding of shares in other companies and they must be obliged to redistribute all dividends received.
   (2) Where 25 per cent or more is held (a substantial participation), dividends are exempt, provided the holding has been in existence for the entire accounting period.

(b) *Dividends received from abroad.* Dividends from substantial participations are similarly exempt, provided that the tax system of the paying country is not substantially different from Denmark's. If it is, the dividend is taxable, with credit for the foreign tax paid.

(c) *Dividends paid.* A withholding tax of 30 per cent is deductible from dividends paid to resident and non-resident shareholders, unless the recipient is a parent company exempt from tax on the dividend under the substantial participation rule.

5. Anti-avoidance measures

There is no tax on accumulated earnings and no thin-capitalisation rules. Transfer pricing rules operate to adjust a Danish company's profits to reflect arm's-length prices. There are no provisions similar to the UK's controlled foreign company rules but the substance over form doctrine will look through shell companies etc.

6. Treatment of losses

(a) *Current period.* Trading losses may be set off against income and gains of the current period.

(b) *Future periods.* Trading losses may be carried forward for a maximum of five years.

(c) *Past periods.* No carry back of losses to prior periods is permitted.

(d) *Transferability.* Where there is a more than 50 per cent change in ownership, the ability to set losses carried forward against non-trading income is restricted.

7. Treatment of capital gains

(a) *Treatment.* Capital gains are generally treated as part of the company's income.

(b) *Computation.* Gains are computed by deducting cost (or depreciated net book value) from sale proceeds. Where plant and machinery is disposed of, no capital gain arises but the sale proceeds are deducted from the value of the pool, thus reducing future depreciation. Gains from immovable business property (ie the excess of proceeds over net book value (where appropriate), as adjusted for inflation (see 3(f) above) disposed of after seven years or more are exempt; for a disposal between four and seven years, there is a sliding scale of reductions. Gains on disposals before four years of ownership are fully chargeable, as are gains attributable to depreciation, whatever the period of ownership.

(c) *Roll-over.* There is no deferral of capital gains on reinvestment in new assets.

(d) *Special treatment for shares.* Where shares have been held for three years or more, the gain is usually exempt from tax. However, restrictions apply to the exemption for shares in foreign companies. Where the purpose of acquiring the shares was to make a capital gain, or the foreign company's business was largely financial or its income was subject to tax at a substantially lower rate than in Denmark, the exemption does not apply and the gain is fully liable to corporate income tax at 40 per cent.

8. Treatment of groups

A parent company together with its 100 per cent directly or indirectly owned subsidiaries may opt for joint taxation. Where they do so:

(1) Profits and losses of subsidiaries are added to (consolidated with) the taxable income of the parent. Pre-consolidation losses of subsidiaries can only be carried forward against their own future income, however,

(2) results of an accounting period in which a subsidiary enters or leaves the group must drop out of the consolidation.

(3) there is no tax-free transfer of assets between group members.

(4) the results of foreign subsidiaries may be consolidated. The 100 per cent ownership rule is relaxed where the law of the

foreign country insists on a minimum home country participation. Joint taxation of foreign subsidiaries means that losses incurred by foreign subsidiaries can be set off against Danish source income and gains and that foreign tax credits can be more effectively used. Furthermore, the foreign trading relief (see 3(c) above) is also available and extends to the whole of the subsidiary's income.

(5) dividends received from subsidiaries within a group are exempt from Danish corporate income tax, unless received from subsidiaries resident in tax havens.

9. Treatment of branches

A Danish branch of a non-resident company is treated effectively as if it were a Danish resident company. The branch's taxable income will include capital gains from assets located in Denmark. There is no withholding tax on remittances of profits from the branch.

10. Other taxes

(a) A hydrocarbon tax (*kulbrinteskat*) is levied in addition to corporate income tax on income arising from North Sea oil and gas activities.

(b) There is no general tax on capital or net worth for companies but there is a local property tax of between approximately 1 and 2.5 per cent.

(c) *Turnover taxes.* A value added tax (*mervaerdiafgift*) is charged on the supply of goods and services. There is a single rate of 22 per cent. Exports are exempt. There is also a labour market contribution (*arbejdsmarkedsbidrag*) of 2.5 per cent (with credit for input tax) on the value of goods and services, charged on the same basis as VAT.

(d) *Transaction taxes.* There is a capital duty of 1 per cent on additional capital subscriptions in a Danish company, and stamp duty on various transactions such as share transfers (1 per cent) and property sales (1.2 per cent).

(e) *Payroll taxes.* There are no general payroll taxes on the employer but financial companies are currently subject to a 2 per cent levy on 1.9 times the payroll.

Finland

Average rate of exchange y/e 31.3.90: £1 = FMk 6.7413

1. The tax year: nature and rates of tax

(a) The tax year is the calendar year. The profits of an accounting period other than a calendar year are taxable wholly in the year in which the accounting period ends.

Accounting period: year ended 30 September 1990. Profits: FMk 300,000.
Taxable: FMk 300,000 in tax year 1990 (ending 31 December 1990).

(b) Companies are liable to national income tax (*valtion tulovero*) at a flat rate of 25 per cent on both distributed and undistributed income. Lower rates are charged for taxable profits of below FMk 100,000. The rate of national income tax for 1991 is likely to be 23 per cent. Local taxes are also payable on income (see 10(a) below).

2. Residence and territoriality

Finnish resident companies are taxable on their worldwide income. A company is resident in Finland if it is *registered* there or if its central management and control is exercised in Finland. *Incorporation* in Finland does not necessarily denote residence.

3. The tax base

(a) *Method of calculation.* Taxable profits are based on the profit reported in the accounts. Income is calculated separately according to its source: business income (including non-trading income that arises from business assets and capital gains), [non-business] property income and agricultural income. Income from woodlands is taxed in a similar fashion to the UK's former Schedule B, the amount being based on the area of the woodland.
(b) *Disallowable items.* Entertaining expenses are non-deductible if 'unreasonable' in relation to turnover; local and church taxes are not deductible in computing profits for national income tax purposes. Charitable donations are not deductible for local or church taxes and their deductibility for national income tax is limited.

(c) *Exempt income/special deductions.* For dividends, see 4 below. For the inventory reserve, see 3(e) below. For the investment allowance, see 3(f) below. A non-specific doubtful debt reserve, of up to 2 per cent of trade debtors, may be established. Contributions to an operating reserve up to a maximum of 30 per cent of payroll are also tax deductible.
(d) *Interest paid.* Loan interest is deductible on an accruals basis. Where interest is paid to affiliates or shareholders, it is deductible only if there is a genuine loan. For thin-capitalisation rules, see 5 below. Interest paid to non-residents is generally not subject to withholding tax.
(e) *Stock.* Stock is valued at the lower of cost and market value on a FIFO basis. Where stock, including work in progress, is manufactured or generated internally, only direct costs are attributable. An inventory reserve of up to 25 per cent is deductible. If there is also an operating reserve (see 3(c) above), the inventory reserve may be restricted.
(f) *Depreciation.* Different methods are prescribed for different types of asset. (1) Buildings are depreciable on the reducing balance basis at rates of between 5 and 20 per cent. (2) Machinery and plant is also depreciable on a reducing balance basis at rates of up to 30 per cent. Machinery and plant is pooled and sale proceeds deducted from the pool value (see also 7 below). (3) Intangible assets are depreciable on the straight-line basis at rates of between 10 and 20 per cent. Free depreciation is available in certain designated regions and for assets with a useful life of less than three years.

4. Treatment of dividends

(a) *Dividends received from Finnish companies.* These carry a tax credit of 21/29 of the net dividend (based on an approximate combined national, local and church tax liability of 42 per cent). The excess tax credit is repayable if the total tax due on the company is less than 42 per cent. Consonant with the planned reduction of national income tax to 23 per cent in 1991, the tax credit for that year is likely to be 2/3 (40/60).
(b) *Dividends received from abroad.* These are generally exempt under treaty, but where there is no treaty the dividend, grossed up by the foreign withholding tax paid, is included in taxable income. The foreign withholding tax paid is available as a tax credit, provided the tax system in the source country is broadly similar to Finland's.

(c) *Dividends payable to residents.* Dividends payable to residents of Finland carry a tax credit of 21/29 of the net dividend. However, the paying company must have paid income tax (national, local and church) of at least the amount of the credit on the income out of which the dividend is paid. Any shortfall must be paid to the tax authorities as a 'complementary tax'; it is possible to cover a complementary tax liability by taxes paid in the preceding five years, beginning with 1989.

(d) *Dividends payable to non-residents.* Non-residents of Finland are not entitled to the tax credit. A withholding tax of 25 per cent is deductible instead, subject to a reduced rate provided by a double tax treaty.

5. Anti-avoidance measures

There are no taxes on accumulated earnings. A thin-capitalisation rule is operated with regard to Finnish subsidiaries of foreign companies. At least 25 to 35 per cent of the subsidiary's capital must consist of equity. Failing this, the excess loan capital is treated as equity and interest corresponding to the excess is deemed to be a dividend. Transfer pricing rules are applied to transactions (including interest payments) with foreign affiliates to adjust them to arm's-length values. There are no provisions similar to the UK's controlled foreign company legislation.

6. Treatment of losses

(a) *Current period.* There is no set-off of losses in the current period because of the 'schedular' system. If the aggregate profits and losses from all sources amount to a loss, the aggregate loss is carried forward.

(b) *Future periods.* The aggregate loss can be carried forward and set off against total taxable profits for national income tax purposes for a maximum of five years. For local income tax, a loss arising from any one source can be carried forward and set off against profits from that source for a maximum of five years. For both national and local income tax losses arising during the first five years of a business may be carried forward for a maximum of ten years.

(c) *Past periods.* Carry back of losses is not permitted.

(d) *Transferability.* A cessation of a business or trade does not cut off losses brought forward but a change of ownership of more than 50 per cent causes brought forward losses to be terminated.

7. Treatment of capital gains

(a) *Treatment.* Capital gains are treated as income.
(b) Computation rules are complicated. Broadly:

(1) Real property used for business purposes. If the property has been owned for at least ten years, the gain is computed by deducting the book value for 60 per cent of the net sale proceeds. Where the property has been owned for less than ten years, 100 per cent of the net sale proceeds are brought into the computation.

(2) Real property not used for business purposes. Where the property has been held for at least ten years, the gain is computed by deducting the greater of cost and 50 per cent of the sale proceeds from the sale proceeds. The gain is further reduced by an allowance of FMk 210,000 and the taxable gain is 40 per cent of the resulting figure. Where the property has not been held for ten years, the FMk 210,000 allowance is not given and the percentage of the gain taxable depends on the length of ownership (eg 100 per cent if under four years).

(3) Plant and machinery. See 3(f) above.

(c) *Roll-over.* There are no roll-over provisions as such, but a replacement reserve can be established with the gain from disposal of a building, so deferring the gain. Unless the reserve is used within three years to write down the cost of a replacement building, it is added back to taxable profits for the third year.
(d) *Special treatment of shares.* The gain on the sale of shares is computed in the same way as for real property, except that the key period of ownership is five (and not ten) years. Non-residents are generally not liable to tax on capital gains arising from the sale of shares in a Finnish company.

8. Treatment of groups

A tax group may be formed by a holding company and its 91 per cent subsidiaries, all of which must be resident in Finland, for the purpose of shifting profits and losses around the group by means of tax-deductible contribution payments (taxable in the hands of the recipient). Contribution payments may only be made between active companies that have both been members of the group for the whole of the accounting period in question and whose accounting periods are coextensive. The payment must be made during the accounting period in question.

9. Treatment of branches

It is comparatively rare for a non-resident company to set up a Finnish branch, as opposed to a Finnish resident subsidiary. However, such a branch would be subject to income tax in much the same way as a resident company. It would also be liable to national net worth tax (see 10(b) below), unless exempted by treaty. There is no withholding tax on remittances of profit abroad.

10. Other taxes

(a) *Local income tax (kunnallisvero).* This has already been referred to. It is levied on a similar base to national income tax. The rates vary between 14 and 19.5 per cent. There is also a church tax (*kirkollisvero*) of between 1 and 2 per cent on the local income tax base. Neither local tax nor church tax are deductible in computing national income tax liability and the same is true vice versa.

(b) *Taxes on capital.* Non-resident companies are in principle liable to national net worth tax (*varallisuusvero*), at 1 per cent on the net value of assets situated in Finland.

(c) *Turnover taxes.* There is a sales tax (*liikevaihtovero*) of 17 per cent on the sale price of goods and certain services, inclusive of the tax itself. This results in an effective rate of 20.48 per cent on the net consideration. In a manner analogous to VAT, sales tax paid on purchases is deductible from a vendor's sales tax liability. Exports are not subject to the tax.

(d) *Transaction taxes.* A duty of 6 per cent is payable on the transfer of real property and a 1.6 per cent duty is payable on a share transfer. This duty is reduced if the transfer takes place on the stock exchange and is not payable on a transfer between non-residents.

(e) *Social security.* Employers pay contributions of between 23 and 25 per cent of payroll. In addition, statutory holiday pay of 14–17 per cent is payable.

France

Average rate of exchange y/e 31.3.90: £1 = FF 9.88

1. The tax year; nature and rates of tax

(a) The tax year is the calendar year. Profits of an accounting period other than a calendar year are taxed wholly in the year in which the accounting period ends.

Accounting period ending 30 September 1990. Profits: FF 500,000
Taxable: FF 500,000 in tax year 1990 (ending 31 December 1990)

(b) Corporate income tax (*impôt sur les sociétés*) is charged at 42 per cent on distributed income and at 37 per cent on undistributed income. There is effectively a minimum tax of FF 5,000, since all companies must make non-refundable advance payments of corporate income tax of at least that amount. A reduced rate of 19 per cent (in some instances, 25 per cent) is payable on long-term capital gains (see 7 below). For the equalisation tax (*précompte mobilier*) on certain distributed profits, see 4 below.

2. Residence and territoriality

French resident companies pay corporate income tax on all income arising in France. Most foreign income (and capital gains) is exempt (see further 3(c) below). Companies may, if they wish, apply to the Minister of the Economy for permission to be taxed on their worldwide income (*bénéfice mondial*) (thereby obtaining relief for worldwide losses). This permission is seldom given.

A company is resident in France if it is incorporated under French law or its central control and management are found in France.

3. The tax base

(a) *Method of calculation.* The taxable profit is based on the profit reported in the accounts.
(b) *Disallowable items.* The major disallowable items are: transfers to the general and statutory reserve (*réserve légale*), costs of providing certain benefits to employees, the excess of charitable donations over 0.2 per cent or 0.3 per cent of turnover.
(c) *Exempt income/special deductions.* For dividends, see 4 below. For profits from foreign branches (exempt), see 9 below.

Contributions to pension schemes are deductible as are some dividends on new shares (see 4(c) below). Formation expenses may be deducted in the period in which they are incurred or amortised over a period of five years. Contributions by companies to the compulsory profit sharing plan are deductible. The only classes of foreign income fully liable to tax in France are interest, royalties, portfolio dividends unconcerned with a permanent establishment abroad and rental income from real property (although the latter is often exempt under a tax treaty).

(d) *Interest paid.* Interest is deductible under either an accruals or a paid basis. Interest paid to loan creditors who are also shareholders is allowed, provided certain conditions are satisfied and the rate is not excessive (ie not in excess of the average rate on private company bonds).

(e) *Stock.* Stock and work in progress are valued at the lower of cost and market value on a FIFO or average cost basis. A measure of stock relief is provided by a tax-deductible reserve that may be set up in a year in which the unit price of items has increased by over 10 per cent over the accounting period. The provision must be written back over a maximum of six years.

(f) *Depreciation.* Tax depreciation may be calculated on either a straight-line or a reducing balance basis, at rates fixed by the tax authorities. Land is not normally depreciable. Special depreciation allowances are available in certain industries (eg newspaper publishing) and accelerated depreciation allowances are available for, *inter alia*, buildings used solely for scientific research (50 per cent in the first year). There is no pooling of assets.

4. Treatment of dividends

(a) *Dividends received from French companies.* An imputation system operates in France, under which dividends paid by French companies carry a tax credit (*avoir fiscal*) of 50 per cent of the net dividend. This is transferred to the recipient company's own shareholders when it pays a dividend. However, a French company holding a minimum of 10 per cent of the paying company's share capital is entitled to an exemption from tax of 95 per cent of the gross dividend and the *avoir fiscal* corresponding to the exempt 95 per cent is not repayable. Where the recipient company's holding is less than 10 per cent the dividend received is subject to the full 42 per cent rate of corporate income tax on distributed income on the gross amount of the dividend. Dividends within a group (see 8 below) are tax free.

(b) *Dividends received from abroad.* The same rules apply as under (a) above. However, a dividend received from a foreign company in which the French recipient holds less than 10 per cent may retrospectively qualify for the 95 per cent exemption if the holding is increased to 10 per cent or more within three years of receipt of the dividend.

(c) *Dividends paid to residents.* There is no withholding tax on dividends paid to French resident shareholders. However, where dividends are paid out of profits that have not suffered the full 42 per cent rate of corporate income tax (eg dividends received qualifying for the 95 per cent exemption – see (a) above) or out of profits taxed at 42 per cent more than five years previously, an equalisation tax (*précompte mobilier*) of 33.3 per cent on the gross value of the dividend (ie dividend plus *avoir fiscal*) is payable by the distributing company. The purpose of the *précompte* is to ensure that the shareholder's *avoir fiscal* (tax credit) is only available where full tax has been paid by the paying company. Where the French company has suffered foreign tax on the profits out of which the dividend is paid, the foreign tax may be set against the *précompte* if there is a tax treaty in force with the foreign country.

(d) *Dividends paid to non-residents.* Non-residents of France are, in general, not entitled to the *avoir fiscal*. A withholding tax of 50 per cent (reduced where appropriate by treaty) is deductible from the dividend. French holding companies with foreign subsidiaries do not have to pay the *précompte* (see 4(c) above).

5. Anti-avoidance measures

There are no taxes on accumulated earnings. Thin-capitalisation rules are applied where interest is paid to foreign lenders, to ensure that where loans from foreign shareholders exceed 150 per cent of the share capital (a debt-equity ratio of 1.5:1), interest on the excessive part of the loan is treated as a dividend. There also measures similar to the UK's controlled foreign company legislation. In certain circumstances, French companies with an interest of 25 per cent or more in a foreign company established in a territory with a 'low tax' régime may be required to include in their income taxable in France their corresponding share of the foreign company's profits. A low tax régime is one under which the company pays 66.6 per cent or less of the tax it would have paid in France. Among European countries, Luxembourg and Switzerland are included in the list (not updated since 1975) as well as the usual offshore etc tax havens. The carrying on in the low tax jurisdiction of genuine commercial activity will usually earn an exemption from these attribution provisions. There are also transfer pricing rules in operation. Any transactions carried out with entities (affiliated or otherwise) in low tax régime jurisdictions will be adjusted for tax purposes to arm's-length values. Transactions with any foreign affiliate that transfer profits abroad by granting an unfair advantage (eg non-arm's-length prices, excessive loans) will also be adjusted to eliminate that advantage.

6. Treatment of losses

(a) *Current period.* Trading losses may be set against income and capital gains of the same period.

(b) *Future periods.* To the extent that they have not been used in the current period or in past periods (see (c) below) losses may be carried forward against taxable income for a maximum of five years. Any depreciation deferred in a year of loss (*amortissement différé*) may be carried forward indefinitely.

(c) *Past periods.* Trading losses may be carried back against undistributed income or gains of the three preceding years. The tax reduction obtained by the application of losses carried back creates a tax credit available for carry forward in an analogous way to a loss carried forward or for sale to a bank.

(d) *Transferability.* There are restrictions on the use of losses carried forward following certain mergers.

7. Treatment of capital gains

(a) *Treatment.* Capital gains are subject to corporate income tax, but at reduced rates in certain cases. French law distinguishes between short- and long-term gains.

   (1) Short term gains (the whole of the gain on an asset held for less than two years and that part of the gain on depreciable assets held for two years or more attributable to depreciation) less short-term losses (see (2) below) are taxable at the appropriate full rates of corporate income tax (37 per cent and 42 per cent).

   (2) Short-term losses are losses on non-depreciable assets held for less than two years and losses on all depreciable assets, no matter how long the term of ownership.

(3) Long-term gains are gains on assets held for at least two years less, in the case of depreciable assets, that part of the gain attributable to depreciation. Where long-term gains exceed long-term losses (of the current period and as brought forward) the net amount is taxable at a reduced rate of 19 per cent (25 per cent for gains from building land). The gain net of tax must be credited to a special reserve. If the reserve, less any net long-term capital losses, is distributed to shareholders, it is added back to taxable income and taxed at the full rate, with a credit for the tax paid.

(4) Net short-term losses in any accounting period, to the extent that they exceed taxable profits and long-term gains, may be carried forward as an ordinary trading loss (see 6(b) above). Net long-term losses may be used to reduce the special long-term gain reserve (see (3) above) or carried forward to set against long-term gains of the following ten years.

(b) *Computation*. Gains are computed by deducting the cost (or net book value where depreciation has been claimed) from sale proceeds.

(c) *Roll-over*. There is no roll-over against the cost of replacement assets.

(d) *Special treatment of shares*. Shares are identified on a FIFO basis to determine whether gains are long- or short-term. Where a non-resident makes a capital gain on disposal of shares in a French company, the gain is taxed at 17 per cent if the holding has exceeded 25 per cent at any time in the five years preceding disposal. Exemption for gains on the sale of shares is conferred by most of France's tax treaties.

8. Treatment of groups

A French parent company and any of its 95 per cent subsidiaries may elect for group treatment (*intégration fiscale*), under which they may consolidate their profits and losses. The election must be made *before* the first accounting period concerned and has effect for five years. All companies must have the same year end and be members of the group throughout the period concerned. Transfers of assets may be made tax free and dividends paid free of tax (that is, without a *précompte* and without the right to the *avoir fiscal*) within the group.

9. Treatment of branches

French branches of non-resident companies are liable for corporate income tax in the same manner as French resident companies. However, there is also a 25 per cent withholding tax on branch profits, all of which are deemed to be remitted for this purpose; this tax is subject to the terms of a tax treaty (eg the withholding tax on profits to the UK is nil).

10. Other taxes

(a) A local tax known as *taxe professionnelle* is levied at varying rates on a special tax base, which is 18 per cent of gross salaries (including fringe benefits) plus the annual rental value of the company's property, reduced by 16 per cent. The maximum payable is 4 per cent of the added value for the year.
(b) There is no net worth tax but a number of local property taxes are in force.
(c) *Turnover taxes.* There is a value-added tax (*taxe sur la valeur ajoutée*) on the supply of goods and services. The standard rate is 18.6 per cent and there is a reduced rate of 5.5 per cent and a luxury rate of 28 per cent.
(d) *Transaction taxes.* There are various taxes on the transfer of assets and on capital subscriptions. There is a 1 per cent duty (maximum FF 430) on share capital on incorporation and a registration tax (transfer duty) on, *inter alia*, the sale of a business as a going concern (11.4 per cent) and on the transfer of real property (16.6 per cent).
(e) *Payroll taxes.* Employers' social security contributions of approximately 39 per cent are payable as is a special residential housing levy of 0.85 per cent on payroll and an apprenticeship tax of 0.6 per cent of payroll.
(f) Other taxes include a special additional tax on company cars payable by the company. The tax varies according to vehicle size, ranging from FF 4,800 to FF 10,500.

Germany

Average rate of exchange y/e 31.3.90: £1 = DM 2.9144

1. The tax year: nature and rates of tax

(a) The tax year is the calendar year. The profits of an accounting period other than a calendar year are taxed wholly in the year in which the accounting period ends.

Accounting period ending 30 September 1990. Profits DM 150,000
Taxable: DM 150,000 in year 1990 (ending 31 December 1990)

(b) Corporation tax (*Körperschaftsteuer*) is levied at 50 per cent on a company's undistributed income; the rate applied to distributed income is 36 per cent.

2. Residence and territoriality

German resident companies are liable to corporation tax on their worldwide income. A company is treated as resident in Germany if it is incorporated there or has its principal place of management in Germany.

3. The tax base

(a) *Method of computation.* Taxable profits are computed by comparing the company's net worth at the beginning and end of the accounting period.
(b) *Disallowable items.* The major disallowable items (add-backs) are gifts, 20 per cent of business entertaining expenses, formation expenses, taxes on non-deductible expenses and other expenses incurred in connection with non-taxable income or gains.
(c) *Exempt income/special deductions.* For dividends, see 4 below. Deductions in assessing net worth include capital contributions, the share premium on shares issued in the period and certain investment grants, pension fund contributions, other taxes (including the trade tax and property tax: see 10(a), (b) below), charitable donations within the statutory limits and 'stock relief' (see (e) below).
(d) *Interest paid.* Interest is deductible on an accruals basis. For thin-capitalisation rules, see 5 below. Interest is disallowed if incurred in connection with income and gains that are permanently exempt from German tax (eg borrowings to finance a foreign branch, the

profits from which are exempt under a treaty). Interest paid to shareholders and affiliates is deductible but the amount may not exceed arm's-length rates.

(e) *Stock.* Stock and work in progress is valued at the lower of cost and market value. LIFO is now available if used for accounting and reporting purposes also. Fungible stock items may be valued on a weighted average cost basis.

(f) *Depreciation.* A variety of methods (straight-line, reducing balance and others) is permitted and the rates vary over different types of asset. Assets may be pooled in limited cases only (eg loose tools). Accelerated depreciation is available on certain expenditure. The gain or loss on sale of depreciable equipment forms part of taxable income.

4. Treatment of dividends

(a) *Dividends received from German companies.* Dividends received from German companies are subject to corporation tax on the gross amount of the dividend (net dividend plus tax credit of 9/16ths – representing the 36 per cent corporation tax paid on the distribution by the paying company). The tax credit may be set against the recipient company's own corporation tax liability and is repayable where appropriate. The gross dividend is also subject to the trade tax (*Gewerbesteuer*): see 10(a) below, but exemption is granted if the recipient has a holding of at least 10 per cent in the paying company. The net dividend will also have been subject to 25 per cent withholding tax. This withholding tax is creditable against the recipient's corporation tax liability.

(b) *Dividends received from abroad.* These dividends are subject to corporation tax and trade tax. Where the German company has a holding of at least 10 per cent in the foreign paying company, there is no trade tax liability and most tax treaties exempt the dividend from German tax. Where there is no exemption, any foreign withholding tax can either be used as a tax credit or, for trading companies, deducted as an expense. A holding of at least 10 per cent will generally ensure that the underlying foreign tax (ie corporation tax payable on the profits out of which the distribution is made) can be credited.

(c) *Dividends paid to German residents.* Distributed profits are taxed at the lower rate (36 per cent) of corporation tax. A record of 'distributable net equity' must be kept so that dividends can be identified as coming from taxed or untaxed profits. Dividends are presumed to stem in the first place from taxed profits. Since these profits will have suffered corporation tax at the retained profits rate of 50 per cent, a refund of 14 per cent will be made to the paying company. Where dividends are identified as coming from untaxed profits, however, the paying company must pay 36/64ths of the net dividend (36 per cent of the gross) as corporation tax. The net dividend is further subject to 25 per cent withholding tax (see 4(a) above).

(d) *Dividends paid to non-residents.* The same rules apply except that the foreign shareholder is not generally entitled to the 36 per cent tax credit. Where the distribution is made out of untaxed foreign income or out of earnings accumulated prior to 1 January 1977, however, the 36 per cent corporation tax is repaid to the non-resident shareholder (so that the only effective tax is the 25 per cent withholding tax). The withholding tax of 25 per cent is reduced by Germany's tax treaties.

5. *Anti-avoidance measures*

There is no special tax on accumulated earnings, which are already subject to the higher 50 per cent rate of corporation tax in any case. There are no statutory thin-capitalisation rules and the government's attempt to introduce them is of doubtful constitutional validity. Legislation is a distinct possibility. Transfer pricing rules operate on transactions between a German company and a foreign related party (where one has a substantial participation in the other or the same third party has a substantial participation in both). Such transactions are adjusted to their arm's-length values.

There are also complex controlled foreign company rules, under which certain undistributed income and gains of a foreign company in which German resident persons directly or indirectly own more than 50 per cent of the shares or voting power and which is taxed at a rate lower than 30 per cent, are taxable in the hands of those residents.

6. *Treatment of losses*

(a) *Current period.* Trading and capital losses are automatically offset against profits of the same period by virtue of the net worth basis of calculating taxable profits (see 3(a) above).

(b) *Future periods.* To the extent that an overall tax loss has not been set off against prior periods, it is carried forward indefinitely.

Losses arising before 1985 may only be carried forward for a maximum of five years, however.

(c) *Past periods.* Where a tax loss arises in any period, it is automatically set against non-distributed income and gains of the two preceding periods, up to a maximum of DM 10 million. There is no carry back for the business tax (see 10(a) below), however.

(d) *Transferability.* Where a change of ownership takes place after 23 June 1988, losses brought forward will continue to be available only where there has been no change of legal or economic identity. Economic identity is regarded as changed where more than 75 per cent of the shares change hands and the company restarts business with predominantly new assets.

7. Treatment of capital gains

(a) *Method of computation.* Gains are computed by deducting the cost (or net book value, where appropriate) of an asset from the sale proceeds.

(b) *Treatment.* Capital gains are treated as income.

(c) *Roll-over.* Gains may be rolled over where they arise from the disposal of real property, depreciable movable property with a minimum useful life of 25 years and shares, held for a minimum of six years. Reinvestment of the sale proceeds must take place in qualifying replacement assets within four accounting periods of the disposal (six in the case of real property). The tax deferred in this way is 50 per cent (100 per cent in the case of real property).

(d) *Special treatment for shares.* See (c) above.

8. Treatment of groups

There is no general recognition of groups for tax purposes but 'integrated companies' (*Organschaften*) may consolidate profits and losses for subsidiaries. For an *Organschaft* relationship to exist, the parent company must own at least 50 per cent of the subsidiary's shares throughout the accounting period in question and the subsidiary's business must be integrated with the parent's on a financial, organisational and economic basis. The subsidiaries must be resident in Germany and a profit and loss pooling agreement must actually be in force and designed to last for at least five years.

9. Treatment of branches

The profits of a German resident branch of a non-resident company are computed according to the rules for a resident company but only German source income and gains are taxable. There is a special flat rate branch tax of 46 per cent instead of the two-tier structure applying to German resident companies (see 1(b) above). Branches are also liable to the net worth tax (see 10(b) below) and the trade tax (see 10(a) below) on their German income and assets. There is no withholding tax on remittances of branch profit abroad.

10. Other taxes

(a) A two-tier trade tax (*Gewerbesteuer*) is payable as a local tax on a company's taxable income and capital.

 (1) The base for the income element of the tax is the corporation tax profit as adjusted for, *inter alia*, long-term debt and dividends from German and certain foreign companies. The basic rate is 5 per cent multiplied by a factor of between 2 and 4.8, depending on the locality.
 (2) The base for the capital element of the tax is the net worth tax base (see (b) below) as adjusted. A deduction of DM 120,000 is available to reduce the adjusted base. The basic rate is 0.2 per cent multiplied by the same factor as in (1) above.
 (3) The trade tax is deductible in computing the tax itself.

(b) *Taxes on capital.* In addition to the capital element of the trade tax, there is also a net worth tax (*Vermögensteuer*) on the worldwide assets of resident companies. Shareholdings of 10 per cent or over in other resident companies or non-dormant foreign companies are exempt. The tax base for branches of non-resident companies is limited to their assets situated in Germany. The tax is charged at a rate of 0.6 per cent on 75 per cent of the adjusted base in excess of DM 125,000. The net worth tax is not deductible for trade tax or corporation tax purposes.

 There is also a local property tax (*Grundsteuer*) on the assessed value of property at a basic rate of between 0.25 and 0.6 per cent multiplied by a local factor of between 1.8 and 3.7. The property tax is deductible for corporation tax purposes.

(c) *Turnover taxes.* There is a value-added tax (*Mehrwertsteuer*) on the supply of goods and services at a single rate of 14 per cent.

(d) *Transaction taxes.* There is a real property transfer tax of 2 per cent and a capital duty of 1 per cent on the incorporation of a company. There is also a transfer tax of 0.25 per cent on share transfers. Capital duties are to be abolished by 1993.

(e) *Payroll taxes*. Employers are obliged to pay certain social security premiums, based on a percentage of gross monthly salary up to a ceiling (eg DM 6,100 for pension insurance). The rates are 9.35 per cent for pension insurance, approximately 6.5 per cent for sickness insurance and 2.3 per cent for unemployment insurance. One half of the amount paid may be recovered from the employee.

Greece

Average rate of exchange y/e 31.3.90: £1 = Dr 264.15

1. The tax year; nature and rates of tax

(a) The tax year is the calendar year. Almost all accounting periods end either on 31 December or 30 June. The appropriate tax year is the year in which the accounting period ends.

(b) The corporation tax is levied at a standard rate of 46 per cent on the income of an *anonymos etairea*, or AE (equivalent to a French SA). A limited liability company (*etairea periosmenis efthinis*), or EPE, is not subject to corporation tax and its income is imputed to its partners, although the company pays a 15 per cent withholding tax, which is credited against their liability. The description below is restricted to the *anonymos etairea* (a 'company'). Lower rates apply to some types of company incorporated in Greece. Quoted manufacturing and mining companies and unquoted manufacturing and mining companies that have made investments in certain development areas pay corporation tax at 35 per cent. Other manufacturing and mining companies and other companies that have made investments as above pay at 40 per cent. For Greek holding companies, see (c) below.

Only undistributed income is liable to corporation tax. Dividends are taxable in shareholders' hands only and dividend payments are therefore deductible expenditure for the company (see 4(c) below).

(c) *Special régime for Greek holding companies.* Holding companies, investment holding companies and mutual trusts are exempt from all major direct taxes on capital and income.

2. Residence and territoriality

Greek resident companies are taxable on their worldwide income. A company is resident in Greece if it is incorporated there or has its central place of management in Greece.

3. The tax base

(a) *Method of computation.* Taxable profits are based on the profit reported in the accounts. Unrealised foreign exchange gains and losses are recognised for tax purposes. Exchange losses on long-term loans may be capitalised.

(b) *Disallowable items.* In general, expenses must be related to the business to be deductible. The major disallowable items include the corporation tax itself (most other taxes are deductible), gifts to political parties, compulsory payments to the statutory reserve (5 per cent of profits must be set aside each year until the reserve amounts to one-third of the company's equity capital) and payments to the (optional) extraordinary reserve.

(c) *Exempt income/special deductions.* The following income is exempt, *inter alia*: interest from deposits with Greek banks, profits from newspaper and periodical publishing, profits from property sales, income from shipping operating under the Greek flag. For dividends, see 4 below. Deductions are allowed for bad debt provisions for debts written off and charitable donations. For investment allowances, see (f) below.

(d) *Interest paid.* Interest is deductible on an accruals basis. Loan interest payable to shareholders is deductible in the normal way, if the loan was incurred for business purposes. Interest payments to resident companies must be made under deduction of 25 per cent withholding tax.

(e) *Stock.* Stock is valued at the lower of cost and market value on a consistent basis. Both FIFO and LIFO are permissible.

(f) *Depreciation.* Depreciation is on the straight-line basis on cost, according to fixed rates for different types of asset, eg buildings 5–8 per cent, plant and machinery 10–15 per cent. Assets held in 1982 were revalued at specified rates to provide swifter depreciation. Land is not depreciable. Pooling is allowed but the valuation of each asset must be made separately. Spare parts and tools and expenditure on research and development may usually be written off in full immediately. Accelerated development is available, depending on which of the four economic areas of the country the investment takes place in and the number of working shifts in which the assets are put to use. The normal depreciation rates are increased by between 20 and 150 per cent.

For investment in the three more disadvantaged areas of the country, an investment allowance of between 40 and 70 per cent of the amount invested may be set against a percentage (varying from 60 to 90 per cent) of taxable profits. The allowance is available only for the first Dr 1,600 million (£6,050,000) invested.

Both the investment allowance and accelerated depreciation are to be withdrawn after 31 December 1992. Various other investment incentives exist.

4. Treatment of dividends

(a) *Dividends received from Greek companies.* Dividends received from other Greek companies are exempt from corporation tax. However, they are paid under deduction of withholding tax at rates of between 42 and 50 per cent. If the dividend payment comes from a company quoted on the Athens stock exchange, the first Dr 50,000 will also be exempt from the withholding tax, up to a maximum of Dr 200,000 in any year for the recipient company. This withholding tax is not repayable but may be set against the withholding tax for which the recipient company must account on its own distributions.

(b) *Dividends received from abroad.* These may be taxed in Greece if the treaty with the source country so provides. In the absence of a treaty, the dividends will usually not be taxable in Greece where the Greek company has a permanent establishment in the source country. A foreign tax credit is available for foreign taxes paid, but it cannot exceed the Greek tax payable had the income been earned in Greece.

(c) *Dividends paid.* Dividend distributions to both residents and non-residents are deductible in computing profits for corporation tax purposes. The paying company must deduct withholding tax from the dividend payment. For companies quoted on the Athens stock exchange, the rate is 42 per cent for registered shares and 45 per cent for bearer shares. For companies not quoted on the stock exchange, the rates are 47 per cent for registered shares and 50 per cent for bearer shares. The rates may be reduced for quoted companies that have increased their capital for the first three years after they do so.

5. Anti-avoidance measures

The only significant anti-avoidance legislation in Greece concerns transfer pricing. Transactions between two or more related companies must be made at arm's length. Where the tax authorities consider profit is being reallocated prejudicially, particularly to foreign affiliates, the profits of the Greek company will be adjusted to reflect the arm's length position. There are no special taxes on accumulated earnings (the tax system already provides exemption for distributed earnings), no thin-capitalisation rules and no provisions similar to the UK's controlled foreign company legislation. Strict exchange controls have been the authorities' main weapon against international tax avoidance in the past; the coming of the Single Market and abolition of exchange controls within the Community may therefore lead to the introduction of specific anti-avoidance legislation.

6. Treatment of losses

(a) *Current period.* Losses (including capital losses) may be set off against profits of the same period.
(b) *Future periods.* Any losses unrelieved in the current period may be carried forward for a maximum of five years (industrial or productive companies) or three years (commercial companies). Capital losses may not be carried forward.
(c) *Past periods.* Carry back of losses is not permitted.

7. Treatment of capital gains

(a) *Treatment.* Most capital gains are taxed as income at normal corporation tax rates, but gains from certain types of asset are taxed separately from business profits and at one of two lower rates.

    (1) Gains from the disposal of immovable property and ships (unless these assets are stock in trade) are exempt.
    (2) Gains from the disposal of other fixed assets are taxed as ordinary income but may be deferred (see (c) below).
    (3) Gains from the assignment of trade marks, patents etc are taxed at 30 per cent, but see (4) below.
    (4) Gains from the disposal of an entire business (including intangible assets) or its shares are taxed at 20 per cent.

(b) *Computation.* Gains are computed by deducting cost from sale proceeds.
(c) *Roll-over.* Gains in category (2) may be deferred if credited to a special reserve to be used for the acquisition of replacement assets within two years of the disposal. Where the reserve is used, the depreciable cost of the replacement asset is reduced accordingly. Any part of the reserve unused at the end of two years is written back to taxable income in that year.
(d) *Special treatment of shares.* Gains from the disposal of shares can be deferred by being transferred to a reserve account for set-off against future losses from the disposal of securities. If distributions are made out of the reserve, it is added back to taxable income.

8. Treatment of groups

There is no concept of grouping in Greek law so every company in a group must account for its own tax, and payments between group companies do not benefit from any tax privileges or exemptions. Transfer pricing rules must be taken into account (see 5 above). For the taxation of holding companies, see 1(c) above.

9. Treatment of branches

In general, the Greek branch of a non-resident company is subject to tax in the same manner as a Greek resident company. The branch is therefore subject to corporation tax, but at the standard 46 per cent rate, on its worldwide income. A special deduction of 2 per cent of profits can be made to represent head office expenses in administering the branch. There is no withholding tax on remittances of profits from the branch.

10. Other taxes

(a) There are no other taxes on the income of an AE. For the treatment of income of an EPE, see 1(b) above.
(b) *Taxes on capital.* There is no net worth tax but Greek companies are subject to an annual tax on the value of immovable property. It is levied on the value of the property as at 1 January, as reduced by any outstanding charges against the property or loans taken out for its acquisition or improvement. The first Dr 40,000,000 (£151,400) is free of tax and the remainder is taxed at 1.5 per cent. Some buildings (but not the underlying land) used by industrial, craft and tourist enterprises are exempt.
(c) *Turnover taxes.* There is a value-added tax on the supply of goods and services. The standard rate is 18 per cent with reduced rates of 3 per cent and 8 per cent and a luxury rate of 36 per cent. Interest is exempt from VAT but royalties are charged at a special rate of 18 per cent. The transfer of shares or participations in an *EA* or *EPE* are exempt.
(d) *Transaction taxes.* There is a tax on the transfer of immovable property, generally at 11 per cent of the value. There is also a capital duty of 1 per cent on the capital subscribed to a company and on further issues. A stamp duty of 2.4 per cent is levied on the payment of loan interest and on various insurance transactions. A 1.2 per cent stamp duty is payable on directors' fees.

(e) *Payroll taxes.* Employers are obliged to pay social security contributions. The rate depends on the type of work performed by the employee but is generally 22.45 per cent for office and white-collar workers and can rise to 24.15 per cent in the manufacturing industry on monthly salaries of up to Dr 238,475 (£903). As formerly in the UK, no additional contributions are payable on the excess above this figure.

Ireland

Average rate of exchange y/e 31.3.90: £1 = IR£1.0963

1. The tax year; nature and rates of tax

(a) The financial year is the calendar year but corporation tax rates are set for years ending on 31 March. Profits of an accounting period ending other than on 31 March are apportioned on a time basis between the relevant tax years.

Accounting period ended 30 September 1990. Profits IR£50,000
Taxable: year 1989 (ending 31.3.90): £50,000 × 6/12 = £25,000
year 1990 (ending 31.3.91): £50,000 × 6/12 = £25,000

(b) The corporation tax is levied at a rate of 43 per cent on distributed and undistributed income. The rate will be reduced to 40 per cent from the year 1991. A special rate of 10 per cent applies to manufacturing companies until 31 December 2010 and to companies providing certain financial services in the Customs House area of Dublin to non-Irish residents. The manufacturing rate applies to income from the worldwide sale of goods manufactured in Ireland. A wide variety of activities constitutes manufacturing, but the following activities are, *inter alia*, excluded: the breaking down of materials acquired in bulk, the preparation of food intended for immediate consumption and the improvement or alteration of articles without changing their character. Companies wishing to benefit from the 10 per cent rate for the Customs House area must obtain a licence from the Minister for Finance. Permitted activities include global money management, dealings in commodity futures and financial assets and ancillary trading and informatics activities.

2. Residence and territoriality

Irish resident companies are liable to corporation tax on their worldwide income and gains. A company is resident in Ireland if its central management and control is exercised there; its country of incorporation is irrelevant.

3. The tax base

(a) *Method of computation.* Taxable profits are based on the profit reported in the accounts. Foreign exchange gains and losses are recognised only if they relate to 'circulating' and not 'fixed' capital. Non-trading income (eg interest and rents) and foreign trading income are liable to corporation tax but are computed separately from trading profits.

(b) *Disallowable items.* The major disallowable items are expenditure not incurred wholly and exclusively for the purposes of the trade, non-staff entertaining, capital expenditure and depreciation (for capital allowances, see (f) below) and general provisions.

(c) *Exempt income/special deductions.* For dividends, see 4 below. For capital allowances, see (f) below. Income from Irish registered patents is exempt if the work leading to the patent was carried out in Ireland. A special deduction of up to IR£600,000 over three years is available for investment in Irish resident film production companies.

(d) *Interest paid.* Interest paid is normally deductible on an accruals basis. Where interest is paid other than to a bank, the company must deduct income tax at the basic rate (ie a withholding tax of 30 per cent) from the payment. This withholding tax is regularly reduced to zero under the terms of a tax treaty. Where interest is paid by an Irish resident company to an overseas parent with a participation of 75 per cent or over, it is non-deductible and treated similarly to a dividend payment (although no ACT (see 4(c) below) is payable. Certain profit-related interest ('section 84 interest') is treated as a dividend payment but the use of section 84 loans as a means of tax avoidance by the payee has now been restricted.

(e) *Stock.* Stock and work in progress is valued at the lower of cost and market value on a FIFO basis. LIFO is not permissible. There is no stock relief for inflationary increases, except for farmers.

(f) *Depreciation.* Accounts depreciation is not deductible for tax purposes. There is instead a system of capital allowances for specified classes of assets.

   (1) Plant and machinery (other than motor vehicles) are entitled to an accelerated allowance of 50 per cent in the first year and an annual allowance in the first and subsequent years of 10, 12.5 or 25 per cent on a reducing balance basis. Accelerated allowances can be disclaimed and will be phased out entirely by 1993.

   (2) Motor vehicles are depreciated by an annual allowance of 20 per cent per annum on a reducing balance basis. The depreciation of private vehicles is based on a maximum cost of IR£7,000.

(3) Industrial buildings are entitled to an accelerated allowance of 50 per cent in the first year and to an annual allowance of 4 per cent of the original cost on a straightline basis. The accelerated allowance will be completely phased out by 1993. Hotels have an annual allowance of 10 per cent. Office and retail premises do not qualify for capital allowances.

(4) Urban renewal allowances of up to 100 per cent are available on construction expenditure in certain areas. The above reductions in the accelerated allowance do not apply to expenditure in designated areas.

Capital allowances are deductible in computing profits.

4. The treatment of dividends

(a) *Dividends received from Irish companies.* Dividends received from Irish resident companies are exempt from corporation tax. The tax credit attaching to them (28/72 of the net dividend – see (c) below) may be used to reduce the advance corporation tax payable by the company on its own dividends. Dividends from companies paying the reduced 10 per cent (see 1(b) above) carry a tax credit of 1/18 of the net dividend.

(b) *Dividends received from abroad.* Where the recipient company's holding is 10 per cent or more, dividends received from abroad are liable to corporation tax on their gross amount (net dividend received plus withholding tax plus underlying tax borne on the profits out of which the dividend is paid). A foreign tax credit is available amounting to the withholding tax and the underlying tax but this may be used against Irish tax on that income alone. Where the holding is less than 10 per cent, there is no credit for underlying tax, but treaties may provide for a tax credit.

(c) *Dividends paid to Irish residents.* Advance corporation tax (ACT) is payable at a rate of 28/72 of the net dividend and an equivalent tax credit is available to the recipient. ACT is indeed an advance payment of corporation tax, in that it may be used (as reduced by the tax credit on incoming dividends) to reduce the company's corporation tax liability on its income (although not its capital gains). If there is a surplus of ACT after set-off in the current period, the surplus may be carried back to the previous accounting period or carried forward indefinitely to future accounting periods. If there is a surplus of 'franked investment income' (ie the tax credit on dividends received exceeds the ACT on dividends paid), the surplus may be carried forward.

(d) *Dividends paid to non-residents.* The company must still pay ACT but non-residents are not entitled to the tax credit represented by ACT. However, dividends paid by 75 per cent subsidiaries to a parent resident in a treaty country are free of ACT. There is no withholding tax.

5. Anti-avoidance measures

There are measures designed to prevent the accumulation of profits in 'close' (primarily family-owned) companies. Such companies are charged to an additional 20 per cent tax on their after-tax 'passive' income (eg investment income and rents, not trading income), unless a distribution is made of that income within 18 months of the end of the accounting period. There are no thin-capitalisation rules as such but note the treatment of interest paid to 75 per cent parents (see 3(d) above). Transfer pricing legislation exists and is of particular application to manufacturing companies benefiting from the reduced 10 per cent rate of corporation tax (see 1(b) above). There is no equivalent to the UK's controlled foreign company legislation but, as in the UK, there are wide-ranging measures to prevent avoidance by transfer of income abroad. There is also a general anti-avoidance power (absent in the UK) allowing the tax authorities to counteract transactions carried out primarily to create an artificial tax benefit.

6. Treatment of losses

(a) *Current period.* Trading losses may be set off against all income and gains of the same period, except gains from development land.

(b) *Future periods.* To the extent that they remain unrelieved in the current or preceding periods, trading losses may be carried forward indefinitely against profits from the same trade.

(c) *Past periods.* A trading loss may be carried back and set against all income and gains of the preceding period, except gains from development land.

(d) *Transferability.* Loss carry forward is denied where there is a more than 50 per cent change in ownership of a company and a major change in the nature of the trade (including its outlets etc).

For capital losses, see 7 below.

7. Treatment of capital gains

(a) *Treatment.* A company's capital gains are assessable to corporation tax but are scaled up or down in order to tax them effectively at the same rate as the capital gains tax charge on individuals. Gains on assets held for three years or less are taxed at 50 per cent (scaling up factor 50/43), gains on assets held for more than three years but not more than six are taxed at 35 per cent (scaling down factor 35/43) and gains on assets held for more than six years at 30 per cent (scaling down factor 30/43). Development land is taxed at different rates and the indexation allowance for inflation (see 7(b) below) is restricted.

(b) *Computation.* Capital gains are computed by deducting the adjusted cost from sale proceeds. The cost of acquisition is adjusted for inflation beginning from a point one year after acquisition.

(c) *Roll-over.* Deferral of a gain by rolling it over against the cost of replacement assets is possible in many situations. Roll-over relief is not available for gains from development land.

(d) *Special treatment of shares.* There is no special treatment of shares as such but a deferral of the capital gain on a *bona fide* commercial share-for-share exchange where the issuing company ends up by owing more than 50 per cent of the other company.

8. Treatment of groups

Group treatment is available along UK lines for a parent company and its 75 per cent subsidiaries, providing all are resident in Ireland. Tax losses of the current period may be transferred to other companies in the group and assets may be transferred between group companies free of capital gains tax. Losses from manufacturing companies benefiting from the special 10 per cent rate of corporation tax (see 1(b) below) are effectively 'ring fenced' and may be used to reduce manufacturing profits only. Dividends and interest may be paid free of ACT or income (withholding) tax and surplus ACT may be surrendered within a 51 per cent group (ie only a 51 per cent relationship is required for these facilities). A single group registration for VAT is available for a 51 per cent group.

9. Treatment of branches

The profits and gains of an Irish branch of a non-resident company are computed in the same way as those of an Irish resident company but tax is charged on Irish source income only. The special 10 per cent rate is available under the same conditions. There is no withholding tax and no ACT on remittances of profits from the branch.

10. Other taxes

(a) There are no other taxes on income or capital except the local authority rate levied on the annual (rental) value on the occupier of property located in the authority's area.

(b) *Turnover taxes.* A value-added tax is charged on the supply of goods and services. There is a standard rate of 23 per cent and lower rates of 2.3 and 10 per cent. Exports are zero rated.

(c) *Transaction taxes.* There is a capital duty of 1 per cent on share issues and stamp duties on the transfer of shares and other property. The rate for share transfers is 1 per cent; the duty on the transfer of real property of over IR£60,000 is 6 per cent.

(d) *Payroll taxes.* Social security contributions are payable by employers at 12.2 per cent on salaries of up to IR£18,600 per annum. No contributions are payable by the employer on the excess of salaries over IR£18,600.

Italy

Average rate of exchange y/e 31.3.90: £1 = L 2,142

1. The tax year; the nature and rates of tax

(a) The tax year is the calendar year. Profits of accounting periods other than calendar years are taxable wholly in the year in which the accounting period ends.

Accounting period year ended 30 September 1990. Profits L 100,000,000
Taxable: L 100,000,000 in year 1990 (ending 31 December 1990)

(b) Italian companies are liable to both national income tax (*imposta sul reddito delle persone giuridiche*, or IRPEG) and local income tax (*imposta locale sui redditi*, or ILOR). IRPEG is charged at a single rate of 36 per cent and ILOR is charged at 16.2 per cent. New industrial undertakings setting up in the Mezzogiorno (the south of Italy) receive a ten-year exemption from IRPEG.

2. Residence and territoriality

Companies resident in Italy are liable to IRPEG on their worldwide income and gains. ILOR is levied on Italian source income and gains only. A company is resident in Italy if it is incorporated there, if its legal or administrative headquarters is in Italy or if its principal business is carried on there.

3. The tax base

(a) *Method of calculation.* Taxable profits for IRPEG and ILOR are based on the profit reported in the accounts.
(b) *Disallowable items.* The major disallowable items are expenses incurred in relation to non-taxable income, two-thirds of entertaining expenses and pension contributions. Repairs and maintenance deductions are limited in the current period to a maximum of 5 per cent of the cost of depreciable assets at the beginning of the accounting period. Deduction for the excess is deferred.
(c) *Exempt income/special deductions.* For dividends, see 4 below. A maximum of 0.5 per cent of trade debtors may be deducted as a provision against doubtful debts but the total provision may not

exceed 5 per cent of trade debtors. The ILOR liability is deductible in computing liability to IRPEG.

(d) *Interest paid.* Interest is deductible on an accruals basis. See (b) above for interest incurred in connection with non-taxable income. A withholding tax of 12.5 per cent (treated as an advance payment of IRPEG) must be deducted on interest payments to residents.

(e) *Stock.* Stock is valued at the lower of cost and market value. Generally, a LIFO basis is used. Work in progress is valued at a percentage of completion value. There is no stock relief for inflationary increases in stock values.

(f) *Depreciation.* Depreciation is on the straight-line basis at rates prescribed by the tax authorities. The depreciable base is cost before any relevant grants. Accelerated depreciation is available for tangible assets in the first three years of use. There is no pooling of assets. The excess of sale proceeds over net book value of assets disposed of is included in taxable income, as are any losses arising. Expenditure on assets costing less than L 1,000,000 (£467) may be written off in the year it is incurred.

4. Treatment of dividends

(a) *Dividends received from Italian companies.* These are subject to IRPEG only. For IRPEG purposes, the dividend is grossed up for withholding tax (10 per cent: see (b) below) and a tax credit of 9/16 (56.25 per cent). Both the withholding tax and tax credit can be set off against the resulting IRPEG liability. The result, with a refund of the withholding tax, is that the dividend is effectively tax free. Both the tax credit and the withholding tax are repayable in the event that the IRPEG liability is zero or less than full (eg if there are losses to be set off: see 6 below).

(b) *Dividends received from abroad.* Dividends received from foreign companies are liable to IRPEG in Italy. The foreign tax paid on the dividend can be used as a credit against IRPEG but any excess is not available for set-off elsewhere or carry forward. Where the Italian company has a participation of 10 per cent or more in the paying company (or 5 per cent where the paying company is quoted), 60 per cent of the dividends received are exempt from IRPEG.

(c) *Dividends paid to Italian residents.* A withholding tax of 20 per cent must be deducted from dividends payable to residents of Italy. In addition, if the paying company distributes more than 64 per cent of its income liable to IRPEG or distributions are made from income that has not suffered the full rate of IRPEG (eg foreign dividends from a substantial participation), the paying company must pay an equalisation tax (*imposta di conguaglio*) by way of additional IRPEG at 56.25 per cent on the excess. This ensures that the tax credit available to the recipient does not exceed the IRPEG paid on the income by the paying company.

(d) *Dividends paid to non-residents.* Withholding tax at 32.4 per cent must be deducted from dividends paid to non-residents; this rate is reduced under the terms of most treaties.

5. *Anti-avoidance measures*

There are no taxes on accumulated earnings and no thin-capitalisation rules. Transfer pricing provisions do operate, however, to adjust transactions between Italian companies and foreign affiliates to arm's-length values. Italy has no provisions similar to the UK's controlled foreign company legislation.

6. *Treatment of losses*

(a) *Current period.* Trading and capital losses may be set off against other income and gains of the same period.
(b) *Future periods.* For IRPEG purposes only, losses may also be carried foward against income and gains for a maximum of five years. ILOR does not recognise losses carried foward.
(c) *Past periods.* Loss carry back is not permitted.
(d) *Transferability.* There is normally no restriction of loss carry forward on a change of ownership.

7. *Treatment of capital gains*

(a) *Treatment.* Capital gains are treated as taxable income.
(b) *Computation.* Gains are computed by deducting the cost of the asset (or, for depreciable assets, their net book (depreciated) value) from sale proceeds. There is no adjustment for inflation. If the asset disposed of is real property, the property tax (INVIM: see 10(b) below) is a deductible expense.
(c) *Roll-over.* Where the disposal proceeds are reinvested in replacement assets, the gain realised may be spread over a maximum of five years.
(d) *Special treatment of shares.* There is no special treatment of shares.

8. Treatment of groups

Italian tax law does not recognise the group concept, so the results of each group member must be treated separately. Grouping is allowed for VAT, however. The members of a 51 per cent group may net off liabilities and amounts refundable. The aggregate liability or refund is paid by or repaid to the parent company.

9. Treatment of branches

The profits and gains of the Italian branch of a non-resident company are computed in the same way as those of a resident company. The branch will be liable to IRPEG and ILOR on its Italian source income and gains. There is no withholding tax on remittances of profit from the branch.

10. Other taxes

(a) Whereas ILOR is a local tax with an invariable national rate (16.2 per cent), the local property tax INVIM (*imposta comunale sull'incremento di valore degli immobili*) varies locally. It is both a transaction tax, chargeable on the vendor of real property, and a decennial capital tax on property. As its name suggests, it is levied on the increase in value of real property over its acquisition cost. The rate also varies according to the period of ownership and, on the occasion of a disposal, to the proportion the gain bears to the cost. INVIM is a deductible expense in calculating the capital gain on disposal of real property and in computing liability to IRPEG and ILOR.

(b) *Turnover taxes.* Value added tax (*imposta sul valore aggiunto*) is charged on the supply of goods and services. The standard rate is 19 per cent; there are lower rates of 2 and 9 per cent and a luxury rate of 28 per cent. Exports are zero rated.

(c) *Transaction taxes.* There are various transfer taxes. A 1 per cent registration tax is payable by the purchaser on the transfer of real property; a 1 per cent capital duty is charged on the issue of shares and a 0.14 per cent transfer tax is payable on share transfers. When a business is transferred as a going concern, a 3 per cent registration tax is payable.

(d) *Payroll taxes.* Employers' social security contributions amount to between 35 and 45 per cent of gross payroll.

Luxembourg

Average rate of exchange y/e 31.3.90: $1 = LF 60.943

1. The tax year; nature and rates of tax

(a) The tax year is the calendar year. Profits of accounting periods other than calendar years are apportioned on a time basis between the tax years in which they fall.

Accounting period year ended 30 September 1990: Profits LF 3,000,000
Taxable: tax year 1989 (ending 31 December 1989) LF 3,000,000 × 6/12 = LF 1,500,000
tax year 1990 (ending 31 December 1990) LF 3,000,000 × 6/12 = LF 1,500,000

(b) Companies are liable to corporate income tax (*impôt sur le revenu des collectivités*) at a standard rate of 34 per cent (plus a supplementary levy of 2 per cent of the tax itself) on distributed and undistributed income. Taxable profits of below LF 1,312,000 ($21,530) benefit from lower rates. For Luxembourg holding companies, (see 1(c) below). A communal business tax is also payable on income (see 10(a) below).

(c) *Special régimes.* Luxembourg has special taxation régimes for 'coordination centres' and Luxembourg-based holding companies.

(1) Coordination centres of multinational groups enjoy special tax status. Luxembourg's coordination centre rules are broadly similar to Belgium's (qv, §1(c)). Coordination centres are Luxembourg companies providing administrative services to members of a multinational group. The group must have members in at least two other countries and the ultimate parent must be resident outside Luxembourg in a jurisdiction in which it is subject to a corporate income tax similar to Luxembourg's. Qualifying coordination centres pay corporate income tax not on their profits but on 5 per cent of relevant expenses, with a minimum tax for this purpose of LF 75,000.

(2) Luxembourg holding companies are Luxembourg incorporated companies benefiting from a special fiscal status under a law of 1929. They are companies with a minimum share capital of LF 1,250,000 (for an SA) or LF 1,000,000 (for an SARL) with prescribed activities (eg holding and trading in shares of other companies (both Luxembourgeois and foreign), currency

holding, financing subsidiaries and holding licences and patents). Certain activities (eg industrial or commercial activity, brokerage or banking) are proscribed. Companies qualifying as Luxembourg holding companies are completely exempt from corporate income tax (on both income and gains), communal business tax, net worth tax etc. Their only tax liability is to capital duty and the annual capital tax (at a special rate of 0.2 per cent) (see 10(d) below).

2. Residence and territoriality

Luxembourg resident companies are liable to corporate income tax on their worldwide income; for Luxembourg holding companies, see 1(c) above. A company is treated as resident in Luxembourg if its registered office or principal place of business is in Luxembourg.

3. The tax base

(a) *Method of calculation.* Taxable profits are derived by comparing the net worth of the company at the beginning and end of the accounting period. Unrealised exchange gains are left out of account.

(b) *Disallowable items.* Contributions to capital and dividends paid during the accounting period must be deducted when computing taxable profits. The major disallowable expense items are excess expenses paid to related parties (treated as a dividend payment), general provisions for bad debts, expenses incurred in relation to non-taxable income, other taxes (except the communal business tax), fees to directors and others for supervisory services and excessive gifts.

(c) *Exempt income/special deductions.* For dividends, see 4(a) below. Pension provisions are deductible within certain limits, as are specific bad debt provisions and provisions for certain, but unquantified, losses. Unrealised exchange losses are deductible.

(d) *Interest paid.* Interest paid is deductible under an accruals basis, provided it is not attributable to exempt income (eg dividends from a substantial participation: see 4(a) below, or foreign dividends exempt by treaty). Interest paid to related parties (eg shareholders and affiliates) is deductible only to the extent of arm's-length rates.

(e) *Stock.* Stock is valued at the lower of cost or market value. In valuing fungible items, any reasonable method is permissible. There is no stock relief for inflationary increases in stock values.

(f) *Depreciation.* Either the straight-line or reducing balance methods may be used, but once the straight-line basis has been adopted for any particular asset, it is not possible to switch to the reducing balance method, although a switch in the reverse direction is permitted. The depreciable base is cost net of government grants. The annual rates used, which must be related to the useful life of the asset, may be individually agreed with the tax authorities, although there is a spread of rates in general use for particular types of asset. Accelerated depreciation is available for certain types of asset; expenditure on assets costing under LF 25,000 (£415) or with a useful life of less than one year may be written off in full immediately. There is no pooling of assets. Tax credits are available in addition for many types of asset. A credit of 12 per cent is available on the difference in value of an asset taken at the end of an accounting period and its average value over the preceding five years – for this purpose, the minimum average value is LF 75,000. A further tax credit on acquisition of assets with a useful life of over four years is available. The credit is 6 per cent on the first LF 6,000,000 plus 2 per cent on the balance over that amount.

4. Treatment of dividends

(a) *Dividends received from Luxembourg companies.* Dividends are received after a deduction of 15 per cent withholding tax (see (c) below). The withholding tax is credited against the company's corporate income tax liability. However, dividends from 'substantial participations' are exempt from withholding tax and corporate income tax in the recipient company's hands. A substantial participation is a direct holding of 10 per cent or more (or LF 50m) in the paying company, held throughout a period of 12 months immediately preceding the end of the accounting period.

(b) *Dividends received from abroad.* Unless the dividends stem from a substantial participation (see (a) above), they are subject to corporate income tax; any foreign tax paid is allowed as a tax credit, but only up to the amount of Luxembourg corporate income tax payable on the income. Dividends from a foreign company in which the Luxembourg company has a substantial participation are exempt, under the same conditions as in (a) above. A further condition is that the foreign paying company is subject to corporate income tax corresponding to that in Luxembourg.

(c) *Dividends paid to Luxembourg residents.* A 15 per cent withholding tax must be deducted from dividends paid, unless the recipient has a substantial participation (see (a) above), in which case the dividend is paid gross.

(d) *Dividends paid to non-residents.* The rate of withholding tax will often be reduced under the terms of a treaty. Of the European and major world economies, Australia, Canada, Greece, Japan and Portugal have no treaty with Luxembourg.

5. Anti-avoidance measures

There is no special tax on accumulated earnings and no thin-capitalisation rules. Transfer pricing rules are operated to adjust all transactions with affiliates to arm's-length values. There are no provisions similar to the UK's controlled foreign company legislation.

6. Treatment of losses

(a) *Current period.* Trading and capital losses of the same period are automatically set against each other by virtue of the net worth basis of computation (see 3(a) above).
(b) *Future periods.* A loss (representing a decrease in net worth, as adjusted) may be carried forward for a maximum of five years.
(c) *Past periods.* Carry back of losses is not permitted.
(d) *Transferability.* There is no restriction on loss carry forward on a change of ownership but losses cannot be transferred to another company.

7. Treatment of capital gains

(a) *Treatment.* Capital gains are taxed as income.
(b) *Computation.* Gains are computed by deducting book value from sale proceeds. Gains and losses are automatically netted with other income by virtue of the net worth computation for the corporate and communal business tax (see 3(a) above).
(c) *Roll-over.* Gains on assets held for a minimum of five years can either be rolled over into the cost of replacement assets or frozen until the company as a whole is sold. Where the replacement asset is acquired within the same accounting period as the disposal, the gain is deducted from the cost of the replacement asset. If replacement occurs within the next two accounting periods, the gain can be transferred to a special reserve and is deferred until the company changes hands.
(d) *Special treatment for shares.* There is no special treatment for

shares. The income exemption for substantial participations (see 4(a) above) does not extend to capital gains. Luxembourg holding companies (see 1(c) above) do not pay tax on gains.

8. Treatment of groups

It is possible to consolidate the profits of a parent company with its 99 per cent subsidiaries, providing the subsidiary is integrated with the parent in an economic and organisational sense. All companies must be Luxembourg resident and have coextensive accounting periods. Intra-group dividends are free of withholding tax and will almost certainly qualify for exemption under the substantial participation rule from corporate income tax (see 4(a) above). Transfers of assets remain subject to tax, however. If consideration equal to their book value passes from the acquirer, there is no gain.

9. Treatment of branches

The taxable profits of a Luxembourg branch of a non-resident company are computed on the same basis as those of a resident company. However, the branch's tax base is limited to its assets situated in Luxembourg. The lower corporate income tax rates for profits of LF 1,312,000 or less (see 1(b) above) apply only if the non-resident company's worldwide income is within the limit. The branch will be liable to communal business tax and national net worth tax (see 10(a), (b) below). There is no withholding tax on remittance of branch profits.

10. Other taxes

(a) *Communal business tax* (*impôt commercial*) is payable on the same base as corporate income tax, as specially adjusted. The tax has two components – one based on profits and one on net worth.

   (1) The income element is levied on the corporate income tax base, as adjusted for, *inter alia*: salaries and fees payable to shareholders owning 25 per cent or more of the share capital, 60 per cent of the interest on 'permanent' debts and all payroll costs (added back); the income element of the communal tax itself, 10 per cent of the assessed value of business real property, losses of the preceding five years, income from a substantial participation and foreign branch profits (deductions). An across-the-board allowance of LF 700,000 is made to all companies. The basic rate is 4 per cent, multiplied

by a factor varying between communes; 2.5 is a common factor.

(2) The net worth element uses the net worth tax base (see (b) below), adjusted for, *inter alia*: 60 per cent of the interest on long-term debts (added back) and the assessed value of business real property, the net assets of a foreign branch and participations of a minimum 10 per cent in resident companies (deducted). An across-the-board allowance of LF 1,800,000 is made to all companies. The basic rate is 0.2 per cent, multiplied by a factor varying between communes.

The communal business tax is deductible in computing corporate income tax liability.

(b) *Taxes on capital*. There is an annual net worth tax (*impôt sur la fortune*) levied on the value of a company's worldwide assets (Luxembourg assets in the case of a branch). Valuations are generally carried out every three years. The rate of the net worth tax is 0.5 per cent. Net worth tax is not deductible in computing corporate income tax liability. In addition to the net worth tax, there is a communal property tax (*impôt foncier*) levied on 5–10 per cent of the market value of property at a rate (which cannot exceed 8 per cent) fixed by the commune.

(c) *Turnover taxes*. A value-added tax (*taxe sur la valeur ajoutée*) is charged on the supply of goods and services. The standard rate is 12 per cent, with lower rates of 3 and 6 per cent. Exports and certain essential commodities are zero rated.

(d) *Transaction taxes*. A capital duty (*droit d'apport*) of 1 per cent is payable on the initial capital subscriptions to a company and on subsequent capital increases. An annual capital tax (*droit d'abonnement*) is payable on the value of securities issued by Luxembourg resident companies at a rate of 0.36 per cent for an SA (*société anonyme*) or 0.18 per cent for an SARL (*société à responsabilité limitée*). There is also a transfer tax on the transfer of real property at a rate of 6 or 9 per cent on the sale price.

(e) *Payroll taxes*. Social security premiums for employers are set at between 12.575 and 18.075 per cent of salary for office etc staff and between 14.65 and 20.15 per cent for manual workers.

Netherlands

Average rate of exchange y/e 31.3.90: £1 = DFl 3.2821

1. The tax year; nature and rates of tax

(a) The tax year is the calendar year but companies may adopt a different year-end. Profits of accounting periods other than calendar years are apportioned on a time basis over the tax years concerned.

Accounting period year ended 30 September 1990. Profits DFl 150,000
Taxable: in the year 1989 (ending December 1989): 3/12 × DFl 150,000 = DFl 37,500
in the tax year 1990 (ending 31 December 1990): 9/12 × DFl 150,000 = DFl 112,500

(b) Dutch companies are liable to corporation tax (*vennootschapsbelasting*) at a combination of two rates: at 40 per cent on the first DFl 250,000 and at 35 per cent on the remainder.

2. Residence and territoriality

Netherlands resident companies are liable to corporation tax on their worldwide income. A company is resident in the Netherlands if it is incorporated under Netherlands law or is deemed to be situated there (eg if its central control and management is located there).

3. The tax base

(a) *Method of calculation.* Taxable profits are based on the comparison of net worth at the beginning and end of the accounting period and also by reference to the company's net worth over its entire existence. Exchange gains and losses are recognised for tax purposes but gains and losses related to long-term assets are recognised only on realisation of the assets. Contributions and withdrawals of capital are left out of calculation as are distributions of profit.
(b) *Disallowable items.* In general, expenses are allowable as long as they relate directly or closely to the conduct of the business. Payments made to related parties are deductible only to the extent that they do not exceed arm's-length values. Any excess over

arm's-length is non-deductible and treated as a deemed dividend, subject to any applicable withholding tax. Withdrawals of capital and dividend payments must be added back.

(c) *Exempt income/special deductions.* For dividends, see 4(a) below. Capital contributions must be deducted from net worth. A general bad debt provision is allowable if it can be justified in the light of previous experience and must be capable of subsequent verification. A tax-deductible reserve to cover variable future expenditure may be set up. For the investment deduction see (f) below.

(d) *Interest paid.* Interest is deductible on an accruals basis but no deduction is possible for interest related to the cost of funding a subsidiary that produces non-taxable income (eg income exempt under the participation exemption: see 4(a) below). Other costs relating to such subsidiaries, other than exchange losses, are also non-deductible. See under (b) for the arm's-length rule.

(e) *Stock.* The preferred method of valuation is at the lower of cost and market value on a FIFO, LIFO or base stock basis, but valuation at cost or market value alone is possible, if it can be justified under the 'sound business practice' (*goed koopmansgebruik*) rules, to which tax computations are subject. There is no stock relief for inflationary increases in stock values.

(f) *Depreciation.* Depreciation is usually provided on a straight-line basis (although the reducing balance basis is permissible) according to the estimated useful life of the asset so as to leave a residual value. Generally, both depreciation periods and rates are at the option of the taxpayer and approval will not be withheld by the tax authorities unless what is proposed is unreasonable. Once a particular method is agreed, it must be adhered to consistently. Land is not depreciable. A special investment deduction (of between 0.25 and 16 per cent) for investment in assets of up to DFl 1,162,000 annually is also available.

4. Treatment of dividends

(a) *Dividends received from Netherlands companies.* Dividends not qualifying for the participation exemption are generally taxable. However, dividends qualifying for the 'participation exemption' are paid gross and are exempt from tax in the hands of the recipient company. To qualify for a participation exemption, a holding must amount to at least 5 per cent of the issued share capital of the investee company. The investing company must be resident in the

Netherlands or be the Netherlands branch (permanent establishment) of a non-resident company and neither company can be a passive investment company.

(b) *Dividends received from abroad.* Shareholdings in foreign companies may qualify for the participation exemption as in (a) above, but additional conditions are attached. The investee company must be subject to a corporate income tax (no matter at what rate) in its country of residence and the shareholding must not be a portfolio or passive investment. The tax authorities may insist, when giving their advance ruling on participation exemption status, that the investor company report a profit of at least 25 per cent of the costs of managing the foreign shareholding per annum and that it finance the purchase of a qualifying subsidiary with a minimum of 15 per cent shareholders' equity. Where the shareholding does not qualify for the participation exemption, the dividend is subject to corporation tax. Foreign tax paid is credited against the Netherlands corporation tax liability, but where no treaty or other means of double tax relief exist between the Netherlands and the source country of the dividends, the foreign tax may be set against general income as an expense, which may give rise to a tax loss. Unused foreign tax credits may be carried forward to future accounting periods.

(c) *Dividends paid to Netherlands residents.* Withholding tax of 25 per cent must be deducted from dividend payments to resident individuals.

(d) *Dividends paid to non-residents.* Withholding tax of 25 per cent must be deducted. Where the recipient is resident in a treaty country, the treaty will often prescribe a zero or lower rate of withholding tax. The Netherlands has treaties with all other members of the EC, the USA, Canada, Australia, Japan and many former Eastern bloc countries.

5. *Anti-avoidance measures*

The Netherlands has no extra tax on accumulated earnings. While there are no statutory thin-capitalisation provisions, the tax authorities may insist on a minimum proportion of equity (see, for example, the participation exemption condition for shareholdings abroad – 3(b) above). Transfer pricing provisions exist in practice to ensure that all transactions with affiliates be conducted, for tax purposes, at arm's-length values. There are no provisions similar to the UK's controlled foreign company legislation.

6. Treatment of losses

(a) *Current period.* Losses of whatever description are automatically netted off against income of the same period by virtue of the net worth basis of calculating taxable profits (see 3(a) above).
(b) *Future periods.* Net losses may be carried forward for a maximum of eight years. Losses incurred during a company's first six years may be carried forward indefinitely.
(c) *Past periods.* Losses may be carried back against profits of the past three years.
(d) *Transferability.* Carry forward of losses is denied on the occasion of a 70 per cent or more change of ownership but only if there has been a prior cessation or near cessation of activities.

7. Treatment of capital gains

(a) *Treatment.* Capital gains are treated as income for tax purposes.
(b) *Computation.* Gains are computed by deducting cost (or net book – depreciated) value from sale proceeds. There is no adjustment for inflation.
(c) *Roll-over.* Gains on the sale of tangible or intangible assets may be rolled over against the cost of similar replacement assets, which must be acquired within four years of the disposal. The gain rolled over is placed in a reserve, used to write down the cost of the replacement asset, both for depreciation purposes and future capital gains computations. The reserve will be written back to taxable income after the end of four years.
(d) *Special treatment of shares.* There is no special treatment as such, but gains arising from a holding qualifying for the participation exemption (see 4(a), (b) above) are exempt from corporation tax.

8. Treatment of groups

A Netherlands holding company and its 100 per cent Netherlands resident subsidiaries may form a single fiscal unit (tax group). The accounting periods of all the companies in the group must be coextensive and the group relationship must have persisted throughout the accounting period in question. Within such a group, profits and losses are pooled for tax purposes and assets may be transferred free of capital gains, VAT and stamp duty. Dividends paid intra-group are exempt from tax, and the transfer pricing rules (see 5 above) do not apply. There may be a tax clawback where group membership ceases.

9. Treatment of branches

The profits of the Netherlands branch of a non-resident company are computed in the same way as those of a resident company. The branch will be liable to corporation tax on profits arising in the Netherlands, computed on the basis of its assets located in the Netherlands. There is no withholding tax on remittances of profit from the branch.

10. Other taxes

(a) There are no other taxes on the income of a company.
(b) *Taxes on capital.* There is a local property tax based on the economic value or size of the property.
(c) *Turnover taxes.* A value-added tax (*belasting over de toegevoegde waarde*) is charged on the supply of goods and services. There is a standard rate of 18.5 per cent and a lower rate of 6 per cent. Exports are zero rated.
(d) *Transaction taxes.* There is a capital duty of 1 per cent on the issue of new shares by a company and a 6 per cent transfer tax payable by the purchaser on property transfers. The tax extends to the sale of shares in a company, 70 per cent or more of whose assets consist of Netherlands real property.
(e) *Pay-roll taxes.* Employers must pay social security premiums.

Norway

Average rate of exchange y/e 31.3.90: £1 = NKr 10.989

1. The tax year; nature and rates of tax

(a) The tax year is the calendar year. Profits of an accounting period other than a calendar year (for which special permission is needed) are taxed in the year in which the accounting period ends.

Accounting period year ended 30 September 1990. Profits NKr 500,000
Taxable: NKr 500,000 in tax year 1990 (ending 31 December 1990)

(b) Income tax is levied on companies at two levels: the national and the county/communal. The national income tax (*inntektsskatt til staten*) rate is 27.8 per cent and the county/communal income tax (*inntektsskatt til fylkeskommunen*) rate is 23 per cent. Under certain conditions, the rate of tax on capital gains may be reduced (see 7 below). The same rates apply to distributed and undistributed income, but undistributed income is effectively taxed at higher rates because of the rules on dividend deduction (see 4(b) below).

2. Residence and territoriality

Norwegian resident companies are liable to national and county income tax on their worldwide income. A company is resident in Norway if it is incorporated in Norway. Companies incorporated under foreign law are therefore non-resident, even where their operations and management are conducted in Norway. There are special rules for shipowning companies.

3. The tax base

(a) *Method of computation.* Taxable profits are based on a comparison of net worth at the beginning and end of the accounting period. Capital contributions and withdrawals are overlooked and profit distributions (dividends) are adjusted for as explained in 4(b) below. Capital gains may need to be isolated where they are charged at a special rate (see 7 below).
(b) *Disallowable items.* The general rule is that expenses must be wholly and exclusively incurred for the purposes of the trade to be

deductible. Specifically, entertaining expenses are disallowable, as are most gifts and charitable donations. An exception is made for gifts to scientific and educational institutes, within certain limits. Most taxes are not deductible, with the exception of the local property tax (see 10(b) below).

(c) *Exempt income/special deductions.* For dividends, see 4(b) below. An annual provision of up to 23 per cent of pre-tax income may be appropriated to a tax-free undistributable reserve (*konsolideringsfond*). If the company operates in a regional development area, a further 15 per cent appropriation may be made to an investment fund to be utilised within five years for investment in the development area.

(d) *Interest paid.* Interest is generally deductible.

(e) *Stock.* Stock is valued at the lower of cost and market value on a FIFO basis. There is no stock relief for inflationary increases in stock values.

(f) *Depreciation.* Depreciation is charged at prescribed rates for different types of asset on a reducing balance basis. Assets of the same type are pooled and, as in the UK, the depreciable base includes additions during the year and is net of sale proceeds of assets disposed of, subject to capital gains roll-over provisions (see 7 below). Rates are as follows: (1) industrial buildings: 7 or 11 per cent; (2) hotels and restaurants: 6 or 10 per cent; (3) plant and machinery (excluding private cars): maximum of 30 per cent; (4) private passenger cars: 20 per cent; (5) ships, oil rigs etc: 25 per cent; (6) aircraft: 15 per cent. Assets with a useful life of less than three years and costing less than NKr 10,000 (£910) may be written off to revenue. Special rules apply to intangible assets. Higher rates are available in northern Norway.

4. Treatment of dividends

(a) *Dividends received from Norwegian companies.* There is no withholding tax on dividends from Norwegian companies and in the hands of the recipient company they are liable to the national income tax only; they are exempt from the county income tax. The effective rate of tax on Norwegian source dividends is thus 27.8 per cent.

(b) *Dividends received from abroad.* Dividends from foreign companies are liable to both national and county income tax. Where the source of the dividend is a treaty country, the foreign tax paid may be relieved by way of credit. Where there is no treaty between

Norway and the source country, the foreign tax is treated as an expense, although the company may request the tax authorities to grant relief by way of credit.

(c) *Dividends paid to Norwegian residents.* Dividends payable out of the current year's profits qualify for deduction against the company's national income tax liability. They are not deductible for the purposes of the county income tax. Distributable income is, however, based on the profit per the accounts, as adjusted by a complicated formula. There is no withholding tax on dividends to Norwegian residents.

(d) *Dividends paid to non-residents.* Dividends paid to non-residents also qualify for the deduction against national income tax but withholding tax of 25 per cent (subject to treaty) must be deducted at source by the paying company.

5. Anti-avoidance measures

There is no special tax on accumulated earnings, but see 4(c) above. There are no thin-capitalisation rules at present, except with respect to oil companies. Transfer pricing rules are applied to all transactions between affiliates to adjust them to arm's-length values. There are no provisions similar to the UK's controlled foreign company legislation.

6. Treatment of losses

(a) *Current period.* The net worth basis of computation grants relief for losses against profits of the same period automatically.

(b) *Future periods.* Losses may be carried forward for a maximum of ten years.

(c) *Past periods.* Carry back of losses is not permitted except on a liquidation, when unrelieved losses may be carried back to the two immediately preceding periods.

(d) *Transferability.* A change of ownership or a complete change in the nature of the trade may result in a cut off of losses brought forward.

7. Treatment of capital gains

(a) *Treatment.* Capital gains are treated as income.

(b) *Computation.* Gains are computed by deducting cost from sale proceeds. Gains from the sale of real investment property (ie real property not used for business purposes) are subject to a reduced rate (14 per cent) of national income tax, a reduced rate (16 per cent) of county income tax and a 2 per cent levy, making 32 per cent in all.

(c) *Roll-over.* Gains from depreciable business assets may be effectively deferred by deducting the disposal proceeds from the appropriate depreciation pool. If that results in a negative pool balance, the balance may be transferred to another asset pool with a similar or higher rate of depreciation or carried forward against purchases of the same category for a maximum of four (in some instances, eight) years. Other means exist of dealing with the negative balance.

(d) *Special treatment for shares.* Gains on the sale of shares held for less than three years are subject to a special higher rate (40 per cent) of national income tax (and may not be reduced by losses for this purpose) but are exempt from county income tax. Where shares have been held for three or more years, gains are completely exempt from both national and county income tax unless the 'substantial sale' rules apply. These rules apply where a minimum of 45 per cent of the share capital is disposed of, although the rules will also be applied if at least 30 per cent is being sold and the purchaser as a result acquires a controlling holding. Where the rules do apply, the special 40 per cent rate of national income tax is charged and losses are not available to reduce the gains so chargeable.

8. *Treatment of groups*

A Norwegian resident parent company and any of its 91 per cent Norwegian resident subsidiaries may form a tax group. Where they do so, profits and losses are consolidated and gains rolled over by one company may be utilised by the group as a whole. The existence of a tax group has no effect on intra-group dividends.

9. *Treatment of branches*

The taxable profits of a Norwegian branch of a non-resident company are computed on the same basis as those of a resident company but the base for the tax is limited to Norwegian source profits and gains and assets located in Norway. Branches are liable to both national and county income tax. They are also liable to national and county net worth tax (see 10(b) below). There is no withholding tax on remittances of profit.

10. Other taxes

(a) *Taxes on income.* For the county income tax, see above, *passim.* There is also a petroleum revenue tax of 30 per cent imposed on income from oil exploitation activities etc, in addition to national and county income tax.

(b) *Capital taxes.* There is a national net worth tax (*formueskatt til staten*) at a rate of 0.3 per cent on the assessed value of worldwide net assets. Norwegian resident companies are not liable to the communal net worth tax (*formuesskatt til kommunen*), which is charged at 1 per cent on the same base. Non-resident companies may, however, be exempt from county net worth tax under a non-discrimination clause in a tax treaty. There is also a county property tax at a rate ranging from 0.2 to 0.7 per cent. This tax is deductible for national and county income tax purposes.

(c) *Turnover taxes.* A value-added tax (*merverdiavgift*) is charged on the supply of goods and services, at a single rate of 20 per cent. An investment tax of 7 per cent is charged on some goods purchased by a company that can claim a VAT deduction for the purchase. Exports are zero rated.

(d) *Payroll taxes.* Payroll taxes amount to 16.7 per cent of payroll, with reduced rates applying to employees resident in development areas.

Portugal

Average rate of exchange y/e 31.3.90: £1 = Esc 251.04

1. The tax year; nature and rates of tax

(a) The tax year is the calendar year. Accounting periods other than the calendar year are permitted only in exceptional circumstances, particularly where the company is the subsidiary of a foreign company or in the case of a branch of a non-resident company.

(b) Portuguese companies are liable to corporate income tax (*imposto sobre o rendimento das pessõas colectivas*) of 36.5 per cent, but there is also a local surcharge of approximately 10 per cent on the tax, making for an effective rate of about 40.15 per cent.

2. Residence and territoriality

Portuguese resident companies are liable to corporate income tax on their worldwide income. A company is treated as resident in Portugal if its head office or effective place of management is there.

3. The tax base

(a) *Method of computation.* Taxable profits are based on a comparison of the net worth of the company at the beginning and end of the accounting period.

(b) *Disallowable items.* All properly substantiated business expenses are deductible. Contributions to the statutory and certain other reserves are not allowable.

(c) *Exempt income/special deductions.* Income from a branch in Macau is exempt. For dividends, see 4 below. For stock provisions, see (e) below. A provision for doubtful debts, at fixed percentages, is tax deductible. The 5 per cent withheld on dividend and interest payments on account of the substitute inheritance and gift tax (see 4(a) and 10(a) below) is deductible. Non-resident companies may set up tax-free operations in Madeira or the Azores.

(d) *Interest paid.* Interest payable for business purposes is deductible. Where interest is paid to related parties, there are restrictions, eg the deductible interest on shareholders' loans is limited to a rate based on the Central Bank's prevailing discount rate (domestic) or the LIBOR or international capital market rate (foreign). For the general transfer pricing restrictions, see 5 below.

(e) *Stock.* Stock must be valued consistently according to sound commercial practice by the historic cost method. Special valuation methods (including FIFO) may be used where permission has been granted by the tax authorities. Where the market value of the stock is lower than the cost, the difference may be transferred to a devaluation reserve. This transfer is deductible in computing taxable profits. There is no stock relief for inflationary increases in stock values.

(f) *Depreciation.* Tax depreciation is on the straight-line or reducing balance basis at rates fixed by the tax authorities. The reducing balance basis may be used at the taxpayer's option for tangible fixed assets but is not available for buildings, private cars or office furniture. Plant and machinery, except private cars, are pooled for depreciation purposes. Illustrative straight-line rates are: (1) electronic equipment 20 per cent; (2) office buildings 2 per cent; (3) machine tools 20 per cent; (4) motor vehicles 14.28–25 per cent. Where extraordinary wear and tear can be demonstrated, these rates can be increased by up to 50 per cent.

4. Treatment of dividends

(a) *Dividends received from Portuguese companies.* Dividends are received net of withholding tax (see (b) below) and are taxable.

(1) Dividends on shares quoted in Portugal enjoy an exemption of 20 per cent (before application of the affiliation privilege), ie only 80 per cent of such dividends are liable to corporate income tax.

(2) An exemption of 40 per cent is provided for dividends from newly privatised companies for the first five years.

(3) A tax credit of 20 per cent of the underlying corporate income tax paid by the distributing company is allowed against the recipient company's corporate income tax liability, whether on quoted or unquoted shares.

(4) Under the affiliation privilege, 95 per cent of dividends received from companies where the recipient company has held at least 25 per cent of the share capital for a minimum of two years are exempt.

(5) Domestic dividend income is also subject to the 5 per cent substitute inheritance and gift tax (see 10(a) below), irrespective of the level of participation.

(6) 'Domestic holding companies' qualify for the exemption whatever the level of their holding.

(b) *Dividends received from abroad.* Dividends received from abroad are liable to corporate income tax and the affiliation privilege does not apply. Where there is no treaty with the source country, foreign tax paid on the dividend is treated as an expense (ie the net dividend is included in taxable income) and no foreign tax credit is available. Where there is a treaty, relief will be granted according to the terms of that treaty (normally by credit). The substitute inheritance and gift tax is not payable on foreign source dividends.
(c) *Dividends paid to residents.* Withholding tax is deductible on dividends paid to domestic shareholders at the following rates:

(1) unquoted shares 25 per cent;
(2) quoted shares 20 per cent;
(3) newly privatised companies 15 per cent.

In addition, the substitute inheritance and gift tax (see 10(a) below) must be withheld at source.
(d) *Dividends paid to non-residents.* The same rates of withholding tax, including the 5 per cent substitute inheritance and gift tax (not reducible by treaty, non-creditable and non-deductible), are applicable to distributions to non-resident shareholders.

5. Anti-avoidance measures

There is no special tax on accumulated earnings. Transfer pricing rules operate under which the tax authorities may adjust transactions between related parties to arm's-length values. This is a general power in addition to the specific restrictions on interest and royalty payments to affiliates (see 3(d) above).

There are no thin-capitalisation rules and no provisions similar to the UK's controlled foreign company legislation.

6. Treatment of losses

(a) *Current period.* Losses are automatically netted off against profits of the same period by virtue of the net worth basis of computing profits (see 3(a) above).
(b) *Future periods.* Any aggregate unabsorbed loss may be carried forward for a maximum of five years.

(c) *Past periods.* Carry back of losses is not permissible.

7. Treatment of capital gains

(a) *Treatment.* Capital gains are generally taxable as income.
(b) *Computation.* Gains are computed by deducting cost from sale proceeds. Where the gain arises from the disposal of fixed assets held for more than two years, the cost is adjusted for inflation.
(c) *Roll-over.* Deferral of tax on capital gains on tangible fixed assets is available by roll-over of the disposal proceeds against the cost of replacement tangible fixed assets acquired within two years of the disposal. Partial reinvestment of the proceeds will qualify for roll-over of the corresponding part of the gain.
(d) *Special treatment for shares.* Roll-over is also available for financial fixed assets (including shares). The shares must have been held for at least twelve months and reinvestment must take place in other shares or government bonds within two years of the disposal. The replacement shares etc must not themselves be disposed of for a minimum of two years. Again, partial roll-over is available. Gains realised directly by non-resident companies on the disposal of shares are exempt from tax.

8. Treatment of groups

A holding company and its 91 per cent subsidiaries (all of which must be resident in Portugal) can form a tax group, with permission from the tax authorities. Within a group, profits and losses may be pooled and dividends and interest may be paid free of withholding tax (but not of the 5 per cent substitute inheritance tax deduction). Intra-group asset transfers may be carried out without incurring a charge to tax on capital gains.

9. Treatment of branches

The Portuguese branch of a non-resident company is taxed on the same basis as a resident company. Its taxable base is its profits derived from operations in Portugal, measured with respect to its Portuguese assets. Tax is paid at the general rate of 36.5 per cent (plus the local surcharge). There is no withholding tax on remittances of profit from the branch.

10. Other taxes

(a) *Taxes on income.*Companies are liable to the local surcharge on their corporate income tax liability. The surcharge varies from one local authority to another, with the average rate being about 10 per cent. A further tax on particular income (*inter alia*, dividends and interest) is the substitute inheritance and gift tax, levied at a rate of 5 per cent (see above).

(b) *Taxes on capital.* There is no net worth tax.

(c) *Turnover taxes.* There is a value-added tax (*imposto sobre o valor acrescentado*) on the supply of goods and services. The standard rate is 17 per cent; there is a reduced rate of 8 per cent and a luxury rate of 30 per cent. Lower rates apply in Madeira and the Azores. Exports and basic foodstuffs are zero rated.

(d) *Transaction taxes.* None.

(e) *Payroll taxes.* Social security contributions are payable at a rate of 24.5 per cent on gross salary.

Spain

Average rate of exchange y/e 31.3.90: £1 = Pts 185.851

1. The tax year; nature and rates of tax

(a) The tax year is the calendar year. Profits of accounting periods other than calendar years are taxable in full in the tax year in which the periods end.

Accounting year end 30 September 1990. Profits Pts 10,000,000
Taxable in year 1990 (ending 31 December 1990): Pts 10,000,000

(b) Corporation tax (*impuesto sobre sociedades*) is levied at a flat rate of 35 per cent on both distributed and undistributed income. Special tax régimes operate in Navarre, the Basque country, Ceuta and Melilla. Special tax rates apply to investment fund companies (13 per cent) and those involved in hydrocarbon exploration (40 per cent).

2. Residence and territoriality

Spanish resident companies are taxed on their worldwide income and gains. All companies incorporated in Spain are treated as resident there, as are foreign incorporated companies having their registered office or effective centre of management and administration in Spain.

3. The tax base

(a) *Method of calculation.* Taxable profits are based on the profit as reported in the accounts. Taxable income includes dividends (but see 4 below), capital gains and non-trading income. Foreign exchange gains and losses are recognised. The revenue authorities retain the option to assess a company on the increase in its net worth.
(b) *Disallowable items.* The major disallowable items are some bonuses etc to shareholders and board members and non-charitable gifts. There are special rules for bad and doubtful debts.
(c) *Exempt income and special deductions.* For dividends from substantial participations, see 4 below. Provisions for a fall in investment value and pensions are generally allowable.
(d) *Interest paid.* Interest is deductible on an accruals basis. Interest

payable to foreign lenders must obtain government approval to be tax deductible.

(e) *Stock.* Stock is valued at the lower of cost and market value. FIFO and average cost methods are both generally acceptable. There is no 'stock relief' for inflationary increases in stock value.

(f) *Depreciation.* There are three recognised methods of depreciation (1) a straight-line basis at (maximum) rates published in official tables; (2) a reducing balance basis for new tangible assets with a life of more than three years; (3) on an individual basis proposed by the company and approved by the authorities. An investment credit of 5 per cent is additionally available on the purchase of new assets. The sum of all investment credits is limited to 25 per cent of the company's corporation tax liability. There is no pooling of assets.

4. Treatment of dividends

(a) *Dividends received from Spanish companies.* These form part of taxable income and are subject to 25 per cent withholding tax, which serves as a tax credit for the recipient company. However, where the recipient company has had a holding of more than 25 per cent throughout the previous year, or is a portfolio investment company, the dividends are wholly exempt. Where the holding is 25 per cent or less, there is a 50 per cent exemption.

(b) *Dividends received from abroad.* These form part of taxable income and credit is obtained for foreign taxes directly payable on the dividend; there is no credit for underlying taxes (eg tax on the profits out of which the dividends are paid).

(c) *Dividends paid.* The company must withhold tax at 25 per cent from dividends to residents and non-residents alike.

5. Anti-avoidance

There are no thin-capitalisation rules and no tax on accumulated earnings. However, the profits of some companies can be imputed directly to their shareholders: the companies involved are essentially holding companies and portfolio investment companies controlled by a single family group or by ten or fewer persons and companies serving as vehicles for carrying on a profession.

6. Treatment of losses

(a) *Current period.* Trading losses may be set off against income (but not capital gains) of the current period. Capital losses may be set off against capital gains only.
(b) *Future periods.* Trading losses may be carried forward for a maximum of five years. Capital losses may be carried forward for set off against capital gains.
(c) *Past periods.* There is no carry back of losses.
(d) *Transferability.* There is normally no restriction on the transferability of losses on a change of ownership.

7. Treatment of capital gains

(a) *Treatment.* Capital gains are taxed as income.
(b) *Computation.* The gain is computed by deducting the net book (depreciated) value from the sale proceeds. Costs of sale are also deductible.
(c) *Roll-over.* Roll-over is available for tangible business assets if reinvestment in assets of a similar type is made within two (sometimes four) years.
(d) *Special treatment for shares.* There is no special treatment for shares.

8. Treatment of groups

The results of a group of companies may be consolidated for tax purposes, if permitted by the tax authorities. Such a group must be headed by a Spanish resident company and consist of 91 per cent subsidiaries, which have been owned for a minimum of two years. Preconsolidation losses are available only to the company that incurred them. There is no withholding tax on dividends or interest paid within a tax group.

9. Treatment of branches

Spanish branches are treated in essentially the same way as Spanish resident companies. They are liable to corporation tax on their income and capital gains on assets located in Spain. Remittances of profits are free of withholding tax if corporation tax has already been paid on them; otherwise, the 25 per cent withholding tax is payable as an advance on the corporation tax.

10. Other taxes

(a) A surcharge of 1.5 per cent of the corporation tax is payable to the local chamber of commerce. The surcharge is deductible for corporation tax purposes

(b) *Taxes on capital.* There is a tax of 1 per cent on capital contributions to Spanish companies and branches.

(c) *Turnover taxes.* Value-added tax (*impuesto sobre el valor añadido*) is payable on the supply of goods and services. There is a standard rate of 12 per cent, a reduced rate of 6 per cent and a luxury rate of 33 per cent. Exports are zero rated.

(d) *Payroll taxes.* Social security premiums are payable. The general charge is 24 per cent and there are additional compulsory contributions to umemployment insurance, salary guarantee and professional education funds.

(e) There is a wide variety of local taxes, such as a business licence tax, an opening licence tax, a construction licence tax and a property tax (*contribución*).

Sweden

Average rate of exchange y/e 31.3.90: £1 = SKr 10.292

1. The tax year; nature and rates of tax

The tax year is the calendar year. Companies may also have year ends on 30 April, 30 June or 31 August. The profits of an accounting period ending otherwise than on 31 December are taxable wholly in the tax year in which the accounting period ends.

Accounting period ended 31 August 1990. Taxable profits SKr 500,000
Taxable: SKr 500,000 at 1990 (year ended 31 December 1990) rates, but assessed in 1991

Income tax (*inkomstskatt*) is levied at 30 per cent on distributed and undistributed income of companies from 1991 onwards. The rate was previously 40 per cent.

2. Residence and territoriality

A Swedish resident company is taxable on its worldwide income. Companies registered in Sweden are treated as resident there, as are companies mainly holding or trading in securities that are effectively managed in Sweden and whose shares are held mainly by Swedish resident individuals.

3. The tax base

(a) *Method of calculation.* Taxable profit is based on the profit reported by the accounts.
(b) *Disallowable items.* The major disallowable items are mostly gifts, capital expenditure not related to the company's trade and some entertaining expenses.
(c) *Exempt income/special deductions.* Certain dividends received are exempt and certain dividend payments are deductible – see 4 below. Payments to pension reserves are deductible. A variety of previous tax-deductible reserves have been abolished with effect from 1 January 1991 and replaced by a special tax equalisation reserve (SURV). The reserve will be based on the tax accounting values of certain assets less liabilities and will be limited to a total of 30 per cent of the company's equity capital. Companies with a

small equity capital, especially in the service sector can base their SURV on a maximum 15 per cent of payroll.

(d) *Interest paid.* Normally deductible on an accruals basis. To the extent that interest between affiliated companies exceeds arm's-length rates, it may be treated as a dividend.

(e) *Stock.* Stock is valued on a FIFO basis at the lower of cost and market value. Where valuation is based on cost, a deduction of 3 per cent is allowed for most types of stock. Stock relief has been abolished as part of the national tax reforms.

(f) *Depreciation.* The method of depreciation depends on the asset involved.

(1) For plant and machinery, two methods are recognised. One, compulsory for taxpayers with inadequate records, is to take a straight 25 per cent of the depreciated (net book) value of the pool of assets. The other, open to taxpayers with adequate records (hence, almost invariably, to all companies), compares in any year the closing net book value obtained by applying a straight 30 per cent of the opening net book value of the pool with the closing net book value given by applying a 20 per cent straight-line depreciation on cost, categorising assets by year of acquisition. The alternative giving the lower net book value is the one chosen for that year. The second method takes a straight 25 per cent of the net book (depreciated) value.

(2) Buildings are depreciated on a straight-line basis according to rates fixed by the tax authorities.

(3) Intangible assets are depreciated according to the plant and machinery rules.

4. *Treatment of dividends*

(a) *Dividends received from Swedish companies.* These form part of taxable income. However, where the recipient company holds 25 per cent or more of the paying company, the dividend is exempt. In certain circumstances, dividends from less than 25 per cent holdings are exempted. The exemption is restricted in the case of holding companies. In order to qualify for the exemption, they must either redistribute the dividend or perform services for their subsidiaries (ie not act merely as a pure holding company).

(b) *Dividends received from abroad.* Dividends from foreign companies are often exempt under a double tax treaty.

(c) *Dividends paid.* Dividends paid to non-resident shareholders are subject to a 30 per cent withholding tax. Companies carrying on a trade or engaged in agriculture or forestry may deduct certain dividends paid in calculating taxable income. The nature and scope of the deduction depends on whether the company is quoted or unquoted. For unquoted companies, deduction is only possible where the company is a trading company and the dividend is paid on new shares. Quoted companies may deduct dividends payable on newly issued shares for a maximum of 20 years subject to an annual limit of 10 per cent of qualifying capital and an overriding limit of the total qualifying capital. The deduction is also available where 50 per cent or more of the shares are held by foreign resident companies provided that the dividends are subject to withholding tax.

5. Anti-avoidance rules

There are rules designed to prevent accumulation of profits in companies holding primarily shares or real property. Transfer pricing rules operate to adjust all transactions with foreign affiliates to arm's-length values. There are no thin-capitalisation rules. Controlled foreign company rules will shortly be introduced to attribute profits earned by investment companies resident in low tax jurisdictions and controlled by Swedish residents to those residents holding at least 10 per cent of the foreign company's share capital.

6. Treatment of losses

(a) *Current period.* Trading losses may be set off against income and gains in the current period.
(b) *Future periods.* To the extent that they remain unrelieved in the current period, trading losses may be carried forward against income and gains of future periods up to a maximum of ten years (indefinitely from 1991).
(c) *Past periods.* There is no carry back of losses to past periods.
(d) *Transferability.* Loss transfer is denied where there is a more than 50 per cent change in the ownership of a close company, but not where ownership stays within the same family. Non-close company losses are unaffected by a change in ownership.

7. Treatment of capital gains

(a) *Treatment.* Capital gains are in principle taxed as income. Different rules apply to a company's gains depending on whether they arise from plant, machinery and intangible assets, immovable property or shares. In practice, sale proceeds of plant, machinery and intangibles are reduced not by the cost but by the net book value of those assets, effectively increasing the taxable gain by the amount of tax-deductible depreciation previously given.

(b) *Computation.* Gains on the disposal of immovable property are computed by deducting the adjusted cost from the sale proceeds.

(c) *Roll-over.* There are no special roll-over rules.

(d) *Treatment of shares.* The gain on the disposal of securities is computed by deducting the cost from the sale proceeds. Intra-group sales may be tax free.

8. Treatment of groups

Profits may be adjusted within a group of companies by means of contribution payments, which are tax-deductible to the paying company and taxable in the hands of the payee company. Profit shifting (within Sweden) by means of inter-company pricing is also recognised. A group of companies consists of a holding company and its 91 per cent subsidiaries. The companies must be trading companies or engaged in real estate or agriculture. The holding company must perform services for its subsidiaries. All members of the group must be registered in Sweden.

9. Treatment of branches

The Swedish branch of a non-resident company is treated in much the same way as a Swedish resident company and is liable to income tax on its profits and gains. Branches are also liable, unless exempted by treaty, to net worth tax on the value of assets located in Sweden. There is no withholding tax on remittance of branch profits.

10. Other taxes

(a) *Taxes on capital.* A national net worth tax (*statlig förmögenhetsskatt*) of between 1.5 and 3 per cent is payable by non-resident companies on assets situated in Sweden. Treaties often provide exemption from this tax.

(b) *Turnover taxes.* A value-added tax (*mervärdeskatt*) is payable on the supply of goods and services. There is a standard rate of 20 per cent and reduced rates of 4 and 12 per cent, payable on the net price *plus* VAT.

(c) *Transaction taxes*. Stamp duty is payable at 2 per cent on share issues and at between 1.5 and 3 per cent on the transfer of immovable property. The transfer of shares and debentures is subject to a tax of 1 per cent of the sale price, payable as to half by the transferer and half by the transferee.

(d) *Social security*. Payroll taxes amounting to 38.9 per cent of payroll are payable by employers, in addition to a further tax of 8.9 per cent on staff salaries and 6.1 per cent on the salaries of other employees. A special payroll tax of 22.2 per cent is to be levied in 1991 on certain income of private companies.

Switzerland

Average rate of exchange y/e 31.3.90: £1 = SFr 2.5722

1. The tax year; nature and rates of tax

(a) The tax year is the calendar year. The profits of an accounting period other than a calendar year are generally allocated to the year in which the period ends.

(b) Swiss companies are subject to income tax at three successive levels: communal, cantonal and federal. The federal income tax is charged on the average taxable profits of the two preceding years.

Accounting period ended 30 September 1989. Profits SFr 150,000
Accounting period ended 30 September 1990. Profits SFr 180,000
Taxable in 1991 (and 1992): SFr 165,000.

(c) Federal income tax is levied at progressive rates on a percentage of taxable profits determined according to the proportion profits bear to the total of capital and reserves (net worth). The minimum rate is 3.63 per cent of taxable profits and the absolute ceiling is equivalent to 9.8 per cent of profits. Cantonal and communal income taxes are levied on the same basis, at rates between 17 and 35 per cent.

(d) *Special régime for holding companies.* Holding companies do not attract special privileges as far as federal income tax is concerned, but many cantons exempt holding companies entirely from cantonal and municipal income tax and levy cantonal net worth tax (see 10(b) below) at reduced rates. The definition of a holding company varies from canton to canton but, broadly speaking, a minimum requirement is that 75 per cent or more of the company's income derive from investment in other companies.

2. Residence and territoriality

Swiss resident companies are liable to federal, cantonal and communal income tax on their worldwide income, both distributed and undistributed.

Companies incorporated in Switzerland are treated as resident there, as are companies whose effective management is carried out in Switzerland.

3. The tax base

(a) *Method of calculation.* Taxable profits are based on the profits reported in the accounts.
(b) *Disallowable items.* Any expenditure that is not commercially justifiable (eg most charitable donations) is non-deductible.
(c) *Exempt income/special deductions.* For dividends, see 4 below. Deductions are available for write-downs of share and loan investments and contributions to pension reserves. Long-term exchange gains and losses are recognised. Taxes paid in the period are deductible for federal income tax and in some cantons for cantonal income tax also.
(d) *Interest paid.* Interest is deductible on an accruals basis.
(e) *Stock.* Stock is valued at the lower of cost and market value according to recognised accounting principles. A deduction of up to 33.3 per cent of stock value to cover obsolescence is nearly always available. If the facts justify a higher rate, that rate may be allowed.
(f) *Depreciation.* Either the straight-line or reducing balance method may be used. Permissible rates are published by the authorities for federal income tax purposes and these are usually acceptable for cantonal and communal income tax also. Assets within the same category may be pooled.

4. Treatment of dividends

(a) *Dividends received from Swiss and foreign companies.* Substantial relief or complete exemption from federal (and usually cantonal and communal) income tax is available (under the so-called holding rebate) in respect of dividends from Swiss and foreign companies in which the recipient company holds at least 20 per cent or SFr 2,000,000 in value. The dividends received from such holdings are exempt from tax altogether but they are included in net worth in order to compute the company's federal income tax rate on its other income (see 1(c) above). The overall effect is to reduce the company's income tax rate by the proportion the exempt income bears to total gross income. Most cantons and communes apply the holding rebate to reduce the cantonal and communal income tax liability also. The holding rebate does not apply to reduce the company's federal net worth tax base but individual cantons may allow it to reduce the cantonal net worth tax.

(b) *Dividends paid.* Dividend payments to residents and non-residents are subject to 35 per cent federal withholding tax.

5. *Anti-avoidance*

There are no provisions against accumulated earnings. Thin-capitalisation rules are applied to payments of interest where debt-equity ratios exceed a certain level (eg 2:1, 3:1 or 6:1 for commercial, industrial or financial companies). In these circumstances, interest is treated as a dividend and subject to 35 per cent withholding tax. Transfer pricing rules exist to adjust payments to and from foreign affiliates to arm's-length values. There are no provisions similar to the UK's controlled foreign company legislation.

6. *Treatment of losses*

(a) *Current period.* Trading and capital losses may be set off against income and gains of the current accounting period (which is two years for federal income tax purposes).
(b) *Future periods.* Losses may be carried forward against future profits for a maximum of seven years (federal income tax) and two to five years (cantonal income tax). Some cantons do not allow carry forward.
(c) *Past periods.* Carry back of losses is not permitted.
(d) *Transferability.* There is no restriction on transfer of losses on a change in ownership, provided there are no major changes in the nature of the trade (including its outlets).

7. *Treatment of capital gains*

(a) *Treatment.* Capital gains are treated as income and subject to federal and cantonal income tax (at rates differing from canton to canton). Gains on real property are subject to special treatment in some cantons.
(b) *Computation.* Gains are computed by deducting cost from sale proceeds. Cost is substituted by net book (depreciated) value where depreciation has been claimed.
(c) *Roll-over.* There are no roll-over or deferral provisions.
(d) *Shares.* There is no special treatment for shares.

8. Treatment of groups

There is no tax consolidation for groups of companies. Dividends from subsidiaries will generally be exempt from federal (and often from cantonal and communal) income tax, however, under the holding rebate (see 4 above).

9. Treatment of branches

A Swiss branch is treated for most purposes like a Swiss resident company. Branches pay federal, cantonal and communal income tax on profits arising in Switzerland but the rate depends on the ratio of their worldwide profits and net worth. There is no withholding tax on remittances of profits.

10. Other taxes

(a) A 3 per cent federal tax is payable on some discounts and rebates granted to customers. Some cantons levy a similar tax.
(b) *Taxes on capital.* A net worth tax is levied at a rate of 0.0825 per cent at the federal level and at rates between 0.3 and 1 per cent by the cantons. Branches are liable to this tax in respect of their Swiss net assets. A property tax is levied in some cantons.
(c) *Turnover taxes.* A sales turnover tax is charged on the supply of goods within Switzerland and on imports. Rates are 6.2 per cent (retailers) and 9.3 per cent (wholesalers and importers).
(d) *Transaction taxes.* Federal tax is payable on share issues (at 3 per cent) and on certain share transfers.
(e) *Payroll taxes.* Social security contributions are levied on employers and employees at rates dependent on the age and salary of the employee. The employer's contribution must be at least 50 per cent of the total due.
(f) *Other taxes.* Most cantons levy a church tax (eg 11.87 per cent of the cantonal income tax in Zürich).

Appendix B

European Personal Tax Systems

Introduction

The European personal tax systems as they apply to foreign executives posted to Europe are set out on the following pages. The countries covered are Austria, Belgium, Denmark, Finland, France, Germany, Greece, Ireland, Italy, Luxembourg, Netherlands, Norway, Portugal, Spain, Sweden and Switzerland.

Only the barest essentials of each country's tax system are set out. An executive posted abroad must seek advice both in the UK and in the European country to establish his best tax position.

The table begins with a summary for the UK for ease of comparison with the various aspects of local taxation examined. These are:

- the basis on which liability to taxation can arise;
- the personal tax year (31 December in all cases other than the UK);
- the marginal rates of tax;
- special rules on taxing foreign income;
- whether gains are taxed;
- local taxes;
- wealth tax (in most cases there is none);
- social security;
- special rules for new residents (this point is particularly important);
- exchange controls (again, in most cases none).

UK

Basis of taxation: Residence, ordinary residence, domicile/certain UK sourced income.

Tax year to: 5 April.

Maximum tax rate: 40 per cent.

Tax on foreign income: Foreign investment income of resident but non-domiciled individuals taxed only if received in UK. Income of a non-UK domiciled individual from a foreign employment carried on wholly abroad only taxable if received in the UK. Other income taxable.

Tax on capital gains: Foreign gains of resident but non-domiciled individuals taxed only if received in UK. Other gains taxable.

Local taxes: 'Community charge' at fixed rate of £148–£500 per annum. Additional charges where UK property is owned but unoccupied.

Wealth tax: None.

Social security: Employee's contributions 9 per cent of earnings on salary up to £18,200 (7 per cent where covered by most personal or employer pension schemes). Employer's contributions – 10.45 per cent (no upper limit).

Special rules for new residents: See above. Moving expenses exempt.

Exchange controls: None.

Austria

Basis of taxation: Residence/certain Austrian source income.

Tax year to: 31 December.

Maximum tax rate: 50 per cent.

Tax on foreign income: Taxed in full.

Tax on capital gains:	Not taxed if arising from *non*-business activities (there are exceptions for speculative transactions and sales of 'participations' in businesses).
Local taxes:	Annual real estate tax based on the assessed value of Austrian real estate.
Wealth tax:	1 per cent. There is a special basis of valuation of land and participations in businesses (if no market value is readily available, ie shares not quoted on a stock exchange) which is significantly lower than market value for the purposes of the wealth tax.
Social security:	Employee's contributions 16–17 per cent. Employer's contributions 19–23 per cent. Limited to a maximum of AS 394,800 of earnings.
Special rules for new residents:	Approximately 1/7th of emoluments may remain tax free or be taxed at a maximum rate of 6 per cent for all employees.
Exchange controls:	Usually no problems are encountered with the transfer of a foreign executive's earnings.

Belgium

Basis of taxation:	Residence/Belgian source income.
Tax year to:	31 December.
Maximum tax rate:	55 per cent (excluding local).
Tax on foreign income:	Taxed in full.
Tax on capital gains:	Not generally taxed if non-business but there are exceptions for sales of some land and substantial participations.
Local taxes:	6–10 per cent communal taxes.
Wealth tax:	None.
Social security:	Employee contributions 12.07 per cent. Employer contributions 32 per cent (approx).

Special rules for new residents:	*Per diem* allowances may not be taxable. Special rules apply to senior foreign employees who work in Belgium on a temporary basis who are treated as being non-resident taxpayers. In that case the executive gives up Belgium's tax treaty protection.
Exchange controls	Effectively none.

Denmark

Basis of taxation:	Residence.
Tax year to:	31 December.
Maximum tax rates:	50–68 per cent (including local).
Tax on foreign income:	Taxed in full.
Tax on capital gains:	Taxed at 50 per cent.
Local taxes:	23–32 per cent on income. There is also a local property tax.
Wealth tax:	1.2–1.5 per cent.
Social security:	Employee contributions DKr 1,124 per annum.
Special rules for new residents:	Foreign nationals working in Denmark for a foreign employer are entitled to a deduction of up to 25 per cent of salary.
Exchange controls:	An individual may have to remit Danish-duties salary into Denmark.

Finland

Basis of taxation:	Residence/Finnish source income.
Tax year to:	31 December.
Maximum tax rate:	44 per cent (1989 rates) (excluding local).
Tax on foreign income:	Taxed in full.

Tax on capital gains:	Where real property has been held ten years or shares five years and is sold at a gain, there is a deemed cost of 50 per cent of the proceeds plus FMK 210,000. 40 per cent of the residual gain is taxed as income. The 40 per cent increases if the asset has been held for shorter periods.
Local taxes:	14–19.5 per cent (Also optional 1–2 per cent Church taxes) (1989 rates).
Wealth tax:	0.9 per cent.
Social security:	Resident individuals pay premiums of 3.5 per cent of taxable salary. Employers' social security payments when added to payments for loss through illness can amount to 40–50 per cent of the company's payroll.
Special rules for new residents:	None.
Exchange controls:	There are many detailed and restrictive rules which may prevent the ownership of foreign company shares by Finnish residents and the expatriation of funds.

France

Basis of taxation:	Residence or centre of family, economic or professional interests if in France/French source income.
Tax year to:	31 December.
Maximum tax rate:	56.8 per cent.
Tax on foreign income:	Taxed in full.
Tax on capital gains:	(a) Real property taxed at full rates although tax base reduced over period of ownership; (b) Securities 16 per cent under certain circumstances.
Local taxes:	Local property taxes.

Wealth tax:	0.5 to 1.5 per cent on net worth. First FF 13 million exempt.
Social security:	Employee's contributions 18–20 per cent.
Special rules for new residents:	Moving expenses exempt. Some tax breaks are available to employees of HQs allowing tax on benefits to be paid by the employer only.
Exchange controls:	Effectively depends on length of stay.

Germany

Basis of taxation:	Residence/German source income.
Tax year to:	31 December.
Maximum tax rate:	53 per cent.
Tax on foreign income:	Taxed in full.
Tax on capital gains:	(a) Private real property – exempt if sold after two years' ownership; (b) Securities – exempt if sold after six months' ownership unless a substantial (over 25 per cent) holding. The tax rate is reduced to approximately half the nominal rate for the sale of substantial (ie 25 per cent or more voting power) shareholdings and businesses.
Local taxes:	Local land tax. Business property tax. (Also optional 8–9 per cent church taxes).
Wealth tax:	0.5 per cent net wealth tax.
Social security:	Maximum employer's contributions (covering retirement and unemployment benefits) DM 701.5 per month (1989 rates). Maximum employee's contributions DM 701.5 per month (1989 rates) if salary DM 6,100 monthly. Contributions covering sickness insurance are not compulsory for employees earning over DM 4,575 monthly. (75 per cent of DM 6,100)
Social rules for new residents:	Moving expenses exempt, but all expenses which are job-related are normally deductible

anyway. The tax applying to certain individuals who immigrate to Germany may be levied on an advantageous flat-rate basis during the first three to five years of residence. If there is foreign source income from countries with which Germany does not have a double tax treaty the tax rate can be reduced to zero if foreign taxes are payable and that income is less than 25 per cent of the aggregate income in Germany. Insurance premiums paid to foreign companies are deductible. Employees on international assignments can claim that earned income is attributable to workdays in foreign countries and hence is not taxable.

Exchange controls: None.

Greece

Basis of taxation: Residence.

Tax year to: 31 December.

Maximum tax rate: 50 per cent.

Tax on foreign income: Taxed in full.

Tax on gains: There is no capital gains tax for non-business transactions.

Local taxes: None.

Wealth tax: None.

Social security: 13.25 per cent on a gross monthly salary of up to Dr 190,640 (1989) (deductible in determining net taxable income).

Special rules for new residents: Individuals not earning income in Greece and not considered to be 'permanent' residents may not pay income tax.

Exchange controls: Strict exchange control rules apply with regard to the export of capital. The reporting requirements are onerous. It is proposed to remove exchange controls with other EC members by 31 December 1992 although there is an option to extend this to 31 December 1994.

Ireland

Basis of taxation: Residence, ordinary residence and domicile/certain Irish source income.

Tax year to: 5 April.

Maximum tax rate: 53 per cent.

Tax on foreign income: Non-Irish domiciled but resident individuals are only subject to Irish tax on non-Irish or UK investment income and gains on a remittance basis. Non-Irish domiciled individuals are only liable to Irish tax on foreign (excluding UK) earnings from non-Irish affiliated companies where remitted to Ireland. Remittances out of capital (including all funds owned at the time of arrival) are not taxable.

Tax on gains: Non-Irish domiciled individuals are subject to tax on a remittance basis on foreign (excluding UK) gains. The following rates of tax apply:

Years	*Rate (per cent)*
0–3	50
4–6	35
6 and over	30

Local taxes: Residential property at 1.5 per cent on value in excess of IR £91,000.

Wealth tax: None.

Social security: Employee's contributions (1990) rates:

Income IR£	*Rate on excess (per cent)*
0–16,700	7.75
16,701–17,300	6.5
17,301 and over	1.0

Special rules for new residents: Remittance basis of taxation (see above). Moving expenses exempt.

Exchange controls:	Strict exchange control rules apply. Approval is required, although generally readily given, for the transfer of funds outside the state. Exchange controls with other EC members will be removed by 31 December 1992.

Italy

Basis of taxation:	Residence/Italian source income.
Tax year to:	31 December.
Maximum tax rate:	50 per cent (excluding local).
Tax on foreign income:	Taxed in full.
Tax on gains:	Not normally taxable unless arising from speculative intent or by way of a business.
Local taxes:	16.2 per cent on Italian source income except salaries and dividends.
Wealth tax:	None.
Social security:	Employee contributions 8–9 per cent.
Special rules for new residents:	None.
Exchange controls:	Exchange control approval required although generally given. Exchange controls with other EC countries no longer exist.

Luxembourg

Basis of taxation:	Residence/certain Luxembourg source income.
Tax year to:	31 December.
Maximum tax rate:	56 per cent plus unemployment fund contribution amounting to 1 per cent of taxes.
Tax on foreign income:	Taxed in full.

Tax on gains:	Taxed as normal taxable income although gains on certain property, land and significant shareholding participations held long-term are subject to half the taxpayer's average rate.
Local taxes:	None.
Wealth tax:	0.5 per cent.
Social security:	2.425 per cent for sickness (annual ceiling of LF 1,792,680 [1989 rate]).
Special rules for new residents:	None, other than to foreign nationals who are managers of credit institutions in Luxembourg.
Exchange controls:	None.

Netherlands

Basis of taxation:	Residence/specific Netherlands source income.
Tax year to:	31 December.
Maximum tax rate:	60 per cent (1990 rates), but many reliefs, eg all interest deductible.
Tax on foreign income:	Taxed in full unless foreign employees qualifying for the 35 per cent concession (see below) who are treated as non-residents subject to tax on investmént income from specific Netherlands sources such as rent, and on emoluments *worldwide* only.
Tax on gains:	Only certain gains are taxed, ie (a) those arising from business or professional activities or from speculative intent at the normal progressive rates; (b) on the sale of shares where the vendor has a 'substantial interest' in the company concerned at a fixed rate of 20 per cent. If '35 percenter', not taxed on sale of shares.
Local taxes:	Property tax.
Wealth tax:	0.8 per cent.
Social security:	These fall into two categories: (a) general employee social security regulation premiums

	which are limited to DFl 7,908 on income up to a maximum of of DFl 65,900 (1989 rates); (b) employee social security regulation premiums which are levied on income up to a maximum of DFl 68,380 – the average premium amounts to DFl 7,641 (1989 rates).
Special rules for new residents:	Foreign employees assigned to work in the Netherlands may be granted a tax deduction of 35 per cent from their gross salary income for up to 60 months (which can be extended). Education allowance.
Exchange controls:	Virtually none; an individual's earnings and other funds are freely transferable. Exchange controls with other EC countries no longer exist.

Norway

Basis of taxation:	Residence/Norwegian source income.
Tax year to:	31 December.
Maximum tax rate:	Absolute maximum of 80 per cent (including national (19 per cent), super (8.5 per cent), local (25 per cent), capital (2.3 per cent) and social security (9.2 per cent) Income tax maximum of 59.3 per cent.
Tax on foreign income:	Taxed in full.
Tax on gains:	Taxed as income. Private residences exempt. No tax on shares held for more than three years.
Local taxes:	Substantial.
Wealth tax:	0–1.3 per cent national; 0–1 per cent municipal.
Social security:	16.7 per cent (employers); 7.8 per cent (employees). Special rate for self-employed.
Special rules for new residents:	15 per cent of salary for first four years. *Per diem*, moving expense, housing allowance.

Exchange controls:	Controls probably will not apply to UK executives.

Portugal

Basis of taxation:	Residence/Portuguese sourced income.
Tax year to:	31 December.
Maximum tax rate:	40 per cent.
Tax on foreign income:	Taxed in full.
Tax on gains:	Taxed at various rates. The sale of shares or other negotiable instruments is taxed at 10 per cent. The sale of real estate is taxed at the normal progressive rates but the assessment is restricted to 50 per cent of the gain.
Local taxes:	None, with the exception of municipal tax which is assessed on the registered value of real estate.
Wealth tax:	None.
Social security:	Employer's contributions 24.5 per cent; Employee's contributions 11 per cent. Both apply to total remuneration.
Special rules for new residents:	Relocation and moving expenses exempt.
Exchange controls:	Strict. It is proposed to remove exchange controls with other EC members by 31 December 1992 although there is an option to extend this to 31 December 1994.

Spain

Basis of taxation:	Residence/Spanish source income.
Tax year to:	31 December.
Maximum tax rate:	56 per cent.

Tax on foreign income:	Taxed in full.
Tax on gains:	Taxed in full, although there is a method of spreading the gain over the years for which it accrued to determine the rate of tax to be applied.
Local taxes:	None.
Wealth tax:	0.2–2 per cent.
Social security:	Employees contributions 6 per cent; employer's contributions 30.3 per cent on basic salaries of up to Pts 275,820 per month.
Special rules for new residents:	None.
Exchange controls:	Strict. Foreign workers in Spain are permitted to remit 50 per cent of their gross salary overseas. Exchanger controls with other EC members will be removed under EC regulations by 31 December 1992.

Sweden

Basis of taxation:	Residence/Swedish source income.
Tax year to:	31 December.
Maximum tax rate:	50 per cent (including local) (1991 rates).
Tax on foreign income:	Taxed in full if stay more than six months.
Tax on gains:	Taxed in full at 30 per cent (1991 rates).
Local taxes:	Approximately 30 per cent (assessed together with the national income tax and incorporated in the tax rates above). Also real estate tax on value of property at between 1 and 2.5 per cent.
Wealth tax:	1.5–3 per cent.
Social security:	37.47 per cent of gross income paid in total by employer. Also special payroll tax.

Special rules for new residents:	Concessions only available to special compensation paid to foreign researchers working on assignment in Sweden. Moving expenses exempt.
Exchange controls:	Almost all exchange controls were abolished with effect from 1 July 1989.

Switzerland

Basis of taxation:	Residence.
Tax year to:	31 December.
Maximum tax rate:	11.5 per cent (federal). Mostly cantonal and parish.
Tax on foreign income:	Rental income from real estate situated abroad is tax-exempt for both residents and non-residents.
Tax on gains:	No special concessions to foreign nationals. Capital gains on the disposal of Swiss real estate only subject to tax. Capital gains on movable property realised by employees are tax exempt.
Local taxes:	Canton (Geneva) 3.1–19 per cent (1989 rates). Communal Tax (Geneva City) 45.5 per cent of basic Cantonal tax (1989 rates). Parish tax often 11–13 per cent of basic Cantonal taxes (1989) rates.
Wealth tax:	Canton (Geneva) 0.175–0.585 per cent (1989 rates).
Social security:	5.05 per cent for employees (no limit) plus 0.3 per cent employment insurance on first SFr 81,600 of compensation plus compulsory pension contributions which are much higher. Can be as high as 13 per cent.
Special rules for new residents:	There are no special concessions to foreigners except in some Cantons (eg Geneva) which allows special deductions for expatriates.
Exchange controls:	None.

Appendix C

Eastern Europe

by Zigurds Kronbergs of Stoy Hayward

Introduction

It is now almost trite to say that as recently as 1989, it would have seemed an absurd idea that the seemingly permanent Communist régimes of Eastern Europe, which had lasted for more than 40 years, would be swept away, one by one, in the space of less than a year. The pace of events has been so swift and uncontrollable that any sort of prognostication into even the medium-term future would be extremely unwise. For obvious reasons, the country-by-country summary of tax systems found in Appendix A cannot be repeated here – the existing rudimentary tax systems, based on the old Soviet-style command economy, are being dismantled and the new systems that will replace them do not even, in some cases, exist on paper let alone in reality. What this Appendix does seek to offer is a political and economic overview of the social and financial climate potential exporters to, and investors in, the former Eastern bloc are likely to encounter.

As is only to be expected, developments are taking place at a different pace, and circumstances differ, from country to country. Nevertheless, two distinct patterns seem to be emerging – one that may be called the 'Western model' and the other the 'neo-Communist model'. It so happens that the nations following either model also fall into two distinct geographical regions. So it is that Poland, Czechoslovakia and Hungary conform to the Western model, whereas Romania and Bulgaria, to date, follow the neo-Communist model.

The four remaining countries are all special cases. Albania, for many decades almost completely isolated not only from the West but also from its Communist neighbours, may now be experiencing the first stirrings of its own revolution, and has recently announced that it would welcome foreign investment. For the time being, however, it still remains under the control of the last Stalinist régime in Europe, so will not be discussed further. The German Democratic Republic will also not be discussed further here. Currency union with West Germany has already taken place; full political union, involving the disappearance of the GDR as a sovereign state, took place on 3 October 1990. Yugoslavia, for long the most 'Western-like' of Communist countries, is now lagging behind politically but currently falls somewhere between the two models. Finally, the USSR itself – is in many ways the most difficult to predict. Like Yugoslavia, it exhibits strong fissiparous tendencies and may well cease to exist in its present form in the near future. Whether or not that is the case, it is now probable that the Baltic republics of Estonia, Latvia and Lithuania will shortly re-establish themselves as *de facto* independent nations and they will accordingly be considered separately here.

Poland

Population	37.9m	*Net currency debt*	$35,300m
Density (km^{-2})	124.5	*Exports‡*	$7,700m
GDP	$69,000m	*Debt/export ratio*	535%*
Per capita GDP	$1,818	*Inflation*	5% on month†

Exchange rate (31.3.90): $1 = 15,328 złoty

‡ = convertible currency
* = 1989 preliminary
† = May 1990

Source: *Financial Times*

Political background

Having led the way among its neighbours with the first non-Communist head of government anywhere in the Eastern bloc since 1948, Poland has now fallen behind in the sense that, apart from Yugoslavia, it is the only country not to have had genuinely free elections. The famous 'Round Table' agreement of March 1989 between the Communists and Solidarity led to elections in June 1989 in which 65 per cent of the seats were guaranteed to the Communist Party and smaller satellite parties. The remaining 35 per cent were freely contested and Solidarity-supported candidates won all but a handful. It represented a compromise between a Communist party that had lost all authority and will to govern, and an umbrella opposition grouping that was not yet sure how far Moscow would tolerate Communist loss of power. The government is headed by Tadeusz Mazowiecki, a Catholic intellectual and former editor of the *Solidarity* newspaper.

Disputes over the speed of reform and the legitimacy of the government itself have led to the growth of two separate parties still nominally within Solidarity, but coalescing around the personalities of Mazowiecki on the one hand and Lech Wałęsa, the Solidarity leader, on the other. Broadly speaking, most of the former dissident intelligentsia have rallied behind the Mazowiecki group, which is best described as 'centre left', whereas Wałęsa's following tends more towards the 'centre right'. It is these two men who are the chief contestants in the presidential elections, held on 25 November 1990*, to find a successor to the former communist leader, General Jaruzelski, who retired before the expiry of his term of office. Free parliamentary elections are expected in 1991, by which time Solidarity, as a political grouping, may well have broken up completely.

Economic situation

In January 1990, the Polish economy was in a dire state, perhaps the worst of all Comecon countries. Poland is saddled with an enormous foreign debt burden – as large as the Soviet Union's, which it will never be able completely to repay. The debt was accumulated largely in the 1960s and 1970s to fund investment in large heavy industrial projects, none of which has been particularly successful and all of which now present the country with the usual problems associated with outdated, overmanned, inefficient and environmentally deleterious industrial plant and in funding subsidies in basic foods and energy in an attempt to buy the acquiescence of the population – the least cowed and most restless in the Eastern bloc.

Recognising the depth of the crisis, the government launched what is universally acknowledged to be Eastern Europe's most radical and sweeping economic reform programme on 1 January 1990. Subsidies on food, energy, transport and housing have been cut drastically, the złoty was devalued by nearly 50 per cent, price controls were removed, interest rates were freed, and prohibitive taxation was imposed on excessive wage increases. This programme, which has the approval of the IMF, was intended to slash the hyperinflation that had broken out, eliminate the budget deficit and prepare the ground for substantial privatisation. At the same time, real living standards are expected to fall by 25 per cent in 1990, open unemployment to rise substantially and

* Election results unknown at the time of going to press.

foreign debt to increase in the short term, as the government seeks further credits. The IMF agreed a loan of $725m in February and the World Bank is expected to lend $1,750m by mid-1991.

The austerity programme has had some notable successes. The month-on-month inflation rate has been cut from 80 per cent in January to 5 per cent in May, a record hard currency trade surplus of $780m was achieved in the first quarter of 1990, the currency has been stabilised, and substantial progress has been made, with the help of Western experts, in establishing a modern banking system. However, internally the recession continues and industrial sales have fallen by about 20 per cent. The privatisation law was for a long time bogged down over how great a proportion of an enterprise's shares to offer to its workers, bearing in mind the need to attract foreign capital and technology by granting a substantial degree of control. The Solidarity government feels the dilemma particularly painfully, given Solidarity's history as a trade union and the substantial debt owed to Polish workers for their continued resistance to Communist rule. In the end, workers in an enterprise are to be offered a substantial minority holding but not control.

To date, large commitments from Western companies have been few. Management, consisting largely of Communist placemen rewarded for loyalty rather than managerial skills has, unsurprisingly, been slow to adapt to new conditions.

All observers are agreed that the real hardship for the population is yet to come and that the government's task in persuading it to accept more sacrifice now for the greater good later will become correspondingly more difficult.

Czechoslovakia

Population	15.5m	*Net currency debt*	$3,400m
Density (km^{-2})	121.2	*Exports*‡	$5,800m
GDP	$118,000m	*Debt/export ratio*	58.6%
Per capita GDP	$7,591	*Inflation*	1.5%

Exchange rate (31.3.90): £1 = 26.88 koruny*

‡ = convertible currency
* = commercial rate

Source: *Financial Times*

Political background

After the Soviet invasion of August 1968, the Czechoslovakian régime was one of the most repressive in the Eastern bloc, which made its collapse when faced with mass popular demonstrations in November 1989 all the more remarkable. The Communist government was replaced by an administration dominated by Civic Forum, a broadly based citizens' group. Its leader, the famous playwright and dissident, Václav Havel, became president. Elections were held in June, in which Civic Forum, now standing as a political party (broadly of the centre left) in its own right, won 46 per cent of the vote and a majority in parliament. The main opposition parties, the centre-right Christian Democratic Alliance and the Communists, polled 12 per cent and 14 per cent respectively. President Havel reappointed the former Communist, Marian Čalfa, as prime minister at the head of a Civic Forum government. The 1968 Communist leader, Alexander Dubček, is speaker of parliament. There is little doubt that the government, and particularly the president, commands a great deal of support. The political future is complicated by a strong nationalist movement in Slovakia. The Slovaks, who have their own language, have always felt a degree of resentment towards the Czechs, who have assumed the leading positions in the country since its creation in 1918. Traditionally, care has always been taken to keep a careful balance between Czechs and Slovaks in government. Thus, Mr Havel is a Czech whereas both Mr Čalfa and Mr Dubček are Slovaks. Although demands for an independent Slovakia do not command majority support, they may be expressed more forcefully if Slovakia seems to suffer disproportionately from the cost of economic reforms. Dispute over the speed of those reforms is already threatening a split in Civic Forum, as for Solidarity in Poland. It remains to be seen whether the views of Vaclav Klaus, the Finance Minister, who favours a rapid privatisation programme, will prevail. However, Czechoslovakia was the single country in mainland Europe east of the Rhine to retain a fully democratic form of government throughout the inter-war period and the prognosis for the new democratic institutions is good.

Economic situation

Czechoslovakia was a major industrial and trading nation before the war and has not unreasonable hopes of regaining that status. However, in common with other Soviet bloc economies, it has a surplus of heavy, inefficient industry and a consumer sector which, while impressive by Comecon standards, is feeble when compared with the West.

Czechoslovakia, in common with its neighbours the former GDR and Poland, suffers from heavy pollution and from the handicap that virtually its only indigenous source of fuel is lignite, the most basic and polluting form of coal.

Although there is considerable tension within the government over the pace and scale of economic reform, it is committed to the introduction of a market economy. Several important measures have already been taken. Private businesses may now be set up without permission in any sphere of the economy and there is no limit on the number of employees or capital involved. Joint stock companies, with a 'reasonable' degree of foreign ownership, may be set up. Foreign companies are allowed to operate within Czechoslovakia on the same terms as Czechoslovakian enterprises. State enterprises are to be transformed into joint stock companies; the state will remain as a shareholder and initially retain the right to appoint 50 per cent of board members.

Hungary

Population	10.7m	*Net currency debt*	$16,100m
Density (*km*$^{-2}$)	115.0	*Exports*‡	$5,900m
GDP	$28,000m	*Debt/export ratio*	273%
Per capita GDP	$2,621	*Inflation*	15.6%

Exchange rate (31.3.90): £1 = 106.99 forint

‡ = convertible currency

Source: *Financial Times*

Political background

Hungary slid almost imperceptibly from Communist dictatorship to democracy, without the need either for armed insurrection as in Romania, or for mass street demonstrations as in Czechoslovakia and the GDR. The Communist party gradually and voluntarily relinquished power, renaming itself the Hungarian Socialist party in the process and ridding itself of two general secretaries, János Kádár and Karoly Grosz, who had both initiated reforms and later stood in the way of further change. In the elections in May 1990, the largest number of seats was won by the centre-right Democratic Forum, under the leadership of

József Antall, a former librarian, who is prime minister at the head of a coalition government with the Smallholders' Party and the Christian Democratic People's Party. The main opposition is provided by the left liberal Free Democrat-Fidesz grouping. Paradoxically perhaps, it is the conservative governing coalition that advocated a more measured and less radical economic programme than the Free Democrats.

Economic situation

It was under the leadership of János Kádár, whom Moscow installed as leader following the crushing of the Hungarian revolution in 1956, that Hungary's path towards a Western-style economy began. In return for complete adherence to Soviet foreign policy abroad, Kádár was given leeway to operate a much less rigid economic system at home. The result was to provide Hungarian consumers with a standard and variety of goods unequalled in the Eastern bloc, but at the price of massive foreign debt (the highest *per capita* in the world) and an economy slowly spinning out of control. The former Communist government's own figures put over 20 per cent of Hungarians as living below the poverty line, and in most cases ordinary people need to have two or three jobs just to make ends meet. It was perhaps the realisation of imminent economic collapse that sapped the will of the Communist party to hold on to power.

Nonetheless, the IMF agreed to a $206m stand-by loan in March 1990, even while the Nemeth caretaker Communist administration was still in power, and a further $1,000m may be made available in the next three years. The new government has announced that its target is to return 66 per cent of the economy to private ownership within the next four years. Foreign companies will continue to have the right to hold up to 100 per cent of Hungarian enterprises, to remit profits in hard currency and enjoy freedom to set their own wage and price levels. The bankruptcy of unprofitable enterprises is to be allowed. However, the tax holiday offered to foreign participants in joint ventures is to be phased out. A stock exchange has been opened in Budapest. To date, there are about 1,000 joint ventures with foreign investors (of which only 40 or so are with British companies) and General Electric of the USA has acquired a 51 per cent stake in the light bulb manufacturer, Tungsram.

The Hungarian government wishes to apply for membership of the EC and has announced that its target is full membership of the Community by 1995.

Yugoslavia

Population	*23.6m*	*Gross currency debt*	$17,960m
Density (km^{-2})	*92.3*	*Exports‡*	$12,780m
GDP	$57,000m	*Debt/export ratio*	158%
Per capita GDP	$2,415	*Inflation*	1,256%

Exchange rate (31.3.90): £1 = 19.52 new dinars

‡ = convertible currency
All figures 1989 estimates, except exports and debt/export ratio 1988.

Source: ABECOR

Political background

Yugoslavia is a federal state of six republics, each with its own government handling internal affairs. Internal tensions, suppressed during the role of Marshal Tito, have now risen to the extent that the future of Yugoslavia as a single state is very much in doubt. There are many parallels with the situation in the Soviet Union. The two principal areas of conflict are between Serbia, the largest and most populous republic and the Albanian majority within the formerly autonomous region of Kosovo in the south of the country and between Serbia and the northern republics, Slovenia and Croatia. Serbia's populist leader, Slobodan Milosević, has appealed to Serbian nationalism in an effort to suppress Albanian agitation for Kosovo to be declared a separate republic within the federation. The stridency of his rhetoric has awakened fears of Serbian domination in Croatia and Slovenia. The other three, southern, republics – Bosnia-Herzegovina, Macedonia and Montenegro – tend to side with Serbia. The largely Catholic Croats and Slovenes (Serbs are largely orthodox and the Albanians Moslems) were historically part of the Austro-Hungarian empire and were somewhat reluctant converts to the idea of an all-embracing Yugoslav state in 1918. While, officially, Yugoslavia is still a one-party state and the federal government of Ante Marković (who has now put himself at the head of a federal, non-Communist party) grapples with the country's formidable economic problems, Croatia and Slovenia have gone their own way in abolishing Communist party monopoly. In free elections held in May and June 1990, Slovenes elected a nationalist administration and the Croats an extremist right-wing government under a former partisan general, Franjo Tudjman. The Slovenian parliament has passed a sovereignty law reserving for itself the right to secede completely from Yugoslavia, and Croatia is likely to follow suit. This north-south divide along political lines is deepened by economic differences. Slovenia and Croatia are the most prosperous republics; the south tends to be backward, poor, and have high unemployment. Unless a compromise can be found between the Serbs on the one hand and the Croats, Slovenes and Albanians on the other, perhaps involving an even looser confederation, it is difficult to see how Yugoslavia can survive as such, especially now that the single most powerful cement holding the country together, fear of Soviet invasion, has vanished.

Economic situation

Of the Communist countries, Yugoslavia has traditionally been the most open to Western influence. Neither a member of the Warsaw pact nor of Comecon, Yugoslavia pursued a 'third way', rejecting both the private capitalism of the West and the state capitalism of the Soviet model, in favour of a form of workers' self-management. However, from the 1970s onwards the Yugoslav economy has been struggling and its problems are now quite acute. The estimated annual rate of inflation for 1989 is 2,000 per cent and the net hard currency debt approximately $14,000m. The federal government has introduced or intends to introduce several market-orientated reforms. As in Hungary, foreigners may now invest freely in Yugoslavia, control up to 100 per cent of enterprises and repatriate profits in hard currency. There are plans to introduce joint stock companies, open a stock market and encourage small business. However, if the government is to have any impact on the rate of inflation it needs to assert control over the republican banks, which have been free to pursue their own credit policies; given moves by Slovenia and Croatia towards quasi-independence, this seems an uphill task. Meanwhile, the two northern republics are pressing ahead with full-scale economic reforms of their own and look increasingly towards the EC for eventual full membership. In short, instability and uncertainty appear to be the order of the day for some time to come.

Romania

Population	23.1m	*Net currency debt*	$1,300m
Density (km^-2)	97.3	*Exports‡*	$7,700m
GDP	$71,000m	*Debt/export ratio*	16.9%
Per capita GDP	$3,072	*Inflation*	0.5%

Exchange rate (31.3.90): $1 = 34.22 lei

‡ = convertible currency

Source: *Financial Times*

Political background

The bloody revolution of December 1989, which overthrew the dictatorship of Nicolae Ceauşescu, placed in power a coalition of former Communist functionaries, dissidents, intellectuals and army officers, under the umbrella of the National Salvation Front (NSF), which set itself the task of steering the country until the elections scheduled for May 1990. By the end of January 1990, most of the leading intellectuals and dissidents had left, at about the same time as the NSF (now almost entirely composed of former Communists) declared that it would after all contest the elections as a political party, under the leadership of Ion Iliescu, formerly a leading party official, who had lost favour with Ceauşescu. As the election campaign got under way, there were widespread and repeated allegations of intimidation from the opposition, based largely on the grounds that the broadcast media were firmly in the grip of the NSF, and that, at local level, administration was largely in the hands of the same officials who had held office under Ceauşescu. The elections themselves were judged largely fair by international observers and resulted in an overwhelming victory both for Iliescu as president (with over 80 per cent of the popular vote) and for the NSF, which has a clear majority in parliament, based on over 70 per cent of the vote. The prime minister is Petre Roman, of the National Salvation Front. The immediate post-election period was marred by violence, when the forcible dispersal of a long-standing, anti-NSF demonstration led to rioting, followed by two days of virtual mob rule (including attacks on opposition politicians and destruction of opposition property) by pro-government coal miners, summoned to the capital by President Iliescu. The situation remains tense; although the government has undoubted support from a large majority of voters, a large section of the educated classes, whose contribution to the nation's economic and environmental recovery is crucial, seems to be permanently alienated from it. Ethnic tensions, fostered by the Ceauşescu régime, are still an important factor. Whereas the 700-year-old German minority is dwindling rapidly through emigration, a sizeable Hungarian minority remains in Transylvania. Although there was a brief period of solidarity during and immediately after the revolution, this seems to have evaporated and there have already been clashes between Magyars and Romanians.

Economic situation

The exact status of the economy is very difficult to judge, and Romania's official statistics from the last years of the Ceauşescu régime must be taken with an even larger pinch of salt than most Eastern European data. What is undoubtedly true is that industrial conditions are primitive, agriculture extremely backward and modern health care virtually non-existent. The one goal achieved in the Ceauşescu years, the virtual elimination of hard currency debt, was won at the cost of regress in almost every other sphere, notably in the consumer and welfare sector. Working conditions in the industrial sector and pollution, poor throughout the Eastern bloc, are often quite atrocious.

Although the worst excesses of the Ceauşescu era, such as the grandiose construction projects and the systematisation policy (widespread razing of villages and small towns) have been halted, much of the rest of the command system remains in place. Some economic reforms have been carried out – the leu has been devalued, the foreign exchange market liberalised and small enterprises encouraged, although a ceiling of 20 has been set for private employers. Foreign funding still requires permission from the Ministry of Finance and no decision has yet been taken on large-scale privatisation. Romanian control of joint ventures remains a precondition. Priority before the elections was given to improving the consumer sector; the government's medium-term economic intentions are still unclear and its election rhetoric underplayed the likely short-term costs of thorough-going economic reform, although there are now signs that a fast track liberalisation policy may be adopted. The prices of many staple commodities were doubled in November 1990 as a first step.

Bulgaria

Population	9.0m	*Net currency debt*	$6,600m
Density (km^{-2})	*81.1*	*Exports‡*	$3,200m
GDP	$38,000m	*Debt/export ratio*	206%
Per capita GDP	$4,244	*Inflation*	5%

Exchange rate (31.3.90): £1 = 1.3122 leva

‡ = convertible currency

Source: *Financial Times*

Political background

Palpable popular dissatisfaction, together with the example of reform in the USSR and the crumbling of Communist rule in Hungary and Poland, forced the Communist dictator Todor Zhivkov to resign in November 1989 after 35 years in power. Zhivkov was replaced by the reforming Communist, Petar Mladenov. Under Mladenov's leadership, the Communists renamed themselves the Bulgarian Socialist party and promised to hold free elections in 1990. Those elections took place in June and resulted in a narrow overall majority for the Communists/Socialists. The victors offered the opposition a coalition, which was refused, amid growing controversy about the election result and the personality of Mladenov. Mladenov was forced to resign in July 1990 following revelations that he had been in favour of calling on the army to suppress popular demonstrations in December 1989. With his departure it is possible that the opposition may now join the Communists/socialists in a coalition government. Certainly, parliament unanimously elected the opposition politician, Zhelyu Zhelev, as president to succeed Mladenov on 1 August 1990. There are also ethnic problems with a large Turkish minority, whom the Communists had forced to adopt Bulgarian names as part of a systematic campaign to eliminate their separate Turkish identity.

Economic situation

It is still not clear to what extent the government will liberalise the command administrative model economy. Although foreign trade and investment are being encouraged, rigorous exchange controls, including restrictions on the repatriation of capital, are still in place and the extent, if any, to which state enterprises will be transferred to the private sector is not currently known. The political paralysis that has followed the general election has contributed to the downward slide of the economy.

The Baltic States

Political background

The Baltic States – Estonia, Latvia and Lithuania – are unique among European countries in being the only 'casualties' of the Second World War. Their pre-war independence was brought to an end by Soviet annexation in 1940 and was not subsequently restored.

The freer atmosphere engendered by the policies of Mikhail Gorbachev brought to the surface long-standing nationalist feelings and grievances, culminating in the formation of 'popular fronts', movements drawing support from a broad cross-section of the population, including nationally-minded Communists. Following semi-free elections in February and March 1990, popular front governments took power in all three republics. The Lithuanian declaration restoring independence on 11 March 1990 was followed by Moscow's imposition of an economic blockade in April. The resulting *impasse* seemed to be resolved on 30 June 1990 when the Lithuanian parliament agreed to suspend the declaration for 100 days as and when talks with the Soviet government take place. The governments of all three republics intend to negotiate together but at the time of writing, formal talks have yet to get under way.

Economic situation

Although all three republics were relatively prosperous during independence and have a higher standard of living than the USSR, their economies suffer from all the shortcomings common to the Soviet system. Since planning has been carried out from Moscow, economic development has been forced at a pace and has been of a nature dictated by the perceived needs of the USSR rather than of the republics themselves. As a result, there is widespread pollution and almost complete dependence on the USSR for raw materials and energy. This necessarily means that the Baltic States' economies will remain closely meshed with that of the USSR, or whatever entity or entities replace it, for some time to come. Since the popular fronts are broad coalitions united on the need for independence but on little else, it is too early to predict what the political – and hence economic – landscape of the likely independent states will be once a genuine multi-party democracy emerges. It is hardly conceivable, however, that policies aimed at restoring a market economy will not be followed. In common with other Soviet systems, there is currently an obvious lack of managerial, accounting and entrepreneurial infrastructure.

Appendix D

EC Tax and company law harmonisation

Corporate tax

After many years of frustrated effort, the EC seems finally to have reached agreement on a cross-border corporate tax régime that will meet the fundamental objectives of the single market. The break-through came in April 1990, when the Commission dropped its earlier policy of trying to harmonise corporate tax rates, systems and dividend withholding taxes in favour of a package of proposals designed to eliminate tax penalties on businesses operating across several member states of the Community. Harmonisation has not been abandoned as a long-term desideratum, but the Commission recognises the need to rethink its approach to take into account developments since the original harmonisation proposal of 1975, not least the widespread tax reforms of the late 1980s.

In the Commission's announcement of 18 April 1990, Mme Scrivener, the Commissioner responsible for taxation and customs union, made it clear that all forms of double taxation within the community had to be abolished by 1 January 1993. In order to do this, the Council had to adopt without delay two draft Directives and a convention, two of which had first been laid before the Council in 1969. Those three documents concern:

- the treatment of dividends paid to parent companies resident in other member states;
- the treatment of cross-border mergers, demergers, asset contributions and share exchanges and
- the establishment of an arbitration procedure in tax disputes concerning transfer pricing.

They were duly agreed by the Council of Ministers on 11 June 1990 and the texts have now been finalised. Mme Scrivener also announced that two further draft Directives would shortly be laid before the Council with respect to:

- the elimination of withholding tax on intra-group interest and royalties and
- the set-off of losses from overseas permanent establishments (and possibly subsidiaries) against profits in the country of residence.

Adoption of these five measures would complete the Commission's package of measures for the Single Market. Its new approach is based on the principle of subsidiarity, under which responsibility is devolved downwards from the centre to the member states as far as possible within the confines of centrally agreed principles. Guided by this approach, the Commission will in future be giving priority to mutual recognition and approximation of national legislation where essential for the strengthening of the single market.

Directive on the taxation of parent companies and subsidiaries of different member states (90/435/EEC)

The main intention of this Directive is to eliminate withholding tax on dividends from companies in one member state to companies holding at least 25 per cent of their share capital and resident in other member states. Another provision requires that dividends from such foreign 'subsidiaries' be completely exempt from tax in the recipient's hands, although a maximum of 5 per cent can be added back to taxable profits. As an alternative to exemption, the member state of the recipient company may tax the dividends but give full credit for the tax paid by the distributing company in its home state on the profits out of which the distribution is made and for any residual withholding tax.

Germany, in particular, has always been opposed to this Directive – principally because of its two-tier corporate tax system (see Appendix A), under which distributed profits are taxed at a rate (36 per cent) lower than the rate on undistributed profits (50 per cent). In the absence of a withholding tax, German companies could avoid tax by establishing foreign parent companies. Germany was finally persuaded to drop its opposition on the understanding that it would be allowed to continue charging a withholding tax, at half of the present 10 per cent rate, until 1996, as long as the difference between its two tax rates remains greater than 11 per cent. By then, presumably, it will have reformed its corporate tax system to eliminate this advantage. Greece and Portugal, which have high withholding tax rates on dividends, have also been given longer transitional periods. Otherwise, the Directive must be implemented by the beginning of 1992.

Directive on the taxation of mergers, divisions, transfers of assets and exchanges of shares concerning companies of different member states (90/434/EEC)

This Directive removes any tax charge on the capital gains arising from certain mergers, demergers or asset contributions between companies in different member states. An asset contribution takes place where a company transfers its trade or assets to another without being wound up, whereas in a merger the contributing company is wound up. In a demerger (or 'division' – French *scission*), a company transfers its trade and/or assets to two or more companies. A potential tax charge would arise when assets are transferred in such situations, based on the difference between the market value of the assets and their tax written-down value in the contributing company's books. Whereas most member states allow for deferral of tax where the merger etc takes place between resident companies, deferral is usually not available where foreign companies are involved. The Directive would require deferral to be available on defined types of cross-border mergers etc within the EC, provided that the assets were transferred at the tax written-down values in which they appear in the contributing company's computation. The effect is to defer any capital gains charge until the assets are actually realised. This Directive is also to come into force on 1 January 1992.

Convention on the elimination of double taxation in connection with the adjustment of profits of associated enterprises (C301/4, 21.12.76)

This Convention is designed to cope with tax disputes arising between the revenue authorities of two member states when transfer pricing adjustments in one state are not matched by corresponding adjustments in the other, so that double taxation is likely to result. If the problem fails to be resolved bilaterally, a specially convened arbitration panel, whose decision will be binding on both parties, will intervene. The arbitration panel would consist of an equal number of nominees from both states involved and a number of independent experts.

VAT

While all are agreed that a common system of VAT accounting is imperative for the success of the Single Market, agreement on the final form which the system should take is still some way away. The Commission's latest (May 1990) proposals, themselves a compromise response to the rejection of the original Cockfield proposals, will, it seems, be further changed by the Council of Ministers.

These, the Scrivener proposals, are designed as an interim measure, due to expire on 31 December 1996. As they stand, they envisage that goods consigned from one EC state to another would still be relieved from VAT at despatch. Because there will be no fiscal border controls after 1992, VAT cannot be collected by Customs on arrival at the border. Instead, the purchaser would enter the VAT figure as input and output tax simultaneously in his VAT return. Importers would thus have the important cash flow benefit of being relieved from the need to pay import VAT. At the same time, the importer's duty deferment account can be reduced by the amount equivalent to intra-Community VAT, producing a saving in the guarantor bank's charges.

A trader based in one member state and buying goods in another would have to present the supplier with a certificate issued by Customs confirming his registration for VAT before the supplier would be allowed to zero rate the sale. Businesses not registered for VAT would be charged VAT by the supplier at the supplier's state's appropriate VAT rate for the goods concerned.

Anomalous areas remain under the Scrivener proposals.

- Non-taxable organisations and exempt traders importing goods worth over ECU 35,000 per year would be liable to VAT in the country of destination. Other non-taxable or exempt purchasers woud pay VAT in the country of origin.

- Businesses engaged in 'distance selling' (eg by catalogue or telesales but not, apparently, by magazine or newspaper advertisements) to private individuals in the Community would have to account for VAT in the country of destination, where their sales in all member states combined exceeded ECU 1 million. Mail order businesses would need a fiscal agent to complete VAT returns for them in each member state in which they sell goods.

- VAT on motor cars or motor cycles would be charged in the state in which the vehicle is first registered, so as to block a loophole involving purchases by private individuals in one member state of vehicles in another where the VAT rate was lower.

In order to avoid fraudulent manipulation of the system, currently policed at borders, increased mutual assistance between the member states' fiscal authorities is envisaged. HM Customs and Excise in the UK has stated that this should not increase the burden of compliance on traders. However, there would be an increase in Customs' verification of traders' records to confirm that goods said to have been consigned to a particular trader in another member state have in fact been so consigned.

Company law

Company law harmonisation continues apace. In the UK, the Companies Act 1989 was introduced largely to implement the Seventh and Eighth EC Company Law Directives, although it contains a miscellany of other, unrelated changes.

The Seventh Directive (83/349/EEC) sets out the circumstances and manner in which consolidated accounts must be prepared and published, and complements the Fourth Directive (78/660/EEC) which dealt with the accounts of individual companies. The latter was implemented in the UK by the Companies Act 1981 (subsequently consolidated with earlier Acts in the Companies Act 1985).

The Directive requires there to be detailed rules in law for the preparation and form of consolidated accounts. Although many changes were required in UK law as a result, practice in the UK (through accounting standards) already followed the main principles of the Directive, the main practical effects of which will therefore be experienced in some other Community countries.

The Eighth Directive (84/253/EEC) on the approval, regulation, education and training of auditors, did require significant new departures in UK law. Eligibility to carry out statutory audits is limited to members of recognised supervisory or qualifying bodies (eg the Institute of Chartered Accountants in England and Wales, the Chartered Association of Certified Accountants etc) eligible under the rules of that body to carry out audits. Such bodies must be recognised for the purpose by the Secretary of State for Trade and Industry. Recognition is dependent on the body's having adequate rules on independence, technical standards and professional integrity etc.

On 21 December 1989, the Council adopted two further company law directives – the Eleventh (89/666/EEC) and Twelfth (89/667/EEC). The Eleventh Directive lays down disclosure requirements for branches opened in a member state by certain companies from other member states. The changes should benefit UK companies with branches elsewhere in the Community as some member states impose unduly burdensome disclosure requirements on the branches of foreign companies. However, some disclosure requirements relating to both the company and the branch will have to be added to UK law. The Twelfth Directive provides that single-member limited liability companies shall be legally recognised in all member states. The UK does not currently allow single-member companies (the minimum number of named shareholders being two), so a change in the law will be required. Member states have until 1 January 1992 to implement the Directive.

Directives in force or proposed

Directives are numbered in the order of their adoption as proposals or drafts by the Commission, so the fact that the Twelfth Directive now has the force of law does not connote that all eleven previous Directives are also in force. Set out below is the list of Directives (adopted or proposed) with a brief description and a note, where they have been implemented in the UK, of the legislation which currently does so.

First Directive. Coordination of safeguards required of companies (68/151/EEC). Implemented as part of the Companies Act 1985.

Second Directive. Coordination of safeguards in respect of the formation of public limited liability companies and the maintenance and alteration of their capital (77/91/EEC). Implemented as part of the Companies Act 1985.

Third Directive. Mergers of public limited liability companies (78/855/EEC). Implemented in the Companies (Mergers and Divisions) Regulations 1987 (SI 1987/1991).

Fourth Directive. The annual accounts of certain types of companies (78/660/EEC). Implemented as part of the Companies Act 1985.

Fifth Directive (proposed). (C240/2, 9.9.83). Would require all plcs to adopt one of two board structures (either a single board with a majority of non-executive directors, or two boards – one managing and one supervisory). Would also require employee participation structures in all plcs employing 1,000 or more persons. The relevant working group of the Council intends to remove the worker participation articles and place them in a separate draft directive.

Sixth Directive. The division (demerger) of public limited liability companies. Implemented in the Companies (Mergers and Divisions) Regulations 1987 (SI 1987/1991).

Seventh Directive. Consolidated accounts (83/349/EEC). Implemented as part of the Companies Act 1985 (by the Companies Act 1989). See above.

Eighth Directive. Qualification of auditors (84/253/EEC). Implemented as part of the Companies Act 1985 (by the Companies Act 1989). See above.

Ninth Directive (draft). Conduct of groups of companies. Would provide a harmonised legal structure for the unified management of a plc and of any other undertaking that had a controlling interest in it. Circulated informally in 1984. A new text is in preparation but further progress is not expected for some time.

Tenth Directive (proposal). Cross-border mergers of public limited companies (C23/11, 25/1/85). Would apply to mergers of the share exchange type and include rules for the coordination of the different laws by which plcs are governed and provide, *inter alia*, for worker participation structures.

Eleventh Directive. The disclosure requirements of branches of certain types of company (89/666/EEC). Yet to be implemented in the UK. See above.

Twelfth Directive. Single-member private limited companies (89/667/EEC). Yet to be implemented in the UK. See above.

Thirteenth Directive (proposal). Takeovers and other general bids (C64/8, 14.3.89). Would lay down minimum requirements for the conduct of takeover bids with the overall objective of ensuring equality of treatment of shareholders.

Many other Directives (eg in specialised areas such as banking and insurance) are in force, and professional advice should be sought.

Appendix E

European Withholding Taxes

This Appendix consists of tables of withholding taxes on passive income payments for dividends, interest and royalties between 17 European countries.

Withholding tax on dividends

Country of source	Non Treaty	Austria	Belgium	Denmark	Finland	France	Germany	Greece	Ireland	Italy	Luxembourg	Netherlands	Norway	Portugal	Spain	Sweden	Switzerland	UK
Austria	25		15	10	10	15	25	25	10	15	5/15	0/15	15	15	10/15	10	5	5/15
Belgium	25	15		15	10/15	10/15	15	15	15	15	10/15	5/15	15	15	15	15	10/15	15
Denmark	30	10	15		0/15	0	10/15	30	0	15	5/15	0/15	0/15	10/15	10/15	0/15	0	0/15
Finland	25	10	10/15	0/15		0	10/15	13	0	10/15	5/15	0/15	0/15	10/15	10/15	0/15	5/10	5
France	25	15/25	10/25	0	0		0/25	25	10/25	5[3]/15	5/25	5/25	5/25	15	10/25	5/25	5/15/25/33⅓	5/25
Germany	25	25	15	10/15	10/15	15		25	15	25	10/15	15/25	15/25	15	15	15	10/15/25	15
Greece[4]	42–50	42–50	25	42–50	47	42–50	25		42–50	25	42–50	35	42–50	42–50	42–50	42–50	35	42–50
Ireland	0	0	0	0	0	0	0	0		0	0	0	0	0	0	0	0	0
Italy	32–4	15	15	15	15	5[3]/15	30	25	15		15	0/32.4	15	15	15	10/15	15	5/15
Luxembourg	15	5/15	10/15	5/15	5/15	5/15	10/15	15	5/15	15		2.5/15	5/15	15	5/15	5/15	15	5/15
Netherlands	25	0[1]/15	5/15	0/15	0/15	5/15	10/15	5/15	0/15	0	2.5/15		0[2]/15	25	5/15	0/15	0/15	5/15
Norway	25	15	15	15	15	15	0/15	25	0/10	15	15	0/15		10/15	10/15	15	15	10/15
Portugal	25	15	15	10/15	10/15	15	15	25	25	15	25	25	10/15		10/15	25	10/15	10/15
Spain	25	10/25	15	10/25	10/25	10/25	10/25	25	25	15	15/25	5/10/25	10/25	10/25		10/25	10/25	10/25
Sweden	30	10	15	0/15	0/15	0	15	0	5/15	10/15	5/15	0/15	0/15	30	10/15		5	0/5
Switzerland	35	5	10/15	0	5/10	5	10/15/30	5	0/10	15	35	0/15	10/15	10/15	10/15	5		5/15
UK	0	0	0	0	0	0	0	0	0	0	0	0	0	0	0	0	0	0

The lower rate usually depends on a minimum shareholding in the paying company.

Notes

1. A new protocol awaiting ratification will increase the lower rate from 0 to 5 per cent.
2. Under the new treaty yet to be ratified the lower rate will be increased to 10 per cent.
3. Under the new treaty, awaiting ratification, the lower rate will be 10 per cent.
4. The normal rate of withholding tax in Greece depends upon the nature of the shares, being 42 per cent for quoted registered shares, 45 per cent for quoted bearer shares, 47 per cent for unquoted registered shares and 50 per cent for unquoted bearer shares.

Withholding tax on interest

Country of source	Non Treaty	Austria	Belgium	Denmark	Finland	France	Germany	Greece	Ireland	Italy	Luxembourg	Netherlands	Norway	Portugal	Spain	Sweden	Switzerland	UK
Austria[1]	0		0/10	0/10	0	0	0/10	0	0	0/10	0/10	0	0	0/10	0/5	0	0/5	0
Belgium	25	0/10		0/10	0/10	10	0/10	10	0/10	10	0/10	0/10	0/10	0/10	0/10	10	0/10	10
Denmark	0	0	0		0	0	0	0	0	0	0	0	0	0	0	0	0	0
Finland[2]	30	0	0/10	0		0/10	0	0/10	0	0/15	0	0	0	0/15	0/10	0	0	0
France	0–51	0	0/10	0	0/10		0	0/10	0	0/10	0/10	0/10	0/10	10/12	10	0	10/45	0
Germany	0/25	0/25	0/15	0	0	0		0/10	0	0/25	0	0/15	0	0/10/25	0/10	0/25	0/15	0
Greece	25	0/10	15	25	0/10	5	0		25	0	25	5/7	25	25	25	10	10	0
Ireland	30	0	15	0	0	0	0	30		10	0	0	0	30	30	0	0	0
Italy	15	10	15	15	15	15	0/15	10	10		10	15	15	15	12	15	12½	15
Luxembourg	0/15[3]/38	0	0/15	0	0	0/10	0	0/15/38	0	0/10		0/2.5/15/38	0	0/15/38	0/10	0	0/15/38	0
Netherlands[2]	0/25	0/15	0/5/15	0/15	0/15	0/5/15	0/10/15	0/5/15	0/15	0	0/2½/15		0/15	0/25	0/5/15	0/15	0/15	0/5/15
Norway	0	0	0	0	0	0	0	0	0	0	0	0		0	0	0	0	0
Portugal	20/25	10	15	15	15	12	10/15	20/25	20/25	20/25	15	20/25	15		15	20/25	10	10
Spain	20	5	15	10	10	10	10	26	26	12	10	10	10	15		15	10	12
Sweden	0	0	0	0	0	0	0	0	0	0	0	0	0	0	0		0	0
Switzerland[4]	0/35	0/5	0/10	0	0	0/10	0	0/10	0	0/12½	0/35	0/5	0	0/10	0/10	0/5		0
UK	25	0	15	0	0	0	0	0	0	25	0	0	0	10	12	0	0	

Rates often vary according to the nature of the debt.

Notes

1. The normal rate is 0 per cent. Other rates shown are charged on interest from mortgages on Austrian property.
2. The normal rate is 0 per cent. Other rates shown are charged on interest from profit-sharing loans only.
3. The normal rate is 0 per cent. Other rates shown are charged on interest from bonds or mortgages on real property only.
4. The normal rate is 0 per cent. Other rates shown are charged on interest from bonds and bank interest only.

Withholding tax on royalties

Country of source	Non-treaty	Austria	Belgium	Denmark	Finland	France	Germany	Greece	Ireland	Italy	Luxembourg	Netherlands	Norway	Portugal	Spain	Sweden	Switzerland	UK
Austria	0/10/20		0/10	0/10	0/10	0/10	0	0/10	0/10	0/10	0/10/20	0/10	0/10	5/10	5	0/10	5	0/10
Belgium	25	0/10		0	0/5	0	0	5	0	5	0	0	0	5	5	0	0	0
Denmark	30	0/10	0		0	0	0	0/30	0	0/5	0	0	0	0/10	0/6	0	0	0
Finland	30	0/10	0/5	0		0	0/5	0/10	0	0/5	0/5	0	0	10	5	0	0	0
France	33.3	0/10	0	0	0		0	5	0	0	0	0	0	5	6	0	5/25	0
Germany	25	0	0	0	0/5	0		0	0	0	5	0	0	10	5	0	0	0
Greece	10/20/25	0/10	5	10/20/25	0/10	5	0		10/20/25	0	10/20/25	5/7	10/20/25	10/20/25	10/20/25	5	5	0
Ireland	30	0	0	0	0	0	0	30		0	0	0	0	30	30	0	0	0
Italy	21	0/10	5	5	0	0	0	0	0		10	0	0	12	4/8	5	5	0
Luxembourg	1/12	0/10	0	0	0/5	0	5	1/12	0	10		0	0	1/12	10	0	1/12	5
Netherlands	0	0	0	0	0	0	0	0	0	0	0		0	0	0	0	0	0
Norway	0	0	0	0	0	0	0	0	0	0	0	0		0	0	0	0	0
Portugal	15	5/10	5	10	10	5	10	15	15	12	15	15	10		5	15	5	5
Spain	20	5	5	6	5	6	5	20	20	4/8	10	6	5	5		10	5	10
Sweden	0	0	0	0	0	0	0	0	0	0	0	0	0	0	0		0	0
Switzerland	0	0	0	0	0	00	0	0	0	0	0	0	0	0	0	0		0
UK	25	0/10	0	0	0	0	0	0	0	0	0/5	0	0	5	10	0	0	

Appendix F

Useful Addresses

International tax advice

UK

Richard Citron
Stoy Hayward
8 Baker Street
London W1M 8DA
Tel: 071-486 5888
Fax: 071-487 3686

S Craig
20 Waterloo Street
Birmingham
West Midlands B2 5TF
Tel: 021-634 4024

R Mannion
Oakfield House
Clifton
Bristol
Avon BSS8 2BN
Tel: 0272 237000

J Wylie
James Sellars House
144 West George Street
Glasgow G2 2HG
Tel: 041-331 2811

Mrs E M T Lennox
Century House
29 Clarendon Road
Leeds
West Yorkshire
Tel: 0532 449512

J S Halstead
Peter House
St Peter's Square
Manchester M1 5BH
Tel: 061-228 6791

D Buck
58 Thorpe Road
Norwich NR1 1RY
Tel: 0603 660096

R Moncrieff
Foxhall Lodge
Gregory Boulevard
Nottingham NG7 6LH
Tel: 0602 626578

M Johnson
19 Borough Road
Sunderland
Tyne and Wear SR1 1LA
Tel: 091-565 0565

Overseas tax advice

Austria
Bernhard Vanas
Auditor Treuhandgesellschaft mbH
Börsegebäude
Wipplingerstrasse 34
A 1010 Vienna
Tel: 010 43 222 53133

Belgium
Professor W Missorten
Blanckaert Missorten Sonck Spaenhoven & Co
Meiselaan 71
1020 Brussels
Tel: 010 32 2 268 0835
(Also at: Antwerp)

Denmark
O J Nielsen
Revisionsfirmaet Askgaard Olesen
Stoltenbergsgade 9
DK 1376 Copenhagen K
Tel: 010 45 331 17400
(Also at: Århus, Køge, Roskilde)

H Lindberg
Jägerhorn Lindberg Almqvist & Co
Mannerheimvägen 76B
SF 00250 Helsinki
Tel: 010 358 0 491711

France
Mlle B Leporcq
Horwath & Horwath France
12 rue de Madrid
75008 Paris
Tel: 010 33 1 438 71140
(Also at: Bordeaux, Chalon sur Saone, Lille, Lyon, Montpellier, Nantes, Rennes, Rouen, Tours)

Germany
Herr Dr Kurt Gratz
HHG Horwath & Horwath GmbH
Postfach 103023
7000 Stuttgart 10
Tel: 010 49 711 210580
(Also at: Berlin, Essen, Frankfurt am Main, Hamburg, Munich)

Greece
S Logothetis
Alexander Young & Co
5–7 Filellinon St
18536 Piraeus
Tel: 010 30 1 453 2277

*Hungary**
Dr T Jenei
Saldo Consulting
1518 BF PF 186
H1113 Budapest
Fax: 010 36 1 851 930

*Iceland**
I Johannsson
Löggiltir Endurskodendur hf
PO Box 8191
128 Reykjavik
Tel: 010 354 1 686377

Ireland
F Sheedy
Simpson Xavier & Co
Abbey Court
Irish Life Centre
Lower Abbey Street
Dublin 1
Tel: 010 353 1 731277

Italy
Sga M Sarno
Horwath & Horwath Italia sas
Via Calabria 7
00187 Rome
Tel: 010 39 6 474 1891
(Also at: Milan, Modena)

Luxembourg
F Hoogewerf
Hoogewerf & Co
BP 878
L2018 Luxembourg
Tel: 010 352 27381

Netherlands
N Shelton
Horwath Holland International
PO Box 71730
1008 DE Amsterdam
Tel: 010 31 20 46
(Also at: Alkmaar, Amsterdam, Arnhem, Brummen, Doetinchem, Dordrecht, Ede, Haarlem, The Hague, Heemskerk, Hoogeveen, Hoorn, IJmuiden, Laren, Leiden, Purmerend, Rotterdam, Utrecht, Zaandam, Zutphen).

Portugal
H Leal
Horwath & Horwath Auditorias Lda
Rua Paio Peres Correia 6
1900 Lisbon
Tel: 010 351 1 82 0908

Spain
Sñr JMG Vilafranca
Gassó y Cía
Ronda General Mitre 126
08021 Barcelona
Tel: 010 34 3 211 1900
(Also at: Madrid, Palma (Mallorca), Pamplona, Sevilla, Tarragona)

Sweden
M Åkesson
Horwath & Horwath AB
Box 49046
S-100 28 Stockholm
Tel: 010 48 8 540090
(Also at: Borås, Enköping, Falkenberg, Falun, Göteborg, Haninge, Hofors, Jörn,

Karlshamn, Karlskrona, Kista, Ljungby, Luleå, Lysekil, Malmö, Motala, Olofström, Piteå, Ronneby, Skellefteå, Smögen, Södertälje, Storuman, Strömstad, Täby, Uddevalla, Umeå, Uppsala, Vallentuna, Växjö)

Switzerland
F Seglias
Horwath Treuhand & Revision SAG
PO Box 440
8034 Zürich
Tel: 010 41 1383 5346
(Also at: Geneva, St Gallen)

NB: All telephone numbers are as from the UK.

* = correspondent firms

Advice on raising finance

Rick Sopher
Stoy Hayward
8 Baker Street
London W1M 1DA
Tel: 071-486 5888
Fax: 071-486 3686

John Jenkins
Lloyds Bank plc
Brookgreen House
4 Rowan Road
Hammersmith
London W6 7DU
Tel: 081-748 4050
Fax: 081-748 9776

M G Ranson
Lloyds Bank plc
London International
Business Centre West End
P O Box 620
16A St James's Street
London SW1 1EU
Tel: 071-321 7891
Fax: 071-321 0395

Advice on grants

Martin Brown
IGS (UK) Ltd
Strode House
46–48 Osnaburgh Street
London NW1 3ND
Tel: 071-383 3994

Lloyds Bank Grantfinder
Helpline telephone 0909 501226
Contact your local Lloyds Bank manager

Advice on information technology

John Dennison
Stoy Hayward
8 Baker Street
London W1M 1DA
Tel: 071-486 5888

Advice on feasibility and location studies

Peter Napier
Stoy Hayward
8 Baker Street
London W1M 1DA
Tel: 071-486 5888

Advice on trading conditions overseas

American Chamber of Commerce
75 Brook Street
London W1Y 2EB
Tel: 071-493 0381

Association of British Chambers of Commerce
Sovereign House
212a Shaftesbury Avenue
London WC2H 8EW
Tel: 071-240 5831

Austrian Commercial Delegate
Embassy of the Republic of Austria
1 Hyde Park Gate
London SW7 5ER
Tel: 071-584 4411

Belgo-Luxembourg Chamber of Commerce
6 John Street
London WC1N 2ES
Tel: 071-831 3508

Canada-UK Chamber of Commerce
3 Regent Street
London SW1Y 4NZ
Tel: 071-930 7711

Czechoslovakian Commerical Counsellor
Embassy of the Federal Republic of Czechoslovakia
26 Kensington Park Gardens
London W8 4QY
Tel: 071-727 4918

Danish-UK Chamber of Commerce
55 Sloane Street
London SW1X 9SR
Tel: 071-333 0240

Finnish Commercial Counsellor
Commercial Section
Embassy of the Republic of Finland
30–35 Pall Mall
London SW1Y 5LP
Tel: 071-839 7262

French Chamber of Commerce
Knightsbridge House
197 Knightsbridge
London SW7 1RB
Tel: 071-225 5250

German Chamber of Industry & Commerce
12–13 Suffolk Street
London SW1Y 4HG
Tel: 071-930 7521

Greek Commercial Secretary
Embassy of the Hellenic Republic
1a Holland Park
London W11 3TP
Tel: 071-727 8040

Hungarian Commercial Secretary
Embassy of the Republic of Hungary
46 Eaton Place
London SW1X 8AL
Tel: 071-235 8767

Irish Industrial Development Authority
Ireland House
150 New Bond Street
London W1Y 9FE
Tel: 071-629 5941

Italian Chamber of Commerce
Walmar House
296 Regent Street
London W1R 6AE
Tel: 071-637 3153

Netherlands British Chamber of Commerce
Dutch House
307–308 High Holborn
London WC1V 7LS
Tel: 071-242 1064

Norwegian Chamber of Commerce
Norway House
21–24 Cockspur Street
London SW1Y 5BN
Tel: 071-930 0181

Polish Commercial Counsellor's Office
Embassy of the Republic of Poland
15 Devonshire Street
London W1N 4AR
Tel: 071-580 5481

Portuguese Chamber of Commerce and Industry
New Bond Street House
1–5 New Bond Street
London W1Y 9PE
Tel: 071-493 9973

Spanish Chamber of Commerce
5 Cavendish Square
London W1M ODP
Tel: 071-637 9061

Swedish Trade Council
73 Welbeck Street
London W1M 8AN
Tel: 071-935 9601

Swiss Trade Secretary
Embassy of Switzerland
16 Montagu Place
London W1H 2BQ
Tel: 071-723 0701

Yugoslav Chamber of Commerce
Crown House
143–147 Regent Street
London W1R 7LB
Tel: 071-734 2581

Advice on the Single European Market

Ben Coleman
European Business Unit
Stoy Hayward
8 Baker Street
London W1M 1DA
Tel: 071-486 5888

Commission of the European Communities
Jean Monnet House
8 Storey's Gate
London SW1P 3AT
Tel: 071-222 8122

also at

Windsor House
9–15 Bedford Street
Belfast BT2 7EG
Tel: 0232 240708

The Centre for European Business Information
Small Firms Service
Ebury Bridge House
2–18 Ebury Bridge Road
London SW1W 8QD
Tel: 071-730 8115 (or Freefone Enterprise)

The European Business Centre
Chamber of Commerce
PO Box 360
75 Harborne Road
Birmingham
West Midlands B15 3DH
Tel: 021-454 6171

North of England Euroinfo Centre
The Northern Development Company
Bank House
Carliol Square
Newcastle Upon Tyne NE1 6XE
Tel: 091-261 5131

Centre for European Business Information
25 Bothwell Street
Glasgow G2 6NR
Tel: 041-221 0999

The Small Business Task Force
80 rue d'Arion
B–1040 Brussels
Belgium
Tel 010 32 2 235 0538

Department of Trade and Industry

Department of Trade and Industry
1–19 Victoria Street
London SW1H OET
Tel: 071-215 7877

also at

Industrial Development Board for Northern Ireland
IDB House
64 Chichester Street
Belfast BT1 4JX
Northern Ireland
Tel: 0232 233233

Ladywood House
Stephenson Street
Birmingham
West Midlands B2 4DT
Tel: 021-632 4111

The Pithay
Bristol
Avon BS1 2PB
Tel: 0272 272666

New Crown Building
Cathays Park
Cardiff CF1 3NQ
Tel: 0222 825396

Industry Department for Scotland
Alhambra House
45 Waterloo Street
Glasgow G2 6AT
Tel: 041-248 2855

Priestley House
Park Row
Leeds
West Yorkshire LS1 5LF
Tel: 0532 443171

Sunley Tower
Piccadilly Plaza
Manchester M1 4BA
Tel: 061-236 2171

Stanegate House
2 Groat Market
Newcastle Upon Tyne
Tyne and Wear NE1 1YN
Tel: 091-232 4722

Severns House
20 Middle Pavement
Nottingham NG1 7DW
Tel: 0602 506181

Revenue authorities

Inland Revenue
Somerset House
London WC2R 1LB
Tel: 071-438 6622

Inspector of Foreign Dividends
Inland Revenue
Lynwood Road,
Thames Ditton
Surrey KT7 ODP
Tel: 081-398 4242

HM Customs and Excise
New King's Beam House
22 Upper Ground
London SE1 9PJ
Tel: 071-620 1313

Export credit guarantee department

Export Credit Guarantee Department
Export House
50 Ludgate Hill
London EC4M 7AY
Tel: 071-382 7000

also at

River House
High Street
Belfast BT1 2BE
Northern Ireland
Tel: 0232 231743

Colmore Centre
115 Colmore Row
Birmingham
West Midlands B3 3SB
Tel: 021-233 1771

1 Redcliffe Street
Bristol
Avon
BS1 6NP
Tel: 0272 299971

72–80 Hills Road
Cambridge CB2 1NJ
Tel: 0223 68801

Welsh Office
Crown Buildings
Cathays Park
Cardiff CF1 3NQ
Tel: 0222 824100

Sunley House
4 Bedford Park
Croydon CR9 4HL
Tel: 081-680 5030

Fleming House
134 Renfrew Street
Glasgow G3 6TL
Tel: 041-332 8707

West Riding House
67 Albion Street
Leeds
West Yorkshire LS1 5AA
Tel: 0532 450631

Elisabeth House
St Peter's Square
Manchester M2 4AJ
Tel: 061-228 3621

Other addresses

Association of British Factors
Moor House
London Wall
London EC2Y 5HE
Tel: 071-638 4090

British Export Houses Association
69 Cannon Street
London EC4N 5AB
Tel: 071-248 4444

British Standards Institution
Linford Wood
Milton Keynes
Bedfordshire MK14 6LE
Tel: 0908 320033

Confederation of British Industry
Centre Point
103 New Oxford Street
London WC1A 1DU
Tel: 071-379 7400

Institute of Directors
116 Pall Mall
London SW1Y 5ED
Tel: 071-839 1233

Institute of Export
World Trade Centre
St Katharine's Way
London E1 9AA
Tel: 071-488 4766

Institute of Freight Forwarders
Suffield House
9 Paradise Road
Richmond upon Thames TW9 1SA
Tel: 081-948 3141

Institute of Marketing
Moor Hall
Cookham
Maidenhead
Berkshire SL6 9QH
Tel: 06285 24922

Institute of Patent Agents
Staple Inn Building
London WC1V 7PZ
Tel: 071-405 9450

Institute of Trade Mark Agents
Canterbury House
2–6 Sydenham Road
Croydon CRO 9XE
Tel: 081-686 2052

Simplification of International Trade
Procedures Board
Almack House
26–28 King Street
London SW1Y 6QW
Tel: 071-930 0532

Index